Nebraska
Symposium on
Motivation
1987

Volume 35

University of Nebraska Press
Lincoln and London 1988

Nebraska Symposium on Motivation 1987

Richard A. Dienstbier
Daniel W. Leger

Presenters

Donald A. Dewsbury

Meredith J. West

Martin Daly

Comparative Perspectives in Modern Psychology

Series Editor
Volume Editor

*Professor of Psychology,
University of Florida*

*Professor of Psychology,
University of North Carolina,
Chapel Hill*

*Professor of Biology and
Psychology, McMaster University*

Margo Wilson

Research Associate, McMaster University

Charles T. Snowdon

Professor of Psychology and Zoology, University of Wisconsin, Madison

Sue Savage-Rumbaugh

Associate Professor of Biology, Georgia State University, and Associate Research Professor, Yerkes Regional Primate Research Center, Emory University

Alan C. Kamil

Professor of Psychology, University of Massachusetts, Amherst

*Nebraska Symposium on
Motivation, 1987*, is Volume 35
in the series on
CURRENT THEORY AND
RESEARCH IN MOTIVATION

Preface

*T*his year's Nebraska Symposium on Motivation focuses on comparative approaches to understanding behavior. The editor for this 35th volume is Professor Daniel W. Leger. As is our custom in dividing responsibilities between the series and volume editors, Dan undertook the planning of this volume, and with his remarkable efficiency and organizational skills he attended to the major and minor details required for a successful production. My thanks to him for putting together an excellent volume.

With some interruption in the smooth flow of funds from our usual source of support, this volume of the Symposium was rescued by funds from the Office of the Vice Chancellor for Research and Graduate Studies of the University of Nebraska–Lincoln, For that support and for his strong backing of our symposium in less tangible ways, our thanks and appreciation go to Vice Chancellor John K. Yost.

This Symposium volume, like those of the recent past, is dedicated to the memory of Professor Harry K. Wolfe, who brought psychology to the University of Nebraska. After studying with Professor Wilhelm Wundt, Professor Wolfe returned to this, his native state, to establish the first undergraduate laboratory of psychology in the nation.

RICHARD A. DIENSTBIER
Series Editor

Contents

Introduction

Daniel W. Leger
University of Nebraska–Lincoln

Comparative psychology has for many years suffered from an identity crisis. I know of no discipline that has devoted so much time, effort, and printer's ink to a lengthy debate concerning its territorial limits within the broad expanse of scientific inquiry. On one front, comparative psychology has struggled with its identity relative to other disciplines (most notably ethology) that work on similar topics. On another front, it has sought to find its niche within the rest of psychology. This critical and often painful self-examination has not been fruitless. Indeed, comparative psychology, once declared dead by one of its leading practitioners, Robert Lockard (1971), and predicted by Wilson (1975) to be nonexistent by the year 2000, has undergone a renaissance in recent years, a new vitality marked by the re-creation of its own American Psychological Association journal, the *Journal of Comparative Psychology*. In fact, this volume is evidence that comparative psychology is alive and well.

The identity problem with ethology has been resolved, as Mason and Lott (1976) have already pointed out. Comparative psychologists publish alongside their zoology-trained peers in the major animal behavior journals and frequently work on similar problems. In fact, one is often hard pressed to guess correctly the departmental affiliations of authors in such journals as *Animal Behaviour*, *Ethology* (formerly *Zeitschrift für Tierpsychologie*), and *Behaviour* based solely on the articles' titles. Robert Hinde's highly influential text *Animal Behaviour* (1966) perhaps contributed more to this condition than any other single work. Its subtitle pronouncement was telling: "A synthesis of ethology and comparative psychology." Comparative psychology and ethology had traveled different historical roads but had journeyed to much the same intellectual destination.

Comparative Psychology and the Rest of Psychology

What about comparative psychology's place within its parent discipline? This has, it seems to me, been a more difficult rapprochement than that between comparative psychology and ethology.

The difficulty has been, as is so often the case, one of words. What, exactly, does *comparative* mean? What is *animal* behavior? Is there a difference between comparative psychological research and other research in psychology that uses nonhuman animals as subjects? Let me delve into these issues.

THE COMPARATIVE METHOD

Comparison can imply three distinct processes. One of them is a general intellectual exercise; the others are specific methods of the biological sciences.

The general process of comparison simply entails specifying two or more entities and then describing their similarities and differences on whatever attributes are judged important. Thus we have comparative literature, linguistics, religion, and so on. By some counts, comparative psychology failed to be comparative even in this most general sense because it rarely incorporated more than one entity, the domesticated Norway rat, as its object of study. Consequently Beach (1950), Dukes (1960), and others chastised the field for being so monospecific. Of course comparative psychology was not always so limited. Earlier in its history comparative psychologists studied a more diverse menagerie (Dewsbury, 1984; also see Dewsbury, this volume).

Another comparative method, originally employed in anatomy, is used to help elucidate the phylogenetic relationships among organisms. Similarities and differences are still the key data, but similarities can arise through common ancestry (homology) or through similar selection conditions in the absence of common ancestry (analogy), making this mode of comparison much more difficult than the general comparative process. The logic is that the more closely related two organisms are to each other, the more numerous and detailed their similarities will be.

Comparative psychology has been criticized for not being comparative in this phylogenetic sense because most of its research made no attempt to deduce evolutionary relationships. In fact, comparative psychology was charged with not being concerned with evolutionary issues at all. Hodos and Campbell (1969) reprimanded the field for being nonevolutionary or for espousing an oversimplified and outmoded linear model of evolution, the *scala naturae*. Although my reading of their paper indicates that most of the evolutionary mistakes were made by comparative neuroanatomists, not behaviorists, there is no doubt that comparative psychology in the two or three decades before their paper was languishing in an intellectual cul-de-sac.

The route out lay along the path that Lockard (1971) proposed over 15 years ago when I was enrolled as an undergraduate in my first comparative psychology course: "That students committed to the area should be encouraged to seek training in genetics, developmental biology, evolution, ecology and other biological areas" (p. 176). He also advised biologically trained animal behaviorists to study relevant topics in psychology. My informal conversations with comparative psychologists trained in the past decade or so suggests that this sound advice was followed, and with it came a narrowing of the intellectual cleft between comparative psychology and biology—and later its complete closing.

The third type of comparative method is concerned with *functional* questions about behavior. What is the adaptive significance of a behavior pattern? That is, how does the behavior contribute to survival and reproductive success? This approach, which Lockard (1971) and others call the "ecological method," depends on convergent evolution—the tendency for organisms exposed to similar selection conditions to evolve similar adaptations, at least within the constraints imposed by their other characteristics (Gould & Lewontin, 1979). When unrelated or only distantly related species evolve a similar trait, we can be confident that its functional significance is much the same across species. Similarly, when closely related species evolve dissimilar characteristics (i.e., divergent evolution), it is probably because they have been subjected to different selection conditions imposed by their respective ecologies.

Comparative psychologists tend to favor this third comparative method. As a few examples, we have French's work on reproductive and social processes in tamarins (French, Abbott, & Snowdon, 1984; French & Stribley, 1987), Mason's work on social-emotional variables as they relate to social organization in New World monkeys (e.g., Mason, 1975; Mendoza & Mason, 1986), research on memory processes in food-hoarding birds (Sherry, 1984), and the extensive comparative work reviewed in the chapters of this volume. The functional comparative method is clearly the dominant one in studies of behavior and will probably remain so owing to the great difficulty of inferring homology from behavior (Atz, 1970).

ANIMAL BEHAVIOR

Comparative psychologists usually state that they study "animal behavior." Implicit in this term is the notion that we are studying the behavior of *nonhuman* animals. The contrast between human and nonhuman animal research, which has always been made and is still salient today, is unfortunate because it implies that different principles apply to human behavior than apply to the millions of other animal species, and that we can gain little insight into the behavior of humans from the study of nonhumans. Many scientists assert that the human species is unique and far more complex than any other animal, so that if we want to understand human behavior, we should study only human behavior.

This position has been championed by numerous scholars, some of whom are influential behavioral biologists. For instance, Washburn (1978) points out that because humans and chimpanzees are so similar genetically yet so different phenotypically, genetic analyses of individual differences in behavior are fruitless and, by implication, evolutionary analyses of human behavior are destined to fail. (It is ironic, however, that Washburn seems to accept such analyses when applied to other species, including nonhuman primates.)

Barnett (1983) has taken a similar perspective. He argues that human behavior is subject to cultural and historical influences (and that other species rarely are) and that little can be derived about a cultural/historical species by studying noncultural/nonhistorical species. The gulf created by culture and its cousin, language, is so great, he argues, that the biological comparative methods simply have no place.

Criticisms of this sort (there are numerous others that could be cited) smack of an extreme anthropocentrism—the idea that humans are the center of the universe or at least should be the focal point for scientific enterprises. This position is promoted in some the leading animal-behavior texts by placing explicit discussions of human behavior in a separate chapter, invariably at the end of the book. Alcock (1984) and Gould (1982) are two who take this approach. (One wonders whether this tack is encouraged by publishers and professors who still see the world this way and whether the authors would do it differently if left to their own devices.)

Unfortunately, well-intentioned comparative psychologists often tend to promote this anthropocentrism when discussing their reasons for studying nonhumans. For instance, Snowdon (1983) cites the following reasons for studying animal behavior: as a source of variability in behavior, as models of human behavior disorders, as a guide to development of investigating human behavior in natural settings and in psychiatry, for the protection and breeding of endangered species, for care of pets and for pets as therapists, and to better understand working animals. Miller (1985) has a similar list. Although I agree with all these reasons, the human orientation of most of them contributes to the notion that our *real* agenda is, or should be, to understand humans. In my opinion, comparative psychologists should cease being defensive about their work. We study diverse animals because they are interesting and informative in their own right and because no single species can yield information about general behavioral principles. No claim can be made that the behavior of any species can be fully understood through careful study of other species, even closely related ones. Each species has a unique evolutionary history. However, the patterns, trends, and tendencies we discover in our studies of diverse animal species lead to insights and hypotheses about other species, including our own. No single species should be allowed to figure too prominently in this enterprise, because it is the overall pattern of relationships between species, ecological variables, and behavioral phenotypes that is our main concern.

THE TWO FACES OF ANIMAL
RESEARCH IN PSYCHOLOGY

The notion that comparative psychologists study animal behavior has led to the conclusion that all animal behavior research in psychology is comparative. Far from it. The vast majority of animal research in psychology has taken place in two arenas: physiological psychology and learning. It is the latter that has been most often confused with comparative work. Most learning research has focused on mechanisms of learning, not on understanding or even describing species differences in learning (see Kamil, this volume). Research whose sole objective is to understand mechanisms is not comparative, though the data *could* be used in comparative analyses in which explanation of the diversity of mechanisms might be the objective.

My goals for this volume of the Nebraska Symposium on Motivation have been to provide a forum for presenting some important research programs in comparative psychology and to point out how much comparative psychology has to offer the rest of modern psychology. My view has always been that comparative issues should be integrated into all other psychological subdisciplines. For the record, I do not see this as unique to comparative psychology. For instance, developmental psychology is in a similar position and can and should be incorporated in many disciplines. It is less obvious to many how comparative psychology can contribute to such traditionally human-oriented fields as clinical psychology or personality theory. However, reading such works as Suomi (1982) and Buss (1984) should help point out the relevance.

Of course, with only six chapters one could not hope to be exhaustive in covering the relevance of comparative psychology to the rest of the field. So I have chosen a few representative areas for review. The chapters in this volume are based on presentations made at the University of Nebraska–Lincoln in October 1986 (Dewsbury, West, Daly & Wilson) and in March 1987 (Snowdon, Savage-Rumbaugh, & Kamil). The two sessions centered on different themes. The October session dealt with reproduction, development, and parental behavior; the March session dealt with more cognitive issues (communication, language, and intelligence).

Dewsbury's chapter reviews comparative psychological approaches to monogamy in animals, using several species of voles to illustrate how monogamy is associated with other behavioral characteristics.

West and King use their work on song acquisition and change in brown-headed cowbirds to demonstrate principles of behavioral development. They argue that our understanding of development has been guided and sometimes hindered by our use of several important terms.

Daly and Wilson address the complex problem of variation in parental investment in numerous species, including humans. They conclude that variations ranging from extreme solicitude to infanticide can be understood in the framework of lifetime reproductive success.

Snowdon reviews the naturalistic communication systems of tamarin monkeys from the perspectives of signal production and variation, response of recipients, and ontogeny.

Savage-Rumbaugh also deals with communication, but in a very different way. She reports on new work on the acquisition and use of an artificial communication system by a pygmy chimpanzee.

Finally, Kamil covers the broad topic of intelligence in animals, concluding that learning and memory are not unitary concepts or abilities, but rather are sets of processes that appear independently in animal species and that are predictable given important ecological principles.

Acknowledgments

I want to thank several people whose efforts were instrumental in conducting the Symposium and in producing this volume. Dr. Jeff French of the University of Nebraska at Omaha and my colleagues at the University of Nebraska at Lincoln, especially the series editor, Dr. Dick Dienstbier, helped in numerous ways. My graduate students, Joe Benz, Jacque Walker, and Jody Meerdink took care of numerous details that I could not possibly have handled myself. Finally, I want to thank again the contributors to this volume who delivered six beautifully executed talks and—on time—produced their well-written chapters. I think it is fair to say that comparative psychology at Nebraska (at least) will never be the same.

REFERENCES

Alcock, J. (1984). *Animal Behavior: An evolutionary approach.* Sunderland, MA: Sinauer.
Atz, J. W. (1970). The application of the idea of homology to behavior. In L. R. Aronson, E. Tobach, D.S. Lehrman, & J. S. Rosenblatt (Eds.), *Development and evolution of behavior* (pp. 52–74). San Francisco: Freeman.
Barnett, S. A. (1983). Humanity and natural selection. *Ethology and Sociobiology,* 4, 35–51.

Beach, F. A. (1950). The snark was a boojum. *American Psychologist, 5,* 115–124.

Buss, D. M. 1984). Evolutionary biology and personality psychology: Toward a conception of human nature and individual differences. *American Psychologist, 39,* 1135–1147.

Dewsbury, D. A. (1984). *Comparative psychology in the twentieth century.* Stroudsburg, PA: Hutchinson Ross.

Dukes, W. F. (1960). The snark revisited. *American Psychologist, 15,* 157.

French, J. A., Abbott, D. H., & Snowdon, C. T. (1984). The effect of social environment on estrogen secretion, scent marking, and sociosexual behavior in tamarins (*Saguinus oedipus*). *American Journal of Primatology, 6,* 155–167.

French, J. A., & Stribley, J. A. (1987). Synchronization of ovarian cycles within and between social groups in golden lion tamarins (*Leontopithecus rosalia*). *American Journal of Primatology, 12,* 469–478.

Gould, J. L. (1982). *Ethology: The mechanisms and evolution of behavior.* New York: Norton.

Gould, S. J., & Lewontin, R. C. (1979). The spandrels of San Marco and the Panglossian paradigm: A critique of the adaptationist programme. *Proceedings of the Royal Society of London, B205* 581–598.

Hinde, R. A. (1966). *Animal Behaviour: A synthesis of ethology and comparative psychology.* New York: McGraw-Hill.

Hodos, W., & Campbell, C. B. G. (1969). Scala naturae: Why there is no theory in comparative psychology. *Psychological Review, 76,* 337–350.

Lockard, R. B. (1971). Reflections on the fall of comparative psychology: Is there a message for us all? *American Psychologist, 26,* 168–179.

Mason, W. A. (1975). Comparative studies of social behavior in *Callicebus* and *Saimiri:* Strength and specificity of attraction between male-female cagemates. *Folia Primatologica, 23,* 113–123.

Mason, W. A., & Lott, D. F. (1976). Ethology and comparative psychology. *Annual Review of Psychology, 27,* 129–154.

Mendoza, S. P., & Mason, W. A. (1986). Contrasting responses to intruders and to involuntary separation by monogamous and polygynous New World monkeys. *Physiology and Behavior, 38,* 795–801.

Miller, N. E. (1985). The value of behavioral research on animals. *American Psychologist, 40,* 423–440.

Sherry, D. F. (1984). What food-storing birds remember. *Canadian Journal of Psychology, 38,* 304–321.

Snowdon, C. T. (1983). Ethology, comparative psychology, and animal behavior. *Annual Review of Psychology, 34,* 63–94.

Suomi, S. J. (1982). Abnormal behavior and primate models of psychopathology. In J. L. Fobes & J. E. King (Eds.), *Primate behavior* (pp. 171–215). New York: Academic Press.

Washburn, S. L. (1978). Human behavior and the behavior of other animals. *American Psychologist, 33,* 405–418.

Wilson, E. O. (1975). *Sociobiology: The new synthesis.* Cambridge: Belknap Press/Harvard University Press.

The Comparative Psychology of Monogamy

Donald A. Dewsbury
University of Florida

*A*mong the most important characteristics of animals are their mating and social systems. Many species appear to be monogamous. I hope to show that psychologists have long been interested in the evolution of monogamy; that problems of definition may greatly influence the study of monogamy; that different mating systems can be seen as the result of stable differences in the motivational systems among species; and that it may be possible to place human monogamy within the broad spectrum of our understanding of monogamy in nonhumans.

Animals of different species behave differently. If we are to develop a comprehensive science of behavior, some explanation of species differences must be forthcoming. Many differences result from the action of natural selection, favoring animals bearing alleles that predispose them to display particular behavioral patterns. I shall argue that, as shown in Figure 1, the traits that are most adaptive differ depending on the ecological conditions typically confronting the individuals of each species. The patterns of reproductive and social behavior that lead to maximal reproductive success vary with the mating system. Conversely, however, the mating system can be viewed as the result of the behavioral tendencies and expression of the individual animals that comprise the

Please address correspondence to: D. A. Dewsbury, Department of Psychology, University of Florida, Gainesville, FL 32611.

This research was supported by grant BNS-8520318 from the National Science Foundation. I thank B. Ferguson, J. Eisenberg, D. Leger, J. Pierce, and J. Wolff for comments on a draft of this paper.

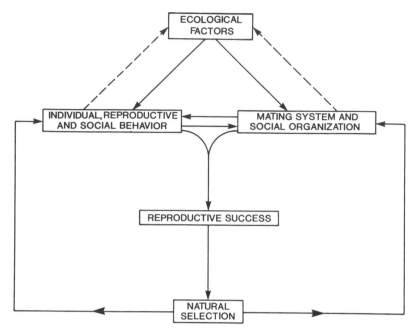

FIGURE 1. Diagram portraying the interaction of factors relating to individual behavior, group structure, and natural selection.

population. There is thus a mutual and reciprocal relationship between the individual and population level of analysis, and we must understand both to understand either. In essence, if we are to understand the diversity of animal reproductive and social behavior, we must place the behavior in an ecological-evolutionary framework. Such is the emphasis in both this paper and this year's Nebraska Symposium, and it constitutes a major emphasis in that part of contemporary comparative psychology that I believe is "mainstream." My focus will be on the comparative method and the mating systems of two species of voles of the genus *Microtus*.

Historical Framework

Comparative psychology is enjoying a renaissance. Signs are visible in publication outlets and organizations, and many vigorous psychologists are conducting insightful studies of animal behavior—as illustrated in the work presented at this symposium. There are also psychologists who either question the place of this approach within psychology or treat it as a new and unique development. I should like to put the comparative/evolutionary approach into historical perspective in order to show that comparative psychologists have long had an interest in these problems and that, contrary to the beliefs of many, evolutionary questions about social behavior have been woven into the fabric of comparative psychology throughout this century.

EVOLUTION IN PSYCHOLOGY

It probably is true, as has often been contended, that evolutionary theory has received less emphasis in comparative psychology than it deserves. However, such influence has been considerable. Darwin's influence provided the raison d'être for the founding of comparative psychology. Whereas many have bemoaned the lack of evolutionary influences, James Rowland Angell wrote a paper asking "how Darwin's radical theories succeeded in gaining such easy access to the psychological sanctuary" (Angell, 1909, p. 152). In the same year, fifty years after the publication of the *On the Origin of Species*, James Mark Baldwin traced the influence of Darwin, crediting him with giving the death blow to "occultism in psychology" (Baldwin, 1909, p. 218). D. T. Howard (1927) again traced Darwin's influence, noting that "we ought to speak of psychology as pre-Darwinian and post-Darwinian, since all that is in any essential degree new in the modern viewpoint is the result, directly or indirectly, of Darwinian influences" (p. 305).

G. Stanley Hall wrote that he "must have been almost hypnotized by the word 'evolution,' which was music to my ear and seemed to fit my mouth better than any other" (Hall, 1923, p. 357). At Clark University, Hall taught a course in "Psychogenesis," which comprised a wide range of evolutionary considerations (Hall, 1923). In 1909 Hall believed, with respect to a perceived theoretical morass in the psychology of the time, that "only a pessimist can doubt that the need will, ere long, bring the man or the men to meet it in the only way it can be met, viz., by a comprehensive evolutionary synthesis in the psychological domain, which by every token seems at present to impend" (Hall, 1909, p. 267).

John B. Watson is most famous for his role in the development of behaviorism; his concern for evolutionary questions is often overlooked.

In the book often credited with beginning behaviorism, however, Watson (1914) devoted two chapters to instincts and their ontogeny and evolution.

Especially relevant to my topic is C. P. Stone's (1943) conclusion to his APA presidential address: "I can think of no better attitude with which to indoctrinate our colleagues of tomorrow who would make animal psychology their speciality than one of constant vigilance for opportunities to study the instincts as they are related to the subject of behavioral ecology" (p. 24).

It is notable that all of those cited were psychologists, and prominent ones at that. Angell, Baldwin, Hall, Stone, and Watson all were presidents of the American Psychological Association.

MONOGAMY AND MATE CHOICE IN PSYCHOLOGY

We can start the discussion of interest in monogamy in psychology with Wilhelm Wundt's (1894) *Lectures on Human and Animal Psychology*. Wundt considered a relationship to be "animal marriage" "when the union of male and female for the fulfillment of the sexual functions is a permanent one, demonstrably based upon individual inclination" (p. 412). He emphasized the importance of free choice in pair formation, noting that males and females kept together in a cage do not always pair. Wundt admitted both monogamous and polygamous animal marriages, noting that in polygamous marriages the females tend the young and the males concentrate on each other. In monogamous relationships males and females share parental duties. He noted that the stability of the relationship seemed to be proportional to the affection for the young. Wundt erroneously believed that most animals are monogamous and, contrary to current information, singled out birds as generally demonstrating polygamy.

In his fieldwork on terns on Bird Key, Florida, John B. Watson provided a model for future field ethologists and psychologists. He used the comparative method in contrasting two closely related species—noddy terns and sooty terns. Both are monogamous. Watson observed the nest-relief ceremonies of male and female and noted differences in the timing of nest relief for the partners in the two species (Watson, 1908). He conducted studies of nest and mate recognition. For his third summer on Bird Key, Watson was accompanied by another future APA president, Karl S. Lashley. Watson and Lashley (1915) refined the studies of nesting in terns and noted that when one partner was removed the mate would generally remain on the nest for at least six days before gradually abandoning it.

A biologist who influenced both Watson and Lashley greatly, Herbert Spencer Jennings, also wrote on the evolution of monogamy (Jennings, 1927). In Jennings's view, the need for the male in parental care was important in the evolution of monogamy. However, he emphasized that this is not the whole story: "Marriage and the family are a complex resultant from the interaction of many functional needs" (p. 275). Such factors as the attraction of the mates for each other and "the effect of habit" were viewed as responsible for maintaining the bond even when no young were present.

Writing in the 1935 *Handbook of Social Psychology*, Friedrich Alverdes distinguished four kinds of monogamous relationships; they could be either seasonal or permanent and either solitary or within a herd. Alverdes believed that permanent mateships within a herd showed the closest affinity to the human condition and thought that some hystricomorph rodents and wild rabbits might show such patterns. Like Wundt, Alverdes emphasized the relationship between monogamy and paternal behavior, noting that "monogamous fathers take more care of their young ones than do polygamous fathers" (Alverdes, 1935, pp. 190–191).

Psychologist David Katz (1937) utilized Alverdes's four categories and cited protoethologist Oskar Heinroth in noting that "the main point of monogamy does not lie in the fact that each male breeds only with one female, but in the care of both for the youngsters" (p. 201). Like Wundt, Katz emphasized that monogamous relationships depend on individual mate preferences that keep particular males and females together.

Relevant observations were made by APA president Robert Yerkes in his long program of research on chimpanzees. Yerkes noted that in the laboratory, where animals have no choice of mates, the chances of ideal pairings are fewer than one in three. He speculated on the relevance of his data for humans and noted that "average or modal trait development and similarity are more favorable than are extremes and sharp contrasts" (Yerkes, 1941, p. 199). Similar individual differences in mate choice were later found in studies of dogs in the laboratory of Frank Beach (e.g., Beach & LeBoeuf, 1967).

C. R. Carpenter (1940), whom Yerkes interested in field research on

nonhuman primates, conducted an extensive field study of monogamous gibbons. Carpenter noted the sharp contrast between gibbons and
the multimale groups of baboons and macaques. Whereas harem formation and male dominance hierarchies characterize the latter, gibbon
groups appear more cooperative with an equivalence of dominance between the sexes. Carpenter observed that, compared with macaques or
chimpanzees, gibbons seem to have a low sex drive but can copulate both
at any season and throughout the menstrual cycle and during pregnancy. Traits such as reduced sex drive and reinforcement of pair-bonds with
repeated copulations have often been attributed to monogamous species.

Ford and Beach (1951) surveyed patterns of mateship in a variety of
human cultures and nonhuman species. They concluded that polygamy was the most prevalent system in human cultures and was shared
by many nonhuman species. Gibbons, wolves, and foxes were singled
out as monogamous species.

The work most relevant to our own is the most recent—that of William Mason. Mason has conducted a long series of studies in which he
contrasts the behavioral patterns of squirrel monkeys, *Saimiri sciureus*,
and titi monkeys, *Callicebus moloch*. Whereas squirrel monkeys live in
variably sized, mixed-sex groups, titis are monogamous and territorial.
In the laboratory, Mason has been uncovering a whole suite of traits that
appear related to the generation of these contrasting social systems in
the field (e.g., Fragaszy & Mason, 1983). For example, in captive male-
female pairs, titis are generally spatially closer, are more often in contact, and display more mutual grooming (Mason, 1974). In choice tests,
attraction to the cagemate is much stronger in titis than in squirrel monkeys (Mason, 1975). Titis showed greater levels of psychophysiological
arousal in a study of separation, presentation of strangers, and reunion
(Cubicciotti & Mason, 1975). These differences may reflect basic contrasts in the organization of the physiological regulatory systems of the
two species (Cubicciotti, Mendoza, Mason, & Sassenrath, 1986).

Our perspective on monogamy and mate choice is now considerably
advanced over that of our forebears. However, I hope I have shown that
the problems with which we are grappling, our interest in evolutionary
questions, and our concern for the naturally occurring behavioral patterns of animals have been characteristic of comparative psychology and
some very prominent psychologists throughout the past century. We are
not as far out of mainstream psychology as some of our colleagues would
have us believe!

What Is Monogamy?

The term "monogamy" is derived from two Greek words, *monos*, single, and *gamos*, marriage. Like many words that have been incorporated into the study of animal behavior from everyday English, however, it has been used in different ways by different workers (see Wickler & Seibt, 1983). Some consideration of these definitional complexities is appropriate, not only in the interest of clarity of communication but because it can help reveal that different "monogamous" species may be doing different things for different reasons.

THREE CASE STUDIES

In developing a definition of monogamy it is useful to have some concrete examples. Consider the following three.

Bank Swallows. Bank swallows, *Riparia riparia*, are insectivorous birds that nest in large colonies (Beecher & Beecher, 1979). They live in pairs, and each pair digs a burrow in a sheer sandbank and builds a nest at the back, in which they rear a single brood. Males and females look much alike and behave very similarly, and both participate in nest building, incubation, and feeding of nestlings. On their frequent flights out from the burrow, however, several males chase single females and sometimes succeed in gaining promiscuous copulations with females that are not their mates.

Mongolian Gerbils. In large outdoor enclosures, and apparently in nature, male Mongolian gerbils establish territories, and females then develop a preference for a male and his territory, coming to spend much time there and eventually chasing other females from the territory (Ågren, 1984). On the day of estrus, however, the female changes her pattern; she spends more time out of the territory and generally mates with other males. The relationship with the single male and his territory is restored as she comes out of estrus. Ågren concluded that her study both demonstrated pair-bonding and gave evidence of "unfaithfulness to the nest-mate on the part of the female" (p. 533).

Elephant Shrews. Rathbun (1979) studied rufous elephant shrews, *Elephantulus rufescens*, in the field and concluded that they were monogamous. They are territorial, with a male and female exclusively occupying a territory and defending it against same-sex intruders. However, except for times of female sexual receptivity and some food-related interactions, the male and female were rarely seen together. The only male involvement in parental care was the protective mobbing of snake predators near juveniles. Although no successful copulations were observed, mating exclusivity has been presumed (e.g., Kleiman, 1977). In this system, then, male and female share an exclusive territory and may mate exclusively, but they rarely associate, and males show little if any paternal behavior.

SOME DEFINITIONS

Which of the systems above are regarded as monogamous depends on one's definition of monogamy. There seem to be as many definitions of monogamy as authors who wrote them. Many incorporate poorly defined terms, such as "reproductive unit," "pair-bond," and "mate," and thus just remove the problem one step. Inferences about monogamy must be based on observable behavior patterns that can be described in terms rendering them clearly identifiable to the observer. I shall consider four classes of definitions.

Population-genetic definitions. For Gowaty (1981), "Monogamy occurs when equal numbers of individual males and individual females contribute gametes to zygotes in any mating season" (p. 852). With this usage there is no consideration of male-female interactions, parental behavior, or exclusivity of mating. The defining attribute of a monogamous system is the relative numbers of males and females that succeed in contributing to zygotes. In principle, one could envisage a population of fishes with external fertilization in which half of the males pair with two females each and half pair with none. Those not pairing might adopt an "alternative mating strategy" and secure a few fertilizations by releasing gametes when the resident and his mates release them. If all contribute to at least one zygote, we must consider this a monogamous system. Although this may be acceptable to the population geneticist, the definition is of little value to one interested in the behavior of individuals. However, it has been adopted by several students of behavior (e.g., Ralls, 1977; Symons, 1979).

Exclusivity of mating. Other definitions focus on the exclusivity of mating by individuals. For Thornhill and Alcock (1983), "Monogamy occurs when a male and female have only a single partner per breeding season" (p. 81). Thornhill and Alcock are explicit in stating that neither a pair-bond nor any other prolonged association between male and female is requisite for a monogamous system. Male and female may meet only at the time of mating. Yet if each mates with just one partner, the system is monogamous. Further, Thornhill and Alcock are unforgiving with respect to occasional trespasses: "a male that is pair bonded with one female but also copulates even once with another female with whom he has only a brief association is a polygynous male, not a monogamous one" (p. 81).

Association. A very different approach is taken by authors who emphasize the unique association between a male and a female as the defining attribute of a monogamous system. For Drickamer and Vessey (1982), "*Monogamy* refers to prolonged association between one male and one female at a time" (p. 243). In an influential review, Wittenberger and Tilson (1980) also gave priority to the male-female association as the key attribute of monogamy. By their definition, monogamy is "a prolonged association and essentially exclusive mating relationship between one male and one female" (p. 198). They continue: "By 'essentially exclusive' we imply that occasional covert matings outside the pair bond (i.e. 'cheating') do not negate the existence of monogamy" (p. 198). This approach is exactly opposite to that of Thornhill and Alcock. The occurrence of cheating does not negate the existence of monogamy as long as the male and female show prolonged association.

Parenthood. Other authors require of a monogamous system not only that male and female associate but that they interact in raising young. For Heinroth (1911/1985), "The crucial point in monogamy lies not in the fact that each male produces progeny with only one female and vice versa, but rather that they stick together and both care for the brood" (p. 262). This view was shared by Wundt, Alverdes, and Katz (see above). For E. O. Wilson (1975), monogamy is "the condition in which one male and one female join to rear at least one brood" (p. 589). For Daly and Wilson (1978), in monogamy "one female and one male form a breeding pair, at least for the rearing of one brood" (p. 82). Rasmussen (1981) considered relationships to be pair-bonds "if paternity of offspring is relatively certain and if the mother and father both invest (in the sense of Trivers, 1972) in their offspring" (pp. 274–275).

In a review of the ambiguous nature of the concept of monogamy, Wickler and Seibt (1983) proposed that there are essentially three "concepts" of monogamy. Their treatment of monogamy as a social system is parallel to my classification of definitions based on association; their treatment of monogamy as a mating system parallels my treatment of exclusivity of mating; and our treatments of the population-genetic approach are similar. They argue that parental care should not be a part of the definition of monogamy: "Producing offspring and caring for offspring obviously are two different things, and monogamy does not generally include co-operation of two parents in rearing offspring" (p. 41). Eisenberg (1981), too, treats monogamy strictly as a mating system and has a separate classification of "rearing systems" with which to consider parental behavior.

The systems of bank swallows and gerbils would be treated as monogamous by all definitions except those based on exclusivity of mating. Classification of the elephant shrew system is difficult. These shrews are monogamous by the population-genetic definitions and appear so with respect to exclusivity of mating. What little male-female association occurs appears to be exclusive. There is also little association in conjunction with parenthood.

THREE DIMENSIONS OF MONOGAMY

Although some definitional differences are trivial and noninstructive, I believe the present ones may be revealing. They reflect differences in both human observers and animals. The definitions were written by individuals of different backgrounds, with different objectives, who use different methods in studying animal behavior. The kinds of information generated are in part a function of the methods used. Thus one's definitions can be constructed to reveal the behavioral differences observed, and these are in turn constrained by what was measured. Some of the differences appear to reflect real differences in animal behavior. "Monogamy" is not unitary; it is inferred from behavior, and different animals may display some but not all of the characteristics that observers tend to label as constituting monogamy. Although they have important subdivisions, there appear to be three basic dimensions to monogamy.

Exclusivity of mating. Exclusivity of mating clearly is one important aspect of monogamy. Most authors treat it as one component. Where they differ is in their treatments of occasional extrapair copulations by individuals that are otherwise monogamously bonded. Although it is relatively easy to observe extrapair copulations, it is difficult to establish that they do not occur. In practice, two different aspects of exclusivity of mating must be considered.

Exclusivity of copulation. By "mating," most writers appear to mean copulation. It is difficult to establish exclusivity of copulation under field conditions. The primary way to tell when and with whom animals copulate is to watch them. Animals must be observed virtually continuously during the breeding season to ensure that there are no extrapair copulations. This is especially a problem because extrapair copulations, like copulations by subordinate males, are likely to occur quickly and in protected sites that may be less accessible to the observer than the sites for copulations within the pair (e.g., Drickamer, 1974). However, because observation of only a single extrapair mating is sufficient, it is relatively easy to reject the hypothesis of complete exclusivity. Thus McKinney, Cheng, and Bruggers (1984) were able to find evidence of extrapair copulations in 26 families of otherwise monogamous birds.

Exclusivity of paternity. Exclusivity of copulation is often inferred from exclusivity of paternity. A genetic marker is used, and the genotypes of a female and her clutch or litter are established. It is often possible to tell whether the male with which she appears bonded is the possible or probable father and whether a litter was of single or multiple paternity. There are several biases in such data. For several reasons, females that copulate with several males may not deliver multiply sired litters (see Dewsbury, 1982; Dewsbury & Baumgardner, 1981). Thus multiple mating may be more common than is suggested by data on multiple paternity.

The genetic marker method has been used effectively. For example, Cheng, Burns, and McKinney (1983) used feather color markers in ducks and established that extrapair copulations could be effective in producing inseminations. Electrophoretic analysis of proteins is an even more useful method. Birdsall and Nash (1973) analyzed the genotypes of litters of deer mice, *Peromyscus maniculatus,* conceived in the field and born in captivity and concluded that a substantial proportion of the litters were of multiple paternity. By contrast, Foltz (1981) used similar methods with the closely related old-field mouse, *P. polionotus,* and found evidence of "a high degree of monogamy."

Joint Parental Care. Determination of male involvement in parental care requires direct observation of the behavior in question. Paternal behavior is relatively easily observed in the laboratory (e.g., Hartung & Dewsbury, 1979). However, males of some species unlikely to display paternal behavior in the field do so when placed in small cages with females and their litters. Thus observations in the field, or at least in seminatural enclosures, appear to be essential. Students of nocturnal, secretive rodents, such as the deer mice and old-field mice just discussed, are unlikely to base inferences about monogamy on paternal care, since it is difficult to observe. By contrast, students of large diurnal birds are more likely to observe the presence or absence of paternal behavior and include it as a characteristic of monogamy.

Paternal behavior has been observed in many species of rodents, albeit frequently under laboratory conditions (Dewsbury, 1985). For other species of small mammals, however, monogamy may exist without direct paternal contributions to the rearing of young, as in elephant shrews (Rathbun, 1979) and Alaskan hoary marmots (Holmes, 1984).

Association. The third dimension of monogamy is association. Monogamy generally entails exclusive, or at least preferential, association between a particular male and female. This may mean that they nest together, travel together, or share the same home range. Because few paternity analyses have been done and both copulations and paternal behavior are difficult to observe in the field, students of small rodents have generally relied on data relating to association as the primary criterion of monogamy.

Joint nesting. Monogamous males and females would be expected to nest together. Clearly this is not the case for elephant shrews, however (Rathbun, 1979).

Because old-field mice often dig visible burrows in roadside hills and sand dunes, it is relatively easy to locate and excavate the burrows. During the breeding season it is common to find male-female pairs with litters (Rand & Host, 1942; Smith, 1966; personal observations). Thus the evidence based on joint nesting is consistent with that based on exclusive paternity. Because the nests of deer mice are more difficult to locate, artificial nest boxes have sometimes been provided, and inferences about association have been based on the occupancy of these nest sites. Although such studies have sometimes indicated joint nesting (e.g., Howard, 1949), the results have been somewhat inconsistent (e.g., Terman, 1961). It is likely, however, that providing a supernormal nesting site may distort normal patterns and lead to excessive male-female joint nesting.

Shared home ranges. It is expected that members of a monogamous pair will generally occupy similar home ranges. In noncolonial species, the home ranges of each sex may be exclusive of others of the same sex. The finding of shared, exclusive home ranges was a primary factor in fostering the belief that elephant shrews and Mongolian gerbils may be considered monogamous. In many field studies of small rodents, trap grids are established. If there is a monogamous system, it is expected that the same male and female will be present in the same section of the trap grid over a period of time. Getz and Hofmann (1986) set traps near known nests of prairie voles and found that the same heterosexual pairs occupied given areas over time.

An alternative method is to place small transmitters on individual animals and use radio telemetry to locate them. Mineau and Madison (1977) used radio tracking to follow a heterosexual pair of white-footed mice, *P. leucopus.* The extensive home-range overlap was an important factor suggesting monogamy. By contrast, in a study of wood mice, *Apodemus sylvaticus,* Wolton (1985) found that males' home ranges appeared to overlap those of females in a random manner, with each overlapping the home range of 5–10 females. There was no indication of long-term bisexual associations.

In pikas the home ranges of the male and female are adjacent, not shared. However, the nesting pattern was used to support the conclusion that pikas are monogamous (Smith & Ivins, 1984).

Joint travel. It is often assumed that the members of monogamous pairs not only share the same home range but travel about together. Traps designed to permit multiple entries can be used to assess such patterns of association during movements about the area. For example, Blaustein and Rothstein (1978) found an excess of male-female harvest mouse pairs in multiple-capture traps and used this as a basis for inferring social bonding. In their radio tracking study of deer mice, Mineau and Madison (1977) found corresponding patterns of movement in addition to the shared home ranges noted above. Blair (1951) found that pairs of old-field mice entered single-catch traps—presumably with simultaneous entry.

Exclusivity of mating, joint parental care, and various forms of association appear to lie at the heart of most inferences of monogamy, with the relative weight given to each varying with the experimenter, the method of study, and the species under study.

SOME COMPLICATIONS FOR INTERPRETATION

One encounters a variety of complications when applying the criteria discussed above. Although detailed consideration is not possible here, brief recognition of their existence is important.

Duration of the bond. For those defining monogamy on the basis of male-female pairing, the question that naturally arises is how long the pair must persist to be regarded as monogamous. Wickler and Seibt (1983) discuss the matter in some detail and in a variety of contexts, such as that of "superfaithfulness"—the persistence of exclusivity when one partner dies. Wittenberger and Tilson (1980) treat monogamy as a *prolonged* association and operationalize this to mean that it should last for at least 20–25% of the breeding season.

Available alternatives. For many workers, if a bond is to be considered monogamous, there must be alternatives. If individuals are very widely spaced or somehow forced together without alternatives, they may not be treated as truly monogamous (e.g., Wickler & Seibt, 1983). Similar concerns were expressed by both Wundt and Yerkes (see above).

Between-population differences. It is a mistake to regard any social or mating system as fixed for all populations of a species; they can vary greatly among populations facing different ecological and other conditions (see Lott, 1984).

Within-population differences. Just as different behavioral patterns may be displayed among different populations, so individuals within a population may vary. One may question how prevalent a pattern must be to be treated as characteristic of the population. In their survey of marriage patterns in humans, Ford and Beach (1951) found that 85% of the 185 societies in their sample permitted polygynous matings. However, in 49% of these, single mateships were the rule; actual polygyny is limited by economic factors and the sex ratio. Thus, although one pattern may be permitted, another may represent the norm.

Between-sex differences. It is possible for mate exclusivity, and perhaps other characteristics, to be sex specific. For example, in honeybees queens mate multiply whereas males mate but once, contributing a "suicidal" donation of a genital plug to the queen (Thornhill & Alcock, 1983).

POSSIBLE SOLUTIONS TO THE DEFINITIONAL PROBLEMS OF MONOGAMY

Having revealed some of the definitional and behavioral complexity of "monogamy," it is appropriate to consider possible solutions for the difficult problems to be faced. Three appear.

Categories of Monogamy. One can hold that monogamy is a useful construct but that there are several forms of monogamy, each with definable characteristics.

Brown (1975). Brown classified monogamous systems with respect to the duration of pairing—as perennial, seasonal, or serial (within a season). This system seems to miss many of the subtleties discussed above.

Kleiman (1977, 1981). Kleiman classified monogamous systems as "facultative" and "obligate." The defining attribute of facultative systems is a looseness of association among the male, female, and offspring that constitute the reproductive unit. Polygyny may occur occasionally, pairs interact rarely, and male parental investment is minimal. By contrast, with obligate monogamy the family unit is more cohesive, males exhibit paternal care, and extrapair matings are rare. Additional characteristics are provided in both papers.

Wittenberger (1979). Wittenberger divided monogamous systems spatially into territorial monogamy, female-defense monogamy, and dominance-based monogamy, and temporally into serial and permanent monogamy.

Wickler and Seibt (1981). Wickler and Seibt differentiated three forms of monogamy. In mutual monogamy both partners prefer a monogamous relationship. In enforced monogamy one partner is forced into monogamy by coercive actions of the partner. In circumstantial monogamy, which Wickler and Seibt regard as equivalent to Kleiman's facultative monogamy, a male is monogamous only because circumstances block his efforts to secure multiple mates.

Evaluation. The goal of delimiting different forms of monogamy appears attractive in principle. The distinction between obligate and facultative monogamy appears to be an important step in recognizing the many forms of monogamy, although the names may not fully reflect the systems they are intended to differentiate. The major difficulty, however, is that the various characteristics do not always covary. As Kleiman (1981) notes, facultative and obligate monogamy are two extreme forms. There are many variants, and different characteristics can be present or absent; there appears to be no obvious hierarchical ordering. In terming pikas facultatively monogamous, for example, Smith and Ivins (1984) noted that they failed to meet Kleiman's criteria in three respects (spacing behavior was not dimorphic, male-female affiliative behavior was more substantial than expected, and parents did not exclude young from home ranges in summer). Thus, although these classification systems provide a good start, none of the systems proposed thus far approaches the richness of variability found in animal mating and social systems.

Polytheticism. Jensen (1970) proposed polytheticism as a solution to definitional complexity in psychology. It is based on the numerical taxonomy used in the classification of species. Whereas with a monothetic classification a single defining attribute identifies an individual as a member of a certain taxon, with a polythetic approach individuals are classified with respect to a cluster of characteristics, no one of which is critical. As proposed by Jensen, "classification divides organisms into *natural groups* on the basis of over-all similarity, and membership in such natural groups is correlated with many characters, no one of which is priori more important than any other" (p. 15). Jensen proposes that such an approach may have wide applicability in biopsychology—as, for example, with regard to the nature/nurture problem.

Applying a polythetic approach to the definition of monogamy would entail elaborating the various characteristics of monogamous systems, such as the "dimensions" of monogamy discussed above, and classifying with respect to the overall fit with a system rather than searching for a single defining attribute.

This appears to be a useful approach in permitting use of the term "monogamy" in a manner that communicates clearly. It could provide a useful introduction, specifying that there are many characteristics of different monogamous systems and that individual systems are classified on the basis of overall fit rather than possession of any single trait. However, polytheticism may have minimal heuristic value for the analysis of the causes of diversity of monogamous mating and social systems.

Recognition of multiplicity. The most heuristic approach seems to be to recognize the diversity of mating and social systems and to search for the underlying mechanisms, developmental pathways, evolutionary history, and adaptive significance of various attributes and combinations of attributes. There may be one set of determinants of paternal care and another set of determinants of association. Glossing over these differences may retard progress in explaining the determination of these various attributes at each of the levels specified. One might then recognize systems with exclusivity of mating, paternal care, and prolonged association and seek their determinants. It may be useful to label the enterprise a study of "monogamy," conceived polythetically, but only so long as it is understood that the various characteristics may have complex and possibly independent determinants and that each must be studied.

Monogamous Species: How Are They Different?

Mating and social systems are the product of the behavior of individual organisms. As noted in Figure 1, these individual behavioral patterns vary with their context and can be seen to be part of a complex web of interrelationships. However, as one part of unraveling this web, one can ask how species that are monogamous in various senses differ from those that are not. Monogamy is best assessed in the field. However, monogamous systems are driven by individual behavioral tendencies that may best be studied under the controlled conditions of the laboratory. Much of the rest of this paper will be devoted to considering how we can reach a better understanding of the characteristics of monogamous species (loosely defined), how they differ from other species, and which individual behavioral tendencies appear to drive the mating and social systems that are observed.

Two fairly general attempts to differentiate these systems will be considered in this section. In the next section a single genus will be examined more intensively.

KLEIMAN'S REVIEW

In an important review of the phenomenon of monogamy in mammals, Kleiman (1977) attempted to differentiate monogamous species from others. Among the possible characteristics she discussed are the following:

1. Adults show little sexual dimorphism, either physically or behaviorally.

2. Established male-female pairs display relatively few social interactions.

3. Courtship in monogamous species may involve relatively little male energy expenditure.

4. Sexual behavior may be less frequent than in other species.

5. Newly formed pairs may interact more frequently than in other species.

6. There are mating preferences for the partner.

7. In monogamous primates males initiate grooming and groom females more often than the reverse.

8. Monogamous primates appear to display more heterosexual grooming than nonmonogamous primates.

9. Females of monogamous species appear to show high levels of both interspecific and intraspecific aggression.

10. Monogamous species may have a low reproductive potential.

11. The young of monogamous species may have a long maturation period.

12. In species with obligate monogamy, the young show delayed sexual maturation in the presence of the parents, and thus only the parents breed.

13. In monogamous species older siblings help rear the young.

14. Males of monogamous species should display paternal behavior,

such as carrying, feeding, defending, and socializing the young. (Kleiman does not regard paternal behavior as intrinsic to monogamy.)

Because some of these characteristics are somewhat complex, a brief listing does not do justice to the more refined treatment Kleiman provided. Interested readers should consult the original paper, which is important as an effort to characterize monogamous mammals and differentiate them from other species.

A MONOGAMY SCALE

I (Dewsbury 1981a) attempted to operationalize some of the characteristics Kleiman proposed and to apply them to 42 species of muroid rodents that had been studied in my laboratory. The characteristics of more monogamous species were considered to be:

1. Monogamous species should display reduced sexual dimorphism.

2. Newly formed pairs should take longer to initiate copulation in laboratory tests of copulatory behavior.

3. They should display more allogrooming during the period preceding copulation.

4. They should display fewer ejaculations in tests of copulatory behavior.

5. There should be no "Coolidge effect," or resumption of copulation when a novel partner is introduced.

6. There may be no copulatory plug deposited when males ejaculate (based on a suggestion of Voss, 1979).

7. Monogamous species should have smaller litter sizes.

8. Males of monogamous species should display paternal behavior.

9. The rate of maturation, as indicated by the age of eye opening, should be slower in monogamous species.

These nine attributes were assessed for all of the 42 species for which data could be found. Species were ranked and scaled on a 5-point scale ranging from -2 to $+2$ with respect to the various dimensions. The scores were summed to give a simple overall scale value. The fit between this rather simple scaling effort and behavior in the field appeared generally reasonable. For example, among the species appearing likely to be monogamous were California deer mice, *P. californicus*, grasshopper mice, *Onychomys*, and old-field mice. All appear to display at least some characteristics of monogamy in the field. Among species scoring low on the monogamy scale were Norway rats, *Rattus norvegicus*, meadow voles, *Microtus pennsylvanicus*, and montane voles, *M. montanus*. All appear unlikely to form stable pair-bonds in nature.

So simple a scaling effort cannot stand up under rigorous, long-term empirical testing. However, it appears to have heuristic value in stimulating further examination of possible correlates of monogamy.

Voles of the genus *Microtus:* A Study in Contrasting Mating and Motivational Systems

Voles of the genus *Microtus* are microtine rodents with a wide-ranging distribution in North America and elsewhere (see Tamarin, 1985). They generally have short tails, rather rounded bodies, and small ears and eyes. They feed on grasses and can be quite an agricultural pest. Voles build tunnels, runways, and nests at or below the surface of fields of various sorts.

Voles are attractive animals for the study of social systems for a number of reasons. First, they are plentiful. Second, they breed fairly well

FIGURE 2. Photograph of montane vole, Microtus montanus (*left*) and prairie vole, M. ochrogaster (*right*).

and adapt to laboratory conditions. Third, several species are native to North America, which makes it possible to coordinate laboratory studies and fieldwork. It is much easier to get good field data on North American species than on species such as Mongolian gerbils or Syrian golden hamsters. Finally, different species within the genus display very different mating and social systems. This renders possible meaningful comparisons at the "species" level, a very powerful method as illustrated by J. A. King (1970) in his Nebraska Symposium paper.

I shall concentrate on two species of voles, pictured in Figure 2. Prairie voles, *Microtus ochrogaster*, inhabit continuous habitat through much of the central prairie of the United States. Montane voles, *M. montanus*, by contrast, inhabit the more mountainous regions of the northwestern United States. I shall also discuss two other species: pine voles, *M. pinetorum*, from the eastern United States, and meadow voles, *M. pennsylvanicus*, which are widely distributed across the northern United States and Canada (Tamarin, 1985).

MATING AND SOCIAL SYSTEMS IN VOLES

Because social behavior can vary greatly under different conditions, mating and social systems can be definitively characterized only in the field. However, observation in laboratory and seminatural settings can provide important corollary data and fill in many of the gaps that are necessarily left when studying a small, secretive species in the field.

Evidence of Monogamy. Evidence suggesting the presence or absence of monogamy has been found for several species of voles.

Prairie voles. Prairie voles show many characteristics of monogamy, at least at some densities. The field data are limited to association patterns. There is no evidence for or against exclusivity of mating, with respect to either copulation or paternity, and there are no direct observations of joint parental care in the field. Male-female pairs of prairie voles tend to travel together, as indicated by their repeated joint entry into multiple-capture traps (Getz, Carter, & Gavish, 1981). Hofmann, Getz, and Gavish (1984) and Getz and Hofmann (1986) monitored breeding units both by radio transmitters attached to voles and by repeat trapping and were able to locate some nests. In the latter study, 50% of the observed breeding units were monogamous, as defined by both joint occupation of a nest and shared home range. These associations were found in both the breeding and the nonbreeding seasons. Thus the social system of prairie voles appears to be monogamous with respect to association based on joint nesting, shared home ranges, and joint travel. Breeding units were "visited" by nonresidents periodically, with males doing more visiting than females (Getz & Hofmann, 1986). Thus there is some potential for multiple-male mating even in this "monogamous" species.

The field evidence is consistent with a growing body of laboratory evidence that suggests monogamy in prairie voles (see Carter & Getz, 1985). For example, males and females from breeding pairs are aggressive toward unfamiliar animals of the opposite sex, and females in postpartum estrus are more likely to mate with familiar than unfamiliar males (Getz et al., 1981; Carter, Getz, & Cohen-Parsons, 1986). In seminatural enclosures prairie voles tend to adopt a monogamous mating system (Thomas & Birney, 1979).

Montane voles. The social and mating system of montane voles is quite different from that of prairie voles (Jannett, 1980). Both males and females are territorial, defending an area against others of the same sex. Males' territories are larger than females' and tend to overlap those of several females. Thus the pattern of home ranges does not suggest monogamy. There is no indication that males and females travel together. Further, males and females almost always nest apart from each other (Jannett, 1982). Jannett (1981) terms this a polygynous system, though he notes that at low densities montane voles can take on the appearance of a monogamous system as a result of spacing (Jannett, 1980). Males tend to shift their movement patterns, as revealed by radioactive tagging, moving to the territory of whichever female is in estrus at the time.

Pine voles. Pine voles live in family units that appear basically monogamous, although more complex associations are possible (FitzGerald & Madison, 1983). As revealed by radio tracking, all family members use one or two nest sites within the home range, and the home ranges of different family groups do not overlap. Thus, patterns of association suggest monogamy. FitzGerald and Madison (1983) noted the following characteristics that suggest monogamy (see discussion of Kleiman, 1977, above): (1) the absence of unrelated conspecifics in territories; (2) reduced sexual dimorphism; (3) continued association between breeders both within and outside the breeding season; (4) delayed maturation of the young in the presence of the parents; (5) shared home ranges of males and females, (6) care of young by older juveniles; and (7) care of young by adult males.

Meadow voles. Extensive data from radio tracking are available for meadow voles (e.g., Madison, 1980a; Webster & Brooks, 1981). Females appear highly territorial and males less so. On average, the ranges of both males and females overlap with those of more than two individuals of the opposite sex. The home ranges of males can be seen to shift as females come into estrus and males move toward them, suggesting male/ male competition over females (Madison, 1980b). Madison (1980b) concluded that "*M. pennsylvanicus* appears to be promiscuous" (p. 65).

Parental Behavior. The field data on these four species suggest monogamy in prairie and pine voles and a nonmonogamous system in montane and meadow voles. However, these conclusions are based primarily on association patterns, with little information on exclusivity of mating or parental care. Such behavioral patterns are difficult to observe in the field but can be studied in the laboratory. There have been several studies of parental care.

When confined in small cages, male and female prairie, meadow, and montane voles all display parental behavior (Hartung & Dewsbury, 1979). This suggests that the potential for paternal behavior is present in all species studied. Nevertheless, species differences are apparent even under these conditions. For example, when the female was removed male prairie voles sat on the nest significantly more than did male montane voles.

Species differences become more apparent in more complex situations. For example, in a comparative study of four species housed in pairs in pens 1.3 m square, the mean amount of time (sec/15 min) males spent in the natal nest was montane 9.40, meadow 3.33, pine 291.66, and prairie 568.84 (McGuire & Novak, 1984, 1986). These observations are consistent with a large body of similar data (Gruder-Adams & Getz, 1985; Oliveras & Novak, 1986; Thomas & Birney, 1979; Wilson, 1982a).

Colvin (1973) compared the responsivity of voles of different species to ultrasonic calls produced by neonates of the species. The measure used was the number of correct choices between sound and no sound in a Y-maze situation. Whereas male and female prairie voles made 57% and 87% correct choices, respectively, male and female montane voles made just 28% and 52% correct choices. This too is consistent with differences in parental behavior between these species.

These observations are impressive because of the consistency generated in different laboratories with different conditions and with animals that were laboratory bred. In addition, they are remarkably consistent with the patterns of field data concerning association with respect to joint nesting, shared home ranges, and joint travel. The differences in mating and social system between prairie and pine voles, on the one hand, and montane and meadow voles, on the other, appear substantial and pervasive.

MONOGAMY AND MOTIVATIONAL SYSTEMS IN VOLES

The differences among mating systems appear to result from stable species differences in the motivational structures or personality profiles of the different species of voles. The behavioral patterns of individuals drive these social systems. It should be possible to analyze these differences and to assess the way they generate differences in social structure. The comparative method is essential because it is only when there is a contrast in the behavioral patterns of different species with different social systems that we have a clue that a characteristic may be important in generating the systems. The laboratory is the appropriate environment for this kind of study, because animals can be reared and tested under controlled conditions so that stable species differences can be revealed. We hope to generate profiles of suites of traits in species with different social and mating systems and thus help understand the ways complex systems are generated from individual behavior.

An Adaptive Profile. During the past 20 years we have worked with 45 species of the superfamily Muroidea in our laboratory. The primary focus has been on reproductive behavior, and we have generated many relevant data. In addition, with the available resource of several related species in a single laboratory at one time, we have conducted a variety of studies of other behavioral patterns, such as digging, climbing, and nest building. In each we have compared the behavioral patterns of a variety of species. The result is a set of scales on which species can be compared. These can be combined, somewhat as in the 16PF personality test (Cattell, Eber, & Tatsouka, 1970), to generate an "adaptive profile" of the personality-motivational structure of a given species. We have

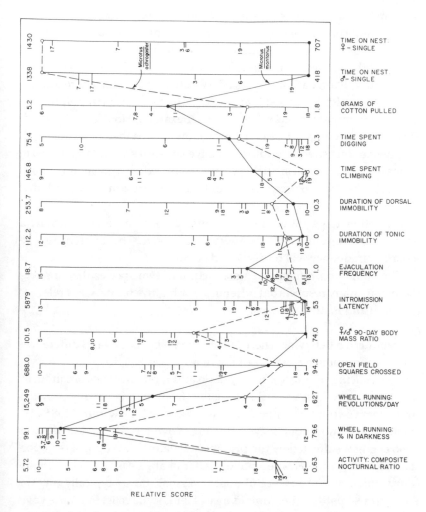

RELATIVE SCORE

FIGURE 3. An adaptive profile of prairie voles and montane voles.

previously done this for both red-backed voles, *Clethrionomys gapperi*, and Djungarian hamsters, *Phodopus sungorus campbelli* (Dewsbury, Baumgardner, Sawrey, & Webster, 1982; Sawrey et al., 1984). An adaptive profile for prairie and montane voles is presented in Figure 3.

For the most part the two lines move closely together, indicating that for most of the behavioral patterns compared, the differences between the species are small. Both species are microtine rodents with similar diets and many similar habits. There are a few striking differences: one is in sexual dimorphism for body mass. At 90 days of age female prairie voles reared under laboratory conditions weighed a mean of 6.2 g less than their brothers; female montane voles weighed 11.0 g less than males (Dewsbury, Baumgardner, Evans, & Webster, 1980). Both theoretical and empirical analyses suggest that across many taxa sexual dimorphism is reduced in monogamous species (e.g., Alexander, Hoogland, Howard, Noonan, & Sherman, 1979). The prevailing view is that males are larger in polygamous species because selective pressures favor large males in competing for females; such pressures are reduced in monogamous species. The data on prairie and montane voles are consistent with that view.

The other large differences in Figure 3 concern parental behavior (Hartung & Dewsbury, 1979), as discussed above. The difference in ejaculation frequency will be discussed below.

The adaptive profile presents a picture of two species that are very similar in many respects but differ in a few highly specific ways relevant to social and mating systems.

Reproductive Behavior. There are also both similarities and differences in the reproductive behavior of the two species.

Reproductive physiology. Both prairie and montane voles are induced ovulators, in which vaginal stimulation from mating usually provides the effective stimulus for ovulation (see Sawrey & Dewsbury, 1985). Females that do not copulate typically do not ovulate. The period of estrus also is greatly affected by the presence of males. Male odors are important in making females receptive (Carter et al., 1986; Sawrey & Dewsbury, 1985). In the absence of males, vaginal smears typically reveal a "diestrous" pattern (i.e., dominance of leukocytic cells) in prairie voles and an estruslike smear (i.e., many cornified cells) in montane voles. The functional significance of this difference is not yet clear.

Male copulatory behavior. At a superficial level the copulatory patterns of male prairie and montane voles appear very similar. Using a classification system found useful in comparing mammalian species (Dewsbury, 1972) both species (1) have no lock (i.e., mechanical tie between penis and vagina during copulation); (2) display repetitive intravaginal thrusting; (3) require multiple intromissions before ejaculating; and (4) attain multiple ejaculations in a test session. Thus both species display pattern 9 as defined by Dewsbury (1972).

There are differences, however. The pacing of thrusting is much slower in prairie voles. Although both display about the same number of thrusts before ejaculating, montane voles have more mounts with intromission and fewer thrusts per intromission. By contrast, the mounts of prairie voles are longer, with more thrusts per intromission and consequently fewer mounts with intromission before ejaculation (see Dewsbury & Hartung, 1982). The briefer copulations of montane voles could be viewed as an adaptation to disruption in male/male competition (e.g., Shively, Clarke, King, Schapiro, & Mitchell, 1982).

It has been customary to conduct "satiety" tests of copulatory behavior, in which pairs are permitted to mate until they reach a criterion of 30 minutes with no copulations. Such a criterion was used by Beach (1956) in an important Nebraska Symposium paper, the thirtieth anniversary of which we celebrate this year. When such tests were conducted a substantial species difference was found, with prairie voles mating for a mean of just 2.0 ejaculations and montane voles for 5.0 ejaculations before satiety (Dewsbury, 1973; Gray & Dewsbury, 1973). This difference appears consistent with Kleiman's suggestion that sexual behavior is less frequent in monogamous species.

In a study with animals from a different population, tested under quite different conditions, it has recently been found that prairie voles sometimes copulate much longer than in the tests of Gray and Dewsbury (1973) (Carter & Getz, 1985). Recent work in our laboratory has confirmed that Illinois prairie voles do copulate longer than our original colony and that the differences between prairie and montane voles may be smaller than the earlier studies suggested.

Coolidge effect. The "Coolidge effect" refers to the tendency of males that have attained a satiety criterion to resume copulation if the original female partner is replaced by a different receptive female (see Dewsbury, 1981b). In tests of the two species a response to novelty was found in montane voles but not prairie voles (Dewsbury, 1973; Gray & Dewsbury, 1973). The failure of prairie voles to resume copulation with a novel female appears quite consistent with a monogamous system and has been so interpreted (e.g., Getz, 1978; Thomas & Birney, 1979).

Female copulatory patterns. When mounted, receptive female voles adopt a posture of lordosis, which enables the male to achieve vaginal intromission. The motor patterns in the females of the two species are quite similar. One apparent difference is that copulations in montane voles tend to be terminated when the female moves away from the male, whereas in prairie voles it is generally the male that terminates the copulation (Diakow & Dewsbury, 1978). It may be that the more prolonged lordosis of prairie vole females permits the longer mount duration by males.

Copulatory plugs. At ejaculation, males deposit in the female's reproductive tract secretions that coagulate to form a copulatory plug. It has been suggested that these plugs serve a "chastity enforcement" function and may be absent or reduced in monogamous species (Voss, 1979). However, the copulatory plugs of prairie and montane voles are nearly identical (Baumgardner, Hartung, Sawrey, Webster, & Dewsbury, 1982).

Pregnancy initiation. Because ovulation is generally contingent on copulation, one can relate the stimulus requirements of females to the copulatory behavior of males. Under test conditions in our laboratory and with females in male-induced estrus, a single complete ejaculatory series was sufficient to trigger pregnancy in 90% of the prairie voles tested (Gray, Zerylnick, Davis, & Dewsbury, 1974). By contrast, a single series triggered pregnancy in just 25% of the montane voles tested; all females became pregnant in prolonged tests (Davis, Gray, Zerylnick, & Dewsbury, 1974). This is consistent with the general correlation found between the prolongation of male copulatory behavior and the stimulus requirements of females (Dewsbury, 1978). It is also consistent with the views of Kleiman (1977) on the reduced extent of copulatory activity in monogamous pairs.

This difference appears to depend greatly on testing conditions, however. When tested in postpartum estrus, for example, a slightly higher percentage of montane than prairie voles become pregnant after one ejaculation (Dewsbury, Evans, & Webster, 1979). Under other conditions, relatively few prairie voles mated for one ejaculatory series become pregnant (Carter & Getz, 1985).

Sperm competition. Because females may often mate with more than one male during a period of receptivity, conditions for "sperm competition" for inseminations may exist. The patterns of sperm competition differ widely among species, with a first-male advantage, last-male advantage, and lack of order effect in various species (Dewsbury, 1984a; Gwynne, 1984). It has been suggested that in species where males display considerable parental effort there will be a last-male advantage in sperm competition. Natural selection might favor males' investing their efforts in young that are more likely to be their own (Gwynne, 1984). Consistent with this expectation, we have found a last-male advantage in prairie voles (Dewsbury & Baumgardner, 1981; Dewsbury & Ward, 1985). We have not yet completed a comparable study in montane voles.

Social interactions. One characteristic that would be expected to foster a monogamous family pattern is contact proneness. The end products of shared home ranges and joint nesting may result, at least in part, from a tendency for animals to remain in contact with each other. This seems generally to be the case. Wilson (1982b) did not study montane voles but compared juvenile prairie and meadow voles in dyadic encounters. Prairie voles showed more body nosing and sitting in contact with each other than did meadow voles.

Working in my laboratory, Lawrence Shapiro has recently compared montane and prairie voles. Unfamilar conspecific male-female dyads were placed together for two hours, and their interactions were then videotaped for the next hour. Whereas the prairie voles spent a mean of approximately 28 of the 60 minutes in contact with each other, the montane voles spent less than 2 minutes.

Under some conditions, the males of one species of *Microtus* will copulate with females of another species. Male meadow voles, for example, will copulate with estrous meadow, prairie, and montane voles (Gray, Kenney, & Dewsbury, 1977). However, the latency to begin copulating was appreciably shorter when the meadow vole males copulated with prairie vole females than when they mated with the other two species. This was because "meadow vole and montane vole females were much more aggressive during the initial approaches of the male, thereby prolonging the time required by the males to mount the female" (p. 1314). This is consistent with the overall contact proneness of the different species.

In another study, groups of two males and two females of eight species were observed for five days in 4 × 8 ft. seminatural enclosures (Dewsbury, 1983). Most species differences were not correlated with the tendency toward monogamy. However, in three of the eight species no litters were produced as a result of mating in the enclosure; all were species for which the possibility of monogamy has been suggested, including prairie voles. This is consistent with the view that monogamous species are slower than polygamous species in initiating reproduction. Consistent with other observations, prairie voles stood out among the eight species as having the most male-female pairs that tended to travel together and be found in contact with each other.

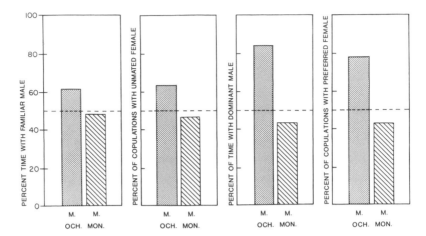

FIGURE 4. Summary of four studies comparing prairie voles (*M. och.*) and montane voles (*M. mon.*). The studies (*left to right*) entailed female preferences for familiar versus unfamiliar males, male preferences for unmated versus mated females, female preferences for dominant versus subordinate males, and male distribution of copulations among four females.

Mate choice. It is in the choice of and fidelity to mates that one might expect the most appreciable differences between monogamous and polygamous species. Such patterns should have their major impact in driving the organization of mating and social systems in the field, but they are the hardest to observe in the field. Our strongest case for the existence of stable adaptations driving mating systems comes from our analysis of mate choice (see Figure 4).

Ideally, mate choice should be tested under the most naturalistic conditions possible. In fact, we have observed differential approach by females to males in an unstructured situation (Dewsbury, 1981c). However, when males are unrestrained, such differences may be more a function of male/male interactions and dominance than of true mate choice. Therefore, it is necessary to restrain stimulus animals so that a free animal of the opposite sex can choose between them. We have used several different test situations. In the tether situation, two individuals of a given sex are restrained in opposite ends of a small test chamber via loose-fitting collars placed around their necks and connected overhead. An animal of the opposite sex is released into the enclosure. The free animal can then move back and forth and copulate with either of the tethered animals (assuming that the females are receptive). Parameters of copulatory behavior appear quite normal under such conditions. In another test situation, several cages are divided in half and connected by tunnels. A free animal can move back and forth between the cages and thus spend time in proximity to either of two animals restrained by wire mesh in the distal half of each cage. The first method has the advantage that copulation can occur, and the second is applicable for a wider range of variables. Active behavior by the stimulus animals can affect the results in both situations. Therefore, in a third situation two animals are anesthetized and placed ventrum up in a test cage. The time spent by a free animal in proximity to the two anesthetized animals can then be determined. Presumably, any preferences are based on chemical cues, as other cues are eliminated by the anesthetization.

Familiarity. A tendency to prefer familiar partners would encourage formation of a monogamous mating system, whereas a preference for novelty, as in the Coolidge effect, might be expected to lead to polygamy. Therefore, mate choice based on familiarity might be expected to discriminate between monogamous and polygamous species. In the first experiment just one male was tethered at the beginning of a test, and a female copulated with him for one ejaculatory series (Shapiro, Austin, Ward, & Dewsbury, 1986). She was then removed from the chamber, and a second male was introduced. The female was then free to copulate with either the familiar male (the one with which she had just copulated) or the unfamiliar male. Female prairie voles spent more time with and copulated more with the familiar male than with the unfamiliar male. By contrast, female montane voles showed no significant preference (Figure 4).

Whereas copulation occurred in the first experiment, familiarity without copulation was examined in the second study. Females were housed across a wire-mesh barrier from a male for a period of two weeks and then tested for a preference for the familiar male versus an unfamiliar male. For a second test in the second experiment, the males were reversed. The female was housed across from the previously unfamiliar male for two weeks and the test was repeated. Familiarity generated in this way had no significant effect on mate choice. The only significant effect was that in the second test females preferred the male from which they received their first ejaculation in the first test, whether he was familiar or unfamiliar. This suggests that copulation may be necessary for the preference based on familiarity to be "stamped in." This is consistent with the views of Carter and Getz (1985), who view pair-bonding as a postcopulatory process.

Recency of Mating. If a male is the only one to mate with a female in an estrous period, all offspring conceived will be sired by him. If other males also mate with the female, however, some of the offspring may be sired by those other males. Therefore natural selection should favor males who can mate exclusively with females (see Parker, 1970). The difference should be more important for males of species that make substantial paternal investments in the care of young than for polygamous species, where there is no such male parental effort. One might thus expect the males of many species to mate preferentially with previously unmated females. However, the difference might be more prominent in males of species with high male parental effort.

In one experiment females were mated with a nonexperimental male for one complete ejaculatory series. Then a mated female and a female not recently mated were tethered at either end of a test chamber and a male was permitted to choose between them. Male prairie voles both copulated more and spent more time with the unmated female than the mated female. The montane vole males showed no significant preference (Ferguson, Fuentes, Sawrey, & Dewsbury, 1986) (Figure 4).

Because mating can engender behavior changes in females, it was possible that the mated and unmated females behaved differently and that males responded differentially not to the difference in previous mating but to differences in proceptivity, receptivity, or resistance correlated with mating. The anesthesia technique was used to eliminate such factors. In the second experiment males chose between an anesthetized mated female and an anesthetized unmated female. Male prairie voles spent more time near the unmated female than the mated female and also sniffed, licked, lay across, and attempted to mount the unmated female more. Although male montane voles did spend more time in the end of the chamber with the unmated female, this was largely due to one anomalous male who showed no contact-related behaviors. No other differences were significant. Thus it appears again that whereas prairie voles show a clear preference, montane voles do not.

Dominance. Animals of many species form stable dominance relationships. Because dominant animals may be better able to accrue important resources and may possess genes that interact with the environment to produce animals more effective in coping with that environment, animals might be expected to prefer dominant mating partners to subordinates. Once more, the preference would be more important in a species with monogamous relationships.

A dominance/subordinance relationship was first established between two males, and then a receptive female, not previously familiar with either male, was permitted to choose between them in the cage-choice apparatus. At least two weeks later the dominance relationship was again tested, and choice was tested in the tether apparatus (Shapiro & Dewsbury, 1986). In both situations female prairie voles displayed a significant preference for the dominant male, spending more time with him and, where possible, mating more with him. Montane voles showed no significant preference (Figure 4).

Choice in montane voles. One possible explanation for the data above is that the test situation is somehow biased against montane voles. If, for example, males reacted very emotionally to the test situation, no reliable discrimination would be observed.

That montane voles can display a preference was demonstrated by Webster, Williams, and Dewsbury (1982). In the tether situation female montane voles displayed a significant preference for intact over castrated male voles. In addition, when permitted to choose between two males that were as equivalent as possible, they tended to display stable preferences and associate selectively with one male or the other.

Copulation in multiple-male test situations. A rather simple test situation entails presenting a single male with several receptive females in order to determine how he allocates his copulations among them. Fuentes and Dewsbury (1984) presented male prairie and montane voles with one, two, or four receptive conspecific females and observed the patterning of copulation. Male prairie voles tended to copulate selectively with one female. In the four-female situation, male prairie voles gave nearly 80% of their copulations to one female. By contrast, male montane voles distributed their copulations more widely among the four females, delivering only 43% to the preferred female (Figure 4). Montane voles also shifted partners more frequently. This difference in fidelity to a single partner is consistent with the difference in mating and social system in the field.

Neuroanatomy. Virtually no neuroanatomical work has been done on the genus *Microtus*. In my laboratory and that of C. M. Leonard, Lawrence Shapiro has been studying the brains of prairie and montane voles. He has found that prairie voles have significantly larger brains and that their cingulate cortex, a structure implicated in the control of maternal behavior, is somewhat larger than in montane voles. This may be related to mating systems.

Related phenomena. Results of other comparative studies on the genus suggest other possible correlates of monogamy. Batzli, Getz, and Hurley (1977) found that in prairie voles the presence of littermates suppressed the offspring's growth and reproduction. This was not the case for meadow voles. The results are broadly consistent with the approach to monogamy of Kleiman (1977).

Gaulin and FitzGerald (1986) reasoned that because the home ranges of males in polygamous species tend to be larger than those of females, spatial abilities might be more important for males, and males might outperform females in laboratory tests of spatial learning. Because the home ranges of males and females in monogamous species tend to be coincident, no such differences would be expected. Results were consistent with this expectation; although male meadow voles (nonmonogamous) outperformed female meadow voles, male pine voles (monogamous) did not differ from female pine voles.

Overview. As summarized in Table 1, there is a growing list of characteristics that appear to differentiate montane voles from prairie voles. These concern such characteristics as sexual dimorphism, parental behavior, reproductive behavior, contact proneness, neuroanatomy, and mate choice based on several criteria. Together these constitute a suite of traits that define very different motivational complexes in these two very similar species.

It should be emphasized that most of these studies were done with laboratory-reared animals bred and raised in conditions that were as similar as possible. There seem to be stable personality differences between the species, and it is these that lead to different individual behavioral patterns, which in turn generate differences in mating and social systems in the field. Natural selection works on individuals, and it is through individual behavior that group structure develops.

One must exercise some care in generalizing from two species. However, as can be seen above, the data that are available for other species in the genus are generally consistent with the view that these behavioral tendencies differentiate monogamous from polygamous species. We plan to extend these studies to additional species.

Table 1 *Some Differences Between Montane Voles* (Microtus montanus) *and Prairie Voles* (Microtus ochrogaster)

Characteristic	Montane Voles	Prairie Voles
Social organization in the field	Generally polygamous	Often monogamous
Sexual dimorphism	Pronounced	Present
Ejaculation frequency	High	Low
Stimulus requirements for pregnancy initiation	High	Low
Sperm competition advantage	?	Last male
Vaginal smears in isolation	Many cornified cells	Few cornified cells
Coolidge effect	Present	Absent
Contact proneness	Low	High
Brain size	Smaller	Larger
Female response to first male approach	High aggression	Low aggression
Male mating with several females	Relatively indiscriminate	Concentrate on few females
Male choice re. Mated females	Relatively indiscriminate	Prefer unmated females
Female choice re. Familiarity	Relatively indiscriminate	Prefer male with which copulated
Female choice re. Dominance	Relatively indiscriminate	Prefer dominant male

Monogamy and Mate Choice in Humans

The primary goals of comparative psychology concern the formulation of general principles concerning the control, development, function, and evolutionary history of behavioral patterns in a variety of species. Comparative psychology does not find its primary justification in the discovery of phenomena that can be generalized directly or simplistically to humans (Dewsbury, 1984b). Comparative psychologists are likely to make maximal contributions to the understanding of humans when they establish general principles and then view humans in the context of those principles rather than extrapolating directly from nonhumans to humans (Beach, 1960). Nevertheless, results from studies of nonhuman animals often suggest important and sometimes counterintuitive hypotheses regarding human behavior. It is often instructive to consider possible implications of comparative research. This can be quite useful so long as generalizations are taken as interesting hypotheses in need of testing rather than as laws of human behavior.

In the process of comparing the behavior of human and nonhuman animals it is important to keep the distinction between proximate and ultimate causation at the fore. There are many behavioral patterns in humans that bear a functional resemblance to those of nonhumans. For example, either a gander or a human male may show "jealous" behavior when a rival male approaches his mate. The functional similarity may be instructive and the responses may have been brought about by similar ecological conditions. However, the underlying processes and complexity in the two species may be quite different. Functionally similar behavior in different species can be generated by very different processes. Further, the behavioral patterns compared must truly be functionally similar; it would be a mistake to compare cognitive processes in humans to overt behavior in nonhumans. Functional similarity can be of great interest—so long as it is not confused with similarity of process.

MONOGAMY IN HUMANS: IS IT THE SAME THING?

Research and writing on humans have been focused on marriage and the family. Often marriage is viewed as a political and economic arrangement bearing little relation to the pair-bonds of nonhumans. For Gough (1971), "The family is a human institution, not found in its totality in any pre-human species" (p. 769). Symons (1979) concluded that "marriage is not remotely adequately described as a pair-bond, that human beings are not monogamous in the sense that gibbons are, and that the human family and the gibbon 'family' are not convergent adaptations" (p. 121).

The definitional problems concerning human marriage are parallel to those of nonhuman mating systems. As noted by Davenport (1976), "So varied is the jural nature of marriage from one society to the next that there is not even a satisfactory legal or sociological definition of marriage that can be applied universally" (p. 139).

Several authors use the great variability of human mating systems as evidence that human mating systems are culturally determined and that the underlying processes are fundamentally different from those in nonhuman animals. That human mating systems are variable is hardly surprising, given the overall plasticity of human behavior and the plasticity of mating systems in nonhumans. That different underlying processes may generate functionally similar behavior does not mean that the functional similarity is not of interest. Behaviorally, there are many similarities between monogamous patterns in human and nonhuman animals. These similarities appear more substantial than suggested by the research cited.

The three dimensions of monogamy. The proposed three dimensions of monogamy can be applied to human mating systems.

Exclusivity of mating. In defining human marriage, mateship, and monogamy, many authors play down the role of sexual motivation in favor of economic and political considerations (e.g., Gough, 1971; Symons, 1979). However, some degree of mate exclusivity is a fundamental characteristic of marriage in virtually all societies. In a cross-cultural and historical review of adultery laws in humans, Daly, Wilson, and Weghorst (1982) found a remarkable consistency of prohibitions of unauthorized sexual contacts by married women. Adultery provides a primary basis for homicide and other violence.

There is considerable variability in the extent of male jealousy and its expression in different cultures. "Few societies attempt to confine all coitus to legitimately married partners" (Davenport, 1976, p. 143). Often, sexual privileges may be granted to designated individuals, generally to kin. A man may have limited rights to intercourse with his wife's sister, or brothers may have rights to each other's wives. In ancient Rome the father of a newly married man had the right of first intercourse with his son's wife. In some Eskimo groups, however, an unaccompanied male visitor is offered the resident's wife as a gesture of hospitality. In all these cases, however, extra pair mating is regulated according to strict rules, and violators are subject to punishment. Of course, not all individuals obey all rules. Although mating is not always completely limited to the pair, a considerable degree of exclusivity of mating is an integral part of pair-bonds in virtually all societies.

Joint parental care. Joint parental care is emphasized by most writers on human monogamy, marriage, and the family. Stephens (1963) treated the family as "a social arrangement based on marriage and the marriage contract, including recognition of the rights and duties of parenthood, common residence for husband, wife, and children, and reciprocal economic obligations between husband and wife" (p. 8). Similarly, Gough (1971) defined the family as "a married couple or other group of adult kinfolk who cooperate economically and in the upbringing of children, and all or most of whom share a common dwelling" (p. 760).

Reproductive success is pivotal in maintaining pair stability in both human and nonhuman animals. Pair-bonded individuals who are not reproductively successful are likely to re-pair whether they are birds or humans (Rasmussen, 1981).

As is so often the case, there are variations and exceptions. Parental obligations can extend beyond one's own children, especially to those of kin. In most societies with permissive premarital sex rules, any children conceived by the female achieve full status when the mother marries (Davenport, 1976). In the Israeli kibbutz the community assumes responsibility for parental care; the parents do not have special responsibility for their children. In the most typical situations, however, parental care goes hand-in-hand with marriage and is an integral part of the relationship.

Association. Whereas a sex-based specialization of labor is nearly universal in human families (Stephens, 1963), joint travel and shared home ranges appear less pervasive than in some species. Indeed, "public prudery" may prohibit such association in public (Stephens, 1963).

However, shared residence, the human analogue of joint nesting, is common in human monogamy, as revealed in the definitions of Stephens and Gough just discussed. This characteristic, too, has its exceptions. "Traditional barriers frequently stand between husband and wife, curtailing their intimacy, sharing, and togetherness. They usually observe avoidance customs when in public; they may sleep in separate beds, own separate property, eat separately, go separately to community gatherings, and . . . work at separate tasks." (Stephens, 1963, p. 278). Stephens estimates that about one-fourth of the world's societies are characterized as mother-child households, with the husband either living in a different house or dividing his time among wives. By contrast, joint residence is a key attribute of marriage in the kibbutz.

Clearly, there is considerable variability in both human and nonhuman systems with respect to mating exclusivity, joint parental care, and association. Nevertheless, the general presence of these dimensions and the range of variability appear as characteristic of human as of nonhuman monogamy.

Other purported differences. Common to many treatments of human monogamy is an emphasis on a marriage contract that is recognized by the society as a whole (e.g., Stephens, 1963). A phenomenon in Western society in recent years is the increased incidence of couples living together without marriage (see Arafat & Yorburg, 1973). As such arrangements have revealed increasing exclusivity of mating, joint parental care, and association, the importance of formal marriage ceremonies for the display of behavioral patterns characteristic of pair-bonds appears to have receded.

A part of Symons's rejection of similarity between human and nonhuman pair-bonds stemmed from the social context of the monogamous bond. He noted that "the gibbon 'family' exists because mated adult males and females repulse from their territory same-sex adult conspecifics," whereas "the human family, on the other hand, does not really exist apart from the larger social matrix that defines, creates, and maintains it" (p. 121). As noted above, there is much variability among both human and nonhuman "monogamous" systems. Extrapolations from one species to another must be made with care. As Alverdes (1935) noted over 50 years ago, nonhuman monogamous relationships can occur either within a herd or in a solitary condition. It is to monogamous relationships in herd dwellers that one should look if one seeks similarities of the sort discussed by Symons. Although gibbons do not provide an appropriate "model" for human monogamy, other species may.

We are left with the conclusion that monogamous relationships in human and nonhuman animals appear functionally and behaviorally more similar than many authors suggest.

PREVALENCE OF AND CONDITIONS FOR HUMAN MONOGAMY

On the basis of some morphological characteristics, one might expect humans to be mildly polygynous. For example, there is a moderate degree of sexual dimorphism, males are slower to mature, more males than females are conceived, and male mortality is higher than that of females (Alexander et al., 1979). Nevertheless, it appears that most individual humans live monogamously. In their cross-cultural survey of human mating systems, Ford and Beach (1951) reported that in 84% of the 185 societies surveyed, men were permitted to have more than one wife at a time. In 14% of these 154 societies approving multiple mateships for males, the only permissible multiple mates were sisters (sororal poly-gyny). Most important, in about half of these societies, although multiple mateships are permitted, monogamous relationships are the rule. Only a few males achieve polygamy. Thus Ford and Beach concluded that, although multiple mateships are permitted in many societies, "most people are in fact monogamous" (p. 123). Gough (1971) provides similar data.

Given that there is variability among the mating systems permitted in different cultures, it is reasonable to search for correlates and determinants of different systems. Several authors have presented evidence of such correlates. Osmond (1965) found monogamy prevalent in societies with complex socioeconomic structures. Weinrich (1977) related mating systems to income predictability. Cunningham (1981) reviewed studies suggesting that the female economic contribution to the marriage affects human mating systems. Wickler and Seibt (1981) called for an economic consideration of human monogamy based on the costs and benefits of alternative patterns.

Alexander et al. (1979) stressed the importance of differentiating "ecologically imposed" monogamy, which may have a long history, from "socially imposed monogamy." They suggest that, consistent with predictions from nonhuman animals, sexual dimorphism is reduced in societies with ecologically imposed monogamy.

Some authors have suggested that this variability implies not a similarity between human and nonhuman monogamy but a dichotomy. Osmond (1965) sought societal correlates of mating systems and "cast doubt on the necessity of evoking [sic] biological or psychological explanations for such preference" (p. 8). According to Cunningham (1981), "It would appear that sociobiology cannot adequately account for human polygamy" (p. 83).

It is important to note, however, that variability in a species's mating system need not imply a lack of evolutionarily based adaptation. Considerable plasticity of mating systems is found within different vertebrate species (Lott, 1984). This within-species variability is predicted and appears to be correlated with the relative costs and benefits of alternative mating strategies under varying conditions of distribution of such factors as mates, predators, and resources (Emlen & Oring, 1977; Lott, 1984).

A search for correlates of mating systems in human and nonhuman species, whether they are the same or different, is likely to be more productive than a debate concerning the applicability of sociobiological principles. It is important to determine whether the factors generating different mating systems in humans and nonhumans are at all related. The real challenge lies in the search for meaningful general principles— at whatever level is supported by the data.

HUMAN MATE CHOICE

I have suggested that population phenomena, such as mating systems, can be viewed as products of individual behavior, such as mate choice. In nonhuman species, patterns of mate choice appear to vary as a function of mating system. As shown above, patterns of mate choice differ in species of voles that can be considered monogamous or polygamous.

The literature on mate choice in humans is very large and well beyond the scope of this paper (e.g., Berscheid, 1985; Buss, 1985). In some societies choices are made by kin rather than by the individuals that are pairing. Where choice occurs, the criteria and preferences can vary greatly across cultures (e.g., Ford & Beach, 1951). Some attempts have been made to understand preferences, such as those for some facial characteristics, in sociobiological perspective (e.g., Cunningham, 1986). The studies of humans that might be most interesting in this context would be analyses of mate choice in human societies with different mating systems. One might suppose that mate choice in humans would differ depending on the level of commitment implied. There is some literature on differential determinants of attractiveness in loved ones versus acquaintances (Berscheid, 1985), and this may provide some insight into the expected relationships. On the other hand, preferences for individuals bearing predictors of traits such as healthiness, locomotor efficiency, and longevity may be universal (Cunningham, 1986; Lott, 1979).

Summary and Conclusions

The phenomenon of monogamy is complex both because different characteristics associated with monogamy are displayed by different species and because different authors tend to focus on different characteristics, in part because of the species they study. The essence of monogamy appears to lie in three dimensions—exclusivity of mating, shared parental care, and association. However, many species that can be treated as "monogamous" may fail to show one or more of these characteristics. No one characteristic can be taken as definitive of monogamy. As a rule of thumb, we might consider a system monogamous if two of the three dimensions of monogamy are present. Monogamy, then, is not a unitary construct, but a general term that is useful in delineating a range of phenomena. A fascinating set of questions concerns the determinants of exclusivity of mating, shared parental care, and different kinds of association and when each is and is not shown. This search can be hindered by overreliance on "monogamy" conceived as a unitary characteristic. I find myself following in the footsteps of Frank Beach's Nebraska Symposium paper of 30 years ago in arguing against a unitary concept of monogamy, just as he argued against a unitary concept of "sex drive."

Mating systems, such as monogamy, are the product of the behavioral patterns displayed by individual organisms. Our work on voles, like that of Mason and his associates on primates, reveals important differences in the motivational systems of monogamous and nonmonogamous species. Animals show both plasticity within species, as individuals encounter different conditions, and remarkably stable species differences, as laboratory-reared individuals vary reliably. The delineation of these personality profiles of species displaying different proclivities toward mating systems illustrates the utility of the comparative method and can help unravel the underlying causes of a variety of psychological differences, from those affecting mate choice to sex differences in spatial learning. They are thus fundamental to a comprehensive understanding of any species.

Although the goal of comparative psychology lies in generating principles of generality concerning behavior rather than in direct extrapolation to humans, results can provide worthwhile hypotheses regarding the evolution of human behavior. Although monogamy and mate choice in humans may be regulated by underlying processes different from those in other species, there are many functional similarities, and both are ultimately the products of natural selection. Viewed behaviorally, characteristics of human marriage in different cultures have a range and variability similar to those of patterns of social and mating systems in nonhuman animals.

In our quest for an understanding of evolutionarily based behavioral adaptations, we follow in a long tradition in comparative psychology.

Comparative psychology was never restricted to the study of rats in mazes; it has been practiced by numerous psychologists with concerns for naturally occurring behavior and a grasp of evolutionary principles. The roster of comparative psychologists interested in the evolution of monogamy includes such names as Carpenter, Watson, Wundt, and Yerkes. They have provided a proud tradition within which we work.

REFERENCES

Ågren, G. (1984). Pair formation in the Mongolian gerbil. *Animal Behaviour, 32,* 528–535.

Alexander, R. D., Hoogland, J. L., Howard, R. D., Noonan, K. M., & Sherman, P. W. (1979). Sexual dimorphisms and breeding systems in pinnipeds, ungulates, primates, and humans. In N. A. Chagnon & W. Irons (Eds.), *Evolutionary biology and human social behavior: An anthropological perspective* (pp. 402–604). North Scituate, MA: Duxbury.

Alverdes, F. (1935). The behavior of mammalian herds and packs. In C. Murchison (Ed.), *A handbook of social psychology* (pp. 185–203). Worcester, MA: Clark University Press.

Angell, J. R. (1909). The influence of Darwin on psychology. *Psychological Review, 16,* 152–169.

Arafat, I., & Yorburg, B. (1973). On living together without marriage. *Journal of Sex Research, 9,* 97–106.

Baldwin, J. M. (1909). The influence of Darwin on theory of knowledge and philosophy. *Psychological Review, 16,* 207–218.

Batzli, G. O., Getz, L. L., & Hurley, S. S. (1977). Suppression of growth and reproduction of microtine rodents by social factors. *Journal of Mammalogy, 58,* 583–591.

Baumgardner, D. J., Hartung, T. G., Sawrey, D. K., Webster, D. G., & Dewsbury, D. A. (1982). Muroid copulatory plugs and female reproductive tracts: A comparative investigation. *Journal of Mammalogy, 63,* 110–117.

Beach, F. A. (1956). Characteristics of masculine "sex drive." In *Nebraska symposium on motivation* (Vol. 4, pp. 1–32). Lincoln: University of Nebraska Press.

Beach, F. A. (1960). Experimental investigations of species-specific behavior. *American Psychologist, 15,* 1–18.

Beach, F. A., & LeBoeuf, B. J. (1967). Coital behaviour in dogs: I. Preferential mating in the bitch. *Animal Behaviour, 15,* 546–558.

Beecher, M. D., & Beecher, I. M. (1979). Sociobiology of bank swallows: Reproductive strategy of the male. *Science, 205,* 1282–1285.

Berscheid, E. (1985). Interpersonal attraction. In G. Lindzey & E. Aronson (Eds.), *The handbook of social psychology* (3rd ed.) (pp. 413–484), New York: Random House.

Birdsall, D. A., & Nash, D. (1973). Occurrence of successful multiple insemination of females in natural populations of deer mice (*Peromyscus maniculatus*). *Evolution, 27,* 106–110.

Blair, W. F. (1951). Population structure, social behavior, and environmental relations in a natural population of the beach mouse (*Peromyscus polionotus leucocephalus*). *Contributions from the Laboratory of Vertebrate Biology, University of Michigan, 48,* 1–48.

Blaustein, A. R., & Rothstein, S. I. (1978). Multiple captures of *Reithrodontomys megalotis:* Social bonding in a mouse? *American Midland Naturalist, 100,* 376–383.

Brown, J. L. (1975). *The evolution of behavior.* New York: W. W. Norton.

Buss, D. M. (1985). Human mate selection. *American Scientist, 73,* 47–51.

Carpenter, C. R. (1940). A field study in Siam of the behavior and social relations of the gibbon (*Hylobates lar*). *Comparative Psychology Monographs, 16* (84), 1–205.

Carter, C. S., & Getz, L. L. (1985). Social and hormonal determinants of reproductive patterns in the prairie vole. In R. Gilles & J. Balthazart (Eds.), *Neurobiology* (pp. 18–36). Berlin: Springer-Verlag.

Carter, C. S., Getz, L. L., & Cohen-Parsons, M. (1986). Relationships between social organization and behavioral endocrinology in a monogamous mammal. *Advances in the Study of Behavior, 16,* 109–145.

Cattell, R. B., Eber, H., & Tatsouka, M. (1970). *Handbook for the 16PF.* Champaign, IL: Institute for Personality and Ability Testing.

Cheng, K. M., Burns, J. T., & McKinney, F. (1983). Forced copulation in captive mallards: III. Sperm competition. *Auk, 100,* 302–310.

Colvin, M. A. (1973). Analysis of acoustic structure and function in ultrasounds of neonatal *Microtus. Behaviour, 44,* 234–263.

Cubicciotti, D. D., & Mason, W. A. (1975). Comparative studies of social behavior in *Callicebus* and *Saimiri:* Male-female emotional attachments. *Behavioral Biology, 16,* 185–197.

Cubicciotti, D. D., Mendoza, S. P., Mason, W. A., & Sassenrath, E. N. (1986). Differences between *Saimiri sciureus* and *Callicebus moloch* in physiological responsiveness: Implications for behavior. *Journal of Comparative Psychology, 100,* 385–391.

Cunningham, M. R. (1981). Sociobiology as a supplementary paradigm for social psychological research. In L. Wheeler (Ed.), *Review of personality and social psychology* (vol. 2, pp. 69–106). Beverly Hills, CA: Sage.

Cunningham, M. R. (1986). Measuring the physical in physical attractiveness: Quasi-experiments on the sociobiology of female facial beauty. *Journal of Personality and Social Psychology, 50,* 925–935.

Daly, M., & Wilson, M. (1978). *Sex, evolution, and behavior.* North Scituate, MA: Duxbury.

Daly, M., Wilson, M., & Weghorst, S. J. (1982). Male sexual jealousy. *Ethology and Sociobiology, 3,* 11–27.

Davenport, W. H. (1976). Sex in cross-cultural perspective. In F. A. Beach (Ed.), *Human sexuality in four perspectives* (pp. 115–163). Baltimore: Johns Hopkins University Press.

Davis, H. N., Gray, G. D., Zerylnick, M., & Dewsbury, D. A. (1974). Ovulation and implantation in montane voles (*Microtus montanus*) as a function of varying amounts of copulatory stimulation. *Hormones and Behavior, 5,* 383–388.

Dewsbury, D. A. (1972). Patterns of copulatory behavior in male mammals. *Quarterly Review of Biology, 47,* 1–33.

Dewsbury, D. A. (1973). Copulatory behavior of montane voles (Microtus montanus). Behaviour, 44, 186–202.

Dewsbury, D. A. (1978). The comparative method in studies of reproductive behavior. In T. E. McGill, D. A. Dewsbury, & B. D. Sachs (Eds.), Sex and behavior: Status and prospectus (pp. 83–112). New York: Plenum.

Dewsbury, D. A. (1981a). An exercise in the prediction of monogamy in the field from laboratory data on 42 species of muroid rodents. Biologist, 63, 138–162.

Dewsbury, D. A. (1981b). Effects of novelty on copulatory behavior: The Coolidge effect and related phenomena. Psychological Bulletin, 89, 464–482.

Dewsbury, D. A. (1981c). Social dominance, copulatory behavior, and differential reproduction in deer mice (Peromyscus maniculatus). Journal of Comparative and Physiological Psychology, 95, 880–895.

Dewsbury, D. A. (1982). Pregnancy blockage following multiple-male copulation or exposure at the time of mating in deer mice, Peromyscus maniculatus. Behavioral Ecology and Sociobiology, 11, 37–42.

Dewsbury, D. A. (1983). A comparative study of rodent social behavior in a semi-natural enclosure. Aggressive Behavior, 9, 207–215.

Dewsbury, D. A. (1984a). Sperm competition in muroid rodents. In R. L. Smith (Ed.), Sperm competition and the evolution of animal mating systems (pp. 547–571). New York: Academic Press.

Dewsbury, D. A. (1984b). Comparative psychology in the twentieth century. Stroudsburg, PA: Hutchinson Ross.

Dewsbury, D. A. (1985). Paternal behavior in rodents. American Zoologist, 25, 841–852.

Dewsbury, D. A., & Baumgardner, D. J. (1981). Studies of sperm competition in two species of muroid rodents. Behavioral Ecology and Sociobiology, 9, 121–133.

Dewsbury, D. A., Baumgardner, D. J., Evans, R. L., & Webster, D. G. (1980). Sexual dimorphism for body mass in 13 taxa of muroid rodents under laboratory conditions. Journal of Mammalogy, 61, 146–149.

Dewsbury, D. A., Baumgardner, D. J., Sawrey, D. K., & Webster, D. G. (1982). The adaptive profile: Comparative psychology of red-backed voles (Clethrionomys gapperi). Journal of Comparative and Physiological Psychology , 96, 649–660.

Dewsbury, D. A., Evans, R. L., & Webster, D. G. (1979). Pregnancy initiation in postpartum estrus in three species of muroid rodents. Hormones and Behavior, 13, 1–8.

Dewsbury, D. A., & Hartung, T. G. (1982). Copulatory behavior of three species of Microtus. Journal of Mammalogy, 63, 306–309.

Dewsbury, D. A., & Ward, S. E. (1985). Effects of albinism on copulatory behavior and sperm competition in prairie voles (Microtus ochrogaster). Bulletin of the Psychonomic Society, 23, 68–70.

Diakow, C., & Dewsbury, D. A. (1978). A comparative description of the mating behaviour of female rodents. Animal Behaviour, 26, 1091–1097.

Drickamer, L. C. (1974). Social rank, observability, and sexual behaviour of rhesus monkeys (Macaca mulatta). Journal of Reproduction and Fertility, 37, 117–120.

Drickamer, L. C., & Vessey, S. H. (1982). Animal behavior: Concepts, processes, and methods. Boston: Willard Grant.

Eisenberg, J. F. (1981). The mammalian radiations: An analysis of trends in evolution, adaptation, and behavior. Chicago: University of Chicago Press.

Emlen, S. T., & Oring, L. W. (1977). Ecology, sexual selection, and the evolution of mating systems. *Science, 197,* 215–223.

Ferguson, B., Fuentes, S. M., Sawrey, D. K., & Dewsbury, D. A. (1986). Male preferences for unmated versus mated females in two species of voles (*Microtus ochrogaster* and *M. montanus*). *Journal of Comparative Psychology, 100,* 243–247.

FitzGerald, R. W., & Madison, D. M. (1983). Social organization of a free-ranging population of pine voles, *Microtus pinetorum*. *Behavioral Ecology and Sociobiology, 13,* 183–187.

Foltz, D. W. (1981). Genetic evidence for long-term monogamy in a small rodent, *Peromyscus polionotus*. *American Naturalist, 117,* 665–675.

Ford, C. S., & Beach, F. A. (1951). *Patterns of sexual behavior*. New York: Harper.

Fragaszy, D. M., & Mason, W. A. (1983). Comparisons of feeding behavior in captive squirrel and titi monkeys (*Saimiri sciureus* and *Callicebus moloch*). *Journal of Comparative Psychology, 97,* 310–326.

Fuentes, S. M., & Dewsbury, D. A. (1984). Copulatory behavior of voles (*Microtus montanus* and *M. ochrogaster*) in multiple-female test situations. *Journal of Comparative Psychology, 98,* 45–53.

Gaulin, S. J. C., & FitzGerald, R. W. (1986). Sex differences in spatial ability: An evolutionary hypothesis and test. *American Naturalist, 127,* 74–88.

Getz, L. L. (1978). Speculation on social structure and population cycles of microtine rodents. *Biologist, 60,* 134–147.

Getz, L. L., Carter, C. S., & Gavish, L. (1981). The mating system of the prairie vole, *Microtus ochrogaster:* Field and laboratory evidence for pair-bonding. *Behavioral Ecology and Sociobiology, 8,* 189–194.

Getz, L. L., & Hofmann, J. E. (1986). Social organization in free-living prairie voles, *Microtus ochrogaster*. *Behavioral Ecology and Sociobiology, 18,* 275–282.

Gough, K. (1971). The origin of the family. *Journal of Marriage and the Family, 33,* 760–771.

Gowaty, P. A. (1981). An extension of the Orians-Verner-Willson model to account for mating systems besides polygyny. *American Naturalist, 118,* 851–859.

Gray, G. D., & Dewsbury, D. A. (1973). A quantitative description of copulatory behavior in prairie voles (*Microtus ochrogaster*). *Brain, Behavior and Evolution, 8,* 437–452.

Gray, G. D., Kenney, A. M., & Dewsbury, D. A. (1977). Adaptive significance of the copulatory behavior pattern of male meadow voles (*Microtus pennsylvanicus*) in relation to induction of ovulation and implantation in females. *Journal of Comparative and Physiological Psychology, 91,* 1308–1319.

Gray, G. D., Zerylnick, M., Davis, H. N., & Dewsbury, D. A. (1974). Effects of variations in male copulatory behavior on ovulation and implantation in prairie voles, *Microtus ochrogaster*. *Hormones and Behavior, 5,* 389–396.

Gruder-Adams, S., & Getz, L. L. (1985). Comparison of the mating system and paternal behavior in *Microtus ochrogaster* and *M. pennsylvanicus*. *Journal of Mammalogy, 66,* 165–167.

Gwynne, D. T. (1984). Male mating effort, confidence of paternity, and insect sperm competition. In R. L. Smith (Ed.), *Sperm competition and the evolution of animal mating systems* (pp. 117–149). New York: Academic Press.

Hall, G. S. (1909). Evolution and psychology. In T. C. Chamberlin (Ed.), *Fifty years of Darwinism* (pp. 251–267). New York: Holt.

Hall, G. S. (1923). *Life and confessions of a psychologist.* New York: Appleton.

Hartung, T. G., & Dewsbury, D. A. (1979). Paternal behavior in six species of muroid rodents. *Behavioral and Neural Biology, 26,* 466–478.

Heinroth, O. (1911/1985). Contributions to the biology, especially the ethology and psychology of the Anatidae. (from Beitrage zur Biologie, namentlich Ethologie and Psychologie der Anatiden, Verhand-lungen des V. Internationalen Ornithologischen Kongresses, Berlin, 1910, *Deutsche Ornithologische Gesellschaft* (1911), pp. 589–702. Trans. D. Gove, & C. J. Mellor in G. M. Burghardt (Ed.), *Foundations of comparative ethology.* New York: Van Nostrand Reinhold, 1985).

Hofmann, J. E., Getz, L. L., & Gavish, L. (1984). Home range overlap and nest cohabitation of male and female prairie voles. *American Midland Naturalist, 112,* 314–319.

Holmes, W. G. (1984). The ecological basis of monogamy in Alaskan hoary marmots. In J. O. Murie & G. R. Michener (Eds.), *The biology of ground-dwelling squirrels* (pp. 250–274). Lincoln: University of Nebraska Press.

Howard, D. T. (1927). The influence of evolutionary doctrine on psychology. *Psychological Review, 34,* 305–312.

Howard, W. E. (1949). Dispersal, amount of inbreeding, and longevity in a local population of prairie deermice on the George reserve, southern Michigan. *Contributions from the Laboratory of Vertebrate Biology, University of Michigan, 43,* 1–50.

Jannett, F. J. (1980). Social dynamics of the montane vole, *Microtus montanus,* as a paradigm. *Biologist, 62,* 3–19.

Jannett, F. J. (1981). Sex ratios in high-density populations of the montane vole, *Microtus montanus,* and the behavior of territorial males. *Behavioral Ecology and Sociobiology, 8,* 297–307.

Jannett, F. J. (1982). Nesting patterns of adult voles, *Microtus montanus,* in field populations. *Journal of Mammalogy, 63,* 495–498.

Jennings, H. S. (1927). From amoeba up: The biological basis of the family. *Survey, 59,* 272–276, 341.

Jensen, D. D. (1970). Polythetic biopsychology: An alternative to behaviorism. In J. H. Reynierse (Ed.), *Current issues in animal learning* (pp. 1–31). Lincoln: University of Nebraska Press.

Katz, D. (1937). *Animals and men: Studies in comparative psychology.* London: Longmans Green.

King, J. A. (1970). Ecological psychology: An approach to motivation. *Nebraska symposium on motivation* (Vol. 18, pp. 1–33). Lincoln: University of Nebraska Press.

Kleiman, D. G. (1977). Monogamy in mammals. *Quarterly Review of Biology, 52,* 39–69.

Kleiman, D. G. (1981). Correlations among life history characteristics of mammalian species exhibiting two extreme forms of monogamy. In R. D. Alexander and D. W. Tinkle (Eds.), *Natural selection and social behavior* (pp. 332–344). New York: Chiron.

Lott, D. F. (1979). A possible role for generally adapted features in mate selection and sexual stimulation. *Psychological Reports, 45,* 539–546.

Lott, D. F. (1984). Intraspecific variation in the social systems of wild vertebrates. *Behaviour, 88*, 266–325.

Madison, D. M. (1980a). An integrated view of the social biology of *Microtus pennsylvanicus. Biologist, 62*, 20–33.

Madison, D. M. (1980b). Space use and social structure in meadow voles, *Microtus pennsylvanicus. Behavioral Ecology and Sociobiology, 7*, 65–71.

Mason, W. A. (1974). Comparative studies of social behavior in *Callicebus* and *Saimiri*: Behavior of male-female pairs. *Folia Primatologica, 22*, 1–8.

Mason, W. A. (1975). Comparative studies of social behavior in *Callicebus* and *Saimiri*: Strength and specificity of attraction between male-female cagemates. *Folia Primatologica, 23*, 113–123.

McGuire, B., & Novak, M. (1984). A comparison of maternal behaviour in the meadow vole (*Microtus pennsylvanicus*), prairie vole (*M. ochrogaster*) and pine vole (*M. pinetorum*). *Animal Behaviour, 32*, 1132–1141.

McGuire, B., & Novak, M. (1986). Parental care and its relationship to social organization in the montane vole (*Microtus montanus*). *Journal of Mammalogy, 67*, 305–311.

McKinney, F., Cheng, K. M., & Bruggers, D. J. (1984). Sperm competition in apparently monogamous birds. In R. L. Smith (Ed.), *Sperm competition and the evolution of animal mating systems* (pp. 523–545). Orlando, FL: Academic Press.

Mineau, P., & Madison, D. (1977). Radio-tracking of *Peromyscus leucopus. Canadian Journal of Zoology, 55*, 465–468.

Oliveras, D., & Novak, M. (1986). A comparison of paternal behaviour in the meadow vole, *Microtus pennsylvanicus*, the pine vole, *M. pinetorum*, and the prairie vole, *M. ochrogaster. Animal Behaviour, 34*, 519–526.

Osmond, M. W. (1965). Toward monogamy: A cross-cultural study of correlates of type of marriage. *Social Forces, 44*, 8–16.

Parker, G. A. (1970). Sperm competition and its evolutionary consequences in the insects. *Biological Reviews, 45*, 525–567.

Ralls, K. (1977). Sexual dimorphism in mammals: Avian models and unanswered questions. *American Naturalist, 111*, 917–938.

Rand, A. L., & Host, P. (1942). Results of the Archbold expeditions. No. 45, Mammal notes from Highlands County, Florida. *Bulletin of the American Museum of Natural History, 80*, 1–21.

Rasmussen, D. R. (1981). Pair-bond strength and stability and reproductive success. *Psychological Review, 88*, 274–290.

Rathbun, G. (1979). The social structure and ecology of elephant shrews. *Advances in Ethology, 20*, 1–77.

Sawrey, D. K., Baumgardner, D. J., Campa, M. J., Ferguson, B., Hodges, A. W., & Dewsbury, D. A. (1984). Behavioral patterns of Djungarian hamsters: An adaptive profile. *Animal Learning and Behavior, 12*, 297–306.

Sawrey, D. K., & Dewsbury, D. A. (1985). Control of ovulation, vaginal estrus, and behavioral receptivity in voles (*Microtus*). *Neuroscience and Biobehavioral Reviews, 9*, 563–571.

Shapiro, L. E., Austin, D., Ward, S. E., & Dewsbury, D. A. (1986). Familiarity and female mate choice in two species of voles (*Microtus ochrogaster* and *Microtus montanus*). *Animal Behaviour, 34*, 90–97.

49
The Comparative Psychology of Monogamy

Shapiro, L. E., & Dewsbury, D. A. (1986). Male dominance, female choice and male copulatory behavior in two species of voles (Microtus ochrogaster and Microtus montanus). Behavioral Ecology and Sociobiology, 18, 267–274.

Shively, C., Clarke, S., King, N., Schapiro, S., & Mitchell, G. (1982). Patterns of sexual behavior in male macaques. American Journal of Primatology, 2, 373–384.

Smith, A. T., & Ivins, B. L. (1984). Spatial relationships and social organization in adult pikas: A facultatively monogamous mammal. Zeitschrift für Tierpsychologie, 66, 289–308.

Smith, M. H. (1966). The evolutionary significance of certain behavioral, physiological, and morphological adaptations of the old-field mouse, Peromyscus polionotus. Doctoral dissertation, University of Florida (University Microfilms No. 67–372).

Stephens, W. N. (1963). The family in cross-cultural perspective. New York: Holt, Rinehart and Winston.

Stone, C. P. (1943). Multiply, vary, let the strongest live and the weakest die—Charles Darwin. Psychological Bulletin, 40, 1–24.

Symons, D. (1979). The evolution of human sexuality. New York: Oxford.

Tamarin, R. H. (Ed.). (1985). Biology of New World Microtus. Lawrence, KS: American Society of Mammalogists.

Terman, C. R. (1961). Some dynamics of spatial distribution within semi-natural populations of prairie deermice. Ecology, 42, 288–302.

Thomas, J. A., & Birney, E. C. (1979). Parental care and mating system of the prairie vole, Microtus ochrogaster. Behavioral Ecology and Sociobiology, 5, 171–186.

Thornhill, R., & Alcock, J. (1983). The evolution of insect mating systems. Cambridge: Harvard University Press.

Trivers, R. L. (1972). Parental investment and sexual selection. In B. G. Campbell (Ed.), Sexual selection and the descent of man, 1871–1971 (pp. 136–179). Chicago: Aldine.

Voss, R. (1979). Male accessory glands and the evolution of copulatory plugs in rodents. Occasional Papers of the Museum of Zoology, University of Michigan, 689, 1–17.

Watson, J. B. (1908). The behavior of noddy and sooty terns. Papers from the Tortugas Laboratory of the Carnegie Institution of Washington, 2 (103), 187–255.

Watson, J. B. (1914). Behavior: An introduction to comparative psychology. New York: Holt.

Watson, J. B., & Lashley, K. S. (1915). Homing and related activities of birds. Papers from the Department of Marine Biology of the Carnegie Institution of Washington, 7 (211), 1–128.

Webster, A. B., & Brooks, R. J. (1981). Social behavior of Microtus pennsylvanicus in relation to seasonal cycles in demography. Journal of Mammalogy, 62, 738–751.

Webster, D. G., Williams, M. H., & Dewsbury, D. A. (1982). Female regulation and choice in the copulatory behavior of montane voles (Microtus montanus). Journal of Comparative and Physiological Psychology, 96, 661–667.

Weinrich, J. D. (1977). Human sociobiology: Pair-bonding and resource predictability. Behavioral Ecology and Sociobiology, 2, 91–118.

Wickler, W., & Seibt, U. (1981). Monogamy in crustacea and man. Zeitschrift für Tierpsychologie, 57, 215–234.

Wickler, W., & Seibt, U. (1983). Monogamy: an ambiguous concept. In P. Bateson (Ed.), Mate choice (pp. 33–50). Cambridge: Cambridge University Press.

Wilson, E. O. (1975). *Sociobiology: The new synthesis.* Cambridge: Harvard University Press.

Wilson, S. C. (1982a). Parent-young contact in prairie and meadow voles. *Journal of Mammalogy, 63,* 300–305.

Wilson, S. C. (1982b). The development of social behaviour between siblings and non-siblings of the voles *Microtus ochrogaster* and *Microtus pennsylvanicus. Animal Behaviour, 30,* 426–437.

Wittenberger, J. F. (1979). The evolution of mating systems in birds and mammals. In P. Marler & J. G. Vandenbergh (Eds.), *Handbook of behavioral neurobiology. Vol. 3. Social behavior and communication* (pp. 271–349). New York: Plenum.

Wittenberger, J. F., & Tilson, R. L. (1980). The evolution of monogamy: Hypotheses and evidence. *Annual Review of Ecology and Systematics, 11,* 197–232.

Wolton, R. J. (1985). The ranging and nesting behaviour of wood mice, *Apodemus sylvaticus* (Rodentia: Muridae), as revealed by radio-tracking. *Journal of Zoology, 206,* 203–224.

Wundt, W. (1894). *Lectures on human and animal psychology.* London: Swan Sonnenschein.

Yerkes, R. M. (1941). Conjugal contrasts among chimpanzees. *Journal of Abnormal and Social Psychology, 36,* 175–199.

Coming to Terms With the Everyday Language of Comparative Psychology

Meredith J. West
University of North Carolina

Andrew P. King
Duke University

We learn more by stooping than by soaring—William Wordsworth

*I*t is the custom of the older generation to inform the younger generation of what it was like in the "olden days." "Olden days" were typically a more difficult time involving long walks to school, endless winters, and long, hot summers. And these days were borne without support from the electronic substrate of appliances and technology that now underlies (undermines?) our existence. So too in science, it is the custom to initiate the young by stories of life before their time.

To students now interested in the comparative study of behavior, some of the stories told might seem like transgenerational tales about the past. Did psychologists really think rats were "the" animal model of human behavior? Did they really think human behavior could be reduced to formulas derived from the behavior of rats? Did the field of comparative psychology really let itself become so unfit that it was de-

We thank the The National Science Foundation and the National Institute of Neurological and Communicative Disorders and Stroke for support of our research.

We dedicate this paper to Harry Levin, who was chairman of the Psychology Department at Cornell during our graduate years. He gave us advice. He gave us money. He gave us knowledge. Taken together, he gave us an excellent definition of motivation.

clared brain dead and then miraculously saved by a shot in the arm from ethology (Eaton, 1970)?

As in all tales of the olden days, the truth and nontruth of these tales are artfully intertwined (see Dewsbury, 1984, for the "true" stories). But those of us who have striven to become comparative psychologists in the past two decades have done so in an unsettled atmosphere. We know of few comparative psychologists who have not wondered at times if they were boarding a sinking ship or, to borrow from Tolman (1945), getting too far out on a phylogenetic limb. Would there be so many "Dear Jack" letters in the *Comparative Psychology Newsletter* if feelings of this sort were not so common?

Our formal entry into psychology as first-year graduate students occurred amid the rising and falling fortunes of comparative psychology. We were spared many of the anxieties suffered by other aspiring comparative psychologists at that time because we were in the Department of Psychology at Cornell University. The department had had peculiar notions about the wisdom of studying animals throughout its long history—sometimes being for it, sometimes against it—but because it had even more peculiar notions about psychology as a whole, students interested in animals were considered no odder than anyone else. The Psychology Department prided itself on being out of the mainstream and went to great lengths to steer its students toward untraveled theoretical and empirical routes.

We begin with the atmosphere of Cornell because it was there that we charted for ourselves a voyage from Ithaca to the tip of South America and back again—we even had a beagle to accompany us. It is now more than ten years later—the beagle is gone, and we have not yet crossed the Rio Grande. We have taken this occasion to confront the issue of our slow progress because we believe it represents a timely example of the phyletic fantasy that besets many would-be comparative voyagers. We thought we needed to travel far and wide to be "comparative." We did not yet know how few steps we would take before encountering unexplored pathways. We begin by describing the rationale for our original plan; then we detail some of the phenomena that diverted us and discuss the role simple words played in the origin and modifications of our plans.

The Cowbirds: Have Eggs, Will Travel

The trip we charted from New York to South America is the reverse of the one made by cowbirds. The three genera of cowbirds range from Argentina to Canada and from California to Nova Scotia (Friedmann, 1929). Naturalists have followed their activities closely because all but one of the species are brood parasites: the female cowbird lays her eggs in the nest of another species, and the foster parents then rear the cowbird along with their own young. Only the southernmost species in South America, the bay-winged cowbird (*Molothrus badius*), displays no parasitism, building nests and rearing young as most vertebrates do. Proceeding north, one encounters a succession of cowbird species that are progressively more successful with a greater number of host species. How brood parasitism evolved puzzled Aristotle, and how it has spread in cowbirds is still not understood.

But what fascinated us were the ontogenetic implications of brood parasitism: we would expect the cowbird to inherit an abundance of problems as a result of its upbringing by a foster species. How do cowbirds find other cowbirds? What kinds of species-identity crises are associated with foster rearing? And how does the degree and extent of an individual species's parasitism affect ontogeny? What we saw was an opportunity to study differences in the acquisition of species-typical behaviors where the subjects represented a narrow genetic category but varied broadly with respect to the young's degree of association with conspecifics during the early phases of ontogeny.

Instead of looking at the role of "early experience" in the pigeon, rat, monkey, and human, we could do what truly comparative psychologists should be doing (and what many had been doing; see Dewsbury, 1984)—looking at microphyletic differences in behavior (Beer, 1974). We would begin by studying the role of early experience in the North American brown-headed cowbirds, the end point, if you will, in terms of the amount and diversity of experience with foster species, because this cowbird parasitizes over 100 species and 200 subspecies (Friedmann, Kiff, & Rothstein, 1977). We would then proceed southward to compare them with the Central and South American species, where more selective parasitism occurs, until we ultimately encountered the other end of the continuum, the nonparasitic bay-winged cowbird.

The choice of the behaviors to be compared could be an essay in itself. It is sufficient here to say that we chose to focus on species-typical communication, and cowbird song in particular, because comparative work in other birds suggested that birdsong is a behavior almost always affected by early experience. No songbird has yet been found that is immune to the effects of postnatal experience. Moreover, the study of song development provides an opportunity to see the effects of experience gradually unfold, because the ability to sing develops slowly over many months. There are many other reasons why comparative psychologists are drawn to vocal communication as a means of comparison across species, genera, or phyla (Snowdon, this volume) but the role of experience early in ontogeny was the key feature for our purposes.

Thus we planned to compare closely related species with respect to the ontogenetic attributes of song development as a function of the kinds of early experiences afforded the young. Where are we now? After more than a decade, we have studied several populations of two of the subspecies in North America. Such superficially slow progress has not, however, dampened our eagerness to compare developmental systems—rather the opposite, since we now begin to understand what it means to compare behaving animals in relation to their ecologies.

Functional Metrics of Song Development

We begin with our most basic methods—Designed for and, in some sense, by our specialty, eastern brown-headed cowbirds, *Molothrus ater ater*, male and female. The touchstones of our work are analyses of female cowbirds' copulatory responses to song and males cowbirds' vocal responses to living and singing in different social contexts. Each method gives us different but internally compatible information about cowbird communication, and the combination allows us to study the perception and production of song as a social enterprise.

FEMALE RESPONSIVENESS TO MALE SONG

Few avian species provide clearer data than cowbirds do about song's proximate role as a regulator of mating interactions and its ultimate role as a potential contributor to reproductive isolation (see also Payne, 1983). Briefly said, the song of the male is a necessary, though not sufficient, condition for mate choice, and the behavior of the female is a proximate and an ultimate regulator of the ontogeny and phylogeny of the male's song.

The female's copulatory response to song is a reflex. When stimulated by the "right" song, she responds with a solicitation posture: her wing feathers are lowered and spread apart, her neck and body are arched, and the feathers around the cloacal area separate. If it is the "wrong" song, she continues about her business with so little disruption that one cannot know by her behavior whether she heard the song.

We have studied this response in two contexts. In playback experiments, females are deprived of male companions to lower their threshold for song, and songs are introduced over a loudspeaker. In mate-choice experiments, females residing in large aviaries with males are observed and the details of all copulations are noted. Playback and aviary females do not respond with copulation solicitation postures to all songs, permitting us to categorize songs, males, or both in terms of song potency; that is, the ability of a song to elicit a copulatory response from a female. The nonsolicitation responses to songs by females in aviaries resemble those of playback females: the aviary females often act as if the male had not sung at all. In both contexts, we also find that some females are more easily aroused than others, a source of individual variation under current investigation (King and West, in press a).

Setting the stage for the observation of copulatory responses in either playback or aviary females requires much preparation. For playback experiments, females are usually obtained nine months before they are to be tested during the female's normal reproductive period of May and June. They are housed socially in sound attenuation chambers that are large by laboratory standards (internal dimensions = 1.3 m cube), permitting the birds room to fly, to forage in the rich seed and insect bed, and to interact with companions.

The playback females are subsequently deprived of male (but not female) companions and thus do not hear song as the breeding season nears. In this way we simulate what happens in the everyday cycle of a free-living female where, during the breeding season, females hear many songs in the morning, fewer as the day goes on, and few or none at night and thus awaken naturally deprived of song. That such deprivation normally lowers the female's threshold for responding to song is indicated by our aviary observations, where we find that all copulations occur in the morning, a finding confirmed by others working with field populations (King & West, 1984; Rothstein, Verner, & Stevens, 1984; Yokel, 1986). Thus the playback females are acoustically deprived of song at a time when they are presumed to be most sensitive to it (a presumption supported by the occurrence of egg laying during this same period). Six or seven songs are then presented daily, separated in time by at least 90 minutes. Playbacks occur for approximately six weeks, the length of the female's normal breeding cycle.

By using the aviary and playback assays, we have been able to ask very specific questions about the role of song. Consider one example: By playing back songs from different geographic regions and from a second subspecies of cowbird, *Molothrus ater obscurus*, which occurs in the Southwest, we learned that our eastern females preferred the songs of their own subspecies and determined which parts of the song contained the information permitting females to distinguish the two subspecies' songs (King & West, 1983a, 1983b, 1983c; King, West, & Eastzer, 1980). Briefly, one feature emerges as critical, the presence of a set of low-frequency notes in the middle of the songs of *M. a. obscurus* males, a feature termed the midsong element (MSE) (Figure 1). This feature is never maintained in the repertoires of wild-caught eastern males, making it a marker of subspecific identity.

In further work, we found that we could induce naïve eastern *M. a. ater* males to sing songs with MSEs by housing them with *M. a. obscurus* males or tutoring them with *M. a. obscurus* song. Such males become bilingual, singing both prototypical *M. a. ater* and *M. a. obscurus* songs (West, King, & Harrocks, 1983). The presence of the MSE marker and the ability to manipulate its presence or absence in an eastern male's repertoire allowed us to ask females more specific questions about the role of song in mate choice. Individual eastern males exposed to *M. a. obscurus* differed in the proportion of *M. a. ater* and *M. a. obscurus* songs in their repertoires. The presence of individual variation allowed a truer test of the role of song in relation to copulatory success. Although we had produced variation in the subspecific "identity" of the songs, we had controlled for the subspecific identity of the males themselves by using all eastern males captured at the same site at the same time.

Would aviary females of each subspecies choose mates according to characteristics of the males' songs or some other male characteristic, such as dominance status? Or, given the constraints of captivity, would they show no selectivity, mating with all available males? Prior work demonstrating assortative mating between the two subspecies in captivity

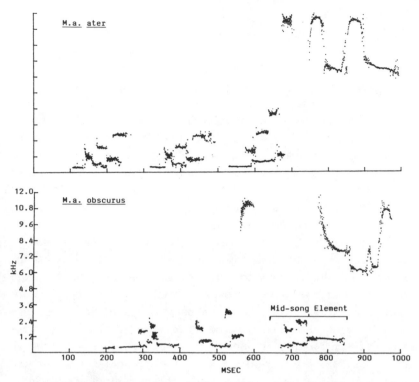

FIGURE 1. Zero-crossings-analyzer displays of *M. a. obscurus* and *M. a. ater* song. Playback experiments to females were used to identify the parts of the song most critical to eliciting the female's copulatory posture (King & West, 1983c). The midsong element (MSE) is most critical to subspecific discrimination, but the interphrase unit (IPU) and other elements in the note clusters of the first phrase contribute to song potency. The second part of the song, the whistle, adds little to song potency and may function in male/male interactions.

suggested that the aviary setting would not prevent females from being highly selective (Eastzer, King, & West, 1985). But on what basis?

Selective mating did occur: *M. a. obscurus* females mated most with the *M. a. ater* males whose repertoires contained the highest proportion of MSE song, and *M. a. ater* females mated most with the *M. a. ater* males singing the fewest song types with MSEs. For the aviary with *M. a. ater* females, the Spearman rank order correlation was +.97, and for the aviary with *M. a. obscurus* females, $r = +.96$ (West et al., 1983). Thus the data directly linked song variation and mate choice.

We also asked essentially the same question of females faced with a range of variation in song content more like what they would normally encounter. Here we observed eastern females assessing eastern males, all of whom had been obtained from the same site. We measured not only what males sang but also how they behaved in terms of courtship behavior and winter dominance interactions with other males (West, King, & Eastzer, 1981a). And we played back their songs to a set of playback females unfamiliar with the individual males. The results demonstrated significant positive correlations among potency, dominance, and copulatory success: males who competed successfully with other males and courted and copulated with the most aviary females sang the songs most often responded to by playback females whose only contact with them was their tape-recorded songs.

Taken together, these studies suggest that cowbird song is a signal of critical importance to females and worthy of developmental study. Our success in getting cowbirds to mate in captivity also meant access to the resource needed for developmental analyses—cowbird eggs. The opportunity to watch an animal go from being an egg to being an egg producer or fertilizer is of course "the" experience for students of ontogeny. But seeing a full revolution of the ontogenetic clock is not always possible in captive populations, because the appropriate circumstances for successful reproduction may not be present. Our desire to see the cowbird's ontogenetic clock move as far as possible directly affected the second method, social rearing in the laboratory.

Kaspar and Kasparina?

Studies of ontogeny are also difficult because developing organisms are moving targets, making measurements of development *during* development hard to come by. The problem obtains for many kinds of social and cognitive development and can easily be seen within the study of the development of birdsong. The customary approach is to obtain birds as young as possible and isolate them from conspecifics, then to record the isolates' songs when they reach maturity. Developmental outcome is assessed most often by judging the structural typicality or lack thereof in the isolates' songs and sometimes by playing back the songs of isolates to wild conspecifics. The housing procedure is the legendary "Kaspar Hauser" condition (Klopfer & Hailman, 1967). Many of the problems with it have been repeatedly explicated, especially the problem of isolating the animal from one particular kind of stimulation without altering any other part of its surroundings.

The problem is really a problem when negative results are obtained: What does it mean when the isolated animal does not perform as well as normally reared animals? Do we conclude that this was caused by isolation per se or the absence of a particular form of stimulation? In most cases we cannot disentangle the two possibilities.

The dilemma of negative data is familiar to all scientists. The somewhat less familiar problem is the interpretation of "positive" data: What can we make of the behaviors produced by isolates? In many animals, particularly primates, the effects of isolation rearing are so obvious in the form of social pathologies that the problem of interpreting outcomes is also obvious. In the study of birdsong the problem is less obvious because the focus has been on only one behavior: the "isolate" song. The isolate song has often been equated with the "innate" song of the species (Thorpe, 1961). The idea is that birds in isolation can consult only their genetic blueprint, and thus the songs that result reveal the contents of that blueprint.

Although reasearch confirms that most songbirds begin the process of song development capable of producing a genetically constrained set of acoustic elements—a significant finding in itself—it cannot reveal whether this is *the* set of acoustic elements that young songbirds of that species normally produce. Isolation experiments cannot by themselves provide this information, because isolation does not preclude the contributions of acoustic self-stimulation to the songs of isolates. Isolated songbirds are living in a highly unusual environment, but not in an environment in which no learning is possible. Kuo (1967) called the behaviors obtained under such conditions "neo-phenotypes": behaviors developed in species-atypical environments that bring out capabilities that may not normally be expressed in the natural environment. The ontogenetically complex nature of neophenotypes has often been discussed, and we need add little except an exposition of how well cowbirds can demonstrate the problem.

First, we must confess that we have never carried out the classic form of the Kaspar Hauser procedure: no bird in our laboratory is ever housed in social isolation during development because we believe this is as pathogenic for a cowbird as it was for poor Kaspar. It is also scientifically wasteful, because it cannot uncover the mechanisms by which cowbirds normally acquire species-typical behavior. Isolation is not a neutral environment, but a biased one affording opportunities for novel experiences. Development proceeds, but in a direction perhaps never encountered normally in a socially reared species.

Given the criticisms ethologists have of the methods of behaviorists, it is ironic to see so many of their criticisms recapitulated in the Kaspar Hauser procedure. For example, some Kaspar Hauser birds have lived in groups of peers, others truly alone, yet little systematic analysis has been carried out to explain the vocal differences that can result from such differences in social housing (but see Marler & Mundinger, 1971). The focus on "appropriate" acoustic stimulation has canalized not only the environments of the subjects, but the methods of the investigators.

To disentangle the effects of isolation from the effects of a particular form of sensory deprivation, we housed acoustically naïve male cowbirds with female cowbirds, which cannot sing and therefore cannot supply the form of experience under study. We also housed some males with members of other species, which could vocalize, but not in a manner species typical for cowbirds. To mix two ethological metaphors, our Kaspars always had "Kumpans" (Lorenz, 1970).

When male cowbirds are so housed they, like all songbirds, develop structurally atypical songs, demonstrating that they must hear other males sing in order to produce species-typical song. But playback females that heard the vocal productions of the song-isolated males liked them, responding twice as often to the atypical songs of the naïve males as to the songs of males reared under the more normal conditions of social housing with both males and females (King & West, 1977). Does this mean acoustic isolation is "good" for cowbirds? If so, why do they live in social groups in the wild?

Here was Kuo's neophenotype: we had biased the environment so that males showed a different behavior than normally-reared conspecifics—but in this case the outcome appeared positive. For reasons we would like to forget, we called this effect the "isolate song effect"— probably because the phrase "isolate song" was common jargon among song researchers and because the males had been isolated from song, which was supposedly the critical variable (West, King, & Eastzer, 1981b). The correct name for the finding is the opposite—the "audience song effect" because all our birds had an audience, and it was the effect of the audience, not auditory deprivation, that was subsequently found to account for the songs' super-potency.

MALE SONG LEARNING:
THE EXPERIENCE OF
INEXPERIENCE

The anomalous finding of higher song potency in naïve males led us to look more closely at their behavior. First we observed such males after they had been housed in acoustic isolation, then we observed them during the period of isolation itself. Such a counterclockwise approach to ontogeny was necessary because it was hard to know what to look for until we had at least glimpsed the outcome.

The results of song deprivation experiments with most passerines are typically evaluated using a single measure of outcome: the male's mature song is examined to determine whether it is structurally "abnormal" (Kroodsma & Baylis, 1982). Such a single measure, however, would not have revealed the songs' higher potency. We added a further test by using our aviary populations—we allowed our song-isolated males to interact with captive colonies. What would male-deprived males do when they had to interact with other males and females?

The "isolate" songs of many species have not been tested in a functional arena because complete isolation often has profound behavioral effects, precluding measures of outcome beyond production of song within the confines of a sound-attenuating chamber. But because our cowbirds had companions and were housed in relatively large chambers, the birds reached sexual maturity in better psychological shape and could be moved to new surroundings for functional tests of their songs. How would a song-isolated male fare when singing to a new audience containing males?

The study swiftly exposed the social naïveté of the song-isolated subjects. Such males readily attempted to sing to the new males and females, but they showed no signs of cowbird etiquette. Socially housed cowbird males form dominance hierarchies, and dominance position affects access to females—the more dominant males court more females and obtain more copulations, and they sing the most potent songs. When the song-isolated males were introduced they too sang their potent songs, but with a different result: they were attacked by the resident males, and had we not intervened they would have been seriously injured or killed (West & King, 1980).

Equally unfamiliar males that had been socially housed with males were also introduced as a control condition. None of those males sang in the presence of the other males, and none were attacked. Living alone with females had not prepared the song-isolated male for an important fact of cowbird life—song potency may be inherited, but the opportunity to sing must be earned (West & King, 1980). Such learning can occur quickly during male/male social interactions: when we reintroduced the song-isolated birds to the same colony a week after their first visit, they did not sing to males or to females when males were nearby, and they were not attacked.

Thus the reason we must rename the "isolate song effect" is the *functional* as opposed to the *structural* outcome of vocal development in acoustic isolation. We had deprived the males of song but enriched their dominance status: in that context they could sing potent songs with impunity, a privilege typically accorded to males that are socially dominant over females *and* males in nature.

"Audience" effects have been studied in a range of species but had hitherto not been considered part of song learning (but see Gyger, Karakashian, & Marler, 1986; Zajonc, 1965). The most common approach was to ask what there was inside the bird's head that guided song learning—the search for sensory templates is a good example. The second most common question was about the effects of fellow performers— adults who might serve as song tutors. To ask about the effects of *non-singing* listeners and to consider such effects part of song learning was in part a theoretical exclusion. If you cannot sing, you cannot be imitated, and song learning had been defined by all as an imitative process (Kroodsma & Baylis, 1982).

Two observations suggested that such a definition was too limited. First, we had found that adult eastern *M. a. ater* males would become bilingual only if housed with *M. a. obscurus* males *and* females, not if housed with *M. a. obscurus* males alone—though juvenile *M. a. ater* males quite readily became bilingual. This observation suggested that the males required both the means (hearing *M. a. obscurus* song) and a motive (the female) to do what juveniles do on the basis of vocal stimulation alone (West et al., 1983).

Second, though we had evidence that eastern *M. a. ater* males could develop highly effective songs without acoustic stimulation from adults, we also had evidence that they did not imitate the songs of other males on the basis of the song's potency to females. To learn about naïve males' copying preferences, we had housed acoustically naïve eastern *M. a. ater* males with other species and tutored them with 12 cowbird songs, six of which were highly effective releasers of the female's copulatory posture and six of which were highly ineffective.

Given that male cowbirds' repertoires rarely exceed six or seven songs, the males would have to choose from among the larger set. Would they copy songs that females independently judged to be more potent? Said another way, would their copying preferences correlate with the copulatory preferences of females? For comparison, we played back the 12 songs to a new set of females as well, to get two samples of females' assessments of their potency.

The results suggested that naïve males profit from experience with both males and females. Although males copied the effective songs more often than the ineffective songs, all regularly sang one or more of the ineffective songs. The correlation between male copying and female assays of potency was low ($r_s = .22$ and $r_s = .38$), in contrast to the significant positive correlation obtained between the two sets of females ($r_s = .82$). Thus, either males know the better songs but choose not to sing them (perhaps to have songs for male/male interaction) or they do not know the "best" songs until after they have used them in social interactions with males and females (West & King, 1986).

We have now repeated the same experiment housing naïve males with conspecific females or males instead of with other species, and the results suggest that both kinds of social interaction have effects. Males housed with other males retained the highest proportion of ineffective songs and developed very little original song, that is, songs structurally dissimilar to any of the tutor songs. In contrast, males housed with females sang the fewest ineffective songs. These males also differed from those housed with other species in that they went beyond the tutor material to develop repertoires containing largely original songs, suggesting that stimulation from the females aroused the males to innovative lengths not seen in males housed with other species (King and West, in press b).

Although we need to learn much more about the role of innovation and improvisation, the data are sufficient to indicate that the nature of the singer's audience affects the process of song acquisition. Given that males sing to attract individual females in order to mate, we must assume that guidance about which songs are most suited to that end is critical. Because females had been studied less than males, we were most curious about their role: Could it be that behind every "great" cowbird song was the proverbial female?

To answer this question, we studied naïve eastern *M. a. ater* males housed with other species, with adult eastern females, or with adult *M. a. obscurus* females for an entire year. Thus the males were all equally deprived of hearing cowbird song but were exposed to different forms of social stimulation. While they were with their respective companions, we recorded the birds' songs twice a month from November through June so that we could begin to determine at what time during ontogeny female guidance might begin to operate.

Let's begin at the end. The breeding-season songs of the three groups differed significantly whether judged by structural measures of acoustic properties or by functional measures of song potency. At the end of this period, the three groups of males had developed structurally and functionally different vocal neophenotypes, though none had ever heard another male sing and all had been obtained as eggs from the same colony (and most likely were full or half-siblings; King & West, 1983a; West & King, 1985).

The performance of the males housed with other species provides a convenient midpoint, because these males experienced abundant social and vocal stimulation from their starling or canary companions but none that was of species-typical relevance. Their repertoires were diverse; they sang some protypical *M. a. ater* and *M. a. obscurus* songs and some highly atypical songs, including imitations of starling and canary vocalizations as well as the sounds of insects. The general or perhaps "generic" nature of their repertoires highlighted the biasing effects of the females in the other two groups. The females' presence led to local song differentiation: the males housed with *M. a. ater* females sang prototypical *M. a. ater* songs; the *M. a. ater* males housed with *M. a. obscurus* females sang predominantly *M. a. obscurus* songs. In nature, such differentiation is undoubtedly also affected by feedback from other males operating as tutors and as filters of what is sung.

But the major point here is that the behavior of females was sufficient for structural and functional differentiation of song structure in the absence of opportunities for modeling or imitation. If song learning were an exclusively imitative and auditory process, the vocal phenotypes of the three groups of male cowbirds should have been indistinguishable, because all were equally deprived of hearing male song and all were operating with presumably quite similar templates. But reliably different neophenotypes occurred, reflecting the contrasting social properties of their environments.

As a further test of the effect of female stimulation, we explored its influence when appropriate auditory input *was* present (King & West, 1983a). Here *M. a. ater* males were tutored with *M. a. ater* song and individually housed either with *M. a. obscurus* females or with canaries. Again the males developed significantly different repertoires. Males housed with other species sang significantly more of the tutor songs than did males housed with *M. a. obscurus* females, who in turn sang reliably more original songs. Thus, even when males were given the "means" to sing their native variant, the behavior of the heterosubspecific female modified the "motive" such that they adopted new variants. Playback tests to *M. a. ater* females confirmed the motivational effect: the songs of the males housed with other species were reliably more effective than those of the males housed with *M. a. obscurus* female companions (West & King, 1985).

It is important to note that all the effects took place before the females came into reproductive condition, and that all data are based on songs recorded before any male had seen a female in a copulatory posture. It is also important to say that however the females affected the differences in the structure and potency of the males' songs, they did *not* do it by singing. In the two experiments just reported, over 32,000 songs were recorded with an observer present: all were sung by males and none by females.

These data show that male cowbirds are open to social influences from their audience and that they react to them with vocal modifications. Analyses of the vocalizations that preceded the final stereotyped songs of the males revealed that males notice their audience from the start. From the earliest point at which vocalizations could be recorded in late fall, the three groups differed. Even in the highly variable and labile vocalizations produced in late fall of the birds' first year, typically called "subsong" and "plastic song," males with different companions sang different kinds of notes. And from the earliest point at which vocalizations could be classed in definitely ordered note sequences with recognizable geographic markers, the males differed in how often they included such markers: males housed with *M. a. obscurus* females or other species included the *M. a. obscurus* markers from the beginning, but males housed with *M. a. ater* females never did so, suggesting that whatever trial-and-error learning is involved can occur very early in development.

Vocal precursors to stereotyped song such as subsong and plastic song are typically not considered communicative behaviors in songbirds. Rather, the period of progressing from subsong to plastic song to crystallized song is considered a sensorimotor activity whereby the bird learns to control his voice by ear (Marler & Peters, 1982). In essence, the idea is that the bird has to learn to sing clearly before he can "say" anything. But the cowbird data challenge this assumption. First, they suggest that the cowbird is learning to control his voice by eye as well as by ear: he not only hears a song's effect, he sees it in the behavior of the listener. Second, the data suggest that cowbirds communicate by song-like vocalizations long before any stereotypy is present. Why would listeners respond differentially if it were not that they found the vocalizations communicative?

Why haven't these earlier stages been studied as communicative behaviors? Probably because the true isolates studied in other species had no one to interact with—the idea that song learning is an auditory but not a social process is so well entrenched that this condition has often been ignored or incompletely analyzed. It is also true that vocal precursors are hard to study—to learn about them in cowbirds involved analyzing more than 34,000 vocalizations and 100,000 individual notes, an analysis exceeding in time the typical life span of a cowbird (and approaching that of a comparative psychologist).

These new data raise an important question: If even the most rudimentary cowbird vocalizations are informative, what is song development for? We were also prompted to ask this after completing an experiment in which we played back samples of vocal precursors obtained from a new sample of males. We also played back the songs of other species. Could females tell a cowbird when the only information was subsong? The answer was a resounding yes (West & King, in press). Although when given a choice females responded more to more developed song, subsong was shown to be a species-identifiable marker. Then why is the male doing all this? If he can already communicate that he is a cowbird, why does song continue to change? To answer this we must return to the earlier theme of song's role in mate selection and consider song development from the perspective of the female.

The Female Cowbird: Cultivating Fine Song

What was most visible about the vocal behavior of the males housed with females in the experiments described above was the number of the males' songs and song attempts that were met with apparent indifference by the females. The seemingly inexhaustible energy of the singing male stood in stark contrast to the passive posture of the "listening" (many would say "snoozing") female as, song after song, she "responded" with not so much as a head movement toward or away from her companion who often was within six inches of her.

The aviary mate-choice experiments had revealed that during breeding season females possess a hierarchy of potential responses to song: they may respond with a copulatory posture, lunge and attack the male, fly away, chatter at the male, or do nothing. They may respond with one or more of these behaviors at different points in a male's courtship sequence of approaching and singing. Although we cannot yet specify how females communicate their likes and dislikes before the breeding season—for example, in early winter—the female's apparent inattention is quite likely one of the more powerful social signals at her command, and it is the one commanding our attention right now.

Inattention is important for many reasons. First, inattention highlights the times when a female does change her behavior by moving toward or away from the male, by moving her wing feathers, or by turning her head. Because of the high incidence of no visible change in her behavior, when changes such as wingflicks or approaches do occur, they undoubtedly have a high "signal-to-noise" ratio. Moreover, the behavior of no change in behavior, or of ignoring, is itself a potent social signal in the communication systems of many organisms.

Second, the response of no response merits study because it is the female's most frequent behavior when sung to by a male. Finally, it is important because females vary in just how responsive or nonresponsive they are, as judged either by playback test data or by responses to actual males. We learned about this by examining the absolute responsiveness to song of the females exposed to the 12 high- and low-potency songs mentioned earlier (West & King, 1986). Although females agreed on which they ranked best to worst, their absolute level of responsiveness differed: some females responded on more days and on more trials.

After the playback season, we housed these same females with males. We tutored the males with the same songs previously played back to the females. The major result was that prior playback nonresponsiveness correlated well with nonresponsiveness to actual males and also correlated with amount of male improvisation. The males given nonresponsive female companions "worked" harder: they improvised more than twice as much as males housed with very responsive females (King & West, in press a).

Returning to the question of the function of song development, the last set of data suggests to us that males sing not so much to inform females of their identity as to arouse the females to notice them in particular. Female arousal was of course the original function assigned to song by Huxley—he termed it the "stimulative" function (Huxley, 1923; Smith, 1977). Focus on the "informative" function came later—probably when the term was infiltrating all the sciences. The "information" function was also more relevant to the situations in which song has been studied most thoroughly—territorial contexts where visual information is less available. If new information is also transmitted when male cowbirds sing to females, it may be information about how well the males can sing. Given that local females agree among themselves about which songs are potent, and given that female stimulation appears to guide males down the same vocal pathways, males face a difficult task. To succeed they have to do more than possess the right songs, because the other males may also know these songs. An individual male may have to sing his songs with "feeling," a subjective measure easy to recognize but hard to define and probably synonymous with Tom Wolfe's concept of the "right stuff."

Females may then participate in song development to become better at detecting or cultivating the "right stuff." By stimulating males to sing the same song material, the females may be able to make finer discriminations among males by judging how well the males sing a song the females know well. If males are to be "socially screened," in West-Eberhard's terms (1983), a screening based on the same material appears to be most advantageous.

It is likely that song is a critical cue for female choice of mates, even more critical than in nonparasitic species, where information about mate quality is available through behaviors in preparation for parental care. Payne (1983) has made similar arguments about the parasitic indigo bird (*Vidua*), documenting his views with data on the pivotal role that male song content plays in female choice of mates. But in cowbirds it may be not song content that females use, but singing ability. The opportunity to demonstrate singing ability, of course, comes after competition among males with respect to dominance: it is the more dominant cowbird males that sing the most potent songs and court the most females. Little is known about the perception of song quality as apart from song structure in any songbird from the listener's point of view. Perhaps the ability to sing well communicates strength or vigor. Might it not also be a sign of good health? Thus males may have to sing what females want to hear not to inform them about their species, subspecies, or individual identity, but to advertise their health, presumed fecundity, and individuality.

DEVELOPMENT IN THE FEMALE:
OPENING A CLOSED PROGRAM

Is the female's ability to stimulate males affected by her early experience, and does the feedback she gives change with experience? We have pursued these questions in parallel with our investigations of male song ontogeny. And in so doing we have encountered other reasons for questioning the everyday language of comparative psychology because, as with the "isolate song effect," we have had to struggle to find the right words to fit the ontogenetic patterns of cowbirds.

In 1983, we published a paper entitled "Female Perception of Cowbird Song: A Closed Developmental Program." In the introduction, we stated that "the female cowbird's preference for her native song variant appears to be highly resistant to environmental modification after hatching" (King & West, 1983c, p. 339). We must now retract that statement on the basis of two experiments. First, we now know that the female's potential for modification cannot be established by comparing the social preferences of females exposed to different social companions during periods of presumed modifiability. Second, we know that different populations of *M. a. ater* females differ in aspects of their ontogeny—we are far from being able to characterize even the behavior of populations within the same subspecies, let alone "the" female cowbird's behavior.

We made the mistake for good reasons. First, the cowbird is often cited as an exemplar of a closed genetic program: it held that "honor" before there were any data on the question (e.g., Lehrman, 1974; Mayr, 1974) and even after the appearance of data to the contrary (e.g., Rothstein, Yokel, & Fleischer, 1986). A nativistic orientation toward this species persists because of the assumption that a brood parasite must depend less on learning and because of the presumed higher probability of errant learning from foster parents or peers.

How does one establish the potential for modification? Most now argue that biologically appropriate stimulus objects are of unquestionable importance (Shapiro, 1980). Recent discoveries of song learning after the end of the presumed sensitive period in white-crowned sparrows (*Zonotrichia leucophrys*) (Baptista & Petrinovich, 1984, 1986) and of sibling influences on the establishment and maintenance of imprinting in ducklings (*Anas platyrynchos*) (Lickliter & Gottlieb, 1985, 1986) attest to the power of socially oriented paradigms to uncover the role of naturally occurring experience during development.

But there is a cost to using animate sources of potential influence, that is, the possibility of reversed and/or reciprocal influence. What if the animal designated the *source* of influence becomes the *subject* of influence as well? That is precisely the situation we uncovered as we tried to study whether females are influenced by their social and acoustic environment.

ESTABLISHING THE ''NONEFFECTS'' OF SOCIAL EXPERIENCE: A CASE OF ''WHO'S ON FIRST?''

Naïve female cowbirds, with no exposure to conspecifics, respond selectively to cowbird song using the bioassay described above, thereby establishing that species identification is possible in the absence of conspecific stimulation (King & West, 1977). But such a finding is easily overinterpreted to mean that subsequent learning is not possible or is not critical to mate choice: perhaps the initial capacity is naturally modified by experience with conspecifics, making the responses of the naïve female just another behavioral neophenotype. Perhaps females *can* identify males with no experience but never do so because they never encounter such a circumstance; males and females congregate together for many months before courtship. Thus, determining whether the females' initial biases are naturally modified and tuned to the geographically and socially distinct variants of song produced by individual males represents the functionally valid level of analysis, because it focuses on how females discriminate song in relation to mate selection.

We first attempted to study how females develop intraspecific selectivity to male song by housing acoustically naïve or wild-caught juvenile *M. a. ater* females for an entire year with *M. a. obscurus* males or with males of their own subspecies.

No effects of experience were apparent: in playback tests, 25 of 26 females responded more often to native *M. a. ater* songs than to *M. a. ob-*

scurus songs (the 26th responded equally), producing a mean response ratio of 2:1 in favor of native song (King & West, 1983b). The selectivity of the females housed with heterosubspecific males was indistinguishable from that of the normally housed females.

In conceptualizing a social system for song development, we saw it as a synergistic one in which social responses from the females stimulated males to modify their vocalizations. We hypothesized that the female served to guide the male's learning because her own song biases were not susceptible to social influence, a conclusion based empirically on the 1983 test of female modifiability and on the responses of a hybrid female that showed the song preferences of her *M. a. ater* mother, not her *M. a. obscurus* father.

But the finding that males are sensitive to female guidance meant that we had not carried out the experiment we supposed in King and West (1983b). If the *M. a. ater* females housed with the *M. a. obscurus* males in that study were instead socially influencing the potency of the songs of their male companions, then the males were not receiving the stimulation intended—that is, potent song stimulation from alien subspecies. This would have been the case if *M. a. obscurus* males, like *M. a. ater* males, are influenced by females. Hence we needed to rethink the results of 1983 and investigate whether the *M. a. obscurus* males used as possible modifiers of the 1983 females' preferences had been modified by their female companions.

To find out we tested the potency of the songs of two groups of *M. a. obscurus* males, the ones used as companions for the 1983b females and a comparison set housed with *M. a. obscurus* females. After social housing, we played back all the males' songs to a new set of *M. a. obscurus* and *M. a. ater* females—the central question was how they would respond to the *M. a. obscurus* males' songs. If the *M. a. ater* females had had an effect, there should be perceptible differences in the potency of the songs of *M. a. obscurus* males housed with *M. a. ater* females.

And there were. The songs of the *M. a. obscurus* males housed with the 1983b *M. a. ater* females were significantly less potent than those of males housed with *M. a. obscurus* females (King & West, 1987).

Thus, although the 1983b females exposed to *M. a. obscurus* males may have begun the year hearing potent song, they ended it hearing ineffective song. The females with the *M. a. obscurus* males may then have retained their preferences because the songs they heard were not sufficiently stimulating to modify their behavior.

Thus we cannot conclude that eastern *M. a. ater* females are not modifiable—nor can we conclude that they are. All we can conclude is that the method was inappropriate because it failed to take into account the possibility of reversed social influence. Given the nature of cowbird song development, alternative strategies are needed to determine who is influencing whom and whose influence comes first.

The data from the last experiment also suggest that our concept of female song perception is too narrow: listening to a male sing is in itself a social interaction in which the singing male learns about singing by observing the listener. The listening female may also be learning in the sense that her initial song preferences are repeatedly reinforced by the male's vocal and social behavior. We chose to pursue the nature of this perception-production-attention cycle in a second study—also carried out in the light of data about differences in the developmental basis of female discrimination of song within the *M. a. ater* subspecies.

Subspecific Differences in the Ontogeny of Song Responsiveness

As part of our efforts to study the eastern female's response to songs from the second subspecies, we also became interested in other populations of *M. a. ater*, especially ones living nearer to populations of *M. a. obscurus*. Thus, for the past several years we have been studying females collected in Oklahoma. These females are morphologically similar to the North Carolina females and are classified as the *M. a. ater* subspecies, but they live nearer to the morphologically described subspecies border between *M. a. ater* and *M. a. obscurus*, a line drawn east to west across northern Texas.

When adult *M. a. ater* females from the Oklahoma site were tested for their discrimination of playback songs from their local area as opposed to songs of *M. a. obscurus*, they showed as strong a native preference as do *M. a. ater* from North Carolina (King et al., 1980; King, West, & Eastzer, 1986). But in contrast to *M. a. ater* from North Carolina (*M. a. ater*–NC), when juvenile *M. a. ater* females from Oklahoma (*M. a. ater*–OK) were housed for a year with *M. a. obscurus* males, their behavior differed from that of Oklahoma females housed with native males. Here we found a "positive" effect of social housing: the experimental group developed no song bias, responding equally often to *M. a. ater*–OK and *M. a. obscurus* song, in contrast to the normally housed females.

A modifiable program for female song perception thus seemed to operate in this part of the subspecies range. Here females appeared initially more susceptible to early postnatal influence from males, thus broadening their song preferences. Considering this finding from the male's perspective, what should be the effect of female modifiability on male modifiability? We should then expect that *M. a. obscurus* males housed with such females would *not* change their songs as did *M. a. obscurus* males housed with NC *M. a. ater* females (King & West, 1983a). Why? Because they should be singing songs in line with the females' preferences.

Song potency should be high if the males' and females' preferences match. We tested this hypothesis by repeating the experimental procedures of King and West (1983a) but with *M. a. ater*–OK instead of *M. a. ater*–NC females. We were in effect asking the question of female modifiability in reverse: If males are singing what females already "like" to hear, do they retain their song patterns even if the females are from another subspecies?

Acoustic analyses of the songs of the *M. a. obscurus* males housed with the *M. a. ater*–OK females had already suggested that males' singing was unaffected, because no clear acoustic differences could be detected in the songs of *M. a. obscurus* males housed with *M. a. ater*–OK females (King et al., 1986).

The playback tests verified the acoustic analyses: new sets of normally housed *M. a. ater*-OK and *M. a. obscurus* females did not find the songs of the *M. a. obscurus* males housed with *M. a. ater*–OK females less potent: no effect on potency was apparent at all (King & West, 1987).

Wild-caught *M. a. ater* adult females from North Carolina and Oklahoma thus apparently both prefer native *M. a. ater* song, but they do proceed along the same ontogenetic pathways leading to the similar adult phenotypes. In the east, *M. a. ater* females may or may not be influenced by males, but they appear to take the lead in determining the direction of effects on song modifiability. In the Midwest, the male's influence seems to dominate. But in both populations social influences occur, with the nature of the social stimulation presumably determined by population differences in their ecologies.

The two populations differ in several ways that may provide clues to why different developmental programs exist. First, cowbirds in Oklahoma represent the central and ancestral part of the species's range, whereas cowbirds have colonized North Carolina within the past half-century (Potter & Whitehurst, 1981). Second, population densities differ; the local populations in the Midwest are much larger than those in the southeastern part of the species's range. Finally, the populations differ in their proximity to cowbirds of the *M. a. obscurus* subspecies, the Oklahoma birds reside within 250 km of a subspecies border. All these differences can affect patterns of song communication in other passerines and represent important areas of future inquiry (Becker, 1982).

At present, our current thinking regarding the population differences in development is that female cowbirds in Oklahoma encounter more males and more potential mates and thus face the problem of assessing song quality at a finer acoustic level of analysis than do females in the East. We make this suggestion because the acoustic analyses of songs from these areas indicate much greater stereotypy in the acoustic properties of the songs in the midwestern population (King et al., 1986). This hypothesis is also supported by other playback experiments showing that OK females prefer their local variants over other within-sub-species *M. a. ater* variants, whereas NC females respond equally to *M. a. ater* variants from local or distant within-subspecies populations.

Because little work has been done on intrasubspecific differences in female responsiveness in other songbirds, it is difficult to evaluate the present work with respect to nonparasitic passerines. But evidence exists on the influences of ecological parameters such as dispersal rate, site fidelity, population density, and migratory patterns on properties of male song development (Becker, 1982; Krebs and Kroodsma, 1980). The role of vocal imitation and improvisation, for example, seem probabilistically tied to opportunities to hear other males. It seems highly likely that the same kind of interdependence between capacity and opportunity would exist in female receptivity.

Other aspects of the NC-OK differences merit attention and further inquiry, but the studies to date seem sufficient to show that differences within subspecies of cowbirds are great enough to make broader levels of comparison highly premature.

The last two experiments demonstrate that in cowbirds an experiment on female modifiability is also an experiment on male modifiability and vice versa. The work reported here showed that the 1983 females modified the experiment we tried to conduct. Given these methodological problems, how can modifiability be studied? A more promising means of investigating the development of perceptual processes in females comes from the methodology reported earlier comparing how different groups of females rank songs in terms of their effectiveness in eliciting copulatory responding. When the two groups of *M. a. ater*–NC females' rankings were compared in West and King (1986), even though the females had heard the songs as part of different playback experiments, their rankings of the songs from high to low potency were highly correlated ($r_s = .82$, $p < .01$). So too, comparisons across two years for the same females produced correlations of $r = .81$ for the same set of songs. The findings suggest that North Carolina females possess a high level of within-sex concordance as to the characteristics of potent songs, a concordance that perhaps can be probed to determine the effects of social experience.

The question to ask now is about concordance across samples of *M. a. ater*–OK females. If our working hypothesis about their more open program is correct, naïve Oklahoma females should show more variability, and hence less agreement, about which songs they perceive as more or less potent. Preliminary data suggest that they do show less agreement.

We have now traveled from North Carolina to Oklahoma with a few excursions into Texas to talk about the *M. a. obscurus* populations we have studied. In terms of our travels, the map contains a few other points. We have studied eastern populations captured from locations other than North Carolina, and we find few acoustic differences in the males' songs and, thus far, little variation in the behavior of females. We have also studied *M. a. obscurus* from California, a population representing the western end of the second subspecies. The data suggest that California *M. a. obscurus* males may show a different pattern of song development. Wild-caught California *M. a. obscurus* males housed in acoustic isolation until their first breeding season produced syntactically atypical song that was functionally less effective when played back to California females than either Texas *M. a. obscurus* or North Carolina *M. a. ater* song. Males from Texas or North Carolina housed identically produce syntactically stable and functionally effective songs at a point in time when the males from the California population were still producing immature song. Thus, the California population appears even more dependent on acoustic and possibly social stimulation for song development to proceed normally, pointing to another ontogenetic difference between cowbird subspecies.

Given such differences within these two subspecies, the reasons for the slow course of the initially planned journey should now be obvious.

We probably will never make it south of the Rio Grande, because we have found a species so full of paradoxes that our desire to travel far has been diminished. We think theoretical advances may come faster if we stay close to home.

Coming to Terms

We shall address these theoretical concerns by turning now to the question of vocabulary. Words steer research voyages, and many of the words we shall discuss have determined the paths we have followed.

The story recounted here could be summarized for a number of current themes in animal behavior. Some of the ones that come quickly to mind are cowbirds and reproductive life history correlates, cowbirds and decision-making processes of mate selection, cowbirds and parental investment or lack thereof, cowbirds and status signaling—all seem to fit. These are popular words chosen by no special strategy. They were the ones most conspicuous in the table of contents of a recent issue of *Animal Behaviour*.

E. B. White (Strunk & White, 1979) issued a warning about such words: "Avoid the elaborate, the pretentious, the coy, and the cute. Do not be tempted by a twenty-dollar word when there is ten-center handy, ready and able" (p. 76). But he also admitted that the most important bioassay of when to use the fancy or the plain is the writer's own ear, citing Abraham Lincoln's use of "Four score and seven," instead of eighty-seven, as a brilliant violation.

Because "ears" are basic to our research, I want to explore White's rule 14, "Avoid fancy words," and also rule 16, "Be clear." It is at that level that some of the everyday words in comparative psychology are worrisome, words that many might consider only "ten-centers" but that do not always ring true.

BEHAVIOR: BRINGING A NOUN TO LIFE

What about "behavior," for example? What could possibly be wrong with it? Nothing at the general level of announcing that what is to be communicated is not chemistry or botany. But at the level of the science of comparative psychology, trouble hovers over it.

A writer once said that in every noun there is a verb trying to escape. In the case of behavior, the verb potentially being smothered is "*behaving*." Consider cowbird song development. Cowbirds may be said to possess a song—a behavior, if you will—but what they do is sing. If there is a redundant message in the many studies of song detailed here, it is that the level of analysis should be the singing male and the listening female, a dynamic duo that is a far cry from the static pair summoned up by the terms song production and song perception. A cowbird cannot succeed by handing his song to the female any more than we can escape the duties of scientific writing by publishing only pages of numbers or sonagrams.

Moreover, the cowbird research suggests that at least in the eastern subspecies, the females may in fact already know the script, perhaps even better than the males themselves. But what arouses them is a stirring performance.

To put it another way, and to borrow from another president, the way to think about cowbird song development is to "ask not what your song can do for you, but what you can do for your song." And what cowbirds can do for their song comes through social interactions where the judge of success or failure is not a human experimenter but other cowbirds.

Although the influence of ethology on comparative psychology has been rejuvenating, its impact on the meanings of words must be carefully considered. Ethologists tend to use the term "behavior" in much the same way that comparative anatomists use the term "organ." When behavior is viewed as an organ, it is easier to accept the nominal form. Such usage may also cause few difficulties when we classify animals into taxa according to their behavioral and morphological adaptations. But to study behavior in action is a harder task. Behaving organisms cannot be pinned down, preserved in formalin, or put on ice to await dissection.

To see "behavior" in its nominal form, visit the Smithsonian Museum of Natural History. There you can gaze at the glassed-in dioramas of other animals or our ancestors. Each organism is fixed in a characteristic posture: an Indian poised to throw a spear, a bear about to roar. No disrespect is meant toward such museum displays, but scientists must work with behavior in ongoing form, and the language of behavior should allow us to communicate the differences between animate and inanimate forms.

The "noun problem" is compounded when the subject matter is developing organisms. There is probably a point at which the anatomist can say that the bird's wing is fully formed. We are less convinced that we know yet how to measure the end point of many behaviors. We can tell you when a cowbird's song becomes structurally stable, if only for one breeding season, but not when a male no longer has the possibility of changing the song's rhythm or musical qualities.

The noun chosen here is concrete—a bird's song can be heard and recorded and a bird's singing directly observed. What about the more abstract cornerstones of our theories, such as "templates," "instincts," "releasers," and "genetic programs"? Don't worry, you say, these are only hypothetical constructs. Or perhaps some would perceive them as metaphors—constructive figures of speech used to help us see similarities. Metaphors play a useful role in science, linking the concrete to the abstract. Sometimes, however, we abuse their "as if" status and exploit them as explanations. "He combs metaphors over the bald spots of his theories," one writer once complained about another. We too should consider the often only cosmetic contributions of such constructs. The challenge is to find the words to capture the ongoing behavioral performances behind the constructs.

"THE" ENVIRONMENT: SEEING THE OBVIOUS

The proper grammatical form for the second term, "environment," is not clear. What is clear is that there is little consensus about its concrete or abstract status. Given the frequency with which psychologists utter phrases such as "the effect of the environment" and the role of "genes and the environment," one would think a clear definition exists. It does not. The term does not appear in Verplanck's (1957) glossary of words used in the "objective science of behavior," though it is used in some of his definitions.

To some the term "environment" summons to mind the variable and unpredictable actions of "Nature" with a capital N, as used in phrases such as "Mother Nature" and "Man against Nature." Here the meaning is the broad set of controlling forces that define the biosphere. Ecologists would label this denotation of environment the "ecotope." This is the environment outside the organism in the broadest sense possible.

But to others the term "environment" defines the particular and unique surroundings of each species. Here the term "habitat" comes closer to what is meant, implying a closer relation between the inside and outside of the organism, which may or may not be considered part of the habitat itself. The difference in meaning between ecotope and habitat is vital, because we speak of organisms as evolving defenses and buffers against an essentially erratic *environment-as-ecotope*, but we speak of them as evolving sensitivities and dependencies on the *environment-as-habitat*.

These differences in usage explain why, for example, cowbirds were and are often cited as exemplars of animals whose behavior is genetically constrained. How else could they avoid mislearning or missing opportunities for learning in the unpredictable environment of their youth? But although cowbirds initially associate with other species, they join conspecifics within their first 50 days and, in that sense, inherit a highly dependable juvenile habitat in which to learn species-typical modes of behaving.

But as long as the environment is viewed only in its general role as an uncontrollable agency, the emphasis will be on buffers and constraints to protect the organism rather than on the invariant features or affordances that educate the organism. We might hope that the view of the environment as erratic is outmoded, but it is not. It appears in especially strong form in sociobiological circles, where the idea of "the phenotype at the mercy of the environment" still flourishes in the 1980s (Stearns, 1982, p. 252; see also Gould, 1982; Marler, 1982).

How then do we communicate about the bounty of the environment-as-habitat? Ontogeny in many organisms relies on *exposure* to such bounty. The chances that a male cowbird will hear another cowbird sing or see a female react are about even with the chances that he will find a pasture and cows and develop a syrinx. In many organisms, sensory development has evolved around the idea that the "average, expectable" environment contains certain kinds of stimulation.

Elsewhere we have proposed the term "ontogenetic niche" to stand for the social and ecological legacies inherited by organisms. We favor "niche" because it complements its conceptual cognates "nature" and "nurture" (West & King, 1987). But more important, the term is attractive because it has stood the test of time as a foundational principle in ecology. It was intended to explain organisms *in relation to* their surroundings, not apart from them, and our research convinces us that psychology must adopt this social perspective. A growing number of scientists have also recognized the ecological usage (e.g., Barker, 1960;

Brunswick, 1955; Gibson, 1966; Schleidt, 1981). Barker (1960) captured this nicely in his Nebraska Symposium address:

> The principles of economics which explain the demand for wheat in Chicago are foreign to the laws of mechanics that account for movement of a train of wheat in Kansas when the pressure on the piston passes a critical point, and this is irrelevant to the reasons water changes to steam and steam expands when heat is applied. Yet in some way these molecular, mechanical, and economic phenomena are related on the Kansas plan. (p. 6).

But until we have a better grasp of the different meanings embedded in the term "environment," it fits only the category of "jargon." And it fits each of the senses of this term with remarkable ease, from "a confused or hybrid language" extending to a "technical terminology" and ending with an "obscure and pretentious language marked by circumlocutions and long words" (*Webster's Ninth New Collegiate Dictionary*).

EXPERIENCE: THE SHORT FORM OR
THE LONG FORM?

Psychologists have been prone to use the term "environment" when what they really mean is "experience." This term too is marked by duplicity. Sometimes the term refers to a conspicuous point in time or to an event of such power that it is remembered or acted upon in a highly specific way—imprinting is a good example. Whatever learning goes on appears to be of a one-trial or few-trial nature and does not appear susceptible to many of the "environmental" influences that define trial-and-error or associative learning. Some types of species-recognition mechanisms may also originate in such "experiences," especially when the species-typical environment is undergoing rapid change in terms of the availability of information or the need to gain the information quickly.

But the term "experience" also refers to events of longer duration, those that transform an animal from a "naïve" to an "experienced" state. Although this usage appears in theories of motor development in the form of the role of practice or rehearsal, it appears less often in theories of social ontogeny. However, anecdotal evidence abounds about changes in animals as a function of age and the knowledge acquired through the "school of hard knocks" (Kaufman, 1975). Objective measures of longer-term experiences are harder to come by.

Do animals, for example, recognize "experienced" conspecifics? And how do they do so? Understanding social recognition at this level would be beneficial. The study of the experience of experience is also critical to understanding what is meant by open or closed ontogenetic programs. Can there be any endogenous program immune to the effects of executing "programmed" behaviors? Although many view hard-wired or closed programs as "fail-safe" or "default" mechanisms to guard against the vagaries of the environment (Gould, 1984), it is difficult to know how such programs can also guarantee a "fail-safe" level of effort on the part of the organism. Anyone who has worked closely with a species, be it bird, monkey, ant, or human, comes away from the experience with the impression that some individuals just do more than others. It is even more likely that members of the same species, enjoying a greater sense of intimacy, also attend to such differences and use such cues in processes such as mate choice.

Stearns has defined fitness as "something everyone understands but no one can define precisely" (1976, p. 4). Every discipline has such words, and "experience" in its second sense may be such a candidate, defined most clearly by example. Here is a cowbird version. In captivity, cowbird males are not successful at courtship unless they sing the "right" song to females after competing with other males. In a series of aviary experiments, we had occasion to introduce the same male, known by his band as 2G, to different aviaries with new males and females. He was usually quite successful in terms of numbers of copulations and mates. Finally we put him in an aviary where, even if he behaved correctly in terms of competing and singing, he was at a disadvantage because the females were of another subspecies. Given no time to learn to sing a new way, what could he do? What he did on several occasions was to wait for a male of the other subspecies to sing and elicit a copulatory posture from a female; then he would fly in from the other side of the aviary, displace the singing male, and copulate. If "finesse" has an avian analogue, this was it. Male 2G was "experienced."

INTERACTION AND ISOLATION:
NUMERICAL FALLACIES

Skinner (1961) believed that part of psychology's problem in establishing itself as a science came from the use of "laymen's" terms. It could only be a source of confusion to attempt to put scientific boundary conditions on terms with strong associative strengths that went beyond their use in science. But whether we like it or not, because many of the other animals that comparative psychologists study behave more like human beings than like machines, using terms from the dictionary of ordinary human behavior may be inevitable.

One alternative to such soft speech is the hard vernacular of mathematics. The terms "interaction" and "isolation" can be found in both lexicons. We worry that the mathematical or statistical meaning has subtly come to prevail so that we begin to think of animals "interacting" the way constructs or numbers do and that models of analysis of variance substitute for models of social behavior. So too, the idea that a variable can be "isolated" by canceling out algebraic units or by partialing variance has dubious connections to "isolating" an animal from a form of stimulation. Computer analogies can also fall short, because although we may be able to identify and understand "subroutines," we may still be far from knowing how the "subroutine" functions with respect to the main program.

Our ineptly named "isolate song effect" aptly illustrates this problem. We made much of the finding that a cowbird housed in the abnormal circumstance of isolation from other males sang a "better" song, as measured by potency, than did a normally housed conspecific. It was, of course, not "better" if measured by males' responses to the singer. We had identified an unusual "subroutine," but it was not until we learned more about the normal course of song learning—the main program—that we could understand the actual significance of the original bits of information.

The term "interaction" is of concern because interactions among real animals resemble interactions among statistical variables about as much as a fine wine resembles diet soda. Animals can interact by fighting, by mating, by grooming, by congregating, or by sensory means we humans cannot even detect. Stripping away all the differences in the means by which animals interact with one another effectively removes the essence of social behavior. It is not that animals interact, it is how, when, where, with whom, and why that satisfies the scientific taste buds.

So too, we should not deceive ourselves into perceiving signs of progress when previously dichotomous terms are joined and said to "interact." Replacing the disjunctive phrases of learning *or* instinct and nature *or* nurture with their conjunctive counterparts only provides the emperor with an alternative set of new clothes.

THE TERM ''ANIMAL'': AN OBITUARY?

A discussion of comparative psychology should start with the word "animal," not end with it. But our concerns here are diverse and ultimately involve endings, not beginnings.

The first set of concerns are with the general and specific meanings of the term "animal." In its most general sense, the word tells us that the subject matter is not vegetable or mineral. Too often, however, it also specifies that the subject matter is not human. As long as our language persists in maintaining the human/animal dichotomy, we guarantee that the next generation of scientists will inherit the burden of engaging in debates about the phylogenetic superiority, inferiority, or linearity of behavioral competencies. Such debates take scientists away from science and in recent years have led investigators and animals alike into great depths of despair (Linden, 1986). And to laypersons, terms such as "infrahuman" and "animal model" suggest an arrogance and exploitation that many now find unpalatable.

Equally serious is the problem the term "animal" poses for comparative psychologists. If generalizations about the role of social stimulation in ontogeny are as yet impossible across subspecies of cowbirds, how do we justify broad levels of comparison? As exhilarating as it may be to soar through the phylogenetic treetops, its value is fleeting compared with what must be accomplished by stooping to the more substantive level of microphyletic comparisons.

What we need to impress on ourselves and others is the value of phyletic comparisons so narrowly conceived that even "bird" or "rodent" seems too vague a designation. The irony is that most scientists and nonscientists find the lives of particular animals extremely interesting—most students we teach seem more fascinated by lectures on the social development of chimpanzees or kittens than on that of humans, and the more details the better. Maybe the level of enthusiasm projected is greater, but perhaps it is the natural inclination to know about "real" animals.

Another concern with the term "animal" is its singular or plural form. Someone once said that "one primate is not a primate" (J. Altmann, pers. comm.). Too often animals are studied alone, with no other species members present—the history of animal learning is largely a history of animals in isolated ivory towers, without the benefits or the costs of learning in the presence of conspecifics. The concern here is not with the study of observational learning but with how, for example, animals learn to find food or water or other resources (the "topic" of most conditioning studies) with conspecifics present, as do their counterparts in nature.

If we had studied cowbirds one by one instead of two by two, we would have deprived ourselves of the flood of knowledge that always comes when we study animals that have something to do and someone to do it with.

How can we bring the language of comparative psychology to life so that it can adequately portray the lives of its subjects? One of the more common complaints about studies of social development is that they do not really study development at all—that is, they do not focus on its ongoing nature. Why? Perhaps the language lulls us into laziness. If you think of all the studies that have employed manipulation of the "early experience" of animals, it is unsettling to realize how few contain any description of early experience. Do "enriched" animals behave differently in a quantitative or qualitative sense? Maybe they just sleep more. If so, it is not what the term "early experience" connotes. But we don't know if we don't look, and we don't look if our words do not demand it.

If, instead of talking about early experience or isolation, we said we biased the development of our subjects, we might be more apt to look. Why? Because bias is a strong word and it elicits strong responses. And if, instead of saying there are parallels between birdsong and human speech, we talk of birds singing to a reactive audience, wouldn't someone be quick to ask about the relationship between the human art of singing or creating melodies and its avian analogues? Such questions would lead to new investigative pathways. Creating effective melodies rests on different criteria than the criteria for effective speech, just as learning to sing and learning to speak are different activities.

To understand the differences, we would have to ask different questions. Human music may not be as "important" a phyletic achievement as learning to speak, but that does not make comparing music making in birds and music making in humans a less important goal. On the contrary, it makes it a more attainable one, because it takes a necessarily strained analogy and converts it into a more concrete question.

All the examples have come from cowbirds—maybe the terms selected are not problems with other animals. On the basis of experiences with studying human infants and our encountering the same problem, we think the words' weaknesses are just as apparent.

The past decade or so of research on infants has focused not on their frailties but on their competencies—the "competent infant" has become a commonplace expression. We do not dispute the data that support this view, but we question the interpretation. A stress on competence obscures the actual enterprise of infancy, an enterprise marked by incompetence, by errors, and more than anything else, by the enormous effort infants expend as they engage their world. The term is also troublesome because it obscures something else quite obvious but vital. Infants by themselves do not possess "the means sufficient for the necessities of life," which is the dictionary definition of competence. Infants possess such means only *in relation to* the cognitive and social competencies of others. An infant alone not only is not competent, it is not capable of surviving.

Let us then convert infant competence into the appropriate verb, to "compete," which connotes something different but more to the mark. Infants must behave to learn about the world. Moreover, infants do not always compete successfully, and they learn as much from their mistakes as from their triumphs. Infants also compete endlessly against themselves in outdoing yesterday's efforts, and hence they discard as many forms of behavior during infancy as they adopt. Infants learn not by trial and error, but by trying and erring—not by "the" environment shaping them, but by themselves patting, twisting, shaking, poking, and provoking the objects and people around them.

Thus human infants share with cowbirds, and with every other social species, the need to act and to perform in order to develop. The elements of cowbird song may be inherited, but the opportunities to sing them and refine them are not. So too, human infants inherit the means to learn to talk but do not do so without effort and intrinsic motivation. Try to teach a toddler how to walk or talk or not to walk or talk. Such a confrontation calls for better words to convey the vitality that characterizes the activities of developing organisms.

Our task as comparative psychologists, then, is to invigorate the discipline by providing it with a steady diet of discoveries and maintaining it on a rigorous verbal fitness regime. Such a regime brings with it the risk of attack or failure. New words can irritate as well as stimulate. But that is the point, because "a theory that cannot be mortally endangered is not alive" (W. A. H. Ruston, quoted in Platt, 1964, p. 349). We need only remember some of the lifeless abstractions of behaviorism, where the species of animal was often only of passing interest, to realize the need for words to repel the circling vultures.

The need for vigor is also a concern at a more basic level and represents the final concern about the term "animal." Although this planet may always contain animals, it will shortly not contain many of the species now present. As humans continue their efforts to configure (some might say disfigure) the earth to fit their needs, more and more of the "infrahumans" must give way. Exhibits of other animals in the Smithsonian and other museums appreciate in value with each passing day. And the burden then falls to scientists, especially comparative psychologists and ethologists, to learn and to communicate about how animals behaved when alive. If for no other reason, so that when we tell the next generation stories about the "olden" days we can talk clearly about what we have lost.

REFERENCES

Baptista, L. F., & Petrinovich, L. (1984). Social interaction, sensitive phases and the song template hypothesis in the white-crowned sparrow. *Animal Behaviour, 32,* 172–181.

Baptista, L. F., & Petrinovich, L. (1986). Song development in the white-crowned sparrow: Social factors and sex differences. *Animal Behaviour, 34,* 1359–1371.

Barker, R. G. (1960). Ecology and motivation. In M. R. Jones (Ed.), *Nebraska symposium on motivation* (Vol. 8, pp. 1–48). Lincoln: University of Nebraska Press.

Becker, P. H. (1982). The coding of species-specific characteristics in bird sounds. In D. E. Kroodsma & E. H. Miller (Eds.), *Acoustic communication in birds.* (Vol. 1, pp. 214–244). New York: Academic Press.

Beer, C. G. (1974). Comparative ethology and the evolution of behaviour. In N. F. White (Ed.), *Ethology and psychiatry* (pp. 173–181). Toronto: University of Toronto Press.

Brunswick, E. (1955). The conceptual framework of psychology. In *International encyclopedia of unified science.* (Vol. 1., pt. 2, pp. 656–750). Chicago: University of Chicago Press.

Dewsbury, D. A. (1984). Comparative psychology in the twentieth century. Stroudsburg, PA: Hutchinson Ross.

Eastzer, D. H., King, A. P., & West, M. J. (1985). Patterns of courtship between cowbird subspecies: Evidence for positive assortment. *Animal Behaviour, 33,* 30–39.

Eaton, R. L. (1970). An historical look at ethology: A shot in the arm for comparative psychology. *Journal of the History of Behavioral Science, 6,* 176–187.

Friedmann, H. (1929). *The cowbirds.* Springfield, IL: C. C. Thomas.

Friedmann, H., Kiff, L. F., & Rothstein, S. I. (1977). A further contribution to the knowledge of host relations in parasitic cowbirds. *Smithsonian contributions to zoology,* no. 235.

Gibson, J. J. (1966). *The senses considered as perceptual systems*. Boston: Houghton Mifflin.

Gould, J. L. (1982). *Ethology: the mechanisms and evolution of behavior*. New York: W. W. Norton.

Gould, J. L. (1984). Natural history of honey bee learning. In P. Marler & H. S. Terrace (Eds.), *The biology of learning*. (pp. 149–180). Dahlem Konferenzen 29. New York: Springer-Verlag.

Gyger, M., Karakashian, S. J., & Marler, P. (1986). Avian alarm calling: Is there an audience effect? *Animal Behaviour, 34*, 1570–1572.

Huxley, J. (1923). Courtship activities in the red-throated diver (Colymbus stellatus Pontopp.): together with a discussion of the evolution of courtship in birds. *Journal of the Linnaean Society of London, Zoology, 53*, 253–292.

Kaufman, I. C. (1975). Learning what comes naturally: The role of life experience in the establishment of species-typical behavior. *Ethos, 3*, 129–142.

King, A. P., & West, M. J. (1977). Species identification in the N.A. cowbird: Appropriate responses to abnormal song. *Science, 192*, 1002–1004.

King, A. P., & West, M. J. (1983a). Epigenesis of cowbird song: A joint endeavor of males and females. *Nature, 305*, 704–706.

King, A. P., & West, M. J. (1983b). Dissecting cowbird song potency: Assessing a song's geographic identity and relative appeal. *Zeitschrift für Tierpsychologie, 63*, 37–50.

King, A. P., & West, M. J. (1983c). Female perception of cowbird song: A closed developmental program. *Developmental Psychobiology, 16*, 335–342.

King, A. P. & West, M. J. (1984). Social metrics of song learning. *Learning and Motivation, 15*, 441–458.

King, A. P., & West, M. J. (1987). Different outcomes of synergy between song perception and song production within the same subspecies. Developmental Psychobiology, 20, 177–187.

King, A. P., & West, M. J. (in press a). The presence of female cowbirds affects vocal imitation and improvisation in males (*Molothrus ater ater*). *Journal of Comparative Psychology*.

King, A. P., & West, M. J. (in press b). Searching for the functional origins of song in eastern brown-headed cowbirds (*Molothrus ater ater*). *Animal Behaviour*.

King, A. P., West, M. J., & Eastzer, D. H. (1980). Song structure and song development as potential contributors to reproductive isolation in cowbirds. *Journal of Comparative Physiology and Psychology, 94*, 1028–1036.

King, A. P., West, M. J., & Eastzer, D. H. (1986). Female cowbird song perception: Evidence for different developmental programs within the same subspecies. *Ethology, 72*, 89–98.

Klopfer, P. K., & Hailman, J. P. (1967). *An introduction to animal behavior*. Englewood Cliffs, NJ: Prentice-Hall.

Krebs, J. R., & Kroodsma, D. E. (1980). Repertoires and geographic variation in bird song. In J. S. Rosenblatt, R. A. Hinde, C. Beer, & M. C. Bushnel (Eds.), *Advances in the study of behavior*. (Vol. 11, pp. 143–177). New York: Academic Press.

Kroodsma, D. E., & Baylis, J. R. (1982). Appendix: A world survey of evidence for vocal learning in birds. In D. E. Kroodsma & E. H. Miller (Eds.), *Acoustic communication in birds.* (Vol. 2., pp. 311–337). New York: Academic Press.

Kuo, Z. Y. (1967). *The dynamics of behavior development: an epigenetic view.* New York: Random House.

Lehrman, D. S. (1974). Can psychiatrists use ethology? In N. F. White (Ed.), *Ethology and psychiatry* (pp. 187–196). Toronto: University of Toronto Press.

Lickliter, R., & Gottlieb, G. (1985). Social interaction with siblings is necessary for visual imprinting of species-specific maternal preferences in ducklings. *Journal of Comparative Psychology, 99,* 371–379.

Lickliter, R., & Gottlieb, G. (1986). Visually imprinted maternal preference in ducklings is redirected by social interaction with siblings. *Developmental Psychobiology, 19,* 265–278.

Linden, E. (1986). *Silent partners.* New York: Times Books.

Lorenz, K. (1970). *Studies in animal and human behaviour.* (Vol. 1). Cambridge: Harvard University Press.

Marler, P. (1982). Some ethological implications for neuroethology: The ontogeny of birdsong. In J. P. Ewert, R. R. Capranica, & D. J. Ingle (Eds.), *Advances in vertebrate neuroethology.* New York: Plenum.

Marler, P., & Mundinger, P. (1971). Vocal learning in birds. In H. Moltz (Ed.), *The ontogeny of vertebrate behavior* (pp. 389–450). New York: Academic Press.

Marler, P., & Peters, S. 1982. Subsong and plastic song: Their role in the vocal learning process. In D. E. Kroodsma & E. H. Miller (Eds.), *Acoustic communication in birds* (Vol. 2, pp. 25–50.) New York: Academic Press.

Mayr, E. (1974). Behavior programs and evolutionary strategies. *American Scientist, 62,* 650–659.

Payne, R. B. (1983). Bird songs, sexual selection, and female mating strategies. In S. K. Wasser (Ed.), *Social behavior of female vertebrates* (pp. 55–90). New York: Academic Press.

Platt, J. R. (1964). Strong inference. *Science, 146,* 347–355.

Potter, E. F., & Whitehurst, G. T. (1981). Cowbirds in the Carolinas. *Chat, 45,* 57–68.

Rothstein, S. I., Verner, J., & Stevens, E. (1984). Radio-tracking confirms a unique diurnal pattern of spatial occurrence in the parasitic brown-headed cowbird. *Ecology, 65,* 77–88.

Rothstein, S. I., Yokel, D. A., & Fleischer, R. C. (1986). Social dominance, mating and spacing systems, female fecundity, and vocal dialects in captive and free-ranging brown-headed cowbirds. In R. F. Johnston (Ed.), *Current ornithology,* (Vol. 3, pp. 127–185). New York: Plenum.

Schleidt, W. M. (1981). The behavior of organisms, as it is linked to genes and populations. In P. P. G. Bateson & P. K. Klopfer (Eds.), *Perspectives in ethology,* (Vol. 4) *Advantages of diversity* (pp. 147–155), New York: Plenum.

Shapiro, L. J. (1980). Species identification in birds: A review and synthesis. In M. A. Roy (Ed.), *Species identity and attachment* (pp. 69–112). New York: Garland.

Skinner, B. F. (1961). The flight from the laboratory. In *Current trends in psychological theory* (pp. 50–69). Pittsburgh: University of Pittsburgh Press.

Smith, W. J. (1977). *The behavior of communicating*. Cambridge: Harvard University Press.

Stearns, S. C. (1976). Life-history tactics: A review of the ideas. *Quarterly Review of Biology*, *51*, 3–47.

Stearns, S. C. (1982). The role of development in the evolution of life histories. In J. T. Bonner (Ed.), *Evolution and development* (pp. 237–258). Dahlem Konferenzen. New York: Springer-Verlag.

Strunk, W., & White, E. B. (1979). *The elements of style*. (3rd ed.). New York: Macmillan.

Thorpe, W. H. (1961). *Bird-song: The biology of vocal expression in birds*. London: Cambridge University Press.

Tolman, E. C. (1945). A stimulus-expectancy need-cathexis psychology. *Science*, *101*, 160–166.

Verplanck, W. S. (1957). A glossary of some terms used in the objective science of behavior. *Psychological Review*, Suppl. 64.

West, M. J., & King, A. P. (1980). Enriching cowbird song by social deprivation. *Journal of Comparative and Physiological Psychology*, *94*, 263–270.

West, M. J., & King, A. P. (1985). Social guidance of song learning by female cowbirds: A test of its functional significance. *Zeitschrift für Tierpsychologie*, *70*, 225–235.

West, M. J., & King, A. P. (1986). Repertoire development in male cowbirds (*Molothrus ater*): Its relation to female assessment of song. *Journal of Comparative Psychology*, *100*, 296–303.

West, M. J., & King, A. P. (1987). Settling nature and nurture into an ontogenetic niche. *Developmental Psychobiology*, *20*, 549–562.

West, M. J., & King, A. P. (in press). Vocalizations of juvenile cowbirds evoke copulatory responses from females (*Molothrus ater*). *Developmental Psychobiology*.

West, M. J., King, A. P., & Eastzer, D. H. (1981a). The cowbird: Reflections on development from an unlikely source. *American Scientist*, *69*, 57–66.

West, M. J., King, A. P., & Eastzer, D. H. (1981b). Validating the female bioassay of cowbird song: Relating differences in song potency to mating success. *Animal Behaviour*, *29*, 490–501.

West, M. J., King, A. P., & Harrocks, T. H. (1983). Cultural transmission of cowbird song: Measuring its development and outcome. *Journal of Comparative Psychology*, *97*, 327–337.

West-Eberhard, M. J. (1983). Sexual selection, social competition, and speciation. *Quarterly Review of Biology*, *58*, 155–183.

Yokel, D. A. (1986). Monogamy and brood parasitism: an unlikely pair. *Animal Behavior*, *34*, 1348–1358.

Zajonc, R. D. (1965). Social facilitation. *Science*, *149*, 269–274.

The Darwinian Psychology of Discriminative Parental Solicitude

Martin Daly and
Margo Wilson
McMaster University

*H*omo sapiens is one of the most intensively parental animal species on this planet, devoting several years and millions of calories to raising each individual offspring. Through human history, most women (and perhaps even men) have probably devoted the absolute majority of their waking hours to foraging for, educating, guarding, and otherwise nurturing their young, often at great cost to their own health and survival. Yet it is a remarkable fact that the previous 34 volumes of the Nebraska Symposium on Motivation do not include so much as a paragraph that specifically concerns parental motivation!

A quick survey in our university library revealed that this neglect is not peculiar to this series. Most of the textbooks and general treatises on motivation that we consulted ignored the subject of parental inclinations altogether. Those works that did not ignore parental motives typically devoted only a page or two to research on the experimental induction of the "maternal state" in rats (getting a rat who initially ignores a stimulus pup to retrieve it and sit over it). A couple of texts briefly discussed whether the maternal "drive" is a product of pressure in the mammary glands.

We believe that this important realm of motivation has been so generally avoided by empirical psychologists because they have lacked a theoretical framework for considering the facts of variable parental effort and inclination. But the requisite framework has long been available: it is the Darwinian view that motivational mechanisms are products of natural selection and can thus be understood as strategic means to the end of genetic posterity.

Darwinian Psychology and Parental Investment

The characteristics of all extant organisms persist by virtue of the historical contributions those characteristics have made to *fitness:* the replication and hence preservation of particular heritable elements that have exerted a causal influence upon the development of these characteristics, in competition with alternative heritable elements tending to induce the development of alternative characteristics. This differential replicative success of traits and their heritable substrates is what is meant by natural selection. It follows that the adaptive function of all organismic attributes is in a sense reproductive, not simply to "preserve the species" but to have one's genotypic elements proliferate and replace those of one's rivals, *within* one's species or population. Relatively proximal goals like eating, breathing, and copulating have evolved to be valued only because attaining these goals has contributed to fitness.

More specifically, we may expect any creature's species-typical attributes to have been shaped by selection in such a way that their typical consequences in "natural" environments (those not crucially different from the environments in which the history of selection has occurred) will be the production of genetic relatives (*reproduction*) and the channeling of benefits to those relatives (*nepotism*). This expectation applies to psychological attributes no less than to morphological ones. It follows that a Darwinian psychology is both possible and desirable (see, e.g., Symons, 1987; Tooby & Cosmides, in press): a psychology in which the logic of fitness maximization will be treated as metatheory for the construction of motivational hypotheses about the mechanisms instantiating adaptive strategies. Parental motivation is an especially apt subject for such a Darwinian approach.

Parental behavior is a sphere of activity with direct, obvious links to fitness: offspring are the vehicles of parental fitness. However, not all offspring are equally capable of utilizing parental nurture to promote the long-term survival of parental genetic materials. It follows that selection should have favored discriminative mechanisms of parental psychology, mechanisms that will assess the probable utility to the parent of alternative ways of allocating parental effort.

This way of thinking inspires an "economic" metaphor. Animals have limited amounts of time or energy to allocate among competing demands, and selection should have favored mechanisms that optimize allocation decisions so as to maximize expected fitness. Sir Ronald Fisher (famous among psychologists for his contributions to inferential statistics) developed this economic metaphor by considering animals to be "investors" of current "reproductive value" (phenotype-specific expected future reproductive success) in the pursuit of present reproduction (Fisher, 1958). Robert Trivers (1972, 1974; Trivers & Willard, 1973) brought the economic metaphor into the conceptual arsenal of behavioral scientists with his discussions of "parental investment," which refers to any sort of parental effort (whether of time, energy, or risk to self) that enhances the fitness of particular offspring while diminishing the parent's capacity to make alternative investments.

According to the Darwinian view of life, fitness is the ultimate basis of self-interest and of our proximal perceptions thereof. Two individuals have a fundamental commonality of interest insofar as that which enhances one's fitness does likewise for the other; moreover, they are likely to have evolved psychological mechanisms such that they *perceive* their interests as harmonious. Conversely, two individuals have a conflict of interest insofar as that which enhances one's fitness detracts from the other's, and again, they may be expected to *experience* the relationship or circumstance as conflictual. Since fitness entails the relative replicative success of the focal individual's genetic materials, it follows that commonality and conflict of interest will be largely a matter of genetic relationship (r, the probability that a rare allele in the genotype of one of the two will also be present in the other as a result of descent from a recent common ancestor). Genetically identical individuals ($r = 1.0$) have identical interests because their fitnesses are identical; unrelated individuals ($r = 0$) are competitors for genetic posterity; and in general the degree of relatedness is an index of common cause. For present purposes, the interesting implication is that parent and offspring, highly but imperfectly related ($r = .5$), have inevitable commonality *and conflict* of interests. Parent/offspring conflict is an endemic feature of sexually reproducing organisms (Trivers, 1974).

The reason for this conflict is that the allocation of resources that would maximize a parent's fitness is seldom identical to that which would maximize a particular offspring's fitness. From the mother's perspective, two offspring of equal reproductive value are equally valuable vehicles of fitness, each carrying half of the maternal genotype. But from the perspective of either offspring, one's self is twice as valuable as one's sibling if there is common paternity, and four times as valuable if the fathers are different and unrelated.

Suppose that mother brings home a couple of food items to her brood of two, and that each youngster can enhance its reproductive value by four arbitrary units if it consumes the first goody and by an additional three units if it eats the second as well. (Such diminishing returns of increased energy consumption are essential to the argument and constitute a realistic assumption in a wide range of circumstances.) The optimal allocation from mother's perspective is one item apiece, thus increasing the reproductive value of her brood by eight units. But from the perspective of either offspring (ego), any gains to the sibling (sib) are devalued relative to ego's own gains by virtue of sib's lesser genetic relationship to ego than ego's relationship to himself. Mother's preferred distribution will get ego his four units, but the four gained by sib add only two to ego's expected fitness if sib is his full sibling ($r = .5$) and only one if sib is his half-sibling ($r = .25$), for a total gain of either six or five units. The optimal solution for ego is to eat both items himself, thus gaining seven units. Sib, of course, is no less selfish. The combined effects of maternal coercion and a standoff between the competing siblings will often produce an equitable distribution. However, both youngsters may be expected to subvert that equity when they can.

This explication of the logic of parent/offspring conflict may seem ploddingly specific and artificial, but the implications are of great generality and interest. The first important implication is that there is no reason to expect a harmonious meshing of offspring demand and parental nurture: selection will generally favor inclinations in both parties to achieve one's own optimum against the wishes and efforts of the other. Thus is explained the seemingly costly and maladaptive phenomenon of weaning conflict. Indeed, the two parties may be expected to disagree about the magnitude of parental investment at every stage, and regardless of whether multiple young are raised simultaneously or sequentially.

A further implication concerns divergent perspectives on the appropriateness of the offspring's social attitudes and behavior. We have already illustrated why mother looks askance at sibling rivalry, and the same logic extends beyond the nuclear family. From mother's perspective, for example, a niece (full sister's daughter) is a relative of degree .25 and is therefore half as valuable as her own offspring. But from the offspring's perspective, said "niece" is a mere cousin ($r = .125$) and only one-eighth as valuable as self. It follows that parents will commonly perceive their offspring as unduly selfish and will encourage them to take a benevolent interest in collateral kin whom they are relatively inclined to disdain when left to their own devices.

This sort of evolutionary logic suggests a radically different perspective on "socialization" than is prevalent in developmental psychology. The fact that parental and offspring interests are imperfectly coincident means that socialization of the young is likely to be at least partially manipulative rather than selfless. One cannot fully trust even one's parents as a source of information about how to pursue one's interests in a complex world full of competing interests. It follows that creatures who are heavily dependent upon social learning must have evolved buffered mechanisms for accurately apprehending their best interests and resisting manipulation, even while accepting instruction from self-interested tutors. The implications of this evolutionary logic for the study of human development are vast and have barely begun to be explored. Trivers (1985), for example, suggests that human adolescence is a time of "identity reorganization" because the achievement of independence means that the offspring are no longer obliged to pursue parental agendas and can define priorities that more accurately reflect their own self-interest.

It is of course incumbent upon the parent as well as the child to make correct assessments in the face of self-interested misinformation. A gaping songbird nestling communicates its need and stimulates parental feeding, for example, but it may also exaggerate its needs. In general, the most strenuously gaping nestling gets the worm, but in at least some species, parents are careful to feed those whom their more vigorous siblings would starve out (Stamps, Clark, Arrowood, and Kus, 1985). The chronic circumstance of parent/offspring conflict may be conducive to an evolutionary "arms race" of ever-escalating offspring demands and compensatory parental discounting of begging signals. Because offspring are always prepared to utilize at least a little more investment than the parent is prepared to provide, the chronically soliciting young may lack satiety mechanisms altogether; rat pups will drown in milk before they will stop ingesting it (Galef, 1981).

Human children often "regress" upon the birth of a sibling, demanding parental assistance they had outgrown, reverting to baby talk, and generally exaggerating their helplessness and dependency as a way of competing for the newly divided parental attention (Dunn & Kendrick, 1982). However, there is brinksmanship in exaggerating one's helplessness. The more advanced offspring is the more valuable fitness vehicle, and to mimic one younger and more helpless than oneself may invite parental abandonment in times of danger or shortage, as we shall see. Parents have evolved to assess offspring quality as well as need and to cut their losses by terminating investment in offspring whom they perceive to be poor candidates to repay that investment in eventual fitness.

In general, then, a parental psyche that has been shaped by selection will be a discriminative psyche, investing parental effort preferentially where it is likely to yield the greatest returns. We shall divide our further discussion of discriminative parental solicitude by first considering the issue of distinguishing one's own offspring from others and then considering the various reasons why a parent might be expected to discriminate even among its own young.

Own Versus Alien

THE BANK SWALLOW

The bank swallow is a migratory, insectivorous bird that breeds in North America and Europe. Bank swallows nest colonially in burrows dug out of the vertical earthen walls of eroded banks and excavations. Hundreds or even thousands of active nesting burrows may exist in a single large colony, and their entrances are often just a few centimeters apart. Each burrow is occupied by one monogamous pair, who will raise a brood of up to about half a dozen young.

For the first two weeks after hatching, both parents bring back beakloads of insects, captured in flight, to feed the flightless nestlings deep in their burrow. Eventually the youngsters begin to await their parents and beg at the burrow entrance, and then, two weeks or a little more after hatching, they make their first flight. But they are still far from capable of surviving without parental assistance.

Once the fledglings become airborne, opportunities for mixups might seem to be rampant. But the parents recognize and favor their own young (Beecher, Beecher, & Lumpkin, 1981; Hoogland & Sherman, 1976). Some fledglings enter burrows other than their own, whether accidentally or in desperation after their own parents have been preyed upon or have otherwise failed to return. Such intrusions seldom succeed, since the intruders are attacked and evicted. Some fledglings get lost, but their parents commonly find them and feed them, even in strange burrows. Large numbers of unrelated fledglings may roost together in a "crèche" with a small number of adult "sitters"; when parents return to the chaotic crèche situation, they seek out and feed their own offspring.

So bank swallows recognize their newly fledged young as individuals and nurture them preferentially. This individuality is not the product of cumulative exposure over weeks; instead, it develops abruptly. If an experimenter swaps eggs between burrows, the birds are none the wiser and raise the fostered young as their own. Perform the same experiment with nestlings two weeks after hatching, and the result is the same. But in just another two or three days, at precisely the time when the young fledge and spontaneous mix-ups become possible, the species-typical immature begging call is replaced by an individually distinctive "signature call," and experimental fostering will no longer work (Beecher, Beecher, & Hahn, 1981).

RECOGNIZING MOBILE YOUNG

The bank swallow's individualized recognition of its offspring cannot be understood as the incidental by-product of some generalized learning capacity. Instead it is a specific adaptation to the species-typical breeding situation. The convergence of two lines of evidence warrants this conclusion. The first is manifest adaptive "design." The birds' discriminatory capabilities fit situational demands that can be identified without appeal to knowledge of those capabilities. If swallows are to promote their fitness and avoid squandering their nurturant effort to the benefit of others, then they *need* to be able to recognize their own offspring from about the 17th day after hatching, and that is precisely when the capability matures. Such evident design is the sine qua non for inferring evolutionary adaptation (Williams, 1966). However, the persuasiveness of such evidence depends upon an intuition of the improbability of such a "fit" by chance, and this is an intuition that is not readily quantified. In the present case, the temporal correspondence between the utility of parental discrimination and its appearance could be attributed to mere coincidence were it not for the second line of evidence, which is comparative.

Different bird species breed in a variety of circumstances, which are associated with a variety of characteristic schedules of mobility and hence of the potential mixing of broods. It turns out that the variable timing of the emergence of individual recognition of own offspring neatly matches the variable timing of the demand for it.

Colonial ground-nesting gulls, whose precocious offspring can wander onto neighboring territories within a few days after hatching, already discriminate against strange chicks by the third day (Beer, 1970). The kittiwake gull, by contrast, nests on irregular little ledges on the faces of cliffs, where wandering by a flightless chick would be lethal. The chicks remain nestbound until fully capable of flight at about five weeks, so that there is no issue of mixing up young hatchlings. Kittiwake parents do not need to recognize their chicks individually, and it turns out that they will accept experimentally fostered young even a month after hatching (Cullen, 1957). At the opposite extreme is the related royal tern, who lays a single egg in a nest on open ground, so close to its neighbors that incubating birds can stretch their necks to fence with one another. In this case even the egg is recognized as an individual, presumably by its distinctive speckling pattern. When Buckley and Buckley (1972) switched eggs between adjacent nests, 18 of 20 parents found their own eggs and incubated them where they lay.

Similar variability appears in other families. The guillemot, another ledge-nesting seabird unrelated to the gulls and terns, raises its broods in such close proximity and builds such a rudimentary nest that eggs can be accidentally displaced between adjacent nests. The closely related razorbill nests dispersedly in similar sites and runs no risk of mix-ups. The former species recognizes its chicks and even its eggs, while the latter does not (Birkhead, 1978). Just as in the gulls, so too in this group of birds (the auks): discriminative capabilities exist in those species and at those life stages where they are required.

The mammals also exhibit great variability in parental discrimination, and the variability again seems to reflect demand. Seals that deliver and nurse their young in close proximity generally attack unrelated pups who try to suckle, even while nursing their own (LeBoeuf & Briggs, 1977). Ungulates such as goats raise highly precocious mobile young, often in herd situations where nursing mothers and same-stage youngsters mingle. Recognizing one's own kid is clearly essential and is indeed established in the immediate postpartum (Gubernick, 1981). If the parturient mother is deceived and becomes bonded to an alien kid, she will soon nurture it selectively and reject her own, but there is no evidence that this happens often (or indeed at all) in natural situations; the usually gregarious mother's tendency to seek solitude to give birth may be a specific adaptation to the risk of such confusion.

At the opposite extreme are the many muroid rodents who are oblivious to cross-fostering, blithely giving suck to whomever they encounter in the nest, including youngsters of grossly inappropriate age or even of another species. These indiscriminate rodents are burrow-dwelling animals that are highly aggressive to anyone approaching their burrows during late pregnancy or lactation; it is likely that mixing of litters almost never occurs spontaneously. In a sense, maternal discrimination is not so much absent in these rodents as it is dependent upon cues other than those presented by the young themselves. A mother rat could be said to use her nest site as the cue by which she "recognizes" her offspring. And even rodents will in fact recognize their own young as individuals, and discriminate against same-age conspecifics, once the young are sufficiently mobile to leave the burrow (e.g., Holmes & Sherman, 1983, Muul, 1970).

There are some famous counterexamples to this general picture of adaptive parental discrimination, some of which remain poorly understood. In general, however, the apparent counterexamples have become less puzzling on closer examination. Two exemplary cases are those of the European robin and the Mexican free-tailed bat.

Like most songbirds, robins continue to feed their young for several weeks after fledging. (Selection seems to have favored leaving the nest as early as possible; the chicks routinely fledge when they can barely fly, although they cannot yet feed themselves at all.) At first the fledglings lurk in the underbrush awaiting parental feedings. Later they may follow their parents, begging loudly. Only very gradually do they begin to find their own food.

In one of the great classics of natural history, *The life of the Robin*, David Lack (1965) noted the surprising fact that "parent robins apparently fail to distinguish their own fledglings from those of other pairs" (p. 90) and illustrated the claim anecdotally. Fully cognizant of the Darwinian rationale for expecting discriminative parental solicitude, Lack proposed as an explanation that "owing to the territorial system young robins rarely come into contact with the young of another pair" (p. 92), a situation he explicitly contrasted with that of ground-nesting gulls.

Lack's solution to the conundrum was not altogether satisfactory, however. The rate of fledgling intrusions into neighboring territories— and hence the selection pressure for parental discrimination—does not appear to be trivial. Moreover, there is evidence that robins *can* discriminate among their *own* offspring. Like many songbirds, a pair of robins often splits its fledged brood (Harper, 1985a): each parent assumes primary responsibility for feeding particular fledglings (its "in-chicks") and is more responsive to the begging of those in-chicks than to comparable begging by those of its offspring in the primary care of the mate (its "out-chicks"). Surely, if the birds can thus discriminate even within their own broods they should be expected to discriminate still more strongly against unrelated fledglings. Well, indeed they do: Harper (1985b) found that parents almost invariably fed begging in-chicks and fed begging out-chicks about half the time, but they fed a begging stranger on only 9% of occasions and were almost three times as likely to attack it instead. Lack's suggestion that such discrimination is absent seems to have been based upon the striking impression he garnered from his observations of misdirected feedings rather than upon systematic data. Indeed, Lack himself noted that "while a robin occasionally attacks a strange fledgling, I never saw a parent attack its own young" (p. 91). So the parental robin is by no means indiscriminate after all.

A still more remarkable tale of indiscriminate parenting is that of the Mexican free-tailed bat in Texas. These bats roost in dark caves, sometimes in aggregations of millions of individuals. The female gives birth to a single pup, and within hours of birth she leaves it hanging in a crèche on the cave ceiling or wall while she goes foraging. The crèche is a squirming mass of infant bats: McCracken's (1984) study, described below, was conducted where there were 4,000 infants per square meter! Moreover, the pups crawl around, sometimes moving a meter or more between nursing bouts. How could their mothers hope to find them? Davis, Herreid, and Short (1962) concluded that they cannot, reasoning both from the considerations above and from experiments in which pups avidly latched onto any nursing females held near them and the females then permitted those pups to nurse without rejection. Davis et al.'s conclusion that the females act as an anonymous "dairy herd" has been widely accepted and cited as a remarkable fact (e.g., Riedman, 1982). But the story is astonishing if true. How could continued maternal solicitude be evolutionarily stable in such a case? Davis et al. estimated that the nursing bat delivers 16% of her body weight per day in milk, enduring energetic depletion and risking predation to do so. Surely in such a selflessly nurturant population, selection must favor the female who makes the least lactational effort: the female who deposits her baby in the care of the "dairy herd," dries up, and opts out.

Gary McCracken (1984) set out to determine whether Mexican free-tailed bats really nurse indiscriminately with respect to kinship by genotyping mothers and the infants nursing from them with respect to a couple of heteromorphic blood allozymes. He tested 167 mother-pup pairs, and given the observed frequencies of the discriminable alleles, he was able to predict an expected number of 42.5 mother-pup genetic mismatches if nursing pairs were truly constituted at random. In fact, McCracken found only 7 such mismatches. On the one hand, this is a hugely significant departure from chance, and hence conclusive evidence that mothers somehow manage to preferentially nurse pups genetically related to themselves, which probably means their own. On the other hand, the mismatches demonstrate that many mothers really do get parasitized by unrelated milk thieves. McCracken suggests that the risk of such parasitism is a cost of communal breeding that is offset by its thermal conservation advantages.

"ADOPTION" IN NON-HUMAN ANIMALS

Of course, there *are* errors. About one in 200 loads of insects that a bank swallow brings back for its young in fact finds its way down the gullet of an unrelated chick, presumably by accident (Beecher, et al., 1981). One of Harper's (1985a) male robins adopted an unrelated bird who happened to fledge from a nest just 22 m from the adoptive male's own on precisely the same day as his own brood; the chick in question was never fed by its own parents, and the adoptive father treated it identically with his natural offspring. As for the Mexican free-tailed bats, the chaotic situation in the maternal caves indeed seems to stretch maternal capabilities—whether to find and recognize own pups or to reject others—to near breaking point, for something like 17% of suckling infants really did turn out to be nursing from females other than their mothers (McCracken, 1984). These are costly failures of parental discrimination, to be sure, but they are not such egregious failures as to make the very existence of parental care evolutionarily unstable, as truly indiscriminate feeding would.

As in the case of the adopted robin, some examples of misdirected "parental" nurture surely represent nothing more than rare "mistakes," generated by motivational mechanisms that are usually effective in promoting fitness. But in other cases there is evidence of advantage to at least one of the parties, and the adoption can hardly be called accidental. Some substrate-spawning fishes actively adopt eggs or fry, for example, stealing them from their neighbors to deposit in their own nests. One documented benefit of such adoption is reduced predation upon the parents' own young (McKaye, 1981; McKaye & McKaye, 1977); nest predators are likely to eat only a fraction of the brood before being chased off by the guarding parents, and extra young in the nest absorb some of the risk. Territorial males who kidnap others' eggs enjoy an additional benefit when females preferentially spawn in nests that already contain eggs (Ridley & Rechten, 1981); the female's preference is itself presumably an adaptive response to the reduced risk of predation upon the eggs in such nests. Because parental care in these fishes consists primarily of guarding the young rather than provisioning them, adopting unrelated young has little or no cost. Indeed, by Trivers's (1972) definition, there is no "parental investment" in the adoptees at all, since they do not compromise the parent's capacity to invest in additional young.

In other cases, however, the adoptee clearly diminishes the fitness of its adoptive parent. There is, for example, a surprising incidence of successful adoptive transfers of chicks in those very ground-nesting gulls that we previously described as discriminative: as many as 5% or even 10% of the hatchlings in a gullery may become spontaneous adoptees (Graves & Whiten, 1980; Holley, 1984). It is the chicks, not the parents, who initiate the transfer, and it seems that they do so only in response to necessity: the disappearance of their own parents and imminent starvation. The usual reluctance to transfer is easily understood when one observes how often the attempt may be fatal; that spontaneous adoption is prevalent in some gulleries does not mean that discrimination and attack by the intended adoptive parents never occurs—only that the discrimination sometimes fails or subsides. Hiding behind the resident chicks can afford some protection, and if the intruding chick can get all the way to the nest, parental attack seems to be inhibited there. After a while the parents may habituate to the intruder and begin to respond to its solicitations, even though, as Graves and Whiten (1980) demonstrate, such adoption reduces the parents' expected success rate in fledging their own chicks. Such failures of discrimination sometimes reveal how simple and "irrational" are the behavioral control mechanisms underlying what is usually successful discrimination. But if such a high rate of spontaneous adoption has indeed been chronic for many generations, then the absence of more effective parental discrimination mechanisms is surprising.

Where adoption is costly to the parent there is a conflict, and we may expect the contesting parties to evolve ploys and counterploys. The most dramatic examples of such "evolutionary arms races" involve interspecific brood parasitism, or "cuckooism." About eighty bird species are obligate brood parasites that lay their eggs in another species' nest and then let the duped foster parents do all the work of incubating and feeding their young. Most of these parasitic species are cuckoos, though not all cuckoos are parasitic. The strategy is believed to have evolved independently seven times in seven different avian taxa (Payne, 1977). The parasitized parents (the "hosts") may recognize that something is amiss and abandon the nest. The parasites have therefore evolved certain adaptations to overcome host discrimination, including elaborate mimicry of the colors and markings of the host species' eggs and chicks.

Some obligate brood parasites, such as the brown-headed cowbird of North America, are not specialized on a single host species and try their luck with "acceptor" (relatively indiscriminate) and "rejector" species. One current theory, with some support, is that susceptibility to parasitism (acceptance) is a local and dynamic trait that can rapidly change to rejection where cowbirds become a significant selective force (Rothstein, 1975). Be that as it may, the strenuous efforts of parasitized songbirds to rear nestlings that (at least eventually) look not at all like those of their own species is one of the most remarkable spectacles of failed adaptation in the natural world. In a sense, however, it is no more remarkable than parasitism generally, for parasitism always involves the subversion of the host's adaptive machinery in the service of the parasite; such seeming maladaptation in the host is possible only because its foe is also a biological entity, with its own capacity to adapt evolutionarily.

Birds are probably susceptible to a significant amount of parasitism by members of their own species, too. Ornithologists have long been aware of incidents of "egg dumping" in the nests of conspecifics. Yom-Tov (1980) listed 53 species in which such behavior had been described, but until recently there was almost no evidence on its prevalence. C. R. Brown (1984) inferred from the too-rapid addition of two eggs to a nest that up to 24% of the cliff swallow nests in a colony were parasitized by other cliff swallows; the proportion parasitized increased with the absolute size of the colony. Five banded females who were directly observed to lay parasitic eggs all had nests of their own, where they successfully fledged their broods. Moreover, intruders were sometimes seen to toss out the eggs of residents, which suggests that some parasitism would have escaped Brown's detection and hence that the actual proportion of nests parasitized could be much higher still. Genetic methods of determining parenthood are clearly needed to elucidate the extent of the phenomenon. Gowaty and Karlin (1984) used allozyme analyses to discover that there was multiple parentage in 9% of the broods being cared for by "apparently monogamous" eastern bluebirds. More females (15%) than males (5%) were found to be caring for young who could not be their own, which suggests that the territorial male may sometimes have been complicit in egg dumping by a nestless female with whom he had mated. We anticipate a blossoming of new research and theory concerning the prevalence and selective impact of intraspecific brood parasitism.

In a few species it is normal for more than one female to lay in a communal nest. The situation differs from intraspecific brood parasitism in that the laying females are mutually acquainted and tolerant (to a degree); usually they are both resident on and defensive of a common territory. Exceptionally cooperative as this unusual breeding system may appear, the logic of selection suggests that it should be fertile ground for the evolution of specialized tactics of competition as each female attempts to promote the welfare of her own offspring in competition with those of her nestmates. Recent research suggests that such competition is indeed rampant.

Vehrencamp (1977) noted the peculiar prevalence of eggs strewn around the nests of communally nesting species (as well as the prevalence of nonadaptive explanations in the literature). In groove-billed anis, she discovered, the strewn eggs are actively tossed from the nest by resident females, but only by those who have not yet laid their own first eggs. The last female to commence laying gets the lion's share of the hatchlings, despite laying the fewest eggs. A surprising aspect of the ani story is that the females with fewer eggs in the nest then deliver more subsequent parental care than the last-laying dominant, despite the latter's greater genetic stake in the brood. A male's parental investment, by contrast, is positively correlated with his share of the nest's paternity, as we might expect (Vehrencamp, Bowen, & Koford, 1986).

Females of the communally nesting acorn woodpecker exhibit much the same behavior as anis: they too discard their nestmates' eggs until they begin to lay their own (Mumme, Koenig, & Pitelka, 1983). In this case the nest is in a hole in a tree, and expelling eggs requires quite an effort. A possibly surprising twist in the case of the woodpeckers is that the competing females are often close relatives, even full sisters. Kinship usually dampens lethal conflict (e.g. Daly & Wilson, 1982a; Hamilton, 1979), but in this case there is apparently an upper limit on the number that can be fledged from a territory, and each increment in own offspring must be bought at the loss of a competitor's, however closely related.

Among East African ostriches, two to seven hens lay up to 13 eggs apiece in a huge communal nest, leading to an eventual clutch of about 30 or even 40 eggs. Only one dominant hen then guards and incubates the brood (with some male assistance). She will not incubate more than about 20 eggs, however, and she pushes the rest beyond the periphery of the nest, where they perish. Bertram (1979) demonstrated that the dominant hen selectively retains her own eggs. At three nests where he registered the maternity of each egg, dominants incubated 31 own eggs and 25 laid by others, while expelling just one own egg and 23 others. But why retain the others' eggs at all? The answer is apparently the same as why cichlid fish "adopt": Bertram (citing unpublished data) asserts that "extra eggs buffer the major hen's eggs against predation."

OTHER USES OF PARENT-LIKE BEHAVIOR

Parental investment in unrelated young is sometimes accidental, but it is more often the result of active parasitism, with demonstrable specializations for circumventing parental defenses. Parental effort is a valuable resource, and it is hardly surprising that parasitic adaptations should have arisen to exploit it, just as parasitic adaptations have arisen to exploit other organisms' photosynthetic, metabolic, and foraging efforts. But it does not follow that every act of "parental" investment in young who are not the investor's own is necessarily detrimental to the investor's fitness. Once an organism has a repertoire of parental activities, it may sometimes evolve alternative uses for them.

A classic example of parent-like efforts by nonparents is that of avian "helpers at the nest." In many species of birds, more than two individuals may be observed feeding the nestlings of a single female. While a few of these cases have proved to represent stable polyandrous associations in which two or more investing males have a share in the brood's paternity (e.g., Faaborg & Patterson, 1981), most helpers are celibate contributors to the brood of a monogamous pair (for reviews see J. L. Brown, 1983; Emlen & Vehrencamp, 1983). In most of the cases that have been investigated, the helpers have proved to be close relatives of those they help raise, usually the grown offspring of the nesting pair and hence siblings of the nestlings. One's full sibling is of course as close a relative as one's own offspring ($r = .5$) and is therefore equally effective as a vehicle of one's fitness. (One may wonder, then, why sibling care is so much rarer in the animal world than parental care. One reason is surely that parental mortality and pairing instability assure that mature individuals can seldom depend on a sustained production of full siblings. Another is that helping one's breeding parents must usually offer a lesser incremental impact upon the immature recipient's reproductive value than becoming a parent oneself. Indeed, most avian helpers apparently resort to that strategy only when breeding opportunities are scarce.)

Evolutionary biologists were long content to conceptualize fitness as equivalent to personal reproductive success. Hamilton (1964) upset that particular applecart when he explored the implications of a seemingly obvious fact: that the contributors to a focal individual's genetic posterity include his collateral kin as well as his offspring. Individuals can therefore have an impact upon their fitness without breeding at all, as for example by helping at the parental nest. Selection will favor those strategies that maximize not merely the production and survival of descendants, but the more "inclusive" fitness represented by the replicative success of the actor's alleles in any and all carriers. Hamilton thus broadened the Darwinian conception of the organism from a *reproductive strategist* to a *nepotistic strategist*. A great deal of parent-like investment in nondescendants has now been shown to be effectively nepotistic, promoting the investor's fitness by enhancing the reproductive value of collateral kin (see, e.g., Kurland, 1977; Moehlman, 1979; Rabenold, 1985; Sherman, 1980; Trivers & Hare, 1976; Wilson, 1971; Woolfenden & Fitzpatrick, 1984). Moreover, as predicted, animal nepotists are sensitive to the variable degree of relatedness between themselves and potential beneficiaries of their actions; scrub jays who will remain celibate to help raise full siblings, for example, are likelier to leave and try to breed on their own if their natal territory offers only half-siblings to invest in (Woolfenden & Fitzpatrick, 1984).

However, the fitness advantage of engaging in parent-like investment need not always be achieved through the eventual reproduction of the recipient of the investment. Some avian helpers at the nest feed young who may or may not be close relatives and are later repaid by those they reared, in the form of help with their own broods (Ligon, 1983; Wiley & Rabenold, 1984). Others may be obliged by the breeding pair to pitch in a little as the price for being tolerated on the territory, thereby enjoying both a reduced predation risk and a chance of eventually succeeding to breeding status there (e.g., Reyer, 1986).

In terrestrial group-living monkeys such as baboons and Barbary macaques, males are often solicitous toward infants and may carry them while their mothers forage. Some of this behavior probably represents genuine paternal solicitude toward infants that the male has at least a substantial probability of having sired (Busse & Hamilton, 1981). Some, however, represents essentially exploitative "agonistic buffering" (Deag & Crook, 1971): the infant's presence inhibits other adult males from attacking the carrier, with the result that males often carry infants they could not possibly have sired—indeed run to fetch them—during tense moments and thereby gain some protection for themselves (perhaps especially from those males who really *could* be the sire).

The behavior of baboons is especially intriguing because their social actions, including pseudopaternal care, are sometimes intelligible in terms of long-range social strategies. Among hamadryas baboons, for example, a species with unusually stable "harem" associations, a male may "adopt" and protect an immature female whom he raises to be his mate (Kummer, 1968). In more promiscuous baboons, some males behave "paternally" toward infants they could not have sired as a way of currying favor with those infants' mothers (Smuts, 1986): "friendly" behavior toward a mother and her infant can gain a male preferential access to that mother when next she mates.

THE ANTITHESIS OF PARENTAL NURTURE

Parents are not merely solicitous toward their own young: they are often actively hostile toward alien young as well. We have already mentioned the risk of death incurred by gull chicks who wander onto neighboring territories and the violent rebuffs of milk thieves by nursing goats and seals. But it is not just those who would parasitize parental investment that the parents are likely to attack. Many female rodents will invade neighboring territories to kill other females' young (Brooks, 1984). Unrelated conspecific young, if allowed to live, are potential future competitors of one's own offspring and oneself. Moreover, they can be an easy meal. Nesting gulls do not merely attack chicks who intrude upon their territories, they make cannibalistic raids as well; and some individuals make this their main food source (Parsons, 1971). Many invertebrates (Polis, 1984) and fishes (Dominey & Blumer, 1984) also derive significant nutrition from conspecific young.

Although mammalian females probably kill unrelated offspring more often than do males, attention and controversy have focused on the phenomenon of "sexually selected infanticide" by immigrant males. In a long and growing list of primate species, males who have newly established local dominance may kill nursing young sired by their predecessors and mate with the mothers, who ovulate and conceive sooner than they would have done had lactation continued (for several reviews, see Hausfater & Hrdy, 1984). Similar behavior is well known in lions and suspected in other social carnivores (Packer & Pusey, 1984). Recent studies have documented essentially the same phenomenon in birds, too (Crook & Shields, 1985; Freed, 1986).

Many biologists have asserted that such infanticidal behavior must represent pathology rather than evolved adaptation. However, the positive fitness consequences for the killers are well established, and it seems irrefutable that selection will act to maintain the behavior by penalizing the noninfanticidal male who delays his own reproduction. The reluctance of many writers to consider infanticidal behavior adaptive seems to derive more from the distastefulness of the phenomenon than from evidence or theory; it also reflects the continuing emotional appeal of the thoroughly discredited concept of "group adaptation," the idea that animals should somehow have evolved to be concerned with the welfare of their species rather than with their inclusive fitness.

If infanticidal behavior is to be adaptive, it must of course be discriminatively directed toward young other than one's own. The groove-billed ani or acorn woodpecker who expels eggs from the communal nest until she begins to lay is displaying precisely such discrimination. Other species also follow simple rules of thumb apparently designed by selection to ensure that any young killed are unlikely to be the killer's own. Some potentially cannibalistic fishes simply do not feed at all while the fry they encounter have a high probability of being their own (e.g., Oppenheimer, 1970). Virgin male house mice kill conspecific pups until the specific experience of ejaculating in a female leads to an inhibition of such killing; the inhibition does not appear immediately, however, but begins about 12 days after the copulation and hence a few days before the male's own young could be born (vom Saal, 1985). About two months after his most recent copulatory experience, when any pups he has sired must be weaned and dispersed, the male mouse resumes killing any infants he may encounter.

CUCKOLDRY, JEALOUSY, AND PATERNITY

J. Boswell: "There is a great difference between the offence of infidelity in a man and that of his wife."
S. Johnson: "The difference is boundless. The man imposes no bastards upon his wife."(Boswell, 1779/1953, p. 1035)

Male and female songbirds alike are susceptible to parasitism by the cuckoo, but among mammals only the male is vulnerable to the slightly different sort of parasitism that bears the cuckoo's name. Maternity is a fact, paternity a conjecture. Some unknown proportion of dutifully paternal fathers are in fact investing their efforts in rearing other males' young.

The risk of cuckoldry is a chronic selection pressure for males to reallocate their reproductive efforts by investing less in specifically paternal pursuits and more either in pursuing additional matings or in sequestering the present mate in order to guarantee paternity of her offspring. Male bank swallows follow their females closely on every flight, but only during those few days when the females are fertilizable; otherwise the pair forages separately (Beecher & Beecher, 1979). Male starlings do the same, even though the pair's simultaneous absence from the nest hole makes them vulnerable to parasitic egg dumping by other starlings and entails a possibly costly delay in the initiation of incubation (Power, Litovich, & Lombardo, 1981). Thus parental males certainly behave as if the risk of cuckoldry were genuine and demanding of countermeasures.

Homo sapiens is a species with prolonged, intensive paternal investment, so that cuckoldry can have major fitness consequences. The sexual possessiveness and jealousy of human males is an emotional/cognitive/motivational state that functions to enhance the man's probability (and confidence) of his paternity of those children to whose welfare he contributes. Male jealousy reduces the risk of cuckoldry partly by motivating vigilance and partly by motivating violent resentment that acts as a deterrent. Men's sexual possessiveness and suspicion of wifely infidelity is far and away the leading precipitator of spousal homicide, both in the modern industrial West and elsewhere (Daly & Wilson, 1988). It is also the predominant motive in sublethal wife beating (review by Daly, Wilson, & Weghorst, 1982). The threat of violence is clearly a major deterrent to infidelity by the wife and to sexual poaching by rival males, and its deterrent value is increased where retaliatory violence by cuckolds is condoned or legitimized, as it is to some degree almost universally.

Men in all human societies adopt a proprietary view of female sexuality and resent sexual encroachment, the many efforts of social scientists to discover a counterexample notwithstanding (Daly et al., 1982; Daly & Wilson, 1988). Wherever people have codified law, they have legislated limitations on sexual access. More specifically, they have deemed sexual intercourse between a married woman and a man other than her husband an offense against the husband. The language is usually that of property violation: the adulterer is considered to have damaged the husband's goods and to owe him compensation for the damage.

The cross-cultural conception of adultery as the violation of a husband's proprietary rights cannot be understood merely by considering sexual contact to be a valued good. After all, the woman's capacity to perform as a sexual partner is not diminished by adultery, and yet her value from the male perspective is radically diminished. Indeed, men perceive "their" women to be diminished in value even by the involuntary "adultery" of having been raped. "She was all mine and now she's been damaged," says one participant in a therapy group for men whose partners have been raped. "Something has been taken from me. I feel cheated. She was all mine before and now she's not," says another (Rodkin, Hunt, & Cowan, 1982). Others blame the victim for inadequate resistance. Rape, although manifestly coerced and violent, is grounds for repudiation and divorce in some societies, and where it is not it remains a great source of strain between the victim and her effectively cuckolded mate (see Thornhill & Thornhill, 1983). Men are universally concerned not merely to gain sexual access to attractive, fertile women, but to guarantee the exclusivity of that access (see, e.g., Dickemann, 1981).

Wherever men have gained despotic power, they have used that power to establish harems of nubile women and have invested heavily in securing those women from other men (Betzig, 1985). A breach of harem security may be considered reason to dispose of the women and replace them. Guarded harems, invented independently in stratified societies the world 'round, are the fantastic manifestations of the male psyche when freed from the usual restraints of limited personal power and wealth. While harems are a relatively rare indulgence, polygynous marriage is not (see, e.g., Daly & Wilson, 1983), and it is invariably the most successful men who have the most wives. Some anthropologists have suggested that men aspire to polygyny because of the economic productivity of wives, but this argument puts the matter backward: economic goals are valued ultimately because of their contributions to fitness, and in fact men strive to be polygynists wherever possible, regardless of whether the circumstances are such that wives are economic assets or liabilities. In the social and technological environments in which people evolved, even the most successful men were probably limited to two or three wives, but the urge to acquire just one more would always be adaptive. Like the rat pup who will drown in the overflow from his stomach before he will stop swallowing milk, the human male has apparently experienced no specific selection for an upper limit to his aspirations. The ambition of men, as revealed by the indulgences of despots, is not simply limitless sex, nor even limitless variety of partners, but the sexual *monopolization* of women, and the more the better.

PATERNAL RESEMBLANCE, PATERNAL
CONFIDENCE, PATERNAL LOVE

I think I go run
Every time I go and come is a different son
And what hurting me
Every children she make none resemble me.

from "Mildred Don't Cry," a song by Small
Island Pride, quoted by Rodman, 1971, p. 220.

In all human societies, men contribute significantly to childrearing, whether directly or through investment in reproductive women. Such efforts are predominantly directed toward the men's putative offspring. Since paternity is mistakable, we would expect that a man's willingness to make such investments will be influenced by his confidence that the children are indeed his own. There are two independent sources of information that must contribute to a putative father's confidence of paternity. The first is his confidence of the mother's sexual fidelity; the jealousy and possessiveness we have already discussed have surely been shaped by selection to promote and monitor that fidelity. The second source of relevant information is the phenotypic similarities and dissimilarities of the child to the putative father or his relatives and to possible rivals.

If allegations of phenotypic resemblance were veridical and disinterested, we might expect equal emphases upon paternal and maternal similarities. But maternity is not at issue, and all interested parties scrutinize newborns for paternal features. People are often well aware of this preoccupation and may joke about it, as in this (American) example:

Doctor (delivering baby, and teasing by hesitating to announce the baby's sex): "What do you want?"
Father (who is very bald): "I don't care as long as it's bald. I don't care as long as it's bald."

(Daly & Wilson, 1982b, p. 71)

In other cases the examination of the baby is no joking matter, and the putative father's repudiation can be the infant's death warrant (see, e.g., Daly & Wilson, 1984). The man who is informed that he is an expectant father often adopts a wait-and-see attitude. After all, there might be more than one potential sire, and if so, he can hardly expect the woman to jeopardize the child's support by admitting it (see, e.g., Bledsoe, 1980; Herlihy, 1984; Rodman, 1971; Rubenstein, 1980; Schatkin, 1953). The drama of childbirth is thus augmented by the arrival of long-awaited phenotypic evidence on the question of paternity.

If confidence of paternity promotes paternal investment, then the mother should be especially motivated to perceive paternal similarity and to draw attention thereto. Indeed, this motivation may already be expressed before the birth: in an interview study of pregnant women, Leifer (1977) reported that "in their fantasies, most women imagined the newborn as looking like their husband."

Within minutes of birth, mothers seek and remark upon evidence of paternal resemblance. Macfarlane (1977) published four transcripts of maternal speech at birth; three mothers remarked upon the baby's appearance, all three asserting that it looked like the father. Robson and Moss (1970) interviewed 54 mothers of 3 1/2-month-old infants, asking retrospectively about the process of maternal attachment. Twenty-five women volunteered that a perception of "family resemblance" in the immediate postpartum had contributed to that attachment: 21 of these asserted the child's resemblance to its father, two to the father's father, and just two to the mother herself. Daly and Wilson (1982b) transcribed spontaneous utterances of mothers within about the first 15 minutes after birth. Sixteen mothers remarked upon their babies' similarities to the fathers, and only four upon similarities to themselves. Those fathers who were present at the birth and commented on the babies' appearance were significantly less likely than mothers to assert a resemblance on the paternal side. Several mothers pressed the matter to noncommittal husbands, as in this example:

Mother: "It looks like you."
Father: no evident response.
Mother (a little later): "He looks just like you."
Father: nod.
Mother (to hospital staff): "He's cute. Looks just like Bill."
Father (embarrassed?): "Don't say that."
Mother: "He *does*."
(Daly & Wilson, 1982b, p. 71)

Mothers may be said to have an *assurance-of-paternity* motive: a felt need to promote paternal confidence and involvement. The strength of this motive may be expected to vary in response to predictors of the reliability of male involvement. In a further study in which assessments of resemblance were solicited, Daly and Wilson (1982b) confirmed the existence of predicted variations in assurance-of-paternity behavior. Mothers were especially likely to impute paternal resemblance to first-born babies, for whom maternal confidence about future paternal investment is shakiest. Mothers were also especially likely to impute paternal resemblance to babies who had been given prenatally chosen paternal names, a practice that was interpreted as another manifestation of the assurance-of-paternity motive.

Concern with paternal resemblance is widespread cross-culturally, usually with explicit reference to paternity determination. A staple character in the folk humor of many societies is the simpleton who unwittingly labors to raise a child that everyone else can see is not his. In other cases the attention to paternal resemblance is ostensibly unrelated to paternity determination, yet is intense nonetheless. A particularly interesting instance is that of the Trobriand Islanders of Melanesia, the textbook case of a people alleged to be ignorant of the male's role in procreation (Malinowski, 1929). Tracing kinship matrilineally, Malinowski's informants explicitly rejected the proposition that men have any input into the conceptus, pointing to the regular pregnancies of ugly women as proof. Nevertheless, it is an offense to remark upon the resemblance of a Trobriand child to its uterine kin and polite to assert resemblance to the mother's husband, who is said to influence the child's appearance in utero by his association with the pregnant mother!

In matrilineal societies such as that of the Trobriand Islanders, men's control of their wives is relatively weak. Grounds for paternity doubt are therefore substantial. Men in such societies make their sisters' sons—more distant relatives than own sons, but unmistakable—their principal heirs. The subject has provoked much discussion (and some controversy) among evolutionists (see Hartung, 1985, for references).

The greater certainty of maternal than paternal links can certainly inspire greater solicitude. As one Trinidadian informant told Rodman (1971), "Some people say they has more love for a sister child than for a brother child. (*Why is that?*) Because you certain your sister child is she own, but when is your brother is not the same, you not sure is he own" (p. 97). Smith (1981) found that Canadian grandparents invest more attention in their daughters' children than in their sons' children; differential proximity could not account for the bias. (One may wonder, then, why inheritance is so often patrilineal. We shall return to this question in the section "Differential Treatment of Sons and Daughters," below.)

If paternal affection is sensitive to perceived resemblance, differential treatment of offspring might follow. We have hypothesized that the child least resembling the father is most likely to be scapegoated and abused, whereas resemblance to the mother should be irrelevant (Daly & Wilson, 1981b). The hypothesis has yet to be tested. Discriminative inheritance and other resource allocation also seem plausible and warrant research. The Trobriand case is again especially intriguing. Although the islanders have been typologically described as practicing matrilineal inheritance, men commemorated the death of kinsmen by bestowing gifts upon the deceased man's wife's children and explained their actions by saying they derived consolation from seeing their dead kinsman's face in the children (Malinowski, 1929). It sounds suspiciously as if Trobriand men diverted investment to patrilateral kin, despite the matrilineal ideology, and furthermore did so in direct proportion to paternal resemblance!

If paternal solicitude has indeed evolved to be sensitive to the child's resemblance to the man, then the discriminative psychological mechanism might be activated "automatically" even in the absence of paternity belief. It has been reported, for example, that successful adoption is more likely where parents perceive the child as like themselves (Jaffee & Fanshel, 1970), but possible effects of the adoptive parent's sex were not investigated. We hypothesize that resemblance to adoptive fathers may be more germane than resemblance to adoptive mothers in predicting adoption failure.

Many social scientists have maintained that men are concerned with "biological" paternity only insofar as it confers "sociological" paternity, that is to say, the "jural rights" of fatherhood. When this view is disputed, often by the subject peoples themselves, it is alleged that biological paternity is merely a conventional (and by implication arbitrary) basis for the allocation of these disputed "rights" (e.g., Paige & Paige, 1981; Schneider, 1968). Such a view is hard to reconcile with the ethnographic record, which is replete with powerful, articulate declarations of men's concern to avoid cuckoldry and to invest only in their own children. In several societies a man who acquires a widow with dependent children may order their death or exile, so that she can get on with the business of breeding for *him* (Daly & Wilson, 1984). Even where stepchildren and children of adultery are economic assets and are therefore tolerated, there seems to be a universal and well-founded apprehension that they will be exploited, as we shall see.

The discovery of nonpaternity can turn paternal love to ashes. "I am ill. The symptoms are impotence, rage and hatred," writes a 37-year-old man to a popular advice columnist (Ann Landers) after discovering by accident and verifying by blood test that his 8-year-old daughter and 3-year-old son were adulterously conceived; his letter ends, "Therapy has failed. I once loved my family but now there is only disgust and hate. Can you offer advice that will help me?" (*Boston Globe*, August 30, 1984, p. 78). The revelation of nonpaternity can even be a stimulus to murder. "We were always arguing about her extra-marital affairs. That day was something more than that," explains a Canadian husband who fetched a rifle and shot his wife when she told him, "You are so damned stupid that you don't even know she is someone else's child and not yours" (Chimbos, 1978, p. 54). This husband went to jail for his response, but in many societies his action would have been deemed justifiable and legal.

Why then is the idea that men are primarily concerned with the "pater role" so popular? We suspect that the answer is *because* the idea is so outrageous. Many social scientists seem to feel that commonsense ideas are not worthy of the name "science" and that the best theories are the most counterintuitive. The trouble with this view is that most counterintuitive ideas are wrong.

Folk accounts and Darwinian psychology often produce similar rationales for human inclinations and behavior. A British stepfather, for example, defends his decision to leave the bulk of his inheritance to his sister's children rather than his stepchildren as follows: "Because I do not feel that they *are* my children. They don't look like me. My sister's children look more like me. *They* could be my children" (Maddox, 1975, p. 44). A Trinidadian woman explains why she would rather her child resemble its father than herself: "When it resemble he, no fear" (Rodman, 1971, p. 53). The Wisconsin Supreme Court explains its decision to let elderly grandparents adopt: "They are grandparents who can give natural love and affection and are inclined by ties of blood and human nature to raise this child in his interests" (Young, 1980). Kitcher (1985) has argued that such correspondences between folk rationales and Darwinian psychology make the latter dubious science, but the *lack* of such correspondences would be a good deal more problematic. People are the most cognitive of animals, and the principal strategic arena in which they pursue their fitness interests is social. One of the most important tasks for which selection has shaped the human mind is predicting the probable activities of others. It would thus be astonishing if ordinary human understanding of what moves people were not to some degree accurate.

THE SPECIAL CASE OF STEPPARENTHOOD

We saw earlier that a male baboon may have good reason to treat an unrelated infant gently or even nurturantly, even if he is not at all deceived about paternity. The behavior is in effect a favor to the mother, and it can be adaptive if it inspires reciprocal favors from her. The situation is analogous to that of stepparenthood in our own species: as part of the cost of acquiring a new mate, the stepparent assumes the burden of a parental obligation to the new mate's existing children.

What evidence is there that stepchildren constitute a "cost" or deterrent factor in remarriage negotiations? In the first place, there is the fact that custody of young children reduces the likelihood that a divorcée or widow *will* remarry (Becker, Landes, & Michael, 1977; Knodel & Lynch, 1985; Voland, 1987). Moreover, there is the fact that the presence of stepchildren is associated with an elevated divorce rate, over and above the higher risk of divorce in remarriages as compared with first marriages (White & Booth, 1985); indeed, the presence of children of the current marriage lowers the divorce rate for first and subsequent marriages alike, whereas the presence of children of former marriages raises it (Becker et al., 1977). There is also the fact that both marital partners in step-families say they are looking forward to the children's departure (Burgoyne & Clark, 1982; White & Booth, 1985), and the fact that stepchildren do indeed leave home at an earlier age than those living with their natural parents (Flinn, 1983; Rankin, 1983; White & Booth, 1985). The circumstantial evidence that stepchildren are perceived as liabilities is clearly substantial.

Moreover, there is an enormous, consistent body of direct evidence that step-relationships are aversive. Nadler (1976), for example, found that stepmothers reported more conflict with their husbands' children than did natural mothers, regardless of whether the children were permanently or only occasionally co-resident. Both full-time and part-time stepmothers expressed more ''anxiety, depression and anger regarding family relationships" than did natural mothers. Perkins and Kahan (1979) found that all the parties in stepfather households were much less "satisfied" than their counterparts in natural-father households, even within a volunteer sample, all of whom were alleged to be functioning "successfully." White and Booth (1985) found that the presence of stepchildren substantially elevates the probability of a retrospective opinion that the respondent should never have remarried, even though stepparents were no more dissatisfied with their *spouses* than were remarried people without stepchildren. Indeed, there is a growth industry of scholarly study and exhortative pop psychology on the subject of stepparenting; the unifying theme is *coping with the conflict* (see Wilson & Daly, 1987, for references).

Social scientists who write about step-families commonly attribute their problems to things like "role ambiguity" (Giles-Sims, 1984) and "incomplete institutionalization" (Cherlin, 1978): stress is alleged to be the product of uncertain and conflicting expectations about the stepparent's rights and duties. According to this view, stepparenthood will remain stressful until "society" defines the "role" more clearly. The proponents of this perspective have yet to subject it to the obvious potentially disconfirming tests (see Wilson & Daly, 1987), nor have they considered this commonsense alternative: stepparents find their roles more stressful and less satisfying than natural parents not because they are uncertain of their obligations, but because they derive fewer emotional rewards from carrying out those obligations. The prevalent conception of parenthood itself as a "role" (with stepparenthood being another role, partially overlapping that of natural parenthood) is profoundly misleading in its implication of arbitrary substitutability. A role is something that any competent actor who has studied the part can step into, but parental love cannot be established at will. Parents care profoundly—often selflessly—about their children, a fact with immense behavioral consequences about which the shallow metaphor of "parental roles" is mute.

In many historical and recent societies, high parental mortality made step-relationships common (see, e.g., Hill & Kaplan, 1988; Knodel & Lynch, 1985; Laslett, 1977; Voland, 1988). But although step-relationships were thoroughly "institutionalized" in such societies, they were apparently no less problematic. "Of Domesticall Duties," a 17th-century English forerunner of today's self-help manuals, admonished its readers "to respect the children of an husband or wife as their owne," the author proceeding to complain that

Contrary is the carriage of most [stepparents] . . . so farre are they from performing the forenamed duty, as rather they envy at the prosperity of their husbands and wives children, and secretly endeavour to hinder it in what they can, and cunningly seeke to alienate the naturall parents affection from them: whence fearfull tragedies have beene made, and lamentable mischiefes have followed. What other reason can be given hereof, but a plaine instigation of the devil, who thus laboureth to disunite those whom God hath joyned together. (Gouge, 1626, p. 326)

According to Webster's dictionary, the "step" root itself derives from an old English word meaning "to deprive or bereave."

The folklorist who consults Thompson's (1955) massive *Motif-Index of Folk Literature* under "step-" will encounter such pithy synopses as "Evil stepmother orders stepdaughter to be killed. Irish myth," and "Evil stepmother works stepdaughter to death in absence of merchant husband. India." For convenience, Thompson divides stepfather tales into those about "Cruel stepfathers" and those about "Lustful stepfathers." Through dozens of tales, from every corner of the world, the stepparent comes out the villain every time! What social scientists are pleased to call "the myth of the cruel stepparent" seems to reflect a problem that is endemic to human society.

The anthropological literature abounds with evidence of the universal problem that dependent children pose for a widow or divorcée still young and marketable enough to remarry. The most common solution is to foster the children to other relatives, ideally the maternal grandparents. Remarriage to the dead father's brother (the levirate) is also common, especially in patrilineal societies where the woman's reproductive and other services have already been compensated by the payment of bridewealth. Where the woman is more autonomous, she may choose not to remarry and may go with the children to live with her brother or another close relative. It is universally assumed that placing the child under the care of an unrelated stepparent entails some risk of neglect and consequent disadvantage, if not active exploitation and mistreatment.

This presumption of risk appears to be well founded. In a study of the foraging Ache Indians of the Paraguayan forest, Hill and Kaplan (1988) traced the careers of 67 children who were raised by stepfathers after the deaths of their natural fathers. Twenty-nine (43%) had themselves died, of a variety of causes, before their fifteenth birthday; the comparable figure for children raised by two surviving parents was just 19% (33 of 171). In 17th- and 18th-century Ostfriesland (now part of Germany), remarriage of a widowed parent led to a subsequent increased mortality of children compared with those whose widowed parents did not remarry (Voland, 1988). For other examples, see Faron (1961) and Nwako (1979).

What, then, of the treatment of stepchildren in modern industrial nations with their growing divorce rates? Several years ago, we reviewed the burgeoning literature on child abuse to see what evidence existed on this question, and we were surprised to find almost none. Household circumstances had been described for a few samples of victims, and these seemed generally to include a heavy representation of substitute parents, but no one had tackled the question of victimization rates and relative risk. The main problem was the lack of information for the population at large: census bureaus routinely distinguish "one-parent" from "two-parent" households, but they conflate natural, step, adoptive, and foster parenthood within these categories. However, the senior demographer of the United States Census Bureau, Paul Glick, had published some widely cited estimates, claiming that 10.0% of American children under 18 years of age lived with a stepparent in 1975 and 10.2% in 1978 (Glick, 1979). We combined Glick's estimates with American Humane Association data on abuse victims to arrive at the victimization rates shown in Figure 1. In fact, Glick's estimates of the prevalence of step-relationships are excessive, owing to some false simplifying assumptions made in their derivation (see Bachrach, 1983; Daly & Wilson, 1981a). The difference in risk between the two household types is therefore even greater than Figure 1 suggests.

More recently, we have conducted a more intensive epidemiological study of household compositions and risks to children in the city of Hamilton, Ontario (Daly & Wilson, 1985). Like its American counterpart, the Canadian census bureau does not distinguish stepparents from natural parents, so we surveyed the population at large ourselves and combined the results with household composition data for abused children known to the local children's aid societies. The results are shown in Figure 2.

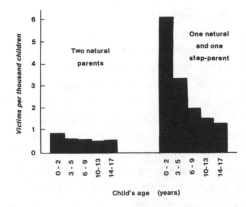

FIGURE 1. Child-abuse victimization rates in the United States in 1976, by household type and age. The data represent validated case reports to the American Humane Association, under a compulsory reporting scheme. Modified from Wilson, Daly, and Weghorst (1980).

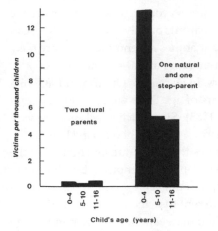

FIGURE 2. Child abuse victimization rates in Hamilton, Ontario, in 1983, by household type and age. The data represent all active cases reported by the local Children's Aid Societies to the Ontario child abuse registry. Modified from Daly and Wilson (1985).

FIGURE 3. The risk of being killed by a natural parent versus a step-parent in Canada in 1974–1983, by age. Modified from Daly and Wilson (1988).

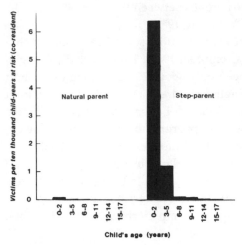

The differences in abuse rate are surely dramatic, but are they valid? One concern is that the effect may reflect a reporting bias against stepparents. Were this so, however, we might reasonably expect such biases, and hence the overrepresentation of step-households, to diminish as we confine attention to increasingly severe and unequivocal forms of maltreatment, up to child murder. In fact, just the opposite is the case. Of the more than 87,000 abuse and neglect cases confirmed by the American Humane Association in 1976, 15% dwelt with a substitute parent. In about a third of those cases, the abuse included physical injury, and when this stricter criterion is employed, the proportion with substitute parents rises to 25%. Finally, just 276 of these children were actually killed, and 43% of this most severely abused group lived with substitute parents. This latter group was so young, on average, as to have an expected incidence of substitute parents of only about 1%. There can be no question that substitute-parent homes are enormously more risky environments for American children than natural-parent homes.

Canadian data tell the same story. In Hamilton, Ontario, in 1983, 16% of child abuse victims under 5 years of age lived with a natural parent and a stepparent (Daly & Wilson, 1985). Since such small children very rarely *have* stepparents—fewer than 1% of preschoolers in Hamilton in 1983—that 16% represents forty times the abuse rate for children of the same age living with both natural parents. Bad enough, but the risk of child homicide at the hands of stepparents versus natural parents (Figure 3) is even more dramatically different than the risk of nonfatal abuse: more than 25% of Canadian children between the ages of 1 and 4 who were *killed* by someone in loco parentis between 1974 and 1983 were the victims of stepparents (Daly & Wilson, 1988).

English data are similar. In a recent study, some 30% of abused children lived with stepparents (Creighton, 1985). The expected value, given their ages, should have been only about 2%, according to a cohort study in which some 3% of English children had acquired a stepparent by age 5 (Wadsworth, Burnell, Taylor, & Butler, 1983). Again we find a hugely elevated risk of abuse in stepparent homes, and again the overrepresentation of stepparents is even more extreme in the fatal cases. Scott's (1973) sample of 29 children murdered by their "fathers" is a still younger group, of whom fewer than 1% would be expected to have a stepfather, and yet 15 (52%) were in fact slain by stepfathers.

Still the conclusion that stepparents imperil children could be hasty.

Might step-relationships be an incidental correlate of some other variable that is the cause of elevated risks? An obvious candidate for such a confound is poverty, but in fact the incidence of stepparenthood is approximately constant across socioeconomic classes in the United States (Bachrach, 1983) and probably in Canada too (Daly & Wilson, 1985). Family size is another predictor of abuse risk, but it too does not differ between step- and natural-parent households (Daly & Wilson, 1985). Maternal age at the child's birth is yet another predictor, and while this factor *is* associated with stepparenthood, it can account for only a small fraction of the stepparent overrepresentation in abuse samples (Daly & Wilson, 1985). Finally, no confounding of step-relationships with chronic dispositional or personality variables can explain the excess risk, since abusive stepparents are almost always discriminative, abusing *only* the stepchildren while sparing their natural offspring within the same household (Daly & Wilson, 1985; Lightcap, Kurland, & Burgess, 1982). No other conclusion seems possible: stepparenthood per se is a major risk factor for child maltreatment, as a Darwinian perspective on parental love would lead one to expect.

ADOPTIVE PARENTHOOD

A robin or gull may adopt and rear an unrelated youngster unwittingly, but people do it on purpose. Such adoption is regularly invoked as an argument against the relevance of evolutionary theory for understanding human action (e.g., Sahlins, 1976), but the typical features of adoption in the various human societies within which it is prevalent are not, in fact, so very anomalous from a Darwinian perspective after all (Daly & Wilson, 1980; Silk, 1980).

The great majority of adoptions occur in one of two contexts. The first is that of unwed motherhood and incapacity to care for the child. A cross-culturally widespread preference in such cases is to place the child with the closest willing maternal relative. The willingness to adopt in such cases can be viewed as straightforward nepotistic solicitude, and where there is *no* nepotistic rationale for such willingness, people are duly wary of the adopter's motives. Children *are*, after all, potentially useful as household help and reciprocal care-givers in the parents' old age. Where the tempering factor of a nepotistic concern for the child's welfare is absent, it is only astute to anticipate that the child may be seriously misused. Even being fostered or adopted out to relatives can be dangerous (e.g., Hobart, 1975).

The second principal context of adoption is stepparenthood, and here the adoption represents the legal removal of parental rights and duties from only one natural parent and their transfer to the other's new mate. Such adoptions are clearly to be understood as part of the give and take of reciprocal concessions between the remarriage partners. If the remarriage fails, the adoptive stepparent commonly attempts to have the adoption abrogated (e.g., Carroll, 1985). We assume that dependent children weaken one's negotiating position in remarriage (witness their negative impact upon its likelihood, noted above). It would be interesting to study whether and how the adoptive stepparent's acceptance of the parental role is reciprocated by the natural parent, in terms of the division of labor and mutual concessions in such households compared with both non-adoptive step-families and two-natural-parent homes.

The seeming anomaly in adoption really applies only to a much rarer variety, namely "adoption by stranger" as practiced in the industrialized West. Such adoptions are overwhelmingly the recourse of childless couples seeking to simulate the experience of natural parenthood. No doubt many succeed. We do not dispute that people are capable of assuming a parental role and developing a true love and solicitude for children not their own. (The psychology of parental love can, after all, even be redirected to a nonhuman pet!) But one may question how generally and how thoroughly the simulation is effective. Adoptions fail, the couple returning the child, more often than is widely realized; marriages fail too, and often neither adoptive parent wants the child (see Festinger, 1986).

In the social environments within which people evolved, mutual dependencies were forged on the basis of both nepotism and reciprocity. Deaths and other crises must frequently have led to adoption and fostering—mostly by close relatives, occasionally by others—as occurs in the remnant foraging societies still in existence. It is hardly surprising, then, that the human mind should be prepared to contemplate adoption. Children are both assets and liabilities, and in any particular case some balance is struck between parental exploitation of and investment in the child. That balance is surely a function of the depth of *child-specific parental love*, and whether adoptions by strangers succeed in effectuating a love comparable to that of natural parents is a question that is important, readily amenable to research, and neglected. The solicitude of adoptive parents might show subtle qualitative differences from that of natural parents, with subtle sequelae. We hypothesize, for example, that adoptive children might exhibit a lower probability of eventual marriage and reproduction than natural children and a higher probability of becoming celibate caretakers to the adoptive parents. We know of no relevant research.

Discriminative Treatment Among One's Own Young

To this point, we have been entirely concerned with the issue of discriminative allocation of parental effort to the benefit of one's own offspring. This is a crucial issue, to be sure, but it is not the only basis for parental discrimination. There are a number of theoretical reasons to expect that parents will treat even their own offspring inequitably.

If, to take a rather obvious example, a particular offspring is moribund and thus manifestly incapable of converting parental investment into reproductive potential, an adaptive parental psychology should be such as to cut losses and invest elsewhere. By and large, animals do curtail investment in failing offspring. The acorn woodpeckers who toss one another's eggs from the communal nest also expel their own yolkless, inviable "runt" eggs (Mumme et al., 1983), for example, and many birds have been observed to desert or expel cracked eggs or those that fail to hatch. Parturient mammals often lick, prod, or otherwise stimulate their newborns and may walk away from (or eat!) those who are not adequately responsive.

Parental passivity may act effectively as discriminative rejection by imposing some requisite threshold of offspring vitality. By continuing to walk and graze, for example, newly parturient ungulates often look indifferent, but they effectively require their young to stand and walk immediately or else succumb. Many authors have remarked with surprise and distaste the phenomenon of some mammalian mother neither helping nor otherwise reacting to a tiny neonate struggling to reach her nipple or some other goal. It is plausible, however, that her passivity has been specifically selected as a test of the offspring's vitality and worthiness. Parental passivity may effectively cull the weak or inviable from a brood, as, for example, when a songbird simply feeds the most strenuous little beggars in its nest and lets those who fall behind starve. Several species of seabirds lay and incubate two eggs but never or hardly ever fledge more than one; the second egg acts as insurance against the loss of the first (see, e.g., Mock, 1984). The action that reduces the brood to one is siblicide by the larger chick, and parental nonintervention is usual. The parents usually could not feed more than one, so that their passivity is not so maladaptive as it may appear.

By interpreting parental *in*action as adaptation, one of course runs some risk of erecting "just-so stories" that are neither testable nor necessary. The best evidence of adaptation in parental passivity would be a facultative switch to more interventionist tactics in predictable circumstances. We have just remarked one apt situation in which to seek such facultative parental response: songbirds commonly feed the most strenuously begging nestlings and thereby let a runt who falls behind starve. Stamps et al. (1985), however, describe budgerigar parents in captivity with ad libitum food stimulating runts to gape and feed and bypassing more active beggars to do so. It would be interesting to determine whether this unusual behavior is a response to superabundance and a resultant parental perception that an exceptionally large brood can all be fledged.

In the case of *Homo sapiens*, the birth of a conspicuously defective child is both motive and justification for infanticide in many nonindustrial societies (Daly & Wilson, 1984; Dickemann, 1975). Where such infanticide is not legitimate and legal sanctions are employed to coerce parents into retaining and nurturing defective children, risks of abuse and abandonment are greatly elevated (reviewed by Daly & Wilson, 1981a).

Many peoples believe that deformed children are ghosts or demons or the progeny thereof. The rationale for infanticide is therefore expressed in terms of a struggle with hostile supernatural forces, and such expressed rationales may distract the anthropologist seeking to understand the practice. Karsten (1932), for example, reports that deformed children are viewed with horror by Chaco Indians because they are the progeny of demons who impregnate women during bathing. Such children are killed at birth. He continues:

> The Indians understand that a sickly or deformed child has scarcely any chance of developing into a strong man and a useful member of society. In the hard struggle for existence under which the Indian lives it may even be merciful to destroy him. I believe however that such considerations play only a subordinate part in the

custom of infanticide, which may first of all be explained by superstition. (Karsten, 1932, p. 78)

But why give explanatory priority to beliefs about demons? Similarly unfortunate mothers in our own society are similarly horrified at the birth of a deformed baby; North Americans have their superstitions too, but a demonic sneak fertilizer in the bathtub is not usually among them. As it happens, mothers dispose "superstitiously" of deformed and sickly babies in many societies, although the details of rationale and ideology vary from place to place. Somehow, people are hardly ever reported to dispose "superstitiously" of well-formed, healthy babies, and when they do the babies are other people's, not their own (Daly & Wilson, 1984). What explanatory force are we then to grant to the concept of superstition?

ON THE VALUE OF A BROOD

Fisher and Trivers introduced the economic metaphors of reproductive *value* (RV) and parental *investment* (PI) because the reproducing individual in question incurs certain "costs" in the pursuit of certain "benefits." The costs are in the form of energy expenditure, predation risk to self, and so forth; the benefits take the form of offspring health, growth, and likelihood of survival. The common currency is fitness: one sacrifices expected future reproduction in order to enhance present reproductive success.

Evolutionary biologists have found this economic metaphor compelling in the abstract but have found it difficult to apply with rigor to specific cases. How can one measure the cost in parental condition, survival, or future reproduction of a present increment in reproductive effort? One cannot simply measure naturally occurring variations and expect to find, for example, that those songbirds who feed their young at the highest rates suffer the greatest overwinter mortality, because the birds adjust their expenditures to their capabilities. Experimental approaches are required, but even these can be confounded by the compensatory responses of the animals (see Daly & Wilson, 1983, chaps. 2 and 8).

The best experimental methodology yet devised for the study of variations in PI involves measuring the response to a standardized artificial threat. To what extent is a parent willing to risk its own life in the defense of offspring? Although the answer cannot be quantified as a maximal tolerable probability of death (since we cannot easily calibrate perceived risk), such experiments provide useful ordinal data: the parent is willing to tolerate *greater* risk (e.g., a closer approach by the threatening stimulus) under one condition than under another.

An exemplary experiment is Pressley's (1981) study of the nest-guarding behavior of male three-spine sticklebacks. In these substrate-spawning fishes, males defend territories, build nests, court gravid females, whom they chase away after spawning, and then care for the eggs, both by guarding them against predation and by a specialized fanning behavior that aerates them. Now from the male's point of view, the expected contribution of a clutch of eggs to his personal fitness is directly proportional to their number. We therefore expect him to tolerate greater risk in defense of his eggs the more numerous they are. And so he does, standing his ground longer and darting more bravely at an approaching model predator the more eggs he has. Carlisle (1985) has replicated this result in an unrelated fish species with similar breeding biology, adding the twist that the parent defends an artificially augmented brood even more strenuously than any natural one; apparently these fish assess the size of the brood and hence its RV by some simple rule of thumb, perhaps CO_2 production.

A more subtle prediction is that the eggs' value to the parent will be an increasing function not only of their number, but also of their *age*. The rationale is this. The risk of egg mortality is high throughout the nest-bound phase. Every day that the offspring survives is a hurdle surpassed, so that the probability of reaching maturity, and hence the immature offspring's own RV, is a monotonic increasing function of age, at least until maturity and possibly beyond. It follows that parental motivational mechanisms should have evolved to effectively cherish offspring more and more intensely as they grow. Pressley's sticklebacks indeed incurred greater risk in defense of their eggs as those eggs drew closer to hatching. An exactly analogous result has been obtained in numerous experimental studies of egg and chick defense in birds (e.g., Andersson, Wiklund, & Rundgren, 1980; Barash, 1975; Curio, Regelmann, & Zimmermann, 1984; Greig-Smith, 1980; Patterson, Petrinovich, & James, 1980).

People, like other animals, seem to be more deeply committed to their older offspring. One apparent manifestation of such differential commitment is the steeply and monotonically declining probability that the parent will kill the child (Daly & Wilson, 1988), which we interpret as evidence of an ever growing reluctance to resort to dangerous violence in conflicts with an ever more valued child. (An alternative interpretation is that older children are simply harder to kill. However, their chance of being slain by anyone *other* than their parents increases steeply while the risk of parental violence declines. Young adults may be maximally formidable in self-defense, but they are also the likeliest *victims* of violence, though hardly ever by their parents; see Daly & Wilson, 1988.)

The claim that parents effectively prefer their elder children may seem contrary to experience, when parents are seen to defend their younger offspring against their older ones or to spoil the last born. But these are not genuine counterexamples. The genetic nonidentity of family members guarantees sibling rivalry, and the parental imposition of equity often involves supporting the younger, weaker competitor, even though the parent would save the older if forced to choose. It is this sort of choice situation that really tests differential valuation of offspring, and while such choices seldom confront affluent westerners, they have often confronted mothers in traditional societies. In a systematic review of ethnographic materials, Daly and Wilson (1984) encountered reports from 11 societies in which newborns were killed if the birth interval was too short or the brood too numerous. There were no societies in which the prescribed solution to such a dilemma was alleged to be the death of an older child. (Indeed, such a report would hardly be credible, which testifies to the strength of our apprehensions of human nature. Everyone already *knows* that people value their growing children increasingly profoundly, although they might not have endorsed the abstract proposition.)

The Darwinian prediction of deepening parental attachment to own offspring has interesting implications for the controversial subject of "maternal bonding." During the 1970s, pediatricians in several countries reported positive effects of immediate postnatal mother-infant contact upon such measures as duration of breast-feeding, complexity of maternal speech to the child during subsequent home visits, and reduced risk of child abuse (references in Daly & Wilson, 1987). The basic design of these studies was that new mothers in the hospital were randomly assigned to either a "hospital-routine" group (baby removed at birth and returned periodically for brief feedings) or an "extra contact" group with just a few more hours of mother-infant contact before hos-

pital discharge. The dramatic results of these studies provided ammu-
nition for the proponents of more natural birth practices, but in the 1980s
the "bonding hypothesis" came under fire in a critical reaction that
threatens to throw the baby out with the bathwater (reviewed by Daly
& Wilson, 1987).

The perspective of Darwinian psychology suggests a compromise
viewpoint that is entirely consistent with present evidence. An evolved
psychology of maternal attachment and affection is likely to entail at least
three distinct processes proceeding over different time courses. The first
is an assessment of the quality of the child and the quality of the occasion, a stage seemingly manifested in the emotional flatness and de-
tachment experienced by many new mothers, perhaps especially those
in poor resource circumstances. The second process to be expected is a
rapidly developing discriminative attachment to *own* child as uniquely
wonderful and worthy of sacrifices. The third expected process of maternal bonding is then a gradual deepening of love and commitment,
proceeding over several years. We have argued elsewhere (Daly & Wilson, 1987) that there is already considerable evidence for the existence
of each of these three processes.

PARENTAL REPRODUCTIVE VALUE

A parent's willingness to risk death or otherwise incur sacrifice for offspring is expected to be a function of the parent's own remaining reproductive value as well as the offspring's. The alternatives to a present reproductive venture shrink as the parent's expected life span passes. If
selection has shaped parental psychology, we would expect a woman
(for example) to be less and less inclined, as her reproductive years slip
away, to devalue a present offspring in terms of its compromising effects upon her future. The psychological trade-off is between the woman's valuation of the baby and her valuation of herself; the latter quantity should have evolved to be a token of her residual reproductive and
nepotistic potential. One prediction from this perspective is that mater-
nally instigated abortion and infanticide will be decreasingly likely the
older the woman. Data on infanticide by women of a Chaco Indian tribe,
the Ayoreo, are supportive (Bugos & McCarthy, 1984). In a nation where
infanticide is illegal and much less frequent—namely, Canada—we see
a very similar effect of maternal age, with the probability of infanticide

dropping steeply after the teenage years (Daly & Wilson, 1984). The impact of maternal age is distinct from that of maternal marital status (Daly & Wilson, 1988).

There are not as many animal studies of parental RV and its impact upon parental effort as there are of offspring RV. Many songbirds nesting in the spring are likely to live to nest again in the same season; by the time of the season's last brood, they are much less likely to live to breed again, owing to high winter mortality. Some students of differential brood defense have therefore predicted greater defense of late-summer broods, when parental RV is low. Results are mixed, perhaps because the RV of the eggs and hatchlings is also seasonally variable (Curio et al., 1984).

The best demonstration of parental sensitivity to own RV in the animal behavior literature is Pugesek's (1981) study of increased reproductive effort in aging California gulls. Older parents left their chicks unattended less than younger parents but nevertheless managed to feed them more, engaged in more territorial defense, and were likelier to fledge them successfully. An alternative explanation might be that older parents are not more committed, but simply more skillful; however, the older parents also continued to feed their chicks longer than the younger birds, a fact that must surely be interpreted as greater parental effort. (There is, however, real potential for confusing low levels of parental motivation with ineptitude. The poor performance and reproductive success of young mothers is often interpreted, particularly in the case of primates, as evidence that parental "experience" is crucial for the development of parental competence. Researchers have seldom considered the alternative hypothesis that young mothers are not less able but only less willing.)

DIFFERENTIAL TREATMENT
OF SONS AND DAUGHTERS

Why do parents so often produce approximately equal numbers of sons and daughters? This question perplexed many early population biologists, particularly with respect to those species in which parental care is provided solely by females and a single male can fertilize many. Why not eliminate superfluous males? Fisher (1958) solved the problem. He pointed out that the parenthood of future generations is equally shared between the sexes, and hence that the sons of the present generation of parents will contribute exactly as much to their eventual genetic posterity as will the daughters. Parents should therefore have evolved to *invest equally* in the production of males and females across the population as a whole. If either sex is less invested in, then that sex will return greater eventual fitness per unit present investment, and selection will favor reallocation of parental efforts until equal investment is restored. Fisher's elegant theory has been elaborated in an equally elegant subfield of evolutionary theory and research on "sex allocation" in plants and animals (see Charnov, 1982).

One of the most interesting elaborations upon Fisher's theory was proposed by Trivers and Willard (1973), who noted that the population equilibrium of equal investment in daughters and sons need not imply that individual parents should behave so equitably. Variable circumstances might favor investment in a daughter this year, in a son next year. In particular, Trivers and Willard considered the case of a large mammal, constrained to produce at most one offspring per annum, in which the fitness of males is more variable than that of females because some males breed with many females while others die barren. In such a species, they suggested, a son's expected fitness will probably increase more steeply or more sustainedly as a function of PI (e.g., maternal milk quality or volume) than will a daughter's. It follows that mothers ought to produce sons when in the best condition and daughters in leaner years.

The evidence for such facultative production of sons versus daughters is weak and mixed (see Clutton-Brock & Iason, 1986; Trivers, 1985), probably because animals such as large mammals are especially constrained in their capacity to make such adjustments, given chromosomal sex determination and a litter size of one. However, once the offspring are produced, there is substantial evidence that sons and daughters indeed absorb different amounts of postnatal PI and that the differential itself varies with the parental resource circumstance. In species that produce mixed-sex litters, active elimination of sons may be observed when resources are tight (McClure, 1981) and active elimination of daughters when resources are abundant (Gosling, 1986). It remains perplexing, however, that these effects appear to be confined to a few taxa and have often not been found in species where they seemed likely.

One of the most puzzling aspects of human society from a Darwinian perspective is the near-universality of the preference for sons. A partial explanation may be derived from the Trivers-Willard theory: a son has greater reproductive *potential* than a daughter, and his expected fitness can profit more than hers from incremental PI beyond that necessary for survival. This provides an explanation for male-preferential inheritance, as has been developed especially by John Hartung (1982, 1985).

The most dramatic manifestation of the human preference for sons is the widespread practice of female-selective infanticide. Dickemann (1979) extended Trivers and Willard's analysis to predict that such infanticide should be especially prevalent among the *upper* classes of stratified societies and has assembled evidence that the practice really was status graded as predicted in the highly stratified societies of India, China, Japan, and mediaeval Europe. However, a strict application of Fisher's sex-ratio theory seems to require that the preference for sons in the upper strata be offset by a preference for daughters in the lower. We have seen no evidence of a switch to male-selective infanticide, but there is some evidence of sex-differential nurture and neglect, amounting to the same thing. Voland (1984) reports that daughters suffered higher mortality than sons among the landholding classes of a European population in the 18th and 19th centuries and that this sex-differential mortality was reversed among the landless. Moreover, the sons of landholders were more marriageable than their daughters, while the daughters of the landless were more marriageable than the sons. Voland interprets these patterns to mean that parents indeed invested preferentially in the sex of greater RV and sometimes practiced the indirect infanticide of severe neglect upon the less desirable sex. Smith, Kish, and Crawford (1987) have shown that Canadian parents leaving larger-than-average estates favor their sons, while those leaving smaller-than-average estates favor their daughters.

Analysis of the fitness consequences of differential treatment of sons and daughters, whether by people or by other animals, becomes a good deal more complicated when we consider the differential post-weaning careers and life histories of the two sexes. Fisher's theory of equal investment presumed a discrete prepubertal termination of parental care and a subsequent mixing of individuals such that each son or daughter was an independent competitor in future mating pools. These simplifications are seldom strictly realized. When sons compete locally for the same pool of matings, for example, a parent may be wise to invest preferentially in daughters (Hamilton, 1967); animals unconstrained by chromosomal sex determination do just that and can exhibit subtle sensitivity to the probable fitness value of each additional son versus daughter (Werren, 1980). Conversely, two sons may be *more* than twice as good as one if they will support each other in conflicts. Yet another complication is that one sex may be likelier than the other to become a competitor not just of its siblings but of the same-sex parent; when sons disperse whereas daughters try to establish a territory near their birth site, crowded mothers may prefer to invest in sons (Clark, 1978). Again, there is a converse situation: one sex may return more than the other in the form of reciprocity or helping and may therefore be preferred. This latter circumstance may be especially relevant to the human preference for sons, particularly in patrilineal societies where sons contribute economically and politically to their parents' ambitions but daughters are "lost" at marriage.

For one reason or another, human parents are often tempted to treat their children inequitably. Grooming one daughter for upward marriage or one son for political power may require manipulating the others to subordinate their interests to those of the elected sibling. Family property and titles may be indivisible, leading to primogeniture or other inequitable inheritance practices and the consignment of other offspring to other careers. A Darwinian analysis can be enlightening even for these most cultural of practices (e.g., Boone, 1988). As we noted earlier, parent-offspring conflict is inevitable, and parental manipulation can be difficult for relatively powerless offspring to resist (Alexander, 1974). The most effective parental manipulation so tips the scales that the best course of action remaining to the offspring becomes accepting and following the parentally prescribed career, even after parental coercion is removed.

OEDIPAL CONFLICT?

The evolutionary view of parent-offspring conflict that informs this chapter is generally accepted among animal behaviorists, but it is not the social sciences' predominant view of what such conflict is all about. Freud's (1900/1953, 1913/1950) Oedipal theory is still with us: that once upon a time the sons rose up and slew their father (the "primal parricide") in order to gain sexual access to their mother (and sisters?), and that parent/offspring conflict remains the "acting out" of that sexual rivalry over Mom.

In developing his primal parricide theory, Freud tried to take account of contemporary knowledge and theory in anthropology, psychology, and animal behavior. These fields have come a long way since 1913, and it is hardly surprising that his scenario now seems hopelessly naïve. Aside from his numerous errors of fact (see Daly & Wilson, 1988), Freud was hobbled by a major conceptual error. Though he respectfully cited Darwin, he never grasped the essential idea of natural selection, namely, that the organismic attributes that survive and proliferate are those that contribute to fitness. One result of this failure was Freud's misconception that psychological mechanisms would evolve merely to achieve mental relief, regardless of the utility of the actions they motivated. Freud's modern followers are no less confused about Darwinian theory and its implications (Daly & Wilson, 1988).

Freud's proposed evolutionary reconstruction (the primal parricide) is unquestionably wrong, but the continuing popularity of his Oedipal theory suggests that it must make some sort of contact with the reality experienced by the faithful. And indeed there *is* conflict between father and son over the wife/mother, though not a sexual rivalry. Young human beings are extremely dependent upon their mothers and are not impatient to be weaned. Daddy has conflicting uses for Mommy: parental sexuality threatens to produce a sibling, and it is not implausible that young children have evolved specific adaptive strategies to delay that event. Much later, father and son may develop a genuine "sexual" conflict, or at least a conflict over the timing of the son's accession to a potentially reproductive status, which must often be subsidized by the father at considerable cost to his own continuing reproductive ambitions (see, e.g., LeVine, 1965). The earlier conflict is not sexual, and the later one is not over the mother. Freud concatenated two distinct father/son conflicts into one.

Is an empirical test between the Freudian and the Darwinian views possible? Well, according to the Darwinian view, the infant's conflict with father is not a function of the infant's sex. Only near maturity does parent/offspring conflict begin to be concerned with same-sex rivalry over reproductive status and with resources of differential utility to daughters and sons. According to Freud's theory, on the other hand, from infancy parent/offspring antagonisms are reducible to rivalry with the same-sex parent over the opposite-sex parent. If the Freudian view were correct, we would anticipate a same-sex contingency in parent/offspring conflict and hence in violence at all ages.

The facts are in accord with the Darwinian account of parent/offspring conflict, but not with Freud's. The proportional representation of sons versus daughters is identical among the victims of mothers versus fathers, whether one considers filicide (Daly & Wilson, 1988) or nonfatal child abuse (Wilson, Daly, & Weghorst, 1983); the rare cases of parricide by prepubertal children also exhibit no same-sex contingency (Daly & Wilson, 1988). It is only after puberty, when sexual rivalry between parent and offspring becomes genuine (though not concerned with the other parent), that a same-sex contingency in violence appears (Daly & Wilson, 1988).

The recent burgeoning of Darwinian theory has produced a renaissance among animal behaviorists and comparative psychologists. No more do we study nonhuman animals as subnormal people or attempt to order them from "lower" to "higher." Comparisons have become principled instead, as witness Dewsbury's treatment of monogamy in this volume. We ask why any particular organism of interest has the traits it has and not others, and the question has become newly meaningful. We look forward to the day when social and developmental psychologists, who scorned the earlier comparative psychology as irrelevant to their interests, will appreciate the enormous relevance of natural selection theory for all the life sciences, including their own.

REFERENCES

Alexander, R. D. (1974). The evolution of social behavior. *Annual Review of Ecology and Systematics, 5,* 325–383.
Andersson, M., Wiklund, C. G., & Rundgren, H. (1980). Parental defence of offspring: A model and an example. *Animal Behaviour, 28,* 536–542.
Bachrach, C. A. (1983). Children in families: Characteristics of biological, step-, and adopted children. *Journal of Marriage and the Family, 45,* 171–179.
Barash, D. P. (1975). Evolutionary aspects of parental behavior: The distraction display of the Alpine accentor, *Prunella collaris. Wilson Bulletin, 87,* 367–373.
Becker, G. S., Landes, E. M., & Michael, R. T. (1977). An economic analysis of marital instability. *Journal of Political Economy, 85,* 1141–1187.
Beecher, M. D., & Beecher, I. M. (1979). Sociobiology of bank swallows: reproductive strategy of the male. *Science, 205,* 1282–1285.
Beecher, M. D., Beecher, I. M., & Hahn, S. (1981). Parent-offspring recognition in bank swallows (*Riparia riparia*): II. Development and acoustic basis. *Animal Behaviour, 29,* 95–101.

Beecher, M. D., Beecher, I. M., & Lumpkin, S. (1981). Parent-offspring recognition in bank swallows (*Riparia riparia*): I. Natural history. *Animal Behaviour*, *29*, 86–94.

Beer, C. G. (1970). Individual recognition of voice in the social behaviour of birds. *Advances in the Study of Behaviour*, *3*, 27–74.

Bertram, B. C. R. (1979). Ostriches recognise their own eggs and discard others. *Nature*, *279*, 233–234.

Betzig, L. L. (1985). *Despotism and differential reproduction: A Darwinian view of history*. Hawthorne, NY: Aldine.

Birkhead, T. R. (1978). Behavioural adaptations to high density nesting in the common guillemot, *Uria aalge*. *Animal Behaviour*, *26*, 321–331.

Bledsoe, C. (1980). The manipulation of Kpelle social fatherhood. *Ethnology*, *19*, 29–45.

Boone, J. L. (1988). Parental investment, social subordination, and population processes among the 15th and 16th century Portuguese nobility. In L. Betzig, M. Borgerhoff Mulder, & P. Turke (Eds.), *Human reproductive behavior*. Cambridge: Cambridge University Press.

Boswell, J. (1953). *Life of Johnson* (R. W. Chapman, ed.). Oxford: Oxford University Press. (Original work published 1779.)

Brooks, R. J. (1984). Causes and consequences of infanticide in populations of rodents. In G. Hausfater & S. B. Hrdy (Eds.), *Infanticide*. New York: Aldine.

Brown, C. R. (1984). Laying eggs in a neighbor's nest: Benefit and cost of colonial nesting in swallows. *Science*, *224*, 518–519.

Brown, J. L. (1983). Cooperation—a biologist's dilemma. *Advances in the Study of Behavior*, *13*, 1–37.

Buckley, P. A., & Buckley, F. G. (1972). Individual egg and chick recognition by adult royal terns (*Sterna maxima maxima*). *Animal Behaviour*, *20*, 457–462.

Bugos, P. E., & McCarthy, L. M. (1984). Ayoreo infanticide: A case study. In G. Hausfater & S. B. Hrdy (Eds.), *Infanticide*. New York: Aldine.

Burgoyne, J., & Clark, D. (1982). Reconstituted families. In R. N. Rapoport, M. P. Fogarty, & R. Rapoport (Eds.), *Families in Britain*. London: Routledge & Kegan Paul.

Busse, C., & Hamilton, W. J. (1981). Infant carrying by male chacma baboons. *Science*, *212*, 1281–1283.

Carlisle, T. R. (1985). Parental response to brood size in a cichlid fish. *Animal Behaviour*, *33*, 234–238.

Carroll, E. N. (1985). Abrogation of adoption by adoptive parents. *Family Law Quarterly*, *19*, 155–177.

Charnov, E. L. (1982). *The theory of sex allocation*. Princeton: Princeton University Press.

Cherlin, A. (1978). Remarriage as an incomplete institution. *American Journal of Sociology*, *84*, 634–650.

Chimbos, P. D. (1978). *Marital violence: A study of interspouse homicide*. San Francisco: R & E Research Associates.

Clark, A. B. (1978). Sex ratio and local resource competition in a prosimian primate. *Science, 201,* 163–165.

Clutton-Brock, T. H., & Iason, G. R. (1986). Sex ratio variation in mammals. *Quarterly Review of Biology, 61,* 339–374.

Creighton, S. J. (1985). An epidemiological study of abused children and their families in the United Kingdom between 1977 and 1982. *Child Abuse and Neglect, 9,* 441–448.

Crook, J. R., & Shields, W. M. (1985). Sexually selected infanticide by adult male barn swallows (*Hirundo rustica*). *Animal Behaviour, 33,* 754–761.

Cullen, E. (1957). Adaptations in the kittiwake to cliff-nesting. *Ibis, 99,* 275–302.

Curio, E., Regelmann, K., & Zimmermann, U. (1984). The defence of first and second broods by great tit (*Parus major*) parents: A test of a predictive sociobiology. *Zeitschrift für Tierpsychologie, 66,* 101–127.

Daly, M., & Wilson, M. (1980). Discriminative parental solicitude: A biological perspective. *Journal of Marriage and the Family, 42,* 277–288.

Daly, M., & Wilson, M. (1981a). Abuse and neglect of children in evolutionary perspective. In R. D. Alexander & D. W. Tinkle (Eds.), *Natural selection and social behavior.* New York: Chiron.

Daly, M., & Wilson, M. (1981b). Child maltreatment from a sociobiological perspective. *New Directions in Child Development, 11,* 93–112.

Daly, M., & Wilson, M. (1982a). Homicide and kinship. *American Anthropologist, 84,* 372–378.

Daly, M., & Wilson, M. (1982b). Whom are newborn babies said to resemble? *Ethology and Sociobiology, 3,* 69–78.

Daly, M., & Wilson, M. (1983). *Sex, evolution, and behavior.* 2nd ed. Boston: Willard Grant.

Daly, M., & Wilson, M. (1984). A sociobiological analysis of human infanticide. In G. Hausfater & S. B. Hrdy (Eds.), *Infanticide.* New York: Aldine.

Daly, M., & Wilson, M. (1985). Child abuse and other risks of not living with both parents. *Ethology and Sociobiology, 6,* 197–210.

Daly, M., & Wilson, M. (1987). Evolutionary psychology and family violence. In C. Crawford, M. Smith, & D. Krebs (Eds.), *Sociobiology and psychology.* Englewood Cliffs, NJ: Erlbaum.

Daly, M., & Wilson, M. (1988). *Homicide.* Hawthorne, NY: Aldine de Gruyter.

Daly, M., Wilson, M., & Weghorst, S. J. (1982). Male sexual jealousy. *Ethology and Sociobiology, 3,* 11–27.

Davis, R. B., Herreid, C. F., & Short, H. L. (1962). Mexican free-tailed bats in Texas. *Ecological Monographs, 32,* 311–346.

Deag, J. M., & Crook, J. H. (1971). Social behaviour and "agonistic buffering" in the wild Barbary macaque, *Macaca sylvana* L. *Folia Primatologica, 15,* 183–200.

Dickemann, M. (1975). Demographic consequences of infanticide in man. *Annual Review of Ecology and Systematics, 6,* 107–137.

Dickemann, M. (1979). Female infanticide, reproductive strategies, and social stratification: A preliminary model. In N. A. Chagnon & W. Irons (Eds.), *Evolutionary biology and human social behavior.* North Scituate, MA: Duxbury Press.

Dickemann, M. (1981). Paternal confidence and dowry competition: A biocultural analysis of purdah. In R. D. Alexander & D. W. Tinkle (Eds.), *Natural selection and social behavior*. New York: Chiron.

Dominey, W. J., & Blumer, L. S. (1984). Cannibalism of early life stages in fishes. In G. Hausfater & S. B. Hrdy (Eds.), *Infanticide*. New York: Aldine.

Dunn, J., & Kendrick, C. (1982). *Siblings*. Cambridge: Harvard University Press.

Emlen, S. T., & Vehrencamp, S. L. (1983). Cooperative breeding strategies among birds. In A. H. Brush & G. A. Clark (Eds.), *Perspectives in ornithology*. Cambridge: Cambridge University Press.

Faaborg, J., & Patterson, C. B. (1981). The characteristics and occurrence of cooperative polyandry. *Ibis, 123*, 477–484.

Faron, L. C. (1961). *Mapuche social structure: Institution reintegration in a patrilineal society of central Chile*. Urbana: University of Illinois Press.

Festinger, T. (1986). *Necessary risk: A study of adoptions and disrupted adoption placements*. Washington, DC: Child Welfare League of America.

Fisher, R. A. (1958). *The genetical theory of natural selection*. 2nd ed. New York: Dover.

Flinn, M. V. (1983). *Resources, mating, and kinship: The behavioral ecology of a Trinidadian village*. Unpublished doctoral dissertation, University of Michigan, Ann Arbor.

Freed, L. A. (1986). Territory takeover and sexually selected infanticide in tropical house wrens. *Behavioral Ecology and Sociobiology, 19*, 197–206.

Freud, S. (1953). *The interpretation of dreams* (J. Strachey, Trans. and Ed.). New York: Basic Books. (Original work published 1900.)

Freud, S. (1913). *Totem and taboo*. (J. Strachey, Trans. and Ed.). New York: W. W. Norton. (Original work published 1913.)

Galef, B. G. (1981). The ecology of weaning. In D. J. Gubernick & P. H. Klopfer (Eds.), *Parental care in mammals*. New York: Plenum.

Giles-Sims, J. (1984). The stepparent role: Expectations, behavior and sanctions. *Journal of Family Issues, 5*, 116–130.

Glick, P. C. (1979). Children of divorced parents in demographic perspective. *Journal of social Issues, 35*, 170–182.

Gosling, L. M. (1986). Selective abortion of entire litters in the coypu: Adaptive control of offspring production in relation to quality and sex. *American Naturalist, 127*, 772–795.

Gouge, W. (1626). *Of domesticall duties: Eight treatises*. London. (No publisher. Houghton Library, Harvard University.)

Gowaty, P. A., & Karlin, A. A. (1984). Multiple maternity and paternity in single broods of apparently monogamous eastern bluebirds (*Sialia sialis*). *Behavioral Ecology and Sociobiology, 15*, 91–96.

Graves, J. A., & Whiten, A. (1980). Adoption of strange chicks by herring gulls, *Larus argentatus* L. *Zeitschrift für Tierpsychologie, 54*, 267–278.

Greig-Smith, P. W. (1980). Parental investment in nest defence by stonechats (*Saxicola torquata*). *Animal Behaviour, 28*, 604–619.

Gubernick, D. J. (1981). Parent and infant attachment in mammals. In D. J. Gubernick & P. H. Klopfer (Eds.), *Parental care in mammals*. New York: Plenum.

Hamilton, W. D. (1964). The genetical evolution of social behaviour. I & II. *Journal of Theoretical Biology, 7*, 1–52.

Hamilton, W. D. (1967). Extraordinary sex ratios. *Science, 156,* 477–488.

Hamilton, W. D. (1979). Wingless and fighting males in fig wasps and other insects. In M. S. Blum & N. A. Blum (Eds.), *Sexual selection and reproductive competition in insects.* New York: Academic.

Harper, D. G. C. (1985a) Brood division in robins. *Animal Behaviour, 33,* 466–480.

Harper, D. G. C. (1985b) Interactions between adult robins and chicks belonging to other pairs. *Animal Behaviour, 33,* 876–884.

Hartung, J. (1982). Polygyny and inheritance of wealth. *Current Anthropology, 23,* 1–12.

Hartung, J. (1985). Matrilineal inheritance: New theory and analysis. *Behavioral and Brain Sciences, 8,* 661–688.

Hausfater, G., & Hrdy, S. B., eds. (1984). *Infanticide: Comparative and evolutionary perspectives.* New York: Aldine.

Herlihy, D. (1984). Households in the early middle ages: Symmetry and sainthood. In R. M. Netting, R. R. Wilk, & E. J. Arnould (Eds.), *Households.* Berkeley: University of California Press.

Hill, K., & Kaplan, H. (1988). Tradeoffs in male and female reproductive strategies among the Ache, Part 2. In L. Betzig, M. Borgerhoff Mulder, & P. Turke (Eds.), *Human reproductive behavior.* Cambridge: Cambridge University Press.

Hobart, C. W. (1975). Socioeconomic correlates of mortality and morbidity among Inuit infants. *Arctic Anthropology, 12,* 37–48.

Holley, A. J. F. (1984). Adoption, parent-chick recognition and maladaptation in the herring gull *Larus argentatus. Zeitschrift für Tierpsychologie, 64,* 9–14.

Holmes, W. G., Sherman, P. W. (1983). Kin recognition in animals. *American Scientist, 71,* 46–55.

Hoogland, J. L., & Sherman, P. W. (1976). Advantages and disadvantages of bank swallow (*Riparia riparia*) coloniality. *Ecological Monographs, 46,* 33–58.

Jaffee, B., & Fanshel, D. (1970). *How they fared in adoption: A follow-up study.* New York: Columbia University Press.

Karsten, R. (1932). *Indian tribes of the Argentine and Bolivian Chaco.* Ethnological Studies. Helsingfors: Societas Scientiarum Fennica.

Kitcher, P. (1985). *Vaulting ambition: Sociobiology and the quest for human nature.* Cambridge: MIT Press.

Knodel, J., & Lynch, K. A. (1985). The decline of remarriage: Evidence from German village populations in the eighteenth and nineteenth centuries. *Journal of Family History, 10,* 34–59.

Kummer, H. (1968). *Social organization of Hamadryas baboons.* Chicago: University of Chicago Press.

Kurland, J. A. (1977). *Kin selection in the Japanese monkey.* Basel: Karger.

Lack, D. (1965). *The life of the robin.* (4th ed.). London: Collins.

Laslett, P. (1977). Parental deprivation in the past. A note on orphans and stepparenthood in English history. In P. Laslett (Ed.), *Family life and illicit love in earlier generations.* Cambridge: Cambridge University Press.

LeBoeuf, B. J., & Briggs, K. T. (1977). The cost of living in a seal harem. *Mammalia, 41,* 167–195.

Leifer, M. (1977). Psychological changes accompanying pregnancy and motherhood. *Genetic Psychology Monographs, 95,* 55–96.

LeVine, R. A. (1965). Intergenerational tensions and extended family structures in Africa. In E. Shanas & G. F. Streib (Eds.), *Social structure and the family: Generational relations.* Englewood Cliffs, NJ: Prentice-Hall.

Lightcap, J. L., Kurland, J. A., & Burgess, R. L. (1982). Child abuse: A test of some predictions from evolutionary theory. *Ethology and Sociobiology, 3,* 61–67.

Ligon, J. D. (1983). Cooperation and reciprocity in avian social systems. *American Naturalist, 121,* 366–384.

Macfarlane, A. (1977). *The psychology of childbirth.* Cambridge: Harvard University Press.

Maddox, B. (1975). *The half-parent.* London: André Deutsch.

Malinowski, B. (1929). *The sexual life of savages in north-western Melanesia.* London: Routledge.

McClure, P. A. (1981). Sex-biased litter reduction in food-restricted wood rats (*Neotoma floridana*). *Science, 211,* 1058–1060.

McCracken, G. F. (1984). Communal nursing in Mexican free-tailed bat maternity colonies. *Science, 223,* 1090–1091.

McKaye, K. R. (1981). Natural selection and the evolution of interspecific brood care in fishes. In R. D. Alexander & D. W. Tinkle (Eds.), *Natural selection and social behavior.* New York: Chiron.

McKaye, K. R., & McKaye, N. M. (1977). Communal care and kidnapping of young by parental cichlids. *Evolution, 31,* 674–681.

Mock, D. W. (1984). Infanticide, siblicide, and avian nestling mortality. In G. Hausfater & S. B. Hrdy (Eds.), *Infanticide.* New York: Aldine.

Moehlman, P. D. (1979). Jackal helpers and pup survival. *Nature, 277,* 382–383.

Mumme, R. L., Koenig, W. D., & Pitelka, F. A. (1983). Reproductive competition in the communal acorn woodpecker: Sisters destroy each other's eggs. *Nature, 306,* 583–584.

Muul, I. (1970). Intra- and inter-familial behaviour of *Glaucomys volans* (Rodentia) following parturition. *Animal Behaviour, 18,* 20–25.

Nadler, J. H. (1976). The psychological stress of the stepmother (Doctoral dissertation, California School of Professional Psychology). *Dissertation Abstracts B,* 5367.

Nwako, F. A. (1979). Child abuse in Nigeria. *Medicine, Science, and the Law, 19,* 130–133.

Oppenheimer, J. R. (1970). Mouthbreeding in fishes. *Animal Behaviour, 18,* 493–503.

Packer, C., & Pusey, A. E. (1984). Infanticide in carnivores. In G. Hausfater & S. B. Hrdy (Eds.), *Infanticide.* New York: Aldine.

Paige, K. E., & Paige, J. M. (1981). *The politics of reproductive ritual.* Berkeley: University of California Press.

Parsons, J. (1971). Cannibalism in herring gulls. *British Birds, 64,* 528–537.

Patterson, T. L., Petrinovich, L., & James, D. K. (1980). Reproductive value and appropriateness of response to predators by white-crowned sparrows. *Behavioral Ecology and Sociobiology, 7*, 227–231.

Payne, R. B. (1977). The ecology of brood parasitism in birds. *Annual Review of Ecology and Systematics, 8*, 1–28.

Perkins, T. F., & Kahan, J. P. (1979). An empirical comparison of natural-father and stepfather family systems. *Family Process, 18*, 175–183.

Polis, G. A. (1984). Intraspecific predation and "infant killing" among invertebrates. In G. Hausfater & S. B. Hrdy (Eds.), *Infanticide*. New York: Aldine.

Power, H. W., Litovich, E., & Lombardo, M. P. (1981). Male starlings delay incubation to avoid being cuckolded. *Auk, 98*, 386–389.

Pressley, P. H. (1981). Parental effort and the evolution of nest-guarding tactics in the threespine stickleback, *Gasterosteus aculeatus* L. *Evolution, 35*, 282–295.

Pugesek, B. H. (1981). Increased reproductive effort with age in the California gull (*Larus californicus*). *Science, 212*, 822–823.

Rabenold, K. N. (1985). Cooperation in breeding by nonreproductive wrens: Kinship, reciprocity, and demography. *Behavioral Ecology and Sociobiology, 17*, 1–17.

Rankin, J. H. (1983). The family context of delinquency. *Social Problems, 30*, 466–479.

Reyer, H.-U. (1986). Breeder-helper-interactions in the pied kingfisher reflect the costs and benefits of cooperative breeding. *Behaviour, 96*, 277–303.

Ridley, M., & Rechten, C. (1981). Female sticklebacks prefer to spawn with males whose nests contain eggs. *Behaviour, 76*, 152–161.

Riedman, M. L. (1982). The evolution of alloparental care and adoption in mammals and birds. *Quarterly Review of Biology, 57*, 405–435.

Robson, K. S., & Moss, H. A. (1970). Patterns and determinants of maternal attachment. *Journal of Pediatrics, 77*, 976–985.

Rodkin, L. I., Hunt, E. J., & Cowan, S. D. (1982). A men's support group for significant others of rape victims. *Journal of Marital and Family Therapy, 8*, 91–97.

Rodman, H. (1971). *Lower-class families*. London: Oxford University Press.

Rothstein, S. I. (1975). Evolutionary rates and host defenses against avian brood parasitism. *American Naturalist, 109*, 161–176.

Rubenstein, H. (1980). Conjugal behavior and parental role flexibility in an Afro-Caribbean village. *Canadian Review of Sociology and Anthropology, 17*, 330–337.

Sahlins, M. (1976). *The use and abuse of biology*. Ann Arbor: University of Michigan Press.

Schatkin, S. B. (1953). *Disputed paternity proceedings*. 3rd ed. Albany, New York: Banks, Bender.

Schneider, D. M. (1968). *American kinship*. Englewood Cliffs, NJ: Prentice-Hall.

Scott, P. D. (1973). Fatal battered baby cases. *Medicine, Science, and the Law, 13*, 197–206.

Sherman, P. W. (1980). The limits of ground squirrel nepotism. In G. W. Barlow & J. Silverberg (Eds.), *Sociobiology: Beyond nature/nurture?* Boulder, CO: Westview Press.

Silk, J. B. (1980). Adoption and kinship. *American Anthropologist, 82*, 799–820.

Smith, M. S. (1981). Kin investment in grandchildren. Unpublished doctoral dissertation, York University, Toronto.

Smith, M. S., Kish, B. J., & Crawford, C. B. (1987). Inheritance of wealth as human kin investment. *Ethology and Sociobiology, 8*, 171–182.

Smuts, B. B. (1986). *Sex and friendship in baboons.* New York: Aldine.

Stamps, J., Clark, A., Arrowood, P., & Kus, B. (1985). Parent-offspring conflict in budgerigars. *Behaviour, 94*, 1–40.

Symons, D. (1987). If we're all Darwinians, what's the fuss about? In C. Crawford, M. Smith, & D. Krebs (Eds.), *Sociobiology and psychology.* Englewood Cliffs, NJ: Erlbaum.

Thompson, S. (1955). *Motif-index of folk literature* (rev. ed. in 6 vols.). Bloomington: Indiana University Press.

Thornhill, R., & Thornhill, N. W. (1983). Human rape: An evolutionary analysis. *Ethology and Sociobiology, 4*, 137–173.

Tooby, J., & Cosmides, L. (in press). Evolutionary psychology and the generation of culture: Part I. Theoretical considerations. *Ethology and Sociobiology.*

Trivers, R. L. (1972). Parental investment and sexual selection. In B. Campbell (Ed.), *Sexual selection and the descent of man, 1871–1971* (pp. 136–179). Chicago: Aldine.

Trivers, R. L. (1974). Parent-offspring conflict. *American Zoologist, 14*, 249–264.

Trivers, R. L. (1985). *Social evolution.* Menlo Park, CA: Benjamin/Cummings.

Trivers, R. L., & Hare, H. (1976). Haplodiploidy and the evolution of the social insects. *Science, 191*, 249–263.

Trivers, R. L., & Willard, D. E. (1973). Natural selection of parental ability to vary the sex ratio of offspring. *Science, 179*, 90–92.

Vehrencamp, S. L. (1977). Relative fecundity and parental effort in communally nesting anis *Crotophaga sulcirostris. Science, 197*, 403–405.

Vehrencamp, S. L., Bowen, B. S., & Koford, R. R. (1986). Breeding roles and pairing patterns within communal groups of groove-billed anis (*Crotophaga sulcirostris*). *Animal Behaviour, 34*, 347–366.

Voland, E. (1984). Human sex-ratio manipulation: Historical data from a German parish. *Journal of Human Evolution, 13*, 99–107.

Voland, E. (1988). Differential infant and child mortality in evolutionary perspective: Data from late 17th to 19th century Ostfriesland. In L. Betzig, M. Borgerhoff Mulder, & P. Turke (Eds.), *Human reproductive behavior.* Cambridge: Cambridge University Press.

vom Saal, F. S. (1985). Time-contingent change in infanticide and parental behavior induced by ejaculation in male mice. *Physiology and Behavior, 34*, 7–16.

Wadsworth, J., Burnell, I., Taylor, B., & Butler, N. (1983). Family type and accidents in preschool children. *Journal of Epidemiology and Community Health, 37*, 100–104.

Werren, J. H. (1980). Sex ratio adaptations to local mate competition in a parasitic wasp. *Science, 208*, 1157–1159.

White, L. K., & Booth, A. (1985). The quality and stability of remarriages: The role of stepchildren. *American Sociological Review, 50*, 689–698.

144

NEBRASKA SYMPOSIUM ON MOTIVATION 1987

Wiley, R. H., & Rabenold, K. N. (1984). The evolution of cooperative breeding by delayed reciprocity and queuing for favorable social positions. *Evolution, 38,* 609–621.

Williams, G. C. (1966). *Adaptation and natural selection.* Princeton: Princeton University Press.

Wilson, E. O. (1971). *The insect societies.* Cambridge, MA: Belknap.

Wilson, M., & Daly, M. (1987). Risk of maltreatment of children living with stepparents. In R. Gelles & J. Lancaster (Eds.), *Biosocial perspectives on child abuse.* New York: Aldine.

Wilson, M., Daly, M., & Weghorst, S. J. (1980). Household composition and the risk of child abuse and neglect. *Journal of Biosocial Science, 12,* 333–340.

Wilson, M., Daly, M., & Weghorst, S. J. (1983). Differential maltreatment of girls and boys. *Victimology, 6,* 249–261.

Woolfenden, G. E., & Fitzpatrick, J. W. (1984). *The Florida scrub jay: demography of a cooperative-breeding bird.* Princeton: Princeton University Press.

Yom-Tov, Y. (1980). Intraspecific nest parasitism in birds. *Biological Reviews, 55,* 93–108.

Young, C. W. (1980). Case notes: Grandparents—adoption. *Journal of Family Law, 18,* 851–857.

A Comparative Approach to Vocal Communication[1]

Charles T. Snowdon
University of Wisconsin–Madison

Why Comparative Psychology?

*T*hose of us who study animals are frequently questioned about the benefits of our research. "Why, with so many human problems still unsolved, should the public support research on nonhuman animals? What can we learn of benefit to human beings?" These questions are asked not only by puzzled citizens like my grandmother, who first posed them when I was a graduate student. Increasingly, as "cognitive science" has become more and more the buzzword of psychology, they are asked by our colleagues as well. Indeed, to many the term "animal psychology" is an oxymoron. Over the years we comparative psychologists have generated many rationalizations about our work: our research shows the continuity of processes between animals and human beings; the study of animals allows us to perform experiments with greater precision of control than would be allowed with human beings; animals are simply

1. The research from my laboratory described in this chapter has been supported by USPHS grants MH 29,775 and MH 35,215 and a Research Scientist Development Award from the National Institute of Mental Health. Additional support has been received from the University of Wisconsin Graduate School Research Committee and the Nave Fund of the Ibero-American Studies Program of the University of Wisconsin–Madison. I am indebted to many people for the development of the ideas in this chapter: W. John Smith first piqued my interest in the study of animal communication. Philip A. Morse taught me much about human language and speech and its ontogeny. Jef-

fun to study, and we should be allowed to pursue whatever research gives us pleasure.

None of these rationalizations are adequate defenses of comparative psychology. The revolution brought about in psychology by the "Garcia effect" made it clear that many aspects of animal behavior were species specific or constrained by biology, and thus one could not assume an easy continuity between nonhuman and human animals in all respects. As comparative psychologists have become more biologically sophisticated over the past two decades, we have recognized that the classical behaviorist model does not apply very well and that we must achieve a better understanding of the animal's natural habitat and its normal social and ontogenetic environment in order to develop sophisticated research questions and the appropriate experiments and observations to answer them.

Increasing concern with the ethics of animal experimentation and the realization that animals have much greater cognitive complexity than previously thought (a point amply illustrated in this volume) makes untenable the argument of using animals for experiments that cannot be performed on human beings. We must recognize the need for humane treatment of animal subjects, and the more we learn about the social and intellectual complexity of animals, the more important it becomes to be cognizant of animal-welfare concerns. In contrast to a popular view of comparative psychologists as exploiters of animals, it is becoming more and more clear that we have much to contribute toward conservation. Many of us work with endangered species, and our behavioral studies show how we can help these animals reproduce and rear their young more successfully in captivity (e.g., Snowdon, Savage, & McConnell, 1985) by understanding the importance of early experience in acquiring parental care skills and by designing appropriate caging and housing. Other comparative research, such as recent work on observational learning of fear of predators (e.g., Mineka, Davidson, Cook, & Keir,

---

frey A. French introduced me to techniques for measuring hormones and indicated the value these techniques might have in understanding the ontogeny of communication. Discussions with Jack P. Hailman have focused my attention on structural aspects of communication, and Irene M. Pepperberg has sharpened my understanding of bird vocalizations and the importance of social interactions. Kim Bauers, Jayne Cleveland, Laura Dronzek, Alexandra Hodun, Patricia McConnell, Yvonne Pola, and Carol Sweet have been excellent research collaborators over the years.

1984), provides examples of what captive animals must learn before they are returned to the wild.

The argument that animal research is fun would be fine if we spent our leisure time studying animals, but it is much less supportable when we try to explain to our department heads, our universities, and federal grant administrators why funds should be spent on what could be viewed as just an interesting hobby. This argument ultimately does not justify our being comparative psychologists.

What then can we use to justify our work? Why should our colleagues pay attention to us? Why should our grandmothers and other citizens be interested in our research findings? I have found the best parallel in the work of cultural anthropologists. Over the past century two groups of people have left the "civilized" world to make contact with people of other cultures. One group, the missionaries, went to convert the heathen to Christianity. When they made contact with a group, they attempted to learn the language so that they could translate the Bible, and then they worked hard to teach the people the language of the missionaries. They attempted to alter the clothing to Western models, and they tried to impose Western mores of social organization. In many cases the effort at conversion was a failure. Once the missionaries left or stopped providing incentives, the group reverted to its original culture. In other cases groups were assimilated, with the loss of their previous culture, and homogenization resulted.

The cultural anthropologists, on the other hand, when they did their job well, participated in the life of the people they studied without imposing Western values or ideas. They learned the language in order to understand the culture; they did not try to teach their own language. Most important, they were content to learn, and the information they brought back helped the rest of us realize the cultural blinders we wore. The forms of social organization we had adopted were not the only ones that worked, and in many cases ours were not even the most efficient. Stereotypes about sex roles were shaken by evidence that other cultures had quite different expectations. Age stereotypes also were undermined when it became clear that other cultures had different expectations about the roles of children, adolescents, and older adults. The reports of the cultural anthropologists greatly expanded our sense of the possibilities available to us. We might still choose to follow the same modes of social behavior, but at least we are now aware that these patterns are open to change.

I see comparative psychologists as extending the work of cultural anthropologists to other species. Our contribution can be to carefully observe other species and to attempt to understand their behavior, not simply to document how they are similar to human beings, but to learn how they differ and to understand the reasons for these differences. Just as cultural anthropologists were able to enrich the possibilities of human behavior by documenting other cultures, so we might enrich our human perspectives by documenting how other species solve problems.

There are many examples of this enrichment, but let me focus on one. Recent popularization of sociobiology has tried to provide a biological basis for the traditional sex-role differences in our society. One version went so far as to claim that human males have "love 'em and leave 'em genes" (Barash, 1979), claiming an explicit genetic basis for sex differences in parental care. However, there are many examples of male nonhuman primates' displaying intensive paternal care even toward unrelated infants, and data from adoptions in species where spontaneous male care has rarely been observed show that male primates are not immunized against parental care by their Y chromosomes. A close reading of the literature on nonhuman primates indicates that males have great interest in helping to care for infants but are frequently excluded by the females. Only in species where females cannot rear their young successfully by themselves is male involvement permitted, and the males of these species display intensive parental care (Snowdon & Suomi, 1982). Here is a case where the investigations of comparative psychologists into the forms and instances of paternal behavior in other species can counter a pernicious view of biological determinism of the absence of male parental care in human beings. By knowing the conditions under which male parental care is allowed in other species, we can better understand what conditions would lead to a more equitable sharing of parental responsibilities in human beings. In addition, research on animal behavior may suggest new areas for research in human behavior that we might never have thought of until prodded by results from animals.

Thus, I argue that documenting and understanding the causes of variation in behavior is the most important contribution that comparative psychologists can make. This means that comparative psychologists collectively should study as broad a range of species as possible, although as West and King (this volume) note, no individual investigator can hope to study closely more than a few species. The species selected should be those that will provide evidence most relevant to the question being examined. Sometimes this means looking at those species most closely related to human beings—chimpanzees, gorillas, and orangutans (see Savage-Rumbaugh, this volume), but at other times problems will be best illuminated by studying species quite different from human beings. Birds, rodents, Neotropical primates, and even invertebrates and fishes can make important contributions to understanding human behavior.

Let me digress for a moment to deal with the frequent accusation that comparative psychologists have not been truly comparative but have primarily studied white rats (Beach, 1950; Dukes, 1960; Lockard, 1971; Porter, Johnson, & Granger, 1981). The evidence from the authors in this volume reflects the great diversity of species studied by comparative psychologists, and each of us has been involved in truly comparative efforts between species. Scanning the articles in the *Journal of Comparative Psychology* and those by psychologists publishing in *Animal Behaviour, Ethology,* and *Behaviour* shows the wide range of species studied.

Among comparative psychologists today we find both of the types represented by the analogy of the missionaries and the cultural anthropologists. Those favoring the missionary approach argue that an appropriate tack is to determine just how humanlike animals might become if provided with an appropriate environment. Thus the performance of animals is judged by human standards. This method has great value in telling us exactly what animals are able to accomplish in human terms and has had great utility in helping the public realize that many animal species are much more complex than previously thought.

I prefer the alternative approach of observing other animals while trying not to impose ideas of human culture on them. This position holds that animals are best studied in natural environments or, if they must be studied in captivity, housed in naturalistic settings and provided with a natural social development and natural social environment. It means that we must learn to understand the language of the animals rather than making them acquire our language, and it means that we must evaluate their performance by the demands of their natural environment rather than by the demands human beings face. There is an increasing trend for comparative psychologists to be involved in field research or in naturalistic studies on captive animals. Today's students in comparative psychology are more likely to have had training in important areas of biology and in field techniques than biology students are to have had training in experimental design and statistical methods.

Models for Studying Vocal Communication

There are two extremes of models available for studying communication in animals. The first derives from the simple models of classical ethology. Either signals are highly stereotyped, or else the animals receiving them use stimulus filters that eliminate much of the variability of signals, so that the signals as perceived are highly stereotyped. This stereotypic perceptual input elicits an equally stereotyped response, known as the fixed action pattern. Signals are species specific, innately determined, and effectively invariant (Mattingly, 1972). Furthermore, animals communicate only about their internal states or emotions. They are unable to use signals symbolically or indicate external referents.

The second model for communication is that of human language, an open, infinitely variable system that makes use of subtle variations in signals and complex syntactic rules to create an enormous variety of signal strings. The responses to these strings can be equally variable. Language is considered a form of communication that is almost entirely symbolic, with internal states being more accurately communicated by nonverbal means.

Although Lloyd Morgan's canon and Occam's razor should incline us toward the simple ethological model, recent research on animal cognition and communication has pointed out its failings. There are several sources for this evidence: variation in signal structure that serves important communicative functions; variations in the perception of signals by animals; the demonstration of referential communication; complex syntax governing call sequences within an animal's utterances and syntactic rules for vocal interactions between animals; social influences on communication; and complex systems of vocal ontogeny. I will discuss each of these points in more detail.

Although I argue that the linguistic model is superior to the traditional ethological model for studying vocal communication in most vertebrates, the use of a linguistic model does not presuppose that the vocal communication systems must be homologous to human speech and language. It would be a naïve biologist or comparative psychologist who would argue for an identity between the communication systems of different species. If we were to discover an alien creature that spoke a human language perfectly, our first inclination would be to classify the alien as humanlike. Our taxonomic identification of a species is often based on commonalities in the communication systems (Hodun, Snowdon, & Soini, 1981; Snowdon, Hodun, Rosenberger, & Coimbra-Filho, 1986). Thus each species should be expected to have developed its own species-specific system. At the same time, we should also expect continuities of processes and similarities of phenomena in related phylogenetic lines. To the extent that vocal communication is best described as complex rather than simple, a linguistic model can be a useful heuristic for study without our having to assume that the communication system being studied is formally like a human language.

Much of the previous work on communication in animals and on human speech and language has focused on the mechanisms governing the production of an utterance or affecting the perception of or response to an utterance. The utterance or signal is the focal point. Until quite recently most scientists neglected the fact that communication is first and foremost a social act that is best studied as an interaction. It is interesting that each of the chapters in this volume dealing with animal communication has described the importance of focusing on social stimulation and social variables on communication (see West & King and Savage-Rumbaugh, this volume). Perhaps what is more amazing is that for so many years we have been aware of the social context of human language without focusing on it in formal studies of either animal communication or human speech and language.

Variability in Signal Structure

The first prerequisite for complexity is signal variability. If indeed signals are highly stereotyped and limited in range, then there is no basis for presuming complexity. However, in the past decade there have been several indications that signal complexity is not merely random variation, but that subtle variations in signal structure have communicative significance. Several studies have been published on birds, mainly warblers, demonstrating that subtle variations in song structure are used in different contexts (Ficken & Ficken, 1967; Kroodsma, 1981; Lein, 1978;

Morse, 1967; Smith, Pawlukiewicz, & Smith, 1978). The premier study with primates was Green's (1975a) study of the coo vocalizations of Japanese macaques (*Macaca fuscata*). Many people studying macaques had described the coo vocalization as a unitary signal used generally in affiliative contexts. However, Green described seven variations of coo call structure that were used in ten different contexts. The distribution of call type by context was far from random. There was a relatively close correspondence between the forms of coo variants noted and the social contexts in which they were used. This result indicated that Japanese macaques had a larger and more complex vocal repertoire than had been thought, and it immediately stimulated the search for vocal complexities in other species.

Pola and Snowdon (1975) described a series of trill-like vocalizations in pygmy marmosets (*Cebuella pygmaea*) that could be divided into four distinct classes (Figure 1). In studies of captive animals two different usages of trill variants were found. One, the open mouth trill, appeared to be used in agonistic situations; its emission was followed with an increased probability of threat displays, approach-withdrawal behavior, or piloerection, in contrast to the closed mouth trill, which appeared to be used as an affiliative vocalization. The structural differences between these two variants were slight. They differed only in duration, with the closed mouth trill having a mean duration of 176 msec while the open mouth trill had a mean duration of 334 msec. The closed mouth trill and the two remaining trills differed from each other in structure much more than the open mouth trill did from the closed mouth trill, yet each appeared to be used, like the closed mouth trill, as an affiliative vocalization, primarily eliciting antiphonal vocal responses from other animals. There did not appear to be differences in the social contexts where these three trill variants were used.

However, it seemed strange that there should be such different structures of trills without any apparent difference in usage. We decided to pursue this issue further with a field study in Peru. The three trill structures suggested predictions about the ability to localize these sounds. (See Wiley & Richards, 1982, for a review of acoustic design features for maximizing and minimizing locatability of vocal signals.) The quiet trill had a very small frequency range (< 1.5 kHz) and was emitted at a lower sound intensity than the other two calls. The closed mouth trill had a moderate frequency range (2.5–4.0 kHz) and was emitted at a greater sound intensity but in all other respects was identical to the quiet trill.

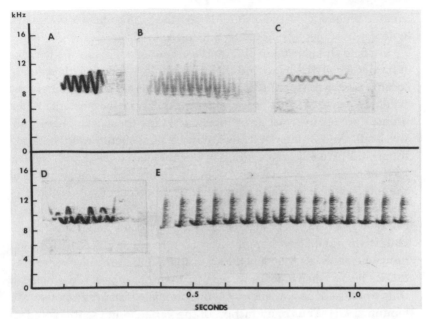

FIGURE 1. Sonagrams of trills of pygmy marmoset: (*A*) closed mouth trill; (*B*) open mouth trill; (*C*) quiet trill; (*D*) juvenile trill; (*E*) J-call.

Finally, the J-call (named for its appearance on sound spectrograms) differed from the other two calls on several dimensions. The J-calls had a much greater frequency range (5–6 kHz), were much longer (> 1.0 sec compared with < 250 msec), and were interrupted with several short notes.

Research on the cues for sound localization in macaques by Brown (1982a) indicated that frequency range was an important cue in sound localization. Adding 400–500 Hz of frequency modulation reduced the error of locatability by 50% in a two-dimensional task. More interesting for our purposes was the finding that when localization was tested with a three-dimensional array, it became necessary to have at least 2 kHz of frequency modulation to significantly reduce error of localization by macaques. The quiet trill of pygmy marmosets has a frequency range below this critical value, making it relatively difficult to localize. Both the closed mouth trill and quiet trill provided a single time-of-arrival cue, whereas the J-call with its series of separate notes provided many time-of-arrival cues. The combination of a greater frequency range with increased time-of-arrival cues should make the J-call quite easy to localize, whereas the quiet trill should be difficult to localize.

In a field situation these differences in sound locatability might make it harder for predators to find the caller while at the same time aiding localization by conspecifics. Thus when animals are close together they would be expected to use the most ventriloquial call, the quiet trill. When animals are relatively far apart they should use the most locatable call, the J-call. And at intermediate distances they should use the closed mouth trill. We followed a group of pygmy marmosets in their natural environment for several weeks, obtaining more than 1,200 examples of these trills where we could identify the location of both the calling animal and the nearest conspecific. When we plotted the distribution of each call type as a function of the distance between caller and nearest recipient, we found that our hypothesis was correct. The quiet trill was used only when animals were less than 5 m apart, and the J-call was the only call we heard when animals were more than 20 m apart. Closed mouth trills were used most frequently at intermediate distances (Snowdon & Hodun, 1981). Thus one function of the variation in the trill vocalizations of pygmy marmosets was to communicate the relative distance between caller and potential recipient.

Adjusting call structure to aid in sound localization over long distances and to minimize location cues over short ones is a nice antipredator strategy. Brown (1982b) presented captive raptors with examples of ventroloquial alarm calls of birds and found that raptors were very inaccurate in localizing the calls. In contrast, playbacks of mobbing calls from the same species were very easily localized by predators. These results suggest a parallel function for the calls of pygmy marmosets. In addition, we found that the frequency range the pygmy marmosets used was not used by other species in the Amazon. The bulk of the sound intensity in the environment (wind noise, insects, birdcalls, etc.) was below the frequency used by pygmy marmosets. Thus these animals appeared to have a unique frequency channel for communication.

The finding that variation in signal structure improves or retards sound localization is interesting, and it seems likely that it might apply to human communication as well. However, to my knowledge there has been little if any study of how human beings might alter their vocal communication to accommodate localization cues. This is one example where a finding from animals suggests some interesting possibilities for further study of human communication.

There have been many other documentations of variability in signal structure with different social contexts. Cleveland and Snowdon (1982) described the vocalizations of the cotton-top tamarin (*Saguinus oedipus*), an endangered monkey from northern Colombia. There are a variety of short frequency-modulated, chirplike vocalizations in this species. Cleveland and Snowdon described eight variants of these chirps found in adult cotton-top tamarins. Although the differences between the chirps were subtle, the contexts in which each chirp type was used were quite different. Thus one chirp was used as a mobbing call, another for intragroup affiliation, a third as a call upon approaching food, a fourth upon taking food, a fifth as an intertroop aggressive call, a sixth as an alarm call, and so on. There was no obvious similarity in the situations over which these similar calls were given. Rather, each subtle variant appears to have been used in a highly specific, but distinct, context.

A playback study involving two of the chirps that were most similar in structure, but most different in context (the F-chirp and the G-chirp), showed that monkeys could distinguish between the calls in the absence of contextual cues from any other source, indicating that the structure of the call was by itself conveying differential information (Bauers & Snowdon, in preparation). Thus these subtle call variations do have functional significance.

Cleveland and Snowdon (1982) also described another set of call variants in the cotton-top tamarin. There were several forms of long-call vocalizations. These are calls that consist of several long whistlelike notes. Four types of long calls were described: the normal long call appeared to be given in response to hearing animals from strange groups, and it was hypothesized to be a territorial call similar to birdsong. The quiet long call had a very different structure and was used in contexts involving within-group cohesion; this call was also given at a very high rate whenever a mated pair were temporarily separated, suggesting that it functioned as a lost call as well. A third form consisted of a normal long call preceded by an F-chirp, the type of chirp used in intergroup encounters. This call appeared to be a grammatical combination of two other calls, and I shall say more about it later. Finally, there was a highly variable form of long call where the whistled segments were preceded by a variety of different chirplike notes. These were called combination long calls because of the mixture of chirps and whistles. They were much more common among sexually immature animals. When these animals were temporarily separated from their group, they emitted these combination long calls at high rates, producing as many as 30 variants over a 45-minute separation.

Snowdon, Cleveland, and French (1983) subsequently developed a discriminant analysis technique to show that the normal long calls and quiet long calls could be discriminated with 98% accuracy. They carried out a playback study demonstrating that cotton-top tamarins could discriminate between the long calls of familiar and unfamiliar animals and that they responded differently to the two types of long calls.

Other studies on monkeys have found subtle variations in vocal structure that correlate with specific contexts. Thus Cheney and Seyfarth (1982) described four types of grunt vocalizations in vervet monkeys (Cercopithecus aethiops) that were correlated with different contexts. Playback studies indicated that vervets perceived each of the grunt types as different and could respond appropriately to them. Gouzoules, Gouzoules, and Marler (1984) described four different screams given by rhesus monkey (Macaca mulatta) infants in agonistic situations and found that they provided information about the relatedness and relative dominance status of the attacker. Through a playback study they showed that the mothers of these infants responded appropriately to each form of scream. Thus among primates, and increasingly among birds, there is evidence that variations in the structure of what have previously been thought to be single call classes are used in predictable ways that effectively increase the vocabulary size of these animals.

Another type of variation important in signal structure is identification information—information that identifies the species, subspecies, or population of a group, information that identifies sex, and information that identifies individuals. Every study that has sought individual differences in call structure has found such individual differences. In chimpanzees (Pan troglodytes; Marler & Hobbett, 1975), grey-cheeked mangabeys (Cecrocebus albigena; Waser, 1977), stumptail macaque infants (Macaca arctoides; Lillehei & Snowdon, 1978), pygmy marmosets (Snowdon & Cleveland, 1980), cotton-top tamarins (Snowdon, Cleveland, & French, 1983), moustached tamarins (Saguinus mystax; Snowdon & Hodun, 1985), and vervet monkeys (Cheney & Seyfarth, 1980) individual differences in call structure have been documented, and in most of these studies playback techniques have demonstrated that the monkeys respond to the playbacks of vocalizations in specific ways, indicating that the monkeys are making distinctions between individuals based on their vocal structure. It is perhaps not surprising that animals living in social groups should recognize one another as individuals and that animals making extensive use of vocal signaling should show differences in vocal structure. Given prior work on individual recognition in birds (Beer, 1970; Brooks & Falls, 1975), it is hardly surprising that monkeys should also display individual recognition. However, I think that the acknowledgment of individual signatures in signals has some important implications for how we view communication. These will be discussed below.

Another issue of special interest is populational variation. Marler (1970a, 1970b) has made excellent use of the geographic variation in the songs of white-crowned sparrows (*Zonotrichia leucophrys*) to provide us with a major model of the ontogeny of vocal communication, a model that has had wide influence in studies of human language acquisition. Among primates there have been fewer demonstrations of vocal variation. Green (1975b) presented brief evidence that Japanese macaques at different sites in Japan gave different calls when food was provided each day. Green argued that these were evidence of a learned vocalization that was culturally transmitted, much like the food-washing behavior of Japanese macaques. However, he was able to gather no evidence on the origin of these different provisioning calls or on their ontogeny within an individual.

Other studies have indicated that vocal differences in primates are much more fixed than they appear to be in birdsong. For example, Marshall and Marshall (1976) have used the differences in the loud calls or choruses of gibbons (*Hylobates* sp.) to make distinctions between species and subspecies. Snowdon, Hodun, Rosenberger, and Coimbra-Filho (1986) found that three separate populations of the endangered lion tamarins (*Leontopithecus* sp.) in Brazil had distinctly different long-call vocalization and that the pattern of differences in these long calls paralleled differences found in more traditional taxonomic measurements of skeletal structure and dentition.

Two populations of squirrel monkeys (*Saimiri sciureus*) exist in the Amazon basin, each with distinctive morphological and vocal features. The gothic arch form, named because of the pattern of the supraorbital arch, is found north and east of the Amazon. The roman arch form is found south and west of the Amazon. Each has been shown to have a distinct type of the isolation peep vocalization—used by infants separated from their mothers or by older animals separated from their groups (Winter, 1969). Subsequent research has shown that these call types can be readily distinguished by a discriminant analysis and appear to be inherited jointly with the supraorbital color pattern (Newman & Symmes, 1982). The two call types elicit different responses from each population. In a playback study Snowdon, Coe, and Hodun (1985) presented groups of squirrel monkeys of each form with infant isolation-peep vocalizations from each type. There was a clear specificity of response to each call type. Roman arch adults responded to the playback of roman arch infants with an increase in locomotion and approach to the speaker, but they showed no change in behavior when the functionally similar call of gothic arch infants was presented. Just the opposite results appeared with the gothic arch animals. Gothic arch adults responded with increased locomotion and approach to the playback of calls from gothic arch infants, but they absolutely ignored the calls of roman arch infants. The Amazon River is a major species-isolation boundary, and the clear patterns of inheritance of call structure and the clear differentiation in response to infant calls by the two populations of squirrel monkeys indicate a sharp separation between species.

However, another example from a different species in the Amazon basin implies a possibility for flexibility in acquisition of vocal variability in monkeys. In the course of traveling through the western Amazon in Peru, Hodun, Snowdon, and Soini (1981) recorded long-call vocalizations from four subspecies of the saddle-back tamarin (*Saguinus fuscicollis* ssp.). Most populations were separated by river barriers, and each population had a long-call structure that differed from those of the others. One animal, however, had an anomalous call. Its long call was an amalgam of the subspecies the animal most clearly resembled and the subspecies found within earshot on the other side of the river. This amalgam call could represent a hybrid of the two subspecies that is reflecting in its calls the genetic background of both populations, or it could result from early learning where the individual was exposed to both types of long calls. To test between these hypotheses we recorded some long calls from captive animals known to be hybrids of the two subspecies found in the field. To our surprise, these hybrids did not give the same type of amalgam call as the wild animal. Instead they had incorporated into their call structure features of a third subspecies, the type that was most populous in the room where these hybrid animals had been housed. The results are seductive, suggesting that the long calls of tamarins, which function much like birdsong, might be susceptible to similar developmental processes.

Perception of Calls: Categorization

There has been a long dispute among students of animal communication over whether call repertoires are discrete or continuous. Marler (1975) suggested a phylogenetic progression toward categorization of communicative signals. Primitive animals tend to have signals that could be distinguished by a discrete set of acoustic parameters. At the next stage, species have a continuous communication system where a single state such as fear or aggression can be coded in intensity or probability by varying a signal along an acoustic continuum. Finally, at the highest level, acoustic continua are divided into perceptually discrete categories.

The phenomenon of categorical perception has long been a mainstay of research into human speech perception (Liberman, 1982). Changing some parameters of production such as the timing of vibration of the larynx relative to expelling air through the lips (voice onset time) or the location of the tongue (place of articulation) allows us to create several different sounds by a few parameter changes. Thus variation in place of articulation gives us /b/, /d/, and /g/, and by adding voice onset time differences we also obtain /p/, /t/, and /k/. Thus variation on two parameters allows us to generate six phonemes. These phonemes must be clearly discriminated from each other, however, and research on categorical perception has shown that when synthesized variants are played to human listeners on a given dimension (say /ba/–/pa/), subjects tend to label them as either /ba/ or /pa/. They do not assign intermediate labels to sounds that are intermediate in structure between the prototypical /ba/ and /pa/; there is a sharp categorization. In addition, when human subjects are asked to discriminate between tokens of /ba/ that differ by some fixed acoustic amount, they are generally unable to do so at better than chance levels. On the other hand, if two stimuli are presented that differ by the same acoustic amount but are chosen so that one is labeled as a /ba/ and the other as a /pa/, then discrimination is virtually perfect. The place where discrimination is greatest and labeling differences are clearest has been described as a category boundary.

The early writers on categorical perception argued that this phenomenon was uniquely human. About 12 years ago Morse and Snowdon (1975) decided to see whether monkeys could perceive speech sounds categorically. We tested rhesus macaques using an habituation/dishabituation paradigm with exemplars from the place-of-articulation continuum. The monkeys made very clear distinctions between sounds that humans would perceive as /ba/ versus /da/, illustrating that they could discriminate the same category boundaries humans used. However, we found that the monkeys could also discriminate between variants of /ba/ and variants of /da/ in a way that human beings were not supposed to do, though the magnitude of the discrimination was not as great. At the same time three other laboratories were working in the same problem. Waters and Wilson (1976) studied rhesus macaques in a more traditional operant paradigm and found that monkeys could discriminate voice-onset time differences in a categorical fashion. More impressively, Kuhl and Miller (1975) showed that even chinchillas could make categorical responses to human phonemes that varied in voice onset time. Sinnott, Beecher, Moody, and Stebbins (1976) tested several species of Old World monkeys and found that monkeys and human beings were equally good at discriminating stimuli both within and between categories. However, the latency for discrimination by human subjects was shorter when discriminations were made across a category boundary than when they were made within a category. Monkeys did not show latency differences correlated with boundary locations. This was the only study to conclude that nonhuman and human animals had different processing systems for speech sounds. In general these results indicated that categorical perception of speech sounds was not unique to human beings.

The more interesting question is how nonhuman animals perceive their own signals. This is interesting for a comparison with human speech perception, but it is also important for addressing the issue of discrete versus continuous communication systems. Our classification of an animal's vocal repertoire is generally based on our human perceptual classification of signals. Only rarely are we able to ask the animals how they classify their signals. Signals that appear to be graded to us may in fact be categorized, just as an alien listening to our speech might hear a highly intergraded series of sounds and not realize how precisely we are able to categorize these sounds as discrete entities.

There have been three studies of categorical perception in nonhuman animals. Ehret and Haack (1981) studied the ultrasonic cries given by mouse pups (Mus musculus) in discomfort and the responses they elicited in the dam—searching and retrieval. Mothers were tested by playing two sounds through different loudspeakers and observing which speaker the dam approached. The dams made significantly more approaches to a natural pup sound than to a 20 kHz control tone in the first experiment. Subsequently the dams were tested with a large number of ultrasonic calls varying in bandwidth from 17.5 to 40 kHz. Each synthesized call was tested against the 20 kHz pure tone. When the bandwidth was varied over a 5 kHz range (from 17.5 to 22.5 kHz), the dams all showed an equivalent significant selection of the speaker emitting the ultrasonic call. However, when the bandwidth was increased by just 1.5 kHz more to 24 kHz, the mice no longer exhibited a preference for the ultrasonic call versus the pure tone. A variation of 5 kHz within the range of natural calls produced no differences in responses, but adding only 1.5 kHz at a critical bandwidth range eliminated the preference for the synthesized pup vocalization. Thus mice dams discriminate categorically between different forms of pup ultrasonic calls.

Masataka (1983) studied Goeldi's monkey (*Callimico goeldi*). This species has five forms of alarm calls, with three forms eliciting freezing responses and the other two serving to rally the other animals and eliciting antiphonal calling. Masataka selected one of each type of call and varied the calls on each of four dimensions while holding other variables constant. Calls with a frequency range between 1.6 and 2.4 kHz were responded to with antiphonal warning calls, and calls with a frequency range greater than 2.6 kHz were responded to with freezing responses. Subsequently, calls with a mean frequency range of 1.6 kHz and 3.0 kHz were used and each of the other dimensions was varied. None of these other manipulations had any effect on responses to calls. The critical variable appeared to be the frequency range. This is another example of categorical-like perception in a nonhuman animal.

Historically, the first demonstration that nonhuman animals categorize their own vocalizations was made by Snowdon and Pola (1978) with the pygmy marmoset. Earlier I described the various trills of pygmy marmosets and I noted that two forms—the closed mouth trill and the open mouth trill—differed only in duration, with all other acoustic parameters the same. As noted earlier, these two calls are used in very different situations; closed mouth trills are used in affiliative contexts, and open mouth trills appear in contexts involving aggression or fear. The structure of these calls is acoustically simple, and we were able to build an inexpensive pygmy marmoset trill synthesizer that allowed us to vary independently each of the parameters of the call—duration, center frequency, frequency range, and rate of frequency modulation. We tested a colony of pygmy marmosets with these calls in a playback paradigm broadcasting the synthesized calls through speakers hidden in the environment. The normal response to a closed mouth trill is an antiphonal trill from some other animal. Hence we used this trill response as an index of whether the animals perceived a given synthesized call as a closed mouth trill or as something else.

The testing showed clear evidence of categorization. Calls varying in duration from 176 to 248 msec were responded to with equivalent rates of antiphonal calls. Calls 257 msec or longer did not elicit antiphonal calling. The response to these longer calls (which included the durations of open mouth trills) was no different from the spontaneous rate of calling heard when no stimulus was present. Thus a difference of only 9 msec in duration was sufficient to produce a very different response to a synthesized trill. This is very similar to the categorical labeling found with human speech. When we classified open mouth and closed mouth trills strictly according to whether the mouth was open or closed when the calls were given, we found nonoverlapping distributions of the durations of the calls. All closed mouth trills were shorter than all open mouth trills. The production boundary was at 250 msec, exactly where the perceptual boundary appeared.

In subsequent studies we tested human beings with the same stimuli and found that they did not categorize the pygmy marmoset sounds but rather showed a continuous discrimination of the sounds. Thus, in contrast to the results on monkeys and chinchillas presented with human speech sounds and showing humanlike categorization, human subjects failed to show marmosetlike categorization of pygmy marmoset trills.

This is a rather odd result. Why should human subjects appear to have a more acute discrimination capacity for pygmy marmoset trills than pygmy marmosets do? Do humans really have a better perceptual system than pygmy marmosets? I do not think so, but the explanation requires more discussion about the importance of social variables in communication. I will discuss this problem in more detail below.

In other studies of how animals perceive their own vocalizations the focus has been not on categorical perception, but rather on whether animals have species-specific adaptations for the perceptual processing of their own sounds. Park and Dooling (1985) used operant techniques to study how budgerigars perceived their own sounds and those of canaries. They found that budgerigars could be trained to discriminate both budgerigar and canary vocalizations but that critical temporal and spectral variables were needed for good discrimination. McArthur (1986) presented song sparrows with songs of varying similarity to their own songs and found greater territorial response directed toward the songs most similar to the birds' own. He hypothesized that song sparrows have an active perceptual recognition of similarity of songs to self-songs and thus have an auditory "self-concept."

Zoloth et al. (1979) tested Japanese macaques and several control species of monkeys with two types of vocalization from Green's (1975a) study of the coo vocalizations of Japanese macaques. The smooth early high and smooth late high coos were chosen, and monkeys were trained in an operant setting to discriminate between various tokens of these calls from different individuals. Although all monkeys eventually learned to make the discrimination, the Japanese macaques learned the task more quickly and performed at higher rates than did the other species. In contrast, when the same tokens were presented and the monkeys were reinforced for discriminating between high-pitch and lower-pitch tokens regardless of the location of the peak frequency, the control species outperformed the Japanese macaques. The authors argued that this result indicated the perceptual specialization of the Japanese macaque for the phonetic feature (location of the peak frequency) that was an important feature of their species-specific calls.

In the same study the investigators also looked at the lateralization of response to these vocal variants. Peterson, Beecher, Zoloth, Moody, & Stebbins (1978) and Petersen et al. (1984) found a significant right-ear advantage in Japanese macaques discriminating coo vocalizations, implying that the locus of the perceptual discrimination was in the left hemisphere. The control species did not show evidence of a right-ear advantage.

Semantic Communication

One of the most exciting areas of communication research in the past few years has been symbolic or semantic communication. Although many of the most interesting results have been obtained in the studies on chimpanzee language learning (see Savage-Rumbaugh, this volume), there have been impressive demonstrations of referential or symbolic communication in other species using their natural communication systems. The first studies to appear were those of Leger and Owings (1978) and Leger, Owings, and Boal (1979) and of Robinson (1980, 1981) on different species of ground squirrels (*Spermophilus beecheyi, Spermo-*

philus beldingii) in the western United States. Both groups of investigators described different forms of alarm calls given in response to potential predators. In general one type of call was given to aerial predators (eagles, hawks, etc.) and a second type was given to terrestrial predators (rattlesnakes, dogs, human beings). There appeared to be a clear context specificity for each call, and each elicited a different behavioral response in other conspecifics.

Subsequently, Seyfarth, Cheney, and Marler (1980) studied the alarm calls of vervet monkeys. There were three distinct predator-alerting calls that were given in response to three different types of predators: a snake alarm call, an eagle alarm call, and a leopard alarm call. Each call was associated with a different behavioral response. When these calls were played back to groups of vervet monkeys in the absence of any predators, the monkeys responded to the playback stimuli as though real predators were present. Thus when the eagle alarm call was played, monkeys ran out of the tree and into shrubs on the ground. Conversely, when a snake alarm call was played animals ran from the ground into trees. The acoustic structure of the call by itself appeared to convey information about the predator.

In a different type of system Gouzoules, Gouzoules, and Marler (1984) studied agonistic screams in rhesus macaques. Rhesus macaque infants have five types of screams used in different contexts, according to whether the infants encounter related or unrelated animals and whether the animals are from a more dominant or less dominant matriline. Gouzoules et al. (1984) developed predictions about when mothers should aid their infants based on these different situations, and in a playback experiment they found that mothers did respond selectively according to the type of scream. They thus argued that the screams of infant macaques form another type of representational call system.

Other studies have focused on food calls as representational calls. Dittus (1984) reported a food call in toque macaques (*Macaca sinica*) that is given when monkeys find a large quantity of a heavily preferred food type (such as ripening figs or other fruits). Other group members respond by running toward the animal who gives the food call. Dittus argues that this call conveys information about the presence of a food source, its relative quantity, and its location. However, he noted that on occasion these calls are also given in response to significant changes in the environment such as the first sunshine after several days of rain or the first rain clouds after months of drought, suggesting that although representational information might be derived from the call by listeners, the call itself may be simply expressing the communicator's elation.

Marler, Dufty, and Pickert (1986a) discovered that domestic cocks (*Gallus domesticus*) give food calls in the presence of hens and that the rate of calling and the number of food calls given are related to the preference rankings of the foods. Females were more likely to approach a cock who was giving frequent food calls. They suggest that this is another example of representational calling. Food calls that are correlated with the preference ratings of food have recently been described for the golden lion tamarin (*Leontopithecus rosalia;* French & Leger, unpublished results) and the pygmy marmoset (Sweet & Snowdon, unpublished results).

Grammar and Syntax

One of the major criteria linguists use to characterize human language is the presence of syntax. It has been argued that animal communication does not contain syntax, and indeed the focal point of much of the controversy over chimpanzee language learning has been over whether apes can form sentences (Terrace, Petito, Saunders, & Bever, 1979). Although no animal system has been demonstrated to have the complete generative capacity of human language, there now exist several demonstrations of syntax in the natural vocal communication systems of animals.

Perhaps the most amazing syntactic system is that of the black-capped chickadee (*Parus atricapillus;* Hailman, Ficken, & Ficken, 1985). Its "chick-a-dee" call, in contrast to common understanding, contains four call notes. In a large sample of chickadee calls, Hailman et al. found 362 different sequences of these four calls. Despite the great variability in the sequence of call types found, it was possible to write a simple grammar for chickadee sequences. If element A is the first note it can be repeated several times, and after one or more A elements the call switches to a D note, which can also be repeated many times. The call ends with a D element. If element B begins a call it can be repeated several times, then it is followed by element C, which can also be repeated, and then by element D, which can be repeated several times. Again the call is terminated with a D element. Out of 3,500 sequences recorded, only 11 failed to follow the rules described. Hailman et al. (1985) used information-theory analysis to show that the number of bits of information per call was 6.7, compared with 11.8 bits per word of English. Thus chickadee is a much simpler language than English. Nonetheless, Hailman et al. argue that both systems are generative—that is, capable of producing a potentially infinite number of sequences. One problem with the chickadee work to date is the lack of any direct semantic relationship to the varieties of sequences that are found.

Working with the song of black-capped chickadees rather than the "chick-a-dee" call, Ratcliffe and Weisman (1986) played normal and rearranged sequences of songs to chickadees and found that the birds could discriminate between the normal and abnormal sequences, demonstrating a syntax to the song of chickadees as well. Nelson (1985) has studied the vocal communication of the pigeon guillemot and has reported a hierarchical syntactic organization in the vocalizations of these birds.

Marler (1977) distinguished two types of syntax: a phonetic syntax that is equivalent to the formation of different words from separate phonemes, and a lexical syntax that is equivalent to the formation of different phrases or sentences from separate words. In this latter form of syntax the sequence produced is equal to the sum of its individual components, whereas in the former, phonetic syntax, the new combinations do not represent the sum of the individual components. Marler wrote that although phonetic syntax was common in animals, he doubted that any species other than humans would display lexical syntax. No sooner had these words been written than studies on monkeys began to indicate the existence of both phonetic and lexical syntax.

Robinson (1979) studied the vocal signals of the titi monkey (*Callicebus moloch*) in South America. Titi monkeys are territorial, and both male and female defend the territory against intruders of the same sex. Robinson found that many of the calls given by the titi monkeys in calling early in the morning or in close encounters with other groups of monkeys involved structuring calls into phrases and then into longer sequences. There were clear regularities to these sequences, and when Robinson recorded some of them, spliced the tapes to form abnormal syntaxes of calls, and played these back to the monkeys, the monkeys displayed an increased number of disturbance behaviors, indicating that they were able to discriminate between normal and abnormal syntax.

Cleveland and Snowdon (1982) found that the communication system of cotton-top tamarins consisted of a few simple elements—short frequency-modulated chirps and longer, unmodulated whistlelike calls. The variation in chirps and in different forms of whistled calls has already been discussed. However, Cleveland and Snowdon also found several cases where series of chirps were produced or where series of whistles or in some cases chirps and whistles were combined to form a longer, more complex sequence. They were able to write a simple structural grammar:

1. All chirps precede all whistled notes in a combination.
2. Chirps or whistles can be repeated several times.
3. Within a sequence each successive call has a lower frequency than the preceding call.

All sequences of calls observed followed these structural rules. While many of the combinations formed by these rules were equivalent to phonetic syntax, there were at least two examples of lexical syntax. One combined an alarm call with a whistle used in calm situations. This combined call appeared after the occurrence of an alarm call when all animals took cover and froze, and it just preceded the animals' moving about freely again. Thus the sequence appeared to combine the semantic elements of both component calls. The other example, the F-chirp plus whistle (F + whistle) was a combination of the F-chirp given toward a strange group and the normal long call used in the same situation. In a simulation study of territorial encounters McConnell and Snowdon (1986) found that females tended to give more normal long calls than males, and males gave more F-chirps than females. Each of these types of calls was the common first response to hearing intruders. As the vocal conflict increased in time and intensity, both males and females ultimately switched to the use of the F + whistle call, which was given equally often by each sex. This also appears to be a good example of lexical syntax.

Robinson (1984) studied the wedge-capped capuchin monkey (*Cebus olivaceus*) in Venezuela and found that this species also has a complex vocal system that involves combining different calls into sequences. He first defined five statistically discriminable classes of calls and subsequently found subtle variations within two of these call classes. Calls were found to occur both in isolation and as part of a sequence. Individual calls could be related to different probable internal motivational states, and he found that there were clear rules that could describe how sequences were formed. Of the calls recorded, 38% were syntactic sequences, and like the examples of the cotton-top tamarin sequences noted above, the sequences Robinson found in capuchin monkeys tended to represent states intermediate between those expressed by either call alone. Thus, here is another example of lexical syntax.

One finding of Cleveland and Snowdon (1982) with cotton-top tamarins, that each note in a sequence is lower than the preceding note, is reminiscent of a general finding in human declarative statements, where there is a steadily decreasing intonation contour throughout the sentence. There is not much evidence that animals have similar patterns in the prosodic features of their calls, but Biben, Symmes, and Masataka (1986) have described prosodic features in squirrel monkey vocalizations. An interesting call in squirrel monkeys is the "chuck" call, used primarily among females who have a close social relationship with each other. Biben et al. (1986) found different types of chuck calls with different acoustic features. Chucks that initiated a sequence of chuck exchanges had lower frequency parameters than did answering chucks that came later in a sequence. Biben et al. termed the first chucks "questions" and the second or later chucks "answers" and argued that the prosodic features differentiating these types of chucks relate to similar prosodic processes found in human speech.

More Complex Models for Communication

The basic model for most of the studies of communication I have described so far has been a simple one focusing on the communicator, the signal produced, and the response made by the recipient (Figure 2A). In reality, though, communication is a much more complex system. There are at least three types of complications that have received relatively little attention.

First, communication is not an isolated instance of a signal passing between communicator and recipient. The previous history of their relationship will affect both the nature of the signal selected in a given situation and the recipient's response to the signal (Figure 2B). The role of prior social history is readily acknowledged in studies of the social organization of primate groups where the past history of dominance-subordinance relations, kinship systems, and other social alliances are all known to be very important. However, there are few studies on the role these relationships play in on the communicative behavior of primates (see Cheney & Seyfarth, 1986, for an exception).

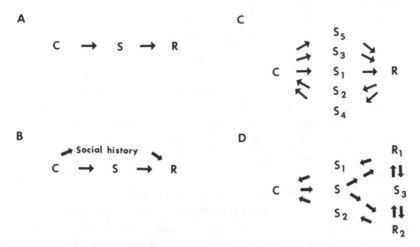

FIGURE 2. Models for the study of communication (C = communicator; S = signal; R = recipient): (A) simple unidirectional model of communication; (B) communication influenced by social history; (C) multiple interactive signals exchanged between communicator and recipient; (D) multiple recipients in interactive communication.

Second, a phenomenon basic to human communication is the conversation. We rarely produce utterances in isolation or, with the exception of the classroom and the scientific conference, as monologues. Instead the socially most natural unit of communication is not the phoneme, the word, or the sentence, but the conversation (Figure 2C). Communication is truly an interactive process, yet in both human linguistics and animal communication we have confined ourselves to the analyses of single utterances. There is good reason for this. We can imagine that many more decades of research would be necessary before we fully understand even a few simple utterances. Yet I suggest that we should start developing techniques for analyzing vocal interactions. Ultimately the comprehensiveness of our understanding of animal communication or human language will require understanding the social interactive processes of communication, not simply single utterances. Duetting between pairs of animals has been studied frequently in birds and primates (see Farabaugh, 1982, for birds; Deputte, 1982, for gibbons). Duetting represents a form of interactive communication. Although the phenomenon of duetting is well known, the process by which mated pairs develop turn-taking behavior and the structural features leading from the utterance of one animal to that of the next, and so forth, have been less well studied. Deputte (1982) presents information on the elaboration of calls through successive interchanges in gibbon duets.

Third, communication frequently is not restricted to the interactions between two individuals but is a multipartite process. An animal may produce one signal for one individual and different signals for others (Marler, Dufty, & Pickert, 1986b). In addition, different individuals hearing the same utterance may respond to it in different ways, and how they respond will have differing effects on the communicator, which in turn will affect the nature of the communicator's next utterance (Figure 2D).

Each of these complications to our traditional model of communication makes our task of understanding vocal communication considerably more difficult, but only when communication is understood in its proper social context will we have a real understanding of it. The remainder of this chapter is concerned with the effects on our understanding of vocal communication when we consider the more complex social environment in which it occurs.

Interactional Communication Among Adults

We have studied two forms of interactional communication in the pygmy marmoset (*Cebuella pygmaea*); both involve the contact trills used by animals as they move through their environment, described earlier in this chapter. The three forms of trills (quiet trills, closed mouth trills, and J-calls) were used by animals to keep in contact with one another as they moved through the home range. They were used to recruit animals to sleeping sites at night and by sentinel animals while others groomed and sunned themselves. The calls are individually distinct, and playback studies have shown that animals respond individually to specific calls (Snowdon & Cleveland, 1980).

The first study involved the use of calls during spontaneous movements through the environment (Snowdon & Cleveland, 1984). If animals use calls to keep in touch with each other, then, we thought, it is likely that there might be some regular pattern of calling so that all animals in a group can keep track of one another. We observed a captive group of three animals and recorded sequences of these contact calls, a total of 295 bouts and 1,315 sequences of three calls each. We noted the order in which animals gave calls, and using information-theory analysis we discovered that there was considerable predictability in calls. Knowledge of which animal had called previously and of which two animals had called previously both provided considerable predictability about which animal would call next. There were orderly patterns to the sequences of calls. Most notably, there was a significant tendency to take turns. That is, each of the three animals would call in sequence much more often than would be expected by chance, and an animal would interrupt a sequence by calling twice in succession considerably less often than would be predicted by chance. One particular sequence of calling of three animals (1, 2, 3) occurred significantly more often than the other sequence of three animals (1, 3, 2) (Figure 3). In the development of human children, turn taking is considered to be a skill of high cognitive achievement. (Passing from egocentricity to the ability to understand another individual's perspective.) It is all the more remarkable that a small primate like the pygmy marmoset is able to exhibit turn-taking behavior.

The second example of interactional influences on communication in pygmy marmosets relates to how monkeys perceive their calls. As I described above, we showed that pygmy marmosets responded in a categorical fashion to two trills that differed from each other only in duration (Snowdon & Pola, 1978). Although there was a clear demonstration of categorization between these calls, the functional significance was considerably less clear. It is odd that animals should neglect information in the call and answer quite different calls with equivalent responses. Thus pygmy marmosets responded equivalently to synthesized trills of 176 msec and 248 msec but quite differently to calls of 248 msec and 257 msec duration. Why should this be? One possibility is that animals did perceive differences in duration within a call category but that the testing situation was not appropriate to determine whether they perceived the differences. Thus if we asked a human subject, "Do you hear a /ba/?" we might be told that two very different /ba/'s were the same. If we were to ask if the same individual produced both /ba/'s, then we might get a response that the two calls were different.

The difference in these two questions can be illustrated by a more concrete example. Suppose you are sitting in a darkened movie theater and you hear a voice shouting "Fire!" It is important that you respond first to the phonetic features of the call and ignore information concerning dialect, age, or sex. A mechanism for categorical sorting of sounds into their proper phonetic categories is essential for a rapid response to

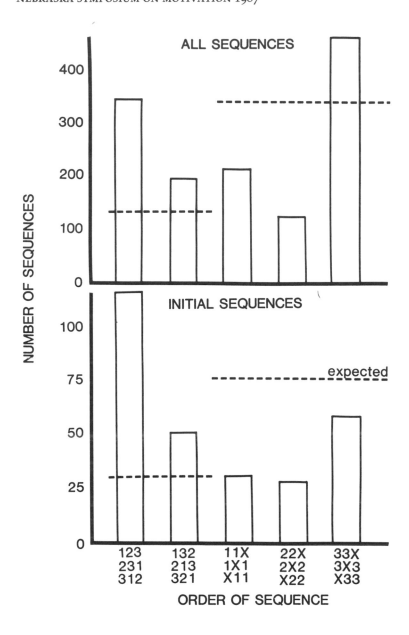

FIGURE 3. Sequences of calls given in a group of three pygmy marmosets: *top*, all sequences of calling; *bottom*, initial sequences of calls in a bout. The number of sequences for each animal calling once within three calls is greater than expected by chance. (From Snowdon & Cleveland, 1984).

a voice yelling "Fire!" Suppose, however, that in the same theater you hear a voice saying "Kiss me, I love you!" Is it sufficient to pay attention to just the phonetic information transmitted? To most of us it is probably important that we identify the age, the sex, and perhaps the individual identity of the speaker (or at least the speaker's degree of familiarity) before we take action. It is also important that we make use of the vocal cues in the speech to determine in which direction we should direct our response. Thus the social demands of the situation determine what features of speech we must attend to before responding. To date almost all studies of human speech perception have used synthesized speech tokens where any individually recognizable features of calls are absent, and all studies, whether using natural or synthesized speech, have tested humans in nonsocial environments. It might be that within-category discrimination of speech sounds by human subjects would be much more likely if the task demands were to focus on within-category information pertaining to dialect or individual recognition.

It seems quite likely that monkeys' apparent categorical perception of their calls might be constrained by the testing environment and the types of questions asked. In the previous study we used a synthesized trill that reflected the averaged parameters of all pygmy marmosets but, in fact, represented no single individual. We also created test demands that asked simply whether the monkeys heard a call as a closed mouth trill. Our experimental procedure did not require them to make or even attempt within-category discriminations.

In light of this thinking we designed a study to address the role of social variables in call perception (Snowdon, 1987). We recorded the closed mouth trills of five pygmy marmosets, newly acquired from Peru, that produced much longer closed mouth trills than those of the animals described previously. Two pairs of animals among the five had closed mouth trills very similar to one anothers', so we took the average stimulus for each of those pairs. After we collected a large sample of trills from each of the two pairs and the single individual, we measured the parameters of the calls and found individual differences between the calls on most of the acoustic variables we measured. We then programmed our synthesizer to produce calls that imitated the individual specific features of center frequency, frequency range, and rate of frequency modulation for each of the three groups and then systematically varied the duration of these calls in 100 msec increments from 100 to 600 msec. To test for individual recognition, we made use of a finding from our previous study (Snowdon & Cleveland, 1980). We had observed that when we played back the call of an individual through a hidden speaker in that animal's cage, then other animals in the colony would give antiphonal calls. However, when we played back the same stimulus through a speaker in a cage in another part of the colony, the animals failed to respond antiphonally. The test animals had formed "expectancies" about the locations of familiar animals, much as the sparrows in Brooks and Falls' (1975) studies had formed expectancies about where their territorial neighbors would be situated. In the present study we played synthesized calls an equal number of times through a speaker in the stimulus animals' home cages and from a speaker in another part of the environment. If we found a significant difference in the response to a call played back in the stimulus animals' home cages and the same call played back from a different part of the colony, we inferred that the stimulus provided cues for individual recognition. If we failed to find a differential response, then that particular stimulus would not have been perceived by the other animals as belonging to a familiar individual.

The colony was presented with 10 trials of each call type at each duration. Any antiphonal trills that occurred within 10 sec of the playback stimulus were counted as part of the response. Table 1 presents the parameters of trills from each of the three stimulus groups (Sally, Val/Marco, and Lana/Don). When we looked at the responses to all stimulus trials combined, calls ranging in duration from 200 to 450 msec were responded to with significant increases in antiphonal calling when played back in the stimulus animals' home cages than when played back through a different speaker. Figures 4 and 5 present separate results for the calls

Table 1.

Parameters of Closed Mouth Trills of Different Pygmy Marmosets

Variable	Individuals		
	Sally	Val/Marco	Lana/Don
Sample size	24	44	41
Duration (msec)	271.0 ± 66.0 (24.3)[a]	254.5 ± 82.5 (32.4)	315.0 ± 120.5 (38.3)
Frequency range (kHz)	4.6 ± 1.4 (30.4)	1.9 ± 0.8 (39.4	2.9 ± 0.9 (31.0)
Center frequency (kHz)	9.1 ± 1.2 (13.2)	10.7 ± 0.4 (3.8)	11.1 ± 1.1 (9.5)
Rate of modulation (Hz)	41.5 ± 3.1 (7.5)	32.8 ± 3.8 (11.6)	38.3 ± 3.1 (8.1)

[a]Mean ± SD (coefficient of variation).

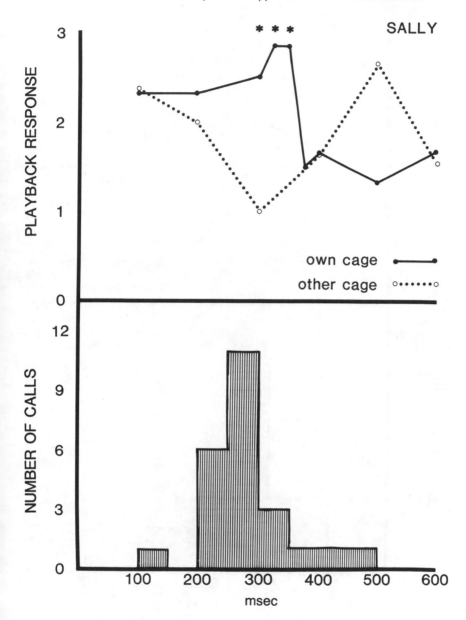

FIGURE 4. *Top,* responses to playback of synthesized calls of Sally from Sally's own cage versus from other cages (*$p<.05$); *bottom,* distribution by duration of Sally's closed mouth trills. (From Snowdon, 1987).

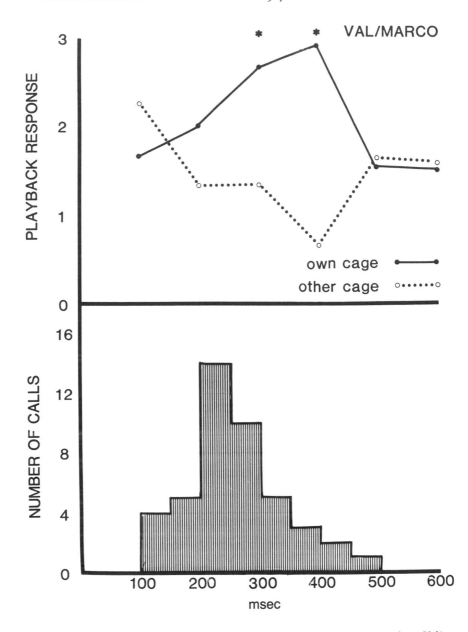

FIGURE 5. *Top,* responses to playback of synthesized calls of Val/Marco from Val/Marco's own cage versus from other cages (*$p<.05$); *bottom,* distribution by duration of spontaneous closed mouth trills from Val/Marco. (From Snowdon, 1987).

of Sally and of Val/Marco, respectively. One can see that Sally had a very narrow distribution of call durations, and the responses of other animals to Sally's calls showed an equally narrow distribution. The duration distributions of calls by Val/Marco were somewhat longer and had more variability than those of Sally's calls, and the responses of other animals to these calls also covered a broader range paralleling the distribution of call durations. Thus, instead of a single categorical response function, there are different response functions that are correlated with the duration distributions of those individual animals.

In our previous study with a 9 msec difference in duration leading to totally different responses, we had hypothesized the existence of neurological feature detectors, a hard-wired system underlying the perceptual responses. In the present study it is clear that a hard-wired system cannot account for the results. Obviously, animals make use of their previous social experience with familiar individuals and construct phonetic boundaries that are appropriate to this past social experience. If a novel trill is heard, the animals may have some hard-wired detector that determines the upper boundaries for responses, but to account for the results of the present study we must posit a flexible phonetic boundary system capable of being modified by social experience with particular individuals. Thus previous social interactions with familiar animals can affect the nature of perceptual responses, and perceptual learning must be involved in the responses to the calls of a familiar individual. It may be that much of the strong evidence for categorical perception that has been obtained in both human and animal studies is due to the use of averaged synthetic sounds that represent no particular familiar individual. If instead subjects are presented with stimuli that match in all other dimensions the characteristics of socially familiar individuals, then the rigidity of the categorical response system might break down.

The last example I have of interactional communication in adults is from a species with which we have worked extensively, the cotton-top tamarin. There have been a few field studies on this species and its closely related subspecies, Geoffroy's tamarin (Dawson, 1979; Neyman, 1977). The species is highly territorial and lives in small groups, and animals encounter other groups at territorial boundaries about once or twice each week. The typical response when animals encounter strange groups is to engage in extensive vocal communication including large numbers of long calls—two- or three-syllable whistled calls that are between 2 and

3 sec in duration. I have described already the several variations of the long calls. Two variants, the normal long call and the F + whistle, are used in territorial encounters with strange groups, and a chirp vocalization and a trilled sequence of the same chirps, the F-chirp and the F-chirp trill are also used in territorial encounters or intergroup conflict situations (Cleveland & Snowdon, 1982).

These territorial encounters are difficult to study in the wild, but descriptions from the field indicated that they might be very fruitful situations in which to study complex vocal interactions between groups. In captive colonies it is possible to record vocalizations simultaneously from two different groups while observing which individuals within a group are giving the vocalizations. We (McConnell & Snowdon, 1986) devised a simple method for stimulating territorial vocal interactions. We reasoned that at the start of a territorial encounter in the wild two groups would move toward each other unaware until they began hearing increasingly louder intragroup vocalizations from the others. To mimic this phenomenon in captivity we simply opened the doors between two colony rooms, which produced a 5 dB increase in the intensity of intragroup vocalizations. We placed microphones in each of the rooms leading to separate channels of the tape recorder so that we could keep track of the sequence of vocalizations within and between rooms. The monkeys did not respond immediately to the door-opening manipulation, but within a mean of 30 sec one or two animals in a group would look in the direction of the other room as if they had just detected the strange group, and then they would begin to give an array of long calls and F-chirps. These calls were quickly answered by the other group, and a complex vocal exchange continued for the duration of the 12 min observation period. Similar observations conducted when the doors were briefly opened and then shut served as control trials.

The animals demonstrated the behavioral changes predicted from observations in the wild. There was an increase in scent marking and piloerection and a decrease in huddling in the experimental conditions compared with the control conditions. There was an increase in all the intertroop vocalizations described by Cleveland and Snowdon (1982). Thus the simple manipulation of opening doors between different colony rooms had the expected effect of stimulating vocal exchanges similar to those in the wild.

The more interesting results are from the analyses of the vocal interactions. There were clear sex and age differences in calling. The participants in the long-calling bouts were primarily paired animals without offspring present. There were many more vocalizations and much more intense vocal interactions among mated pairs without offspring than among family groups. All the territorial vocalizations given were those characteristic of sexually mature animals (see below). There was evidence of a role differentiation. Females gave significantly more long calls than would be predicted by their representation among the subjects, while males gave significantly more F-chirps and F-chirp trills than expected. However, the F + whistle call, which is a syntactic combination of the F-chirp and the long call (see above), was given with equal frequency by both sexes.

Close analyses of the calls given immediately after a particular call indicated that responses were not random. In general, intergroup territorial calls tended to follow one another, and affiliative calls also tended to follow one another. There was no rapid switching back and forth between affiliative calls and territorial calls. Which type of intergroup call was given in response to a territorial call depended on whether the response was from within the same group as the focal caller or from a different group, and the response also depended on the type of intertroop call given. Thus, in response to F-chirps, the call given predominantly by males, the focal animal's group responded with F-chirp trills and F + whistle calls, more intensified variants of the F-chirps, while the other group responded with antiphonal F-chirps or with affiliative calls. In response to long calls from one group the other group tended to respond with more long calls or with F + whistle calls.

A diagram of the response to focal callers is shown in Figure 6. The left side shows the responses given by animals in the same room as the focal caller, while the right side shows the responses of those in the other room. There are very different response patterns. Animals from the same room as the focal caller tended to respond with a different vocalization. There was a reciprocal response between the normal long call and the F-chirp calls that were given by females and males respectively. In addition, however, there was an escalation of response from F-chirp to F-chirp trill or to F + whistle calls by animals in the same room as the focal caller. In contrast, animals in the other room tended to respond with the same type of call as the focal caller. This pattern of escalation of calling intensity within a group and antiphonal imitation of a call between

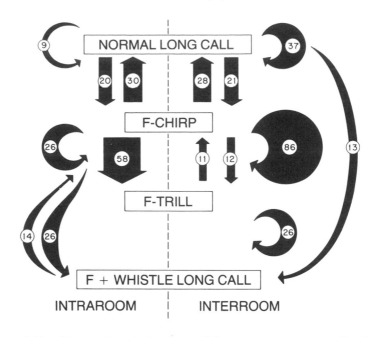

FIGURE 6. Vocal interactions during long-call bouts in cotton-top tamarins: *left*, transitions from call types between callers within the same group; *right*, transitions from call types between callers in different rooms. (From McConnell & Snowdon, 1986.)

groups indicates that different communicative roles are played by different sexes and different responses are given according to whether the last call heard was from one's own group or from the other group. In general there appears to be an inciting within the group to more and more intense versions of intertroop calling and an imitation or even a softening of response with some affiliative calls given between groups. There are some general patterns to calling so that the vocal interactions observed between groups are not random.

This study indicates one simple way vocal interactions between groups can be stimulated, giving us a large body of data for analysis within a very short period. The techniques we have used so far to analyze the patterns of vocal interaction are rather simple modifications of information-theory statistics, but they hold considerable promise for future study of interactive communication.

Importance of Interaction in Ontogeny

I will now argue that understanding the interactive process of communication not only is an important goal in its own right, to provide a more complete description and analysis of adult communicative behavior, but is essential for dealing with the other major underdeveloped research problem in primate communication—ontogeny. To date our information on the ontogeny of vocal communication is very limited. Our major data are from the squirrel monkey, primarily the infant isolation peeps, and the major finding is that call structures are inherited, not learned (Newman & Symmes, 1982). This is an apparent paradox, since we have evidence of clear parallels between the development of birdsong and the development of human speech (Marler, 1970a, 1970b), where the phylogentic distance is much greater.

Why should we find no parallels in the work on primates? I think this might be for several reasons. First, research has tended to focus on a single call type, the isolation peep, which is used by infants separated from their mothers. This is the one type of call that we might expect to be selected as highly conservative. Alarm calls and distress calls, to be effective, should not be subject to great plasticity. Thus it would be more appropriate to look at other call types for evidence of modifiability during development. Second, only a few species have been studied, and in birds many precocial species show little or no evidence of modifiability, whereas most altricial species do show experiential effects on vocal development. Even among altricial species, however, there is a great variety. Some species appear to have a sensitive period for song learning, while others are able as adults to learn components of their mates' songs or call notes (Mundinger, 1970) or to learn the sounds of another species (Pepperberg, 1985, in press). Still other species do not appear to require any learning at all in acquiring songs (Kroodsma, 1984). Third, we might not be applying the proper models to the study of ontogeny.

Historically, there has been a close parallel between our theories about the acquisition of human language and our studies of animal communication. In the 1950s behaviorist psychology was popular in North America, and a chief tenet was that anything could be taught through the appropriate application of rewards. Skinner (1957) proposed a behaviorist theory of verbal behavior, arguing that all language was learned through a series of operant responses and reinforcements. I think it is fair to state that many students of psycholinguistics at first agreed with Skinner's position.

In the same year Chomsky (1957) proposed that no behaviorist theory could account for the complexity of human language and its capacity for generating an infinite number of sentences. Chomsky argued that several innate mechanisms must assist in language acquisition. At the same time the research of ethologists had an increasing influence on thinking in North America, and the early research by Thorpe (1958) and Marler (1970a, 1970b) on birdsong learning suggested an ontogenetic model compatible with Chomsky's ideas. There was a species-specific predisposition to acquire only a certain limited range of song types. These songs, however, had to be presented to birds during a critical period in development. Thus there was a need for learning, but learning occurred only at a certain time, and the types of things that could be learned were restricted by a perceptual template.

It was argued that language acquisition was limited by the range of potential phonemes available to human speakers and by grammatical universals. An infant needed only minimal exposure to sounds, since children born to deaf parents would learn language readily with no signs of deficit, and language learning was limited to a critical period, since children isolated from language for the first 12 years of life failed to learn language (Lenneberg, 1967). Studies on newborn infants indicated a predisposition to categorize speech sounds in the same way as adult speakers, and children could even make perceptual distinctions important in a language different from that spoken by their parents. Their parents could not make the same perceptual distinctions, indicating a reduction of perceptual capacity with disuse.

More recent work on both child language and birdsong suggests a modification of this earlier, ethologically based view. Several writers now argue the importance of close social interaction as a key to language acquisition. The various games and rituals between care-givers and human infants create a context for vocal communication and provide a structure for acquiring syntactic rules (Bruner, 1983; Snow & Ferguson, 1977). Studies indicate that babbling in infants plays an important role in phonetic development (e.g., Oller, Wieman, Doyle, & Ross, 1975), and babbling can be stimulated through social and vocal reinforcement from adults (Dodd, 1972; Todd & Palmer, 1968). Parents use a simplified language in communicating with infants that may serve as a model to help them attain linguistic competence (Ferguson, 1964; Ferguson & Garnica, 1977).

Interactive models of vocal acquisition in birdsong are becoming more common. The chapter by West and King in this volume makes clear the importance of social stimulation in developing song competence in the parasitic cowbird. The presence of a live tutor has been used to extend song learning beyond the usual sensitive period, and parts of allospecific song can be acquired from a live tutor (Baptista & Morton, 1981; Baptista & Petrinovitch, 1984; King & West, 1984; Kroodsma, 1972, 1973; Kroodsma & Baylis, 1982, Pepperberg, 1985, in press; Petrinovitch, 1985; West & King, 1985). In addition, Marler and Peters (1982) have demonstrated the importance of a period of vocal practice (or plastic song) that appears similar in function to the babbling of infants. Lemon (1975) discusses the importance of vocal improvisation in acquiring song dialects. Thus it appears that vocal learning in human beings and in birds not only is more flexible than previously thought but is also highly dependent upon social interaction with other organisms and upon a period of vocal play or practice.

Despite the essentially negative results with squirrel monkey isolation peeps, some recent studies indicate more openness in primate vocal ontogeny. Seyfarth and Cheney (1986) showed that young vervet monkeys do not use their alarm calls in as refined a way as adults. They typically give aerial-predator calls to a variety of birds, not only to those that prey on vervets. However, adults appeared to reinforce young vervet monkeys when the young animals gave an aerial-predator call in the presence of true predators. Infant vervets did not show the differentiated structure of grunts seen in adults (Cheney & Seyfarth, 1982). Initially the calls are more variable, and different parameters reach adult values with different time courses (similar to results on cotton-top tamarins and pygmy marmosets reported below). Grunt vocalizations were not differentiated with respect to context as completely as adult grunts until the infants were three to four years old. The general picture of vervet vocal ontogeny is that in the early months calls are highly variable, with only limited context specificity. With practice and social learning both from observation and from socially reinforced behavior, infants develop a better usage of calls, and they are able to produce calls with a structure close to that of adults.

Role of Social Interactions in Primate Vocal Development

For the past decade we have been studying vocal communication in marmosets and tamarins as well as their social organization, social development, parental care patterns, and reproductive physiology. They have rich and complex vocal repertoires, and they live in close extended family social groups with several caretakers assisting the mother in rearing offspring. In the field they appear to be territorial and to maintain close vocal contact with each other throughout the day. They are good candidates not only for the study of vocal interactions between adult animals as described above, but also for investigating the influence of adult-infant social interactions on the development of vocal communication. These animals use long calls in the same situations in which birdsong is used—for territorial defense and for mate attraction and intragroup cohesion. The infants go through a prolonged phase of babbling in which they appear to practice the phonetics of adult sounds.

We have studied the role of social interactions in vocal development in three systems: the development of trills in pygmy marmosets, the differentiation of chirp types in cotton-top tamarins, and the ontogeny of long-call usage in cotton-top tamarins.

TRILL DEVELOPMENT IN PYGMY MARMOSETS

Over the past two years Carol Sweet and I have been studying the ontogeny of trill vocalizations in pygmy marmosets. We focused on the most common of the trill variants, the closed mouth trill. This call was found in young monkeys in our earliest samples at three weeks of age. However, there were several differences in the structure of these early closed mouth trills compared with the adult form. The earliest trills were much higher in pitch and much shorter in duration, and the frequency envelope was much more irregular than for adult calls. The three parameters of pitch, duration, and regularity of frequency envelope approached adult levels with independent time courses. As seen in Figure 7, pitch was the first variable to reach adult levels, by the sixth week of life. The call duration fell within the range of adult duration somewhere between the 10th and 15th week of age, and the irregularity of the frequency envelope showed a gradual decline toward adult levels over the entire 40 weeks of the study. Coincident with the observations of structural

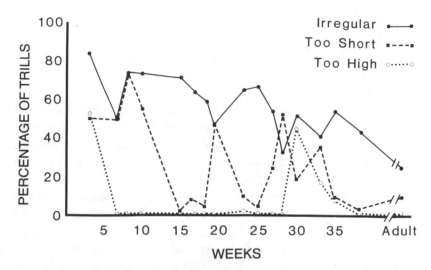

FIGURE 7. Changes in structure of closed mouth trills during first 40 weeks of life in pygmy marmosets. Note the regression to shorter and higher-pitched calls that occurs about 30 weeks of age, when new infants are born.

change, we also observed the contexts in which the calls were used. Typically, adults use closed mouth trills as affiliative contact or location calls, and the trills are never found in conjunction with other types of vocalizations. In contrast, almost all the infant closed mouth trills were found in conjunction with other types of calls, and the trills appeared to be uttered indiscriminately, without regard for the proper context. Gradually the application of the calls changed to appropriate adultlike usage, but not until week 38 of our sampling did any of the pygmy marmosets show both adult structure and adult usage of the trills.

An interesting finding shown in Figure 7 is of a vocal regression that occurred between weeks 28 and 30. At this time the trills became much shorter and the pitch became much higher, regressing to the levels found in the very youngest infants. This period coincided with the birth of new infants in each of the groups we observed, and the regression in form to infantile vocalizations appeared to be the response of the 30-week-old animals to the loss of attention to them resulting from the birth of new infants.

The change in the pitch of the call can be related to physical changes in body size that would result in lower pitch; however, the rapidity of the change in pitch within the first six weeks is not expected by physical growth alone. The alterations in trill duration and in the reduction of ir-regularity of the frequency envelope cannot be related easily to simple maturational changes. The independence of change in each of these pa-rameters and the regression toward infantile call forms with the birth of new infants suggests some flexibility in vocal development that, while possibly not a demonstration of call learning, implies at least some de-velopmental flexibility in call development. The independent changes in call parameters and the failure to use the calls in appropriate contexts until relatively late in infancy closely parallel results reported for vervet monkeys by Seyfarth and Cheney (1986).

During the period before the birth of new infants, we also recorded frequent bouts where the infants monopolized all vocal activity in the colony. These "babbling" bouts occurred when the parents placed in-fants on a branch or rope by themselves while the adults went off to for-age or groom. During the entire period of separation from their care-takers, the infants vocalized continuously. Close analyses of these vocal bouts revealed a wide array of calls, many of which could be identified as imperfect versions of adult calls, although many idiosyncratic calls could be found. The calls were mixed together in highly inappropriate juxtaposition relative to adult usage (see Figure 8). It seems probable that these "babbling" bouts inform the caretakers of the location of the in-fants and also give the young extensive vocal practice.

We have some preliminary data on the ontogeny of the J-call, another form of trill vocalization. This form appears much later in infancy (be-tween week 14 and week 22), and the J-calls do not appear to be as vari-able as the early closed mouth trills. However, J-calls at this age are giv-en in inappropriate contexts just as frequently as are closed mouth trills.

Trill development in pygmy marmosets is not fixed, but there are gradual changes in both structure and usage over time. Different vari-ables of the calls reach adult forms at different times, and there is a regression toward infantile forms with the birth of new infants in the group. The extensive babbling seen in young pygmy marmosets may represent a time of vocal practice whereby adult structure and contexts of different call types can be acquired.

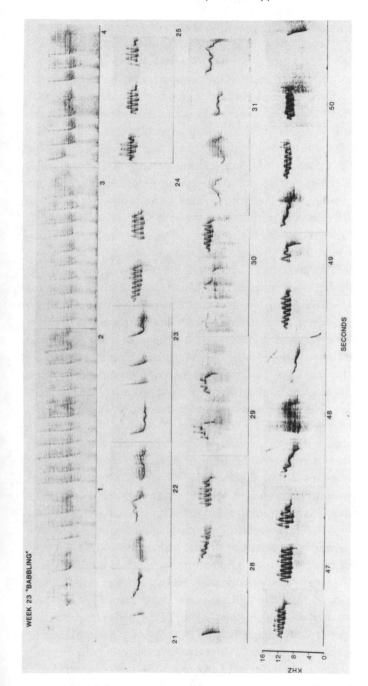

FIGURE 8. Excerpt from a "babbling" bout of an infant pygmy marmoset. Trills are highly variable and irregular in structure and are interspersed with many other call types that would not occur in adults.

CHIRP DEVELOPMENT IN THE COTTON-TOP TAMARIN

Laura Dronzek and I have studied the ontogeny of chirp vocalizations in cotton-top tamarin infants throughout the first year of life. We took twice-weekly vocal samples of several infants, some reared in normal family groups and others hand reared in an incubator during the first month and then gradually reintroduced to an adoptive family during the second month of life. In the adult cotton-top tamarin Cleveland and Snowdon (1982) demonstrated that there were eight variants of chirps that could be statistically discriminated from one another and that appeared to be used in very different contexts. McConnell and Snowdon (1986) have shown that some of the chirp variants used in territorial disputes are uttered only by reproductively mature adults.

Despite the fact that some chirps have been observed only in adults, it seemed likely that some chirp variants would appear in the first months of life. In our vocal recording we took careful note of the context in which the calls were given. We measured the same vocal parameters of infant chirps that had been used to differentiate among the adult chirps and then compared these parameters in chirps given in different contexts by infant cotton-top tamarins. Surprisingly, we found no consistent differences between chirps uttered in different situations, even in 12-month-old infants. Thus the differentiation of chirp structure by context did not appear in the first year of life.

The chirps, even though undifferentiated by context, are also highly variable in structure compared with those of adults. Figure 9 illustrates the changes in the coefficient of variation of three parameters of chirps—start frequency, end frequency, and duration over the first year of life for both normally reared monkeys and those that were hand reared for the first few weeks and then reintroduced to an adoptive family. As with the pygmy marmoset's closed mouth trills, there were different time courses for different variables. End frequency reached adult levels of variation by the fourth to sixth month. Start frequency showed a gradual reduction in coefficient of variation over the course of the first year but had not reached adult levels by the end of the year. The coefficient of variation for normally reared infants was within the adult range by the fifth month but displayed considerable variability. In both duration and end frequency, the hand-reared and reintroduced animals had consistently greater variation in call structure than did normally reared infants.

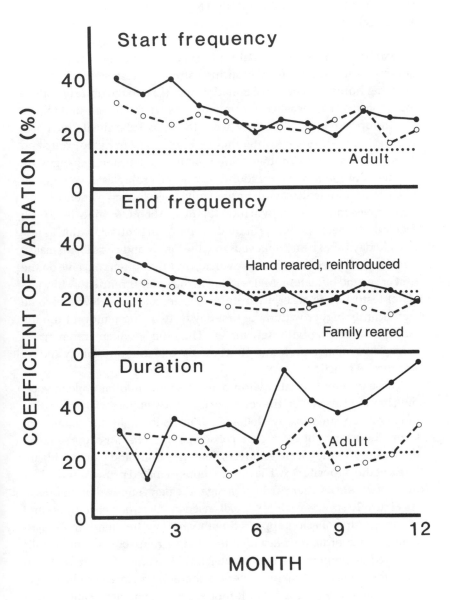

FIGURE 9. Changes in the coefficient of variation in three parameters of cotton-top tamarin chirps over the first year of life: *dotted line,* coefficient of variation of chirps recorded from adults; *solid line,* hand-reared monkeys reintroduced to social groups between six and eight weeks of age; *dashed line,* normally-reared monkeys.

LONG-CALL DEVELOPMENT IN COTTON-TOP
TAMARINS

As part of a study on sexual maturation in cotton-top tamarins, we have developed techniques for measuring estrogens, testosterone, and luteinizing hormone/chorionic gonadotropin (LH) in the urine of cotton-top tamarins. We measured hormonal levels daily in male and female cotton-top tamarins while they were living as subordinate members within a family group and after they were removed from the group and paired with mates in another colony room. The hormonal changes are striking. Although we have found occasional examples of estrogen or LH activity in females living in the family, we saw no evidence of orderly cycles indicative of ovulation (French, Abbott, & Snowdon, 1984; Ziegler, Savage, Scheffler, & Snowdon, 1987). In contrast, within as few as eight days after being removed from the family and paired with males, females have been observed to ovulate, and they often conceive on the first or second ovulation. Males living in the family group show low levels of testosterone and dihydrotestosterone, and these levels become significantly higher within the first day or two after removal from the family and pairing with new mates. Thus the social environment tamarins live in has a profound effect on reproductive physiology and reproductive function.

These different social environments play an important role in vocal development as well. In the course of our study of the social maturation of cotton-top tamarins, we followed animals living in their family environments for eight weeks, then observed the behavior of the same individuals after they were removed from the family and paired with animals of the opposite sex. The observations of mated pairs continued for the first 24 weeks after pairing (Savage, Ziegler, & Snowdon, in press). As Figure 10 shows, each of the calls used in intertroop encounters and in intragroup cohesion appeared with very low frequency in animals living in a subordinate role within the family group, but each of the calls occurred at significantly higher rates after the animals were removed from the family and mated. There is therefore a close correlation between the development of adult reproductive competence and the appearance of these vocalizations. We do not yet know whether there is a causal relationship between hormonal changes and the appearance of the vocalizations or whether both change independently as a function of the change in an animal's social environment. However, there are close

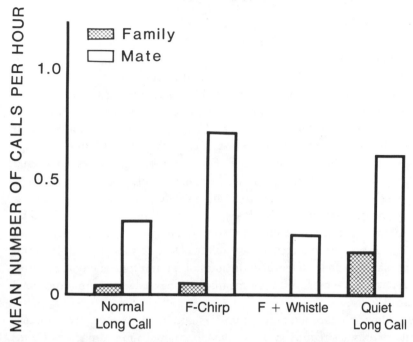

FIGURE 10. Number of calls per hour in cotton-top tamarins while living in family groups and in the first four months after being removed from the family and paired with a mate. Normal long calls, F-chirps, and F+ whistles are used in territorial encounters. Quiet long calls are used as cohesive calls between mates.

parallels between the appearance of these calls with reproductive maturity and the emergence of crystallized birdsong with male reproductive maturation (Marler & Peters, 1982), although Kroodsma (1974) has shown that the Bewick's wren can reach the stage of song crystallization before attaining reproductive maturity. There is also a highly variable form of long call, the combination long call, which has many of the characteristics of subsong and plastic song that Marler and Peters (1982) describe as occurring before reproductive maturity in birds. These earlier phases of song development are thought to represent a period of practice and crystallization of song learning in birds. The close parallel between birdsong ontogeny and the development of adult forms of long calls in cotton-top tamarins suggests a similar ontogenetic process for long-call ontogeny.

Conclusions

In this chapter I have argued that comparative psychology can make its major contribution by documenting and understanding the behavioral variability found in other species. This variability can suggest ways of thinking about behavior that we had not considered possible before, and this in turn can illuminate human behavior. Findings encountered in studies of different animal species can suggest new studies or approaches to human psychology. For example, I have noted here that pygmy marmosets have distinct cues that are added to vocalizations to make calls more locatable when animals are farther apart. There is an extensive literature on the design features of auditory signals used by animals, but no parallel research on human communication. Do we alter our sounds to improve locatability? How do the words or the nonverbal sounds we use travel through different types of environments? What are the most effective means for long-distance communication? And so on.

I have also argued that our understanding of the cognitive complexity of animals requires that we develop more complex models of communication than many animal ethologists have used so far. The model of human language can be illuminating so long as one does not expect any animal species to show all the features of human languages. I have reviewed a variety of studies from many species indicating parallels to such phenomena as phonetic variability, categorical perception, referential communication or semantics, and grammatical organization or syntax. Both among birds and among a few primate species, there are parallels between vocal ontogeny and human speech and language development. The conversations and rule-governed vocal exchanges of primates have parallels in human conversations. It is important to note that while an impressive number of parallels exist, no one species has been shown capable of all aspects of human speech and language. It is only by studying a wide variety of species at different phylogenetic levels and with different social organizations and habitats that we can discover the large number of existing parallels to human speech and language. This is another illustration of the importance of variability that comparative psychologists can bring to the attention of other psychologists.

Although much progress has been made in the comparative study of vocal communication over the past two decades, I have argued that such studies have focused too closely on the utterance produced or on the behavior of the communicator, while little attention has been directed toward the recipient of the utterance and even less to the social environment in which communication occurs. The study of communication needs to be complicated by considerations of the past social history of the communicator and recipient, which can, as I have shown, affect how animals perceive the calls of others. The appropriate metaphor for communication should be not the utterance but the conversation. I have given some rudimentary examples of how exchanges of signals between animals can be studied both in the affiliative antiphonal trilling of pygmy marmosets and in the intertroop calling of cotton-top tamarins.

Social interactions between care-givers and infants play an important role in the ontogeny of human speech and language, and similar social influences should be examined in the ontogeny of primate communication. These studies provide the beginning of a framework for learning how social history and interaction influence communication. We have shown that there are orderly changes in the development of both the closed mouth trills of pygmy marmosets and the chirps of cotton-top tamarins, with different vocal parameters having different developmental time courses. The presence of vocal regression with the birth of new infants, the existence of "babbling" bouts that might allow vocal practice in pygmy marmosets, and the differences in variability of chirp structure between cotton-top tamarins that are hand reared and reintroduced and those that are normally reared suggests that vocal development in these species may be more plastic and flexible than in many of the other monkey species studied to date. Finally, the parallels in long-call production and other territorial calls with hormonal maturation in tamarins compared with song development and hormonal maturation in birds suggests that further study of long calls in tamarins might be a fruitful source of information about vocal ontogeny in primates.

REFERENCES

Baptista, L. F. & Morton M. L. (1981). Interspecific song acquisition by a white-crowned sparrow. *Auk, 98*, 383–385.
Baptista, L. F., & Petrinovitch, L. (1984). Social interaction, sensitive phases, and the song template hypothesis in the white-crowned sparrow. *Animal Behaviour, 32*, 172–181.

Barash, D. P. (1979). *The whisperings within: Evolution and the origin of human nature*. New York: Harper and Row.

Beach, F. A. (1950). The snark was a boojum. *American Psychologist, 5,* 115–124.

Beer, C. (1970). Individual recognition of voice in the social behavior of birds. In D. S. Lehrman, R. A. Hinde, & E. Shaw (Eds.), *Advances in the study of behavior* (Vol. 3, pp. 27–74). New York: Academic Press.

Biben, M., Symmes, D., & Masataka, N. (1986). Temporal and structural analysis of affiliative vocal exchanges in squirrel monkeys *(Saimiri sciureus)*. *Behaviour, 98,* 259–273.

Brooks, R. J., & Falls, J. B. (1975). Individual recognition by song in white-throated sparrows. I. Discrimination of songs of neighbors and strangers. *Canadian Journal of Psychology.* 53: 879–888.

Brown, C. H. (1982a). Auditory localization and primate vocal behavior. In C. T. Snowdon, C. H. Brown, & M. R. Petersen (Eds.), *Primate communication,* (pp. 144–170). New York: Cambridge University Press.

Brown, C. H. (1982b). Ventriloquial and locatable vocalizations in birds. *Zeitschrift für Tierpsychologie, 59,* 338–350.

Bruner, J. (1983). *Child's talk: Learning how to use language*. New York: Norton.

Cheney, D. L., & Seyfarth, R. M. (1980). Vocal recognition in free-ranging vervet monkeys. *Animal Behaviour, 28,* 362–367.

Cheney, D. L., & Seyfarth, R. M. (1982). How vervet monkeys perceive their grunts: Field playback experiments. *Animal Behaviour, 30,* 739–751.

Cheney, D. L., & Seyfarth, R. M. (1986). The recognition of social alliances by vervet monkeys. *Animal Behaviour, 34,* 1722–1731.

Chomsky, N. (1957). *Syntactic structures*. The Hague: Mouton.

Cleveland, J., & Snowdon, C. T. (1982). The complex vocal repertoire of the adult cotton-top tamarin *(Saguinus oedipus oedipus)*. *Zeitschrift für Tierpsychologie, 58,* 231–270.

Dawson, G. A. (1979). The use of time and space by the Panamanian tamarin, *Saguinus oedipus*. *Folia Primatologica, 31,* 253–284.

Deputte, B. L. (1982). Duetting in male and female songs of the white-cheeked gibbon *(Hylobates concolor concolor)*. In C. T. Snowdon, C. H. Brown, & M. R. Petersen (Eds.), *Primate Communication* (pp. 69–93). New York: Cambridge University Press.

Dittus, W. P. J. (1984). Toque macaque food calls: Semantic communication concerning distribution of food in the environment. *Animal Behaviour, 32:* 470–477.

Dodd, J. J. (1972). Effects of social and vocal stimulation on infant babbling. *Developmental Psychology, 7,* 80–83.

Dukes, W. F. (1960). The snark revisited. *American Psychologist, 15,* 157.

Ehret, G., & Haack, B. (1981). Categorical perception of mouse pup ultrasounds by lactating females. *Naturwissenschaften, 68,* 208.

Farabaugh, S. M. (1982). The ecological and social significance of duetting. In D. E. Kroodsma & E. H. Miller (Eds.) *Acoustic communication in birds,* Vol. 2, *Song learning and its consequences,* (pp. 85–124). New York: Academic Press.

Ferguson, C. A. (1964). Baby talk in six languages. In J. Gaumpertz & D. Hymes

(Eds.) *Ethnography of communication.* Suppl. to *American Anthropologist, 66,* 103–114.

Ferguson, C. A., & Garnica, O. K. (1977). Theories of phonological development. In C. Snow & C. Ferguson (Eds.), *Talking to children.* Cambridge: Cambridge University Press.

Ficken, M. S., & Ficken, R. W. (1967). Singing behaviour of blue winged and golden winged warblers and their hybrids. *Behaviour, 28,* 149–181.

French, J. F., Abbott, D. H., & Snowdon, C. T. (1984). The effect of social environment on estrogen excretion, scent marking, and sociosexual behavior in tamarins (*Saguinus oedipus*). *American Journal of Primatology, 6,* 211–214.

Gouzoules, S., Gouzoules, H., & Marler, P. (1984). Rhesus monkey (*Macaca mulatta*) screams: Representational; signalling in the recruitment of agonistic aid. *Animal Behaviour, 32,* 182–193.

Green, S. (1975a). Variation of vocal pattern with social situation in the Japanese monkey (*Macaca fuscata*): A field study. In L. A. Rosenblum (Ed.), *Primate behavior,* Vol. 4, pp. 1–102. New York: Academic Press.

Green, S. (1975b). Dialects in Japanese monkeys: Vocal learning and cultural transmission of locale-specific behavior. *Zeitschrift für Tierpsychologie, 38,* 304–314.

Hailman, J. P., Ficken, M. S., & Ficken, R. W. (1985). The "chick-a-dee" call of *Parus atricapillus:* A recombinant system of animal communication compared with written English. *Semiotica, 56,* 191–224.

Hodun, A., Snowdon, C. T., & Soini, P. (1981). Subspecific variation in the long calls of the tamarin, *Saguinus fuscicollis. Zeitschrift für Tierpsychologie, 57,* 97–110.

King, A. P., & West, M. J. (1984). Social matrices of song learning. *Learning and Motivation, 15,* 441–458.

Kroodsma, D. E. (1972). Variations in the songs of vesper sparrows in Oregon. *Wilson Bulletin, 84,* 173–178.

Kroodsma, D. E. (1973). Coexistence of Bewick's wrens and house wrens in Oregon. *Auk, 90,* 341–352.

Kroodsma, D. E. (1974). Song learning, dialects, and dispersal in Bewick's wren. *Zeitschrift für Tierpsychologie, 35,* 352–380.

Kroodsma, D. E. (1981). Geographic variation and functions of song types in warblers (Parulidae). *Auk, 98,* 743–751.

Kroodsma, D. E. (1984). Songs of the alder flycatcher (*Empidonax alnoran*) and willow flycatcher (*Empidonax trailli*) are innate. *Auk, 101,* 13–24.

Kroodsma, D. E., & Baylis, J. R. (1982). Appendix: A world survey of evidence for vocal learning in birds. In D. E. Kroodsma & E. H. Miller (Eds.), *Acoustic communication in birds,* Vol. 2, *Song learning and its consequences* (pp. 311–337). New York: Academic Press.

Kuhl, P. K., & Miller, J. D. (1975). Speech perception in the chinchilla: Voiced-voiceless distinction in alveolar plosive consonants. *Science, 190,* 69–72.

Leger, D. W., & Owings, D. H. (1978). Responses to alarm calls by California ground squirrels: Effects of call structure and maternal status. *Behavioral Ecology and Sociobiology, 3,* 177–186.

Leger, D. W., Owings, D. H., & Boal, L. M. (1979). Contextual information and differential responding to alarm whistles in California ground squirrels. *Zeitschrift für Tierpsychologie, 49,* 142–155.

Lein, M. N. (1978). Song variation in a population of chestnut-sided warblers (*Dendroica pennsylvanica*): Its nature and suggested significance. *Canadian Journal of Zoology, 56,* 1266–1283.

Lemon, R. E. (1975). How birds develop song dialects. *Condor, 77,* 385–406.

Lenneberg, E. H. (1967). *Biological foundations of language.* New York: Wiley.

Liberman, A. M. (1982). On finding that speech is special. *American Psychologist, 37,* 148–167.

Lillehei, R. A., & Snowdon, C. T. (1978). Individual and situational differences in the vocalizations of young stumptail macaques. *Behaviour, 65,* 270–281.

Lockard, R. B. (1971). Reflections on the fall of comparative psychology: Is there a message for us all? *American Psychologist, 26,* 168–179.

Marler, P. (1970a). A comparative approach to vocal learning: Song development in white-crowned sparrows. *Journal of Comparative and Physiological Psychology Monographs, 71,* 1–25.

Marler, P. (1970b). Bird song and speech development: Could there be parallels? *American Scientist, 58,* 663–669.

Marler, P. (1975). On the origin of speech from animal sounds. In J. F. Kavanaugh & J. E. Cutting (Eds.), *The role of speech in language* (pp. 11–37). Cambridge: MIT Press.

Marler, P. (1977). The structure of animal communication sounds. In T. H. Bullock (Ed.), *Recognition of complex acoustic signals* (Report of the Dahlem Workshop) (pp. 17–35). Berlin: Dahlem Konferenzen.

Marler, P., Dufty, A., & Pickert, R. (1986a). Vocal communication in the domestic chicken. I. Does a sender communicate information about the quality of a food referent to a receiver? *Animal Behaviour, 34,* 188–193.

Marler, P., Dufty, A., & Pickert, R. (1986b). Vocal communication in the domestic chicken. II. Is a sender sensitive to the presence and nature of a receiver? *Animal Behaviour, 34,* 194–198.

Marler, P., & Hobbett, L. (1975). Individuality in a long-range vocalization of wild chimpanzees. *Zeitschrift für Tierpsychologie, 38,* 97–109.

Marler P., & Peters, S. (1982). Subsong and plastic song: Their role in the vocal learning process. In D. E. Kroodsma & E. H. Miller (Eds.), *Acoustic communication in birds,* Vol. 2, *Song learning and its consequences* (pp. 25–49). New York: Academic Press.

Marshall, J. R., & Marshall, E. (1976). Gibbons and their territorial songs. *Science, 193,* 235–237.

Masataka, N. (1983). Categorical responses to natural and synthesized alarm calls in Goeldi's monkey (*Callimico goeldi*). *Primates, 24,* 40–51.

Mattingly, I. G. (1972). Speech cues and sign stimuli. *American Scientist, 60,* 327–337.

McArthur, P. D. (1986). Similarity of playback songs to self song as a determinant of response strength in song sparrows (*Melospiza melodia*). *Animal Behaviour, 34,* 199–207.

McConnell, P. B., & Snowdon, C. T. (1986). Vocal interactions between unfamiliar groups of captive cotton-top tamarins. *Behaviour, 97*, 273–296.

Mineka, S., Davidson, M., Cook, M., & Keir, R. (1984). Observational conditioning of snake fear in rhesus monkeys. *Journal of Abnormal Psychology, 93*, 355–372.

Morse, D. H. (1967). The context of songs in black-throated green and blackburnian warblers. *Wilson Bulletin, 79*, 64–74.

Morse, P. A., & Snowdon, C. T. (1975). An investigation of categorical speech discrimination by rhesus monkeys. *Perception and Psychophysics, 17*, 9–16.

Mundinger, P. (1970). Vocal imitation and individual recognition of finch calls. *Science, 168*, 480–482.

Nelson, D. (1985). The syntactic and semantic organization of the pigeon guillemot (*Cepphus columba*) vocal behavior. *Zeitschrift für Tierpsychologie, 67*, 97–130.

Newman, J. D., & Symmes, D. (1982). Inheritance and experience in the acquisition of primate acoustic behavior. In C. T. Snowdon, C. H. Brown, & M. R. Petersen (Eds.), *Primate Communication* (pp. 259–278). New York: Academic Press.

Neyman, P. A. (1977). Aspects of the ecology and social organization of free-ranging cotton-top tamarins (*Saguinus oedipus*) and the conservation status of the species. In D. G. Kleiman (Ed.), *The biology and conservation of the callitrichidae* (pp. 39–71). Washington DC: Smithsonian Institution Press.

Oller, D. K., Wieman, L. A., Doyle, W. J., & Ross, C. (1975). Infant babbling and speech. *Child Language, 1*, 1–11.

Park, T. J., & Dooling, R. J. (1985). Perception of species-specific contact calls by budgerigars (*Melopsittacus undulatus*). *Journal of Comparative Psychology, 99*, 391–402.

Pepperberg, I. M. (1985). Social modeling theory: Possible framework for understanding avian vocal learning. *Auk, 102*, 854–864.

Pepperberg, I. M. (in press). The importance of social interaction and observation in the acquisition of communicative competence: Possible parallels between avian and human learning. In T. Zentall and B. G. Galef, Jr. (Eds.), *Social learning: A comparative approach*.

Petersen, M. R., Beecher, M. D., Zoloth, S. R., Green, S., Marler, P., Moody, D. B., & Stebbins, W. C. (1984). Neural lateralization of vocalizations by Japanese macaques: Communicative significance is more important than acoustic structure. *Behavioral Neuroscience, 98*, 779–790.

Petersen, M. R., Beecher, M. D., Zoloth, S. R., Moody, D. B., & Stebbins, W. C. (1978). Neural lateralization of species-specific vocalizations by Japanese macaques (*Macaca fuscata*). *Science, 202*, 324–327.

Petrinovitch, L. (1985). Factors influencing song development in the white-crowned sparrow (*Zonotrichia leucophrys*). *Journal of Comparative Psychology, 99*, 15–29.

Pola, Y. V., & Snowdon, C. T. (1975). The vocalizations of pygmy marmosets (*Cebuella pygmaea*). *Animal Behaviour, 23*, 826–842.

Porter, J. H., Johnson, S. B., & Granger, R. G. (1981). The snark is still a boojum. *Comparative Psychology Newsletter, 1* (5), 1–3.

Ratcliffe, L., & Weisman, R. G. (1986) Song sequence discrimination in the black-capped chickadee (*Parus atricapillus*). *Journal of Comparative Psychology, 100,* 361–367.

Robinson, J. G. (1979). An analysis of the organization of vocal communication in the titi monkey (*Callicebus moloch*). *Zeitschrift für Tierpsychologie, 49,* 381–405.

Robinson, J. G. (1984). Syntactic structures in the vocalizations of wedge-capped capuchin monkeys (*Cebus olivaceus*). *Behaviour, 90,* 46–79.

Robinson, S. R. (1980). Antipredator behavior and predator recognition in Belding's ground squirrels. *Animal Behaviour, 28,* 840–852.

Robinson, S. R. (1981). Alarm communication in Belding's ground squirrels. *Zeitschrift für Tierpsychologie, 59,* 150–168.

Savage, A., Ziegler, T. E., & Snowdon, C. T. (1988). Sociosexual development, pairbond formation, and mechanisms of fertility suppression in female cotton-top tamarins (*Saguinus oedipus oedipus*), *American Journal of Primatology,* in press.

Seyfarth, R. M., & Cheney, D. L. (1986). Vocal development in vervet monkeys. *Animal Behaviour, 34,* 1640–1658.

Seyfarth, R. M., Cheney, D. L., & Marler, P. (1980). Vervet monkey alarm calls: Semantic communication in a free-ranging primate. *Animal Behaviour, 28,* 1070–1094.

Sinnott, J. M., Beecher, M. D., Moody, D. B., & Stebbins, W. C. (1976). Speech sound discrimination by monkeys and humans. *Journal of the Acoustical Society of America, 60,* 687–695.

Skinner, B. F. (1957). *Verbal behavior,* New York: Appleton Century.

Smith, W. J., Pawlukiewicz, J., & Smith, S. T. (1978). Kinds of activities associated with singing patterns of the yellow-throated vireo. *Animal Behaviour, 26,* 862–884.

Snow, C., & Ferguson, C. (1977). *Talking to children: Language input and language acquisition.* Cambridge: Cambridge University Press.

Snowdon, C. T. (1987). A naturalistic view of categorical perception. In S. Harnad (Ed.), *Categorical perception* (pp. 332–354). New York: Cambridge University Press.

Snowdon, C. T. & Cleveland, J. (1980). Individual recognition of contact calls in pygmy marmosets. *Animal Behaviour, 28,* 717–727.

Snowdon, C. T., and Cleveland, J. (1984). "Conversations" among pygmy marmosets. *American Journal of Primatology, 7,* 15–20.

Snowdon, C. T., Cleveland, J., & French, J. A. (1983). Responses to context- and individual-specific cues in cotton-top tamarin long calls. *Animal Behaviour, 31,* 99–111

Snowdon, C. T., Coe, C. R., & Hodun, A. (1985). Population recognition of infant isolation peeps in the squirrel monkey. *Animal Behaviour, 33,* 1145–1151.

Snowdon, C. T., & Hodun, A. (1981). Acoustic adaptations in pygmy marmoset contact calls: Location cues vary with distance between conspecifics. *Behavioral Ecology and Sociobiology, 9,* 295–300.

Snowdon, C. T., & Hodun, A. (1985). Troop-specific responses to long calls of isolated tamarins (*Saguinus mystax*). *American Journal of Primatology, 8,* 205–214.

Snowdon, C. T., Hodun, A., Rosenberger, A. L., & Coimbra-Filho, A. F. (1986). Long call structure and its relation to taxonomy in lion tamarins. *American Journal of Primatology, 11*, 253–261.

Snowdon, C. T., & Pola, Y. V. (1978). Interspecific and intraspecific responses to synthesized pygmy marmoset vocalizations. *Animal Behaviour, 26*, 192–206.

Snowdon, C. T., Savage, A., & McConnell, P. B. (1985). A breeding colony of cotton-top tamarins. *Laboratory Animal Science, 35*, 477–481.

Snowdon, C. T., & Suomi, S. J. (1982). Paternal care in primates. In H. E. Fitzgerald, J. A. Mullins & P. Gage (Eds.), *Child nurturance* (Vol. 3, pp. 63–108). New York: Plenum Press.

Terrace, H. S., Petito, L. A., Saunders, R. J., & Bever, T. G. (1979). Can an ape create a sentence? *Science, 206*, 891–902.

Thorpe, W. H. (1958). The learning of song patterns by birds with especial reference to the song of the chaffinch (*Fringilla coelebs*). *Ibis, 100*, 535–570.

Todd, G. A., & Palmer, B. (1968). Social reinforcement of infant babbling. *Child Development, 39*, 591–596.

Waser, P. M. (1977). Individual recognition, intragroup cohesion and intergroup spacing: Evidence from sound playback to forest monkeys. *Behaviour, 60*, 28–74.

Waters, R. S., & Wilson, W. A., Jr. (1976). Speech perception by rhesus monkeys: The voicing distinction in synthesized labial and velar stop consonants. *Perception and Psychophysics, 19*, 285–289.

West, M. J., & King, A. P. (1985). Social guidance of vocal learning by female cowbirds: Validating its functional significance. *Zeitschrift für Tierpsychologie, 70*, 225–235.

Wiley, R. H., & Richards, D. G. (1982). Adaptations for acoustic communication in birds: Sound transmission and signal detection. In D. E. Kroodsma & E. H. Miller (Eds.), *Acoustic communication in birds*, Vol. 1, *Production, perception, and design features of sounds* (pp. 131–181). New York: Academic Press.

Winter, P. (1969). Dialects in squirrel monkeys: Vocalizations of the roman arch type. *Folia Primatologica, 10*, 216–229.

Ziegler, T. E., Savage, A., Scheffler, G., & Snowdon, C. T. (1987). The endocrinology of puberty and reproductive functioning in female cotton-top tamarins (*Saguinus oedipus*) under varying social conditions. *Biology of Reproduction, 37:* 618–627.

Zoloth, S. R., Petersen, M. R., Beecher, M. D., Green, S., Marler, P., Moody, D. B., & Stebbins, W. C. (1979). Species-specific perceptual processing of vocal sounds by monkeys. *Science, 204*, 870–872.

A New Look at Ape Language: Comprehension of Vocal Speech and Syntax

Sue Savage-Rumbaugh

*Georgia State University
and Yerkes Regional Primate
Research Center*

Ape Language: A Brief Review

*T*he language acquisition capacity of apes has been the focus of a number of research projects (Fouts, 1972; Gardner & Gardner, 1971; Miles, 1983; Patterson, 1978; Premack, 1971; Rumbaugh, 1977; Savage-Rumbaugh, 1984a, 1984b; Terrace, 1979). Despite the controversy among these projects regarding the communication modality, there has been general agreement that apes can learn to express simple needs and desires through symbols (Jolly, 1985; Savage-Rumbaugh, 1981; Terrace 1985). Controversy remains over whether these requests are simple conditioned responses or symbolic expressions in which the symbols represent specific items, objects, and events. Controversy over the issue of syntax also remains, but it has assumed a secondary role, since emergence of syntax presupposes the appearance of representation (Savage-Rumbaugh, 1986, in press; Seidenberg & Pettito, in press; Terrace, 1985).

When a word is said to be a member of a child's vocabulary, this generally means that not only can the child produce a recognizable version of that word in the appropriate situation, but he or she can also understand the word when it is used by others (Benedict, 1979; Greenfield & Smith, 1976; McShane, 1980; Nelson, 1978). It is also presumed that the child can use such words to accomplish a variety of communicative functions in addition to requesting (Benedict, 1979; Nelson, 1973; Rescorla, 1976). In fact, children seem to comprehend talk about objects present or absent months before they begin to produce similar expressions (Nelson, 1977).

Studies that have focused specifically upon comprehension have concluded that it precedes production throughout the one-word stage and that some children develop extensive comprehension skills while speaking very little (Benedict, 1979; Gibson & Ingram, 1983; Goldin-Meadow, Seligman, & Gelman, 1976; Greenfield & Smith, 1976; Huttenlocker, 1974; Oviatt, 1980; Snyder, Bates, & Bretherton, 1981). It also appears (Snyder, Bates, & Bretherton, 1981) that children develop the critical concept of linguistic reference as they learn to comprehend the utterances addressed to them. By the time they begin to speak, they are aware of the referential function of words and ready to go about the task of sorting out which utterances refer to objects, events, feelings, and so on.

Representational Competency

Ape-language researchers initially presumed that when a word was classified as a member of a chimpanzee's vocabulary, this meant that the chimpanzee's knowledge about that word was similar to a child's (Gardner & Gardner, 1971; Rumbaugh, 1977; Terrace, 1979). But was this conclusion justified? We began to doubt its validity when we tested two chimpanzees, Sherman and Austin, who had vocabularies they could use to request a wide array of desirable actions, objects, and foods. Tests that controlled for contextual prompting revealed that Sherman and Austin's comprehension skills were minimal (Savage-Rumbaugh, 1986). Not only did comprehension not follow automatically from production, we also found that the chimpanzees seemed to differ from children in other ways. For example, additional tests indicated that Sherman and Austin did not differentiate between the semantic functions of requesting and naming. This was not obvious when they were asked to name something they wanted and it was given to them if they were correct (a typical training technique that confuses requesting with naming). It became obvious when they were asked to name something they wanted and the item was not given to them if they were correct. This resulted in significant confusion among symbols that were thought to be well learned. More revealing was the finding that even though they might be able to use a symbol appropriately when the referent was present, removing the referent often led to inappropriate symbol usage (Sanders, 1985; Savage-Rumbaugh, 1986). These observations forced a serious challenge to the validity of the assumption that chimpanzees and children were using symbols in a similar manner (Savage-Rumbaugh, Pate, Lawson, Smith, & Rosenbaum, 1983; Savage-Rumbaugh, Rumbaugh, & Boysen, 1980; Seidenberg and Pettito, 1979; Terrace, 1985).

Our findings suggested that chimpanzees evidenced more "disjointness" of representational symbol usage than was characteristic of normal children, or at least more disjointness than has been reported in the normal child. In response to this, we devised specific criteria to determine whether a given symbol was being used in a representational manner (Savage-Rumbaugh, 1984b, 1986). These criteria were developed by analyzing the kinds of skills present in the human child during the one-word stage (Bates, 1979; Greenfield & Smith, 1976; Lock, 1980; McShane, 1980; Savage-Rumbaugh, 1986). They required that the chimpanzee demonstrate an ability to (a) appropriately request an item in the correct context, (b) name a displayed item, (c) correctly respond to a request for a particular item by selecting that item from a group of things, (d) demonstrate a behavioral correspondence between action and symbol, (e) announce intended actions, and (f) demonstrate an ability to respond to and make judgments about symbols that were equivalent to the way they would respond to the referent. Additionally, the chimpanzee was required to demonstrate competency on all these tasks with the referent absent (for information on how this was done, see Savage-Rumbaugh, 1986).

It quickly became apparent that the ability to use the proper symbol to request a desired item did not mean the chimpanzee could meet the remaining criteria. However, it did prove possible, by devising additional training tasks that focused on establishing these skills in communicative settings, to enable the chimpanzees to meet the other requirements (Savage-Rumbaugh, 1986). Still, the fact that considerable additional training was required led to the conclusion that symbol acquisition is a multiskill phenomenon that requires learning much more than simply item-symbol associations.

The multiskill requirements of word acquisition are not obvious as the normal child acquires language. Indeed, symbol acquisition seems almost effortless to observers. Presumably this is because a rather lengthy period of comprehension precedes the onset of actual use for any given symbol. During this period of comprehension, the child determines the general meaning of a word as well as a number of different ways the word can function in a communicative setting.

However, chimpanzees, in all cases, were being taught to produce words before they comprehended them (Fouts, 1973; Gardner & Gardner, 1971; Premack, 1971; Rumbaugh, 1977; Savage-Rumbaugh, 1979; Terrace, 1979). Consequently their initial word usage reflected little more than an associative connection between a displayed referent and a symbol. This was why chimpanzees' signs were referred to as "tricks" (Hediger, 1981; Seidenberg & Petitto, 1981; Terrace, 1981). Such signs or "tricks" added no new information to the communicative setting. Instead, they were a means of obtaining a desired incentive, and if it could not be shown that it was possible to use them in the absence of that incentive, they could not justifiably be viewed as representations of it. It was more appropriate to regard them as behaviors elicited by the presence of the incentive (Sanders, 1985).

For the most part, training procedures were inadvertently designed to promote the learning of tricks rather than symbols, because they required chimpanzees to encode situationally obvious things (Sanders, 1985; Savage-Rumbaugh, 1984a, 1984c). For example, if the teacher had an apple and a chimpanzee tried to take a bite of it, the teacher would stop him and ask, "What do you want? Sign, sign." Upon signing, the chimpanzee would be given the apple. Signing (or selecting the correct symbol) in situationally obvious settings is tantamount to performing a "trick," because the teacher knows what is desired before the sign is made.

When such training tactics are used, the chimpanzee cannot learn that the sign "apple" represents an apple because the sign does not stand for apple in that situation. Rather, the meaning of the sign is something more like "Let me have what is in your hand." There is no need to specify the identity of what is desired, since that is obvious. What is being communicated (which is what the sign will stand for if it stands for anything) is the chimpanzee's desire to be given the object. Such training techniques promote confusion among food names, since the sign the chimpanzee must produce to obtain the food varies depending upon what food the teacher has. Yet the information that the chimpanzee is attempting to encode, regardless of the food, is his desire that the food be transferred.

This situation must be very confusing for the chimpanzee, since he has to make sign A to get food on some occasions, sign B to get food on other occasions, sign C on still other occasions. The only thing that he can learn is to produce sign A in the presence of an apple, sign B in the presence of an orange, and so on. Thus the objects themselves come to elicit the signs, but the signs do not stand for the objects. The chimpanzee could easily learn a sign that represented something like "Give that to me," and the sign would represent the act of giving. Indeed, chimpanzees develop such gestures in the wild in exactly the same circumstances—when something they want is being withheld. They do not develop gestures that specify *the name of the object being held,* since the identity of the object is self-evident and need not be encoded in order to be communicated (Goodall, 1986).

Yet typically in such training contexts, it was assumed that if the chimpanzee could sign "apple" to get an apple when the teacher held up an apple and "banana" to get a banana when the teacher held up a banana, the chimpanzee then knew what these signs stood for. The assumption that the chimpanzee was using the sign to "ask for a specific food" was easy enough to test by simply offering a variety of fruits when the sign "apple" was produced and then noting whether the "apple" was selected over other fruits. Unfortunately, attempts to determine whether there was a concordance between what a chimpanzee said and what it then did were absent from all reports except those on Sherman and Austin (Savage-Rumbaugh, 1986).

By looking for a concordance between verbal and nonverbal components in Sherman and Austin's performance (Savage-Rumbaugh, 1984a, 1984b), it was possible to tell whether they were executing a series of behaviors designed to provide themselves with a desired object or event or actually using a symbol to convey a representational message. This method is used all the time by parents who do not understand their children's initial utterances. The parent queries the child, and the child responds gesturally to make his message clear (Bates, 1979; Greenfield & Smith, 1976; Lock, 1980).

The training techniques used with Sherman and Austin *did not* stress the production of situationally obvious messages. Instead, they made it necessary for Sherman and Austin to encode aspects of the situation that were not obvious. Often this was accomplished by spatially or temporally removing the referent (Savage-Rumbaugh, 1986). For example, to teach object symbols, we designed a tool-using task that required making a decision about what sort of tool was needed to open a box. The chimpanzee first learned to select the tool from a group, then to ask a

206

person (or another chimpanzee) to select the tool for him when the tools were in a different room. The use of a symbol in this study encoded specific information about a particular object the chimpanzee wanted. Since this object was not the sole object present and the chimpanzee could not make evident his desire for a tool simply by reaching for it, he had to learn how to encode the specific item.

The chimpanzee learned that tool A was needed when food was blocked by a padlock, tool B was needed when food was out of reach, and so on. He also learned that symbol A-1 caused others to retrieve tool A, symbol B-1 caused them to retrieve tool B, and so forth. The chimpanzee could not just encode the idea "retrieve object for me." He had to encode the identity of the object to be retrieved. This sort of training was coupled with tasks in which the chimpanzee did not ask for the needed tool but retrieved it himself. In this case the experimenter decided which tool was needed and asked the chimpanzee for it. The chimpanzee could not see where the food was placed and so did not know which tool the experimenter needed. He had to observe which tool was requested, go into the next room, select that tool from a group, and bring it to the experimenter. If he did not bring the right tool it would be self-evident, since the wrong tool would not open the site.

Thus the chimpanzee had to learn that when the experimenter uses symbol A-1, he should select tool A. Meanwhile, he was also learning to use symbol A-1 when he needed tool A. The identification of which tool to bring the experimenter had to be accomplished without viewing the tool sites. Similarly, the specification of the symbol A-1, B-1, C-1, and so on, for a particular tool had to be accomplished without seeing the tool at the time the symbol was selected. Thus, the presence of the referent could not trigger the selection of the symbol, and the chimpanzee *could not learn* to select symbol A-1 in the presence of tool A, symbol B-1 in the presence of tool B, and so forth.

Training of this nature was very different from previous studies, and it fostered representational symbol usage far more than the "naming" training used in other studies (Savage-Rumbaugh, Rumbaugh, & Boysen, 1978). Such training also made it possible to demonstrate that Sherman and Austin could make categorical judgments about objects represented by symbols even when the objects were absent (Savage-Rumbaugh, 1981).

Nonetheless, the process of symbol acquisition still depended upon first teaching the chimpanzee to produce the symbol and then teaching a variety of functional uses, including comprehension. The normal child does not need such training because he learns to comprehend symbols *before* he begins to produce them. For the normal child, production is simply a manifestation of part of what he already knows about symbols; for the chimpanzee, it is the acquiring of symbol knowledge itself.

Syntactical Competency

The issue of syntactical competency in chimpanzees has been addressed as though it had no relation to the issue of representational symbol competency (Terrace, Pettito, Sanders, & Bever, 1979). Although it was found that Nim had certain order preferences in his combinations, Terrace dismissed these as being dissimilar to the order found in children's combinations for a number of reasons, including the fact that the information conveyed by Nim's longer combinations was not greater than that conveyed by his shorter combinations. Nim's mean length of utterance (MLU) did not increase steadily as does that of the normal child; many of his combinations seemed to be composed of "wild card" signs such as "Nim" or "me" that were always appropriate; and many of his combinations could be attributed to imitation of the teacher's recent signs. However, since Nim's ability to use any of his signs in a representational manner was questionable (Seidenberg & Petitto, 1979, 1981), the validity of Terrace's syntactical analysis is dubious at best. If Nim did not know what individual name signs represented, it is doubtful that he could accurately form the syntactic classes of agent, action, location, and so on, that were attributed to him. It therefore does not seem surprising that when required by his teachers to produce complex combinations he relied heavily upon imitation.

The Gardners have not specifically addressed the issue of word order and did not keep track of specific sign order during the Washoe project, though more recently they have suggested that chimpanzees may use inflection as a syntactic device (Gardner & Gardner, in press). Lana unquestionably demonstrated the ability to order symbols to a high degree and to produce novel combinations that reflected knowledge of specific ordering rules (Pate & Rumbaugh, 1983). However, because her training stressed the production of stock sentences from the outset, it is not clear that the combinations Lana produced were formed by syntactical rules themselves, as opposed to simple generalizations between stock sentence formats (Savage-Rumbaugh, Rumbaugh, & Boysen, 1980; Thompson & Church, 1980). Also, the representational function of some of Lana's symbols was not well established (Savage-Rumbaugh, 1986). No claim of syntactical competency has been made for Sherman and Austin, though clear demonstrations of representational competency at the single-morpheme level have been provided (Savage-Rumbaugh, 1981, 1984a, 1984b). Indeed, the best explanation of their combinations seems to be that they encode aspects of the situation that are perceived to vary and that they encode multiple sources of variability with multi-symbol utterances (Greenfield & Savage-Rumbaugh, 1984). There is no evidence that they are following syntactical ordering rules.

Language Acquisition Theories

Language acquisition theories universally focus upon production (Bloom, 1973; Brown, 1973; McNeil, 1970). Indeed, regardless of disagreement about a multitude of other factors, most theorists agree that what is yet to be explained about language acquisition is how and why a child comes to produce the linguistic structures that typify human language. No major treatise exists on how and why the child comes to comprehend and appropriately respond to linguistic and nonlinguistic structures.

To gather a large corpus of children's utterances and derive from them hypotheses about how language is acquired is a rather straightforward task. It is much more difficult to gather data on the development of language comprehension. Production occurs in discrete, easily detectable, measurable units. By contrast, comprehension typically occurs without any overt change in the behavior of the listener. Even in cases where some behavior can be discerned, it is difficult to tell what aspects of the communicative context produced the behavior. This is because utterances typically occur in a rich setting that includes gestural information, glances, knowledge of routine, intonation of utterance, and immediate context as well as the phonemic utterance. It is difficult to eliminate these factors and still obtain reliable responses to linguistic communication when dealing with young children.

The focus on language production has led Chomsky (1980a, 1980b) to assert that the syntactic components of human language must be innate and to emphasize that acquisition follows a typical pattern across a wide range of linguistic input settings. Chomsky (1980a, 1980b) takes the position that the major mystery of language acquisition lies in our ability to deduce syntactical rules and apply them in novel situations.

Basic to this view is the idea that language is processed apart from context by a device that is equipped to deduce rules from the surface structure of sentences. This device, which is said to be in the left hemisphere, is thought to permit us to decode the meaning of any sentence. Indeed, the true "meaning" of all sentences is presumed to be represented only one way, regardless of the surface structure of the sentences of the language. This device, thought to be present in all human brains, decodes all languages in a similar fashion. Without it, it is presumed that there would be no language and man would not be man. Chomsky (1980a, 1980b) has made it quite clear that data from chimpanzees who acquire language are irrelevant to the issue, commenting that with regard to apes one thing is missing: that little part of the left hemisphere that is responsible for the specific structures of human language. There is, of course, no neurological evidence to support the view that this particular piece is indeed missing in the chimpanzee brain and present in the human brain. In fact, individuals who have lost left-hemisphere function at an early age go on to develop normal language skills. There is also evidence that individuals lacking normal cortical development of Wernicke's and Broca's areas owing to hydrocephaly still develop language (Lorber, 1980). At the minimum this implies that any sort of language acquisition device is not completely hard wired unless it is a noncortical structure.

Others argue that equally innate is our ability to differentiate phonemic units and syllables (Liberman, 1970; Liberman, Cooper, Shankweiler, & Studdert-Kennedy, 1967; Lieberman, 1984). Lieberman (1984) suggests that the neuropsychological mechanisms that allow us to perceive speech have evolved in concert with the peripheral physical mechanisms that allow us to produce it. While recognizing that the rudiments of speech comprehension stem from general auditory processing mechanisms, Lieberman (1984) argues that many components of speech comprehension require a "phonetic analysis mechanism" that operates at a different neurological level than general auditory processing. This "phonetic processing mechanism" allows us to process speech easily, and is not present in other animals.

In fact, we really do not know how the human child comes to discriminate one phoneme from another or one word from another. Yet differentiating between sounds and words is critical to the perception of speech. Although two phonemes such as /ba/ and /pa/ sound distinct to us, they are really quite similar in terms of sound pattern, differing only in voice-onset time. Human listeners make a sharp discrimination between these two sounds at the 25 msec boundary, calling the sound a [b] if voice onset occurs before 25 msec and [p] if it occurs after 25 msec. That the ability to do this is not just a function of our excellent sensitivity to such auditory input is demonstrated by the fact that we cannot differentiate sounds that are 25 msec apart either below or above this boundary. Our discrimination is good only at this boundary, as though some template filters out these sounds for us into two separate groups (Lieberman, 1984; Snowdon, this volume).

It has been shown that rhesus monkeys can discriminate at least a few of the basic phonemic units of human speech (Morse & Snowdon, 1975; Waters & Wilson, 1976). In these studies, the monkeys tended toward categorical perception of speech sounds, as do humans, though many technical questions still need to be investigated and a far wider range of sounds must be studied before it will be possible to conclude that rhesus monkeys can perceive the phonemic units of speech as we do. Even if rhesus monkeys do prove able to perceive human phonemic units, the question of whether such monkeys could comprehend human speech would still remain unanswered.

Human speech consists not of individual phonemic units but rather strings of such units. Moreover, groupings of phonemes are not arranged like beads on a string; instead, the vowel that follows or precedes any consonant alters the production of that consonant. For this reason, machines that read and translate human speech have been notoriously difficult to build (Lieberman, 1984). Not only are consonants affected by the vowels that precede and follow them, but the form of the vowel is affected by the size of the vocal tract. The human listener must calibrate the size of the speaker's vocal tract in order to know how to decode various vowel sounds, since some vowels overlap. Only by knowing the size of the vocal tract can the type of vowel be distinguished. This is accomplished by utilizing the vowels [i] and [u], which can always be properly discerned and whose frequency serves to identify the size of the speaker's vocal tract (Lieberman, 1984).

Language: Man Versus Animal

The prevailing perspective of our time insists that language is a uniquely human skill. The ability to perceive and decode language sounds is thought to be unique, as is the ability to structure single utterances into meaningful propositions, the singular characteristic of these propositions being that the relationship between the utterances conveys meaning not carried in any of the individual utterances.

It is surprising how little evidence exists to prove that these capacities are indeed uniquely human. Most studies that address these issues show that both speech perception and syntax are highly evolved skills in the human species, but few studies actually attempt to determine whether similar skills exist in other species (Kuhl & Padden, 1986). The neurological evidence used to support Chomsky's (1980a 1980b) position is limited to the finding that language or at least speech processing is typically lateralized in human beings (Kimura, 1961; Molfese, 1978) and that the left temporal planum is larger than the right in most human brains (Wada, Clarke, & Hamm, 1975).

In support of the view that speech is processed by special neurological mechanisms, Lieberman (1984) cites the close relationship between our ability to process voice-onset time distinctions and the presence of consonants in our speech that are matched to these capacities. He also offers the presence of categorical perception and its close link to place of articulation, the phenomenon of adaptation (in which there is a shift in a phonetic boundary toward an adapting stimulus), and lateralization of language as arguments supporting the view that man's acoustic apparatus is specially prewired to understand and produce language in a manner distinct from that of any other animal. In a chapter entitled "Speech Is Special," Lieberman concludes that the "weight of the evidence is consistent with the presence in human beings of neural mechanisms matched to the acoustic characteristics of human speech" (Lieberman, 1984, p. 169). Unlike Chomsky, however, Lieberman goes on to take a biological perspective and to assert that the rudiments of these processing mechanisms are likely to be found in other animals.

The views that language is uniquely determined by an innate parsing device and that speech is similarly decoded by innate processing mechanisms do not go unchallenged (Greenfield & Smith, 1976; Kuhl & Padden, 1986). It must be said, however, that the influence of these views is substantial in the field today, and it is upon the merits of these views that the validity of the accomplishments of symbol-using apes is continually evaluated.

The issue of determining whether other animals can process human phonemes is a complicated one, fraught with methodological problems. On the surface, it seems that those animals that can hear a wide range of frequencies, including those that make up human speech, should be able to hear what we say. But as Lieberman (1984) observes, such may not be the case. These animals may be able to detect the sounds we make but not know where syllables or words begin or end. To them, our speech could sound something like an orchestra in which each instrument is playing a different tune—one could hear all the noises but not be able to identify any specific song.

Although the arguments of categorical perception, place of articulation, adaptation, and lateralization all support the view that language and neurology are closely tied together in man, they do not demonstrate the absence of similar mechanisms in animals. The presence of these phenomena in man is in and of itself insufficient data from which to conclude that speech perception is unique to man. As Kuhl and Padden (1986) argue, though the claim may be made that speech is processed by a special mechanism, this claim can be tested only by examining nonhuman animals' perception of speech. Kuhl and Padden (1986) present data on chinchillas and macaques suggesting that animals probably do share similar tendencies toward categorical perception of speech, with regard to both voice-onset time and place of articulation. There are, however, many other aspects of speech perception, such as context effects, trading relations, syllable perception, talker recognition, and crossmodal perception, that have not yet been tested with animals.

The argument that syntactic capacity is unique to man is somewhat easier to uphold because no animal engages in a behavior we recognize as language. Moreover, the natural communication systems of our closest living animal relatives, the nonhuman primates, are often characterized as heavily prewired and severely limited in function (Wilson, 1975). Although some recent evidence suggests that learning may play at least a moderate role in the development of nonhuman primate vocal skills (Seyfarth, Cheney, & Marler, 1980), at present it appears to be a very constrained type of learning in which any modification that can occur is highly canalized. However, Chomsky's syntactical acquisition device is equally constrained in many ways. Although the words, pronunciation, and surface structure can vary, the deep-structure rules are considered innate and unalterable.

If Lieberman's evolutionary hypothesis is correct regarding the co-development of peripheral organs and central processors, it may be that not only human beings but other animals as well possess neuronal mechanisms that allow them to parse their own calls in unique ways, at both an acoustical and a syntactical level. Cleveland and Snowdon (1982) argued that a structural grammar is not adequate to describe the sequencing of various calls in cotton-top tamarins. Consequently they devised a simple phrase-structure grammar to account for the sequences they documented. They also argued that contextual information was embedded in some call sequences.

If we accept the position that humans understand and speak language only because we are uniquely adapted to do so, then we must also entertain the concomitant possibility that other primates are similarly endowed with their own syntactical encoding devices and auditory processing devices. It also follows that lacking an ability to make the proper acoustical and syntactical distinctions, we will be unable to find relationships between particular sounds and their referents in the vocalizations of other primates. Lacking their special neuronal mechanisms, we are bound to forever perceive their sounds only as a cacophony of emotions, totally unaware of the structure, meaning, and syntax that are present.

However, lest we become too optimistic that language lies only in the ear of the perceiver and has relatively little to do with other aspects of intelligence, it should be noted that no animal has attempted to teach us its language as we attempt to teach other men, or animals, who do not knows ours. Thus, at the very least, it must be said that if other animals possess something akin to human language, they are less aware of its value. Even very young children will attempt to teach words to other children.

Recent Developments in the Field of Ape Language

New evidence has come to the fore that clearly challenges the tenet that both speech processing and syntactical parsing are unique to the human species (Greenfield & Savage-Rumbaugh, 1986; Savage-Rumbaugh, McDonald, Sevcik, Hopkins, & Rubert, 1986; Savage-Rumbaugh, Sevcik, Rumbaugh, & Rubert, 1985). This evidence is provided by the study of a new and little-known species of ape, *Pan paniscus*—the pygmy chimpanzee.

Pygmy chimpanzees are rare both in captivity and in the wild. It is at present illegal to export them from Zaire (the only country in which they are found in the wild), and there are fewer than 50 in captivity. The entirety of their habitat is now severely threatened by logging, and it is expected that they will not be able to survive in the field for more than a few generations.

Unlike other apes, pygmy chimpanzees exhibit close male-female ties, and males participate in the care of the offspring (Kuroda, 1984; Patterson, 1979). The strong male-female ties are maintained, in part, by the continuous receptivity of the female. Ventroventral copulation is common. Social-sexual bonds also exist between individuals of the same sex. Food sharing is frequent, even between adults and especially between males and females (Kuroda, 1984; Thompson-Handler, Malenky, & Badrian, 1984). Eye contact is especially prevalent in pygmy chimpanzees, as are frequent and complex gestures (Savage-Rumbaugh & Wilkerson, 1978; Savage-Rumbaugh, Wilkerson, & Bakeman, 1977). All these traits differentiate the pygmy chimpanzee from other great apes. More important, the traits that separate the pygmy chimpanzee from other apes all exist in modern man. Many of them, such as the continuous receptivity of the female and the prevalent food sharing between adults of different sexes, were formerly presumed to be unique to man.

Recent studies of this species have shown that, unlike other apes, pygmy chimpanzees acquire symbols without training. Like children, they comprehend symbols before they begin to produce them. Not only can they comprehend and use graphic symbols, they can also comprehend human speech. Unlike other chimpanzees, they do not seem to acquire symbols piecemeal. The representational aspects of symbol usage are easily grasped, with no training required. They are able to utilize symbols properly with the referent absent and to differentiate between naming and requesting without being trained to do so. They show definite concordance between symbol usage and their nonverbal behavior (Savage-Rumbaugh, in press; Savage-Rumbaugh et al., 1986; Savage-Rumbaugh, Rumbaugh, & McDonald, 1985; Savage-Rumbaugh et al., 1985). They appear to have the capacity to construct a rudimentary grammar. The present report extends these findings to cover the pygmy chimpanzee's comprehension of synthetic speech and complex sentences.

Method and Subject

The principal subject of this study is a young male pygmy chimpanzee, Kanzi, who is at present 6 years old. Kanzi was born in captivity, at the Yerkes Regional Primate Research Center, on October 28, 1980. Kanzi was assigned to the Language Research Project at 6 months of age, along with his mother, Matata, a wild-caught female who had also served as a subject in previous studies of nonverbal communication (Savage-Rumbaugh & Wilkerson, 1978; Savage-Rumbaugh et al., 1977).

The primary medium of communication used with Kanzi is a visual geometric symbol system that has been described in detail elsewhere (Savage-Rumbaugh, 1986). Geometric symbols are arranged on a board attached to a speech synthesizer. When a symbol is touched, the synthesizer "speaks" the appropriate English word. At present there are 256 symbols on Kanzi's keyboard. He has demonstrated mastery of 150 of these symbols.

Kanzi's human companions provide him with a communicative model by using the keyboard when they wish to talk with him or with each other. Because the keyboard has a limited number of symbols, these models also add speech to the keyboard communications. Examples of sentences directed to Kanzi or to other caretakers are given in Table 1. Those words that are on the keyboard are shown in italics. These symbols are touched as the speaker (and the synthesizer) says the English word. The remaining words are produced in English alone. When conversation is needed but the keyboard is not nearby, English is used. Spontaneous gestures may also accompany English words. Most of these gestures are indicative or iconic, though some American Sign Language signs are used. None of the people who work with Kanzi are fluent signers, though most know some signs and use them when it seems appropriate. Any interpretable communication is accepted from Kanzi, whether it is vocal, gestural, lexical, or nonverbal. If, for example, Kanzi can get his message across by pointing, as is often the case, then pointing is accepted.

There is one exception to this general policy. If Kanzi grabs food or objects from someone, or if he jumps or pulls on them, he is asked to use his keyboard rather than to grab and shove. This exception is made not in the interest of language instruction, but to maintain social harmony. People resent having objects grabbed from their hands or being shoved when no playful intent has been announced. Moreover, Kanzi seems to use grabbing and shoving as a means of contesting authority.

216

NEBRASKA SYMPOSIUM ON MOTIVATION 1987

Table 1

Samples of Lexigrams and English Input Kanzi Receives

I'd like to *ball tickle* Kanzi. (11:08)
Would you like to *ball tickle* also? (11:08:20)

We can *open* some *food*. (11:08:45)
You did want *food?* Let's *open*. (11:09)

We're *outdoors* and we need a *shirt on*.   (11:15:26)
I was *throwing* the *ball*. (11:16:23)

You want to *bite?* OK, I'll *bite* Kanzi. (11:18:48)
You're *grabbing Phil's shoe*. (11:19)
You're *pushing Phil off, push Phil off*. (11:19:20)

Now *Kanzi* has the *ball*. (11:12:42)
Oh, *Kanzi's hiding* the *ball*. (11:21:50)
Look, a *stick*, let's *grab* the *stick*. (11:22:35)

Kanzi, were you trying to say *hide?* (11:23:07)
Are you interested in going to look for a *surprise?* (11:23:45)
Crisscross corner's surprise! (11:23:50)
It might be a *food surprise*. (11:24:10)

Yes, I'll *tickle* and *bite* you. (11:47:39)
Yes, that's your *collar*. (11:48:30)

I was thinking . . . maybe I would *slap Kanzi*. (11:48:40)
You'd like me to *slap* on this area? That's called the *tummy*.
    (11:48:50)
Yes, let's *slap* the *tummy* area. (11:49)

Often, when asked to use his keyboard instead of grabbing an item, he refuses because he does not really want the item. He simply wants to see if he can take it.

Although Kanzi's keyboard (see Figure 1) is portable, it often proves difficult to carry it into parts of the heavily wooded forest that surrounds the laboratory. When this is the case we take along a nonspeech keyboard, reducing the weight from about 10 lbs to a few ounces (Figure 2).

From approximately March to October, Kanzi's food is dispersed daily to 16–20 locations within the 55 acre forest that surrounds the Lan-

FIGURE 1. Kanzi uses his keyboard to tell the experimenter that he sees M&Ms in the picture she is holding. The keyboard is mounted vertically on the wall, and the spoken word "M&M" is produced by a speech synthesizer as Kanzi presses on the symbol.

FIGURE 2. Outdoors the same symbols are used, but speech is not produced. The symbols are displayed photographically and are covered with Durasel to protect them. Here Kanzi is holding the keyboard up with his left hand while commenting "groom" with his right hand before grooming himself.

guage Research Center. To obtain this food, Kanzi travels from place to place with human companions. He uses the keyboard to indicate where he wishes to travel, and he can reliably guide naïve human observers to the locations he indicates (Savage-Rumbaugh et al., 1986). During the day he repeatedly attempts to engage companions in games of hide, keepaway, chase, grab, tickle, play bite, and so on. He often spontaneously helps in simple projects such as gathering sticks for a campfire, pulling weeds from the garden, stringing up a hammock between trees, or clearing new trails. Kanzi is not caged but is with human companions throughout the day. He can visit his mother whenever he wishes for as long as he wants, and he stays with her at night.

Although Kanzi's rearing situation clearly differs from that of a wild chimpanzee, we make every effort to provide as natural an environment as possible. We make no attempt to treat Kanzi as a child, to get him to wear clothes, or to teach him human values. Instead, we try to do the kinds of things that seem to interest him naturally, such as playing chase and finding food in the woods. The days are very loosely structured, with Kanzi's desires generally determining which activity takes precedence during most of the day. We put no pressure upon him to learn or use symbols, and nothing is withheld from him contingent upon symbol usage.

The criterion for determining when a word should be listed as a member of Kanzi's vocabulary differs significantly from that utilized by other researchers (Fouts, 1973; Gardner & Gardner, 1971; Terrace, 1979). These studies required only that symbol production appear to be appropriate and that the sign occur on a specific number of consecutive days. We require not only that Kanzi produce the symbol, but also that he demonstrate he knows what that symbol represents on 9 out of 10 occasions when he is asked to do so (Savage-Rumbaugh et al., 1986).

For example, if Kanzi requested a trip to the "trailer," he would be told, "Yes, we can go to the trailer." However, only if he then led the experimenter to this location would a correct behavioral concordance be scored. If he asked for a specific food, such as "hamburger," he would be presented with a number of favorite foods (apples, hamburger, peanuts, hot dogs, Coke, etc.), and note would be made of whether his requested food agreed with his selected food. Alternatively, a request for "hamburger" might be acknowledged by saying, "Yes, let's go get hamburger." Only if Kanzi then correctly led to the location where hamburger was to be found would a concordance be scored. On still other occasions, if a number of foods had been gathered in the woods and were being carried in the backpack, Kanzi might touch "hamburger" and point to the backpack. We would then answer, "Yes, you can open the backpack and find the hamburger." If Kanzi correctly sorted through the other foods and pulled out the hamburger, a concordance would be scored.

Kanzi was not required to demonstrate a concordance with every single symbol usage, since this would have produced a very unnatural communicative situation. Instead, correspondences were obtained when they seemed to fit naturally, as in the example above where Kanzi asked for hamburger and pointed to the backpack when it happened to be full of a number of foods. If for example, he asked for hamburger while we were cooking it, while we were putting it in the backpack, or while we were eating, it did not seem to make sense to stop the ongoing activity to construct a setting appropriate to obtaining a concordance. In such instances Kanzi was simply given the hamburger, and no concordance was scored.

All of Kanzi's utterances were recorded from the time he began to use the keyboard at 2 years, six months of age until 6 years of age. When Kanzi used the portable keyboard, data were recorded by hand and entered into the computer later. Kanzi's utterances did not occur rapidly. They averaged approximately seven per hour, making the task of taking real-time data feasible. Videotapes were made once a month to validate real-time data (see Savage-Rumbaugh, 1986). All utterances were recorded in the order of occurrence, and multisymbol utterances were recorded in the order in which the symbols occurred. Contextual information was noted for each utterance and particularly for each combination. In addition, each utterance was coded according to communicative function using the following categories: spontaneous request, spontaneous statement, spontaneous comment, structured request, structured statement, structured naming. Structured utterances were those that were elicited in some way by the teacher—for example, by asking Kanzi to name a food he had found. Spontaneous utterances were those that occurred in the absence of any behavior on the part of the caretaker designed to elicit an utterance.

Data were recorded not only on Kanzi's lexigram use but on his comprehension of both single words and complex utterances. Whenever Kanzi demonstrated comprehension of an utterance that was not accompanied by glance, gesture, or other nonverbal signal, that utterance and Kanzi's behavior were recorded. Most of the time either the context or the gestures could not be excluded, and so comprehension of an utterance was not recorded. Generally, utterances that were recorded were made specifically to evaluate Kanzi's comprehension. Throughout the day, Kanzi responded appropriately to many utterances that were made for communicative purposes and not explicitly to test his comprehension. These were not recorded. A number of specific criteria had to be met before comprehension could be scored. These were:

1. The behavior could not be a common one that would be expected in that context.
2. The context itself could not suggest the specific behavior.
3. Glances and gestures that might aid in the comprehension of the utterance could not occur.
4. Kanzi's response had to occur immediately after the utterance.
5. The setting had to support the possibility of a number of alternative behaviors as well.

During part of each day, Kanzi was engaged in some type of formal testing or task-oriented activity. Food reward was not used during any testing. These activities permitted a more structured assessment of the skills Kanzi displayed in the natural interchange that took place during the rest of the day. During formal test sessions, appropriate controls were employed to guard against contextual cuing, since this could not be done during natural exchanges. Stimuli were randomly presented, and Kanzi was asked to make a single response. To date, formal testing has concentrated only upon single-word comprehension and usage. Four types of tests were used in the present study. Food reward was *not* used during any test.

In the first test, Kanzi listened as the experimenter pronounced an English word. He was then shown three lexigrams and asked to select the one he had just heard. The lexigrams were presented so that the experimenter could not see them as Kanzi made his selection (see Figure 3). During this test the alternatives were selected randomly, with the restriction that at least one be from the same category of items as the sample. This restriction was employed because we found that Kanzi could often correctly identify lexigrams he was learning, but did not yet know well, if they were paired with items from very different categories. For example, though Kanzi could not identify the lexigram "kiwi" when it was paired with "grapes" and "M&Ms," he could often select it when it was paired with "key" and "lever." This was because he knew that

FIGURE 3. The basic test format used with Kanzi is illustrated here. Three lexigrams are randomly chosen and arranged in a test booklet for each trial. The experimenter knows the target item but does not know its location, since the items are arranged by another experimenter. The experimenter pronounces the English word, then opens the test booklet so that only Kanzi can see the choices. Kanzi makes his selection by touching the item of his choice, and the experimenter notes whether his arm is in the left, right, or center position. After Kanzi has made his selection, the experimenter looks to determine which item he chose. If Kanzi appears to move his arm so that his selection is unclear, he is asked to repeat the choice before the experimenter views the items.

the "kiwi" lexigram represented a food, but he was not certain which food. Thus the restriction that at least one alternative be from the same class as the sample served to make it more difficult for Kanzi to sort out the lexigrams he knew well from those he was still learning. No target item was presented twice in succession.

We tested a total of 202 lexigrams, presenting each on two to four nonconsecutive occasions. If Kanzi was incorrect on the first two trials, the item was not presented again. If Kanzi was incorrect on one of three trials, the item was presented a fourth time. On each trial the sample lexigram was paired with a different set of alternatives. Items were presented by two different experimenters, and between 5 and 20 items were tested on a given day. Testing took place between April 21, 1986, and July 1, 1986, when Kanzi was 5 years, 6 months old. This test battery was given approximately 18 months after a similar test of speech comprehension that had covered the first 17 months of his lexigram acquisition, as reported in Savage-Rumbaugh et al. (1986). In the intervening period, Kanzi was neither drilled nor formally tested on speech comprehension.

In the second test Kanzi again listened to an English word, but now the word was presented by a speech synthesizer instead of a person (see Figures 4–6). Items selected for this test were those that Kanzi had correctly identified during the first test. Each item was again presented three times, with the restriction that no item follow itself. Alternatives were randomly selected with the restriction that at least one be of the same category as the sample. The alternatives were paired with different samples during each presentation. Synthesized speech was produced by a Votrax synthesizer attached to an Epson computer. Words were typed into the computer to produce a synthesized utterance, whose form depends upon how the word was spelled. If, for example, a vowel did not seem to be pronounced clearly by the synthesizer, the pronunciation could be changed by altering the spelling of the word. In programming this synthesizer, only the text-to-phonemic-conversion capacities were utilized. There was no variation of rate, stress, inflection, or pitch. By eliminating these cues from the speech output, it was possible to preclude the selection of the appropriate lexigram on some basis other than phonemic input.

In the third test, Kanzi listened to the words that were correctly identified in Test 1, but now the word was presented by a tape recorder instead of by the experimenter. Kanzi wore headphones, so that only he knew which word was presented on any given trial (see Figures 7–9). The experimenter did not know any of the alternatives and could not see the lexigrams as Kanzi made his selection. The target item was randomly determined on any given trial and was located on the tape by a second experimenter, who also prepared the test items for presentation to Kanzi. The first experimenter presented the items to Kanzi and recorded his selection; however, she was unaware of the target item and did not view the location of any of the items until after Kanzi had made his choice. As in the earlier tests, alternatives varied for each trial, and no item was allowed to follow itself. One alternative was selected from the same class as the target item. The alternatives used in each of these

Figure 4. Experimenter 1 arranges randomly selected lexigrams in the test folder.

Figure 5. Experimenter 1 passes the test folder to Experimenter 2, who does not know what alternatives are available or where the target item is situated. Experimenter 2 presses a symbol (not visible to Kanzi) that produces synthesized speech, then she opens the test booklet.

FIGURE 6. Kanzi selects a lexigram.

tests varied randomly across all tests and thus differed for all three tests. We administered a total of 112 trials in this test condition.

In the fourth test, Kanzi again listened to an English word pronounced by the experimenter and selected that word from among three alternatives. However, one of the alternatives was now a word that shared either the same initial phoneme, the same terminal phoneme, or both. For example, the experimenter might pronounce "shirt" and then present Kanzi with the lexigrams for "shirt," "shot," and "clover." On a later, nonconsecutive trial, Kanzi would be presented with the word "shot" and the lexigrams for "shirt," "bark," and "shot." Pairs of twenty phonemically similar words were used during this test.

Results

TEST 1

The results of the test of speech comprehension are shown in Table 2. Of the 194 items presented on this test, Kanzi achieved a score of 100% across all three presentations on 109 items and demonstrated 75% correct identification of three of four presentations on 40 items. He was at

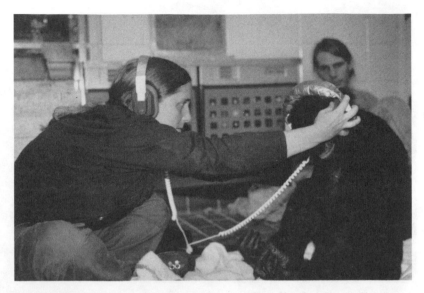

FIGURE 7. The experimenter puts headphones on herself and on Kanzi. She cannot hear the item, but Kanzi feels more comfortable wearing the headphones if others have them on also.

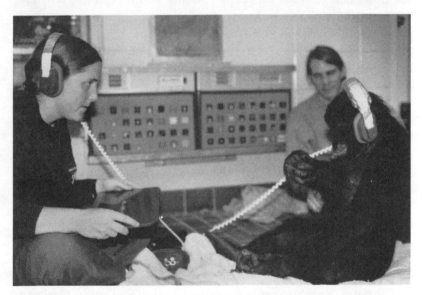

FIGURE 8. The experimenter waits to open the test booklet until Kanzi signals her that he has heard the word and is ready to make his selection. The experimenter does not know what alternatives are in the test booklet, nor does she know which item Kanzi hears.

FIGURE 9. Kanzi listens to the word.

or below chance on the remaining 45 items, and we concluded that he had not yet learned these words. The results of this test revealed that Kanzi's vocabulary had grown steadily during the 18 months since the previous test. Additionally, the results were highly consistent between the two tests. Of the 66 items Kanzi knew at 46 months of age, he scored accurately on all but 3 at 69 months of age.

The three items he missed on the more recent test were "dig," "Sue's office," and "childside" (a term used to refer to the front part of the building and the surrounding area, where research is done with human children). "Dig" was used frequently with Kanzi when he was younger and a garden was regularly maintained. As he grew older and a number of additional chimpanzee subjects were added to the project, the garden was abandoned. The word "dig" was rarely used anymore and apparently dropped from Kanzi's vocabulary. Kanzi had used the term primarily to refer to the location of the garden (where we dig) rather than to the act of digging. At the time of the second test, there was no garden on the laboratory grounds.

Kanzi began to show confusion regarding the "Sue's office" lexigram once he acquired my name. Before this time Sue's office was closely associated with visits to me as I worked in my office. Once my name be-

Table 2

Comprehension of Spoken English

100%			75%	Chance
A-frame	Group room	Refrigerator	Away	Bad
Apple	Hamburger	Rock	Butter	Bedroom
Austin	Hammer	Rubber band	Chase	Blue
Ball	Head	Salt	Chicken	Butt
Balloon	Hide	Scrubby pine	Coconut	Cabinet
Banana	Hot dog	nook	Coffee	Childside
Bark	Hug	Sherman	Dessert	Come
Bean (green)	Ice	Shirt	Go	Dig
Bill	Jeannine	Slap	Gully gushers	Explore
Bite	Jello	Sour cream	Hilltop	Fish
Blackberry	Keys	Sparkler	Hot	Flatrock
Blanket	Kolor	Stick	Jelly	Good
Blueberry	Kool-Aid	Straw	Juice	Grape
Bowl	Leaf	Strawberry	Keepaway	Hat
Bread	Lemonade	Sue	Kiwi	In
Bug	Lettuce	Surprise	Lever	Kanzi
Bunny	Light	Sweet potato	Linda	Kelly
Burrito	Magnet	Taco	Liz	Log cabin
Camper cabin	M&Ms	Tickle	Mary Ann	Lookout point
Can opener	Matata	Tomato	Money	Mary
Car	Melon	Toothbrush	Mop	Midway
Carrot	Milk	Toothpaste	Mouth	Monster
Cereal	Mulika	Turtle	Observation	Nail
Cheese	Mushroom	TV	room	No
Cherry	Mushroom trail	Umbrella	Outdoors	Noodles
Chow	Needle (pine)	Vacuum	Perrier	Now
Clay	Oil	Wash	Phil	Off
Clover	Onion	Water	Pillow	On
Coke	Open	(White) potato	Pomegranate	Orangutan
Collar	Orange		Rain	Pee
Colony room	Orange drink		Sandpile	Phone
Crisscross	Orange juice		Shoe	Pinkie
Dog	Out		Snake	Play
Egg	Paint		Soap	Privet berry
Fire	Paper		Staff office	Push
Food	Pinecone		Sue's gate	Red
Funny face	Peas		Toolroom	Rose
Gibbon	Peaches		Towel	Spoon
Give	Peanut		Trailer	Sue's office
Grab	Play yard		Velvet plant	Sugar
Groom	Raisin		Yogurt	T-room
				Throw
				Trash
				Tummy
				Yellow
Totals:		109	40	45

came a part of Kanzi's working vocabulary, he seemed to have difficulty using the lexigram that referred to my office, as though the office itself had no salient existence for him apart from me. The choice of a single lexigram to represent the place we called "Sue's office" was probably confusing for Kanzi. A separate lexigram was used to represent the location we call "staff office." No single individual was associated with this location. Kanzi presumably identified the sound of "office" with these locations and the sound of "Sue" with me but was confused by the possessive, "Sue's office."

Many of the items Kanzi did not know on the test reflected rather abstract concepts (good, now, and explore), or things that Kanzi typically showed little interest in, such as colors (red, blue, and yellow) or prepositions (off, on, and in). Others were things whose function Kanzi seemed to understand only partially, such as "trash." Typically, when we asked Kanzi to throw something in the trash, he threw it into any handy large container. This container might contain blankets to go to the laundry, dirty dishes to be washed, or trash. He seemed to have no concept of "trash" as something that was to be discarded or was unwanted and consequently found no reason to call something "trash" of his own accord.

Kanzi also understood "hat" in a somewhat ambiguous way. To him, hats served a single purpose; he pulled them down over his eyes and ran around the room unable to see, bumping into things. We tended to refer to this activity as "hide," and Kanzi almost always responded appropriately if we invited him to play "hat hide." He would do the same thing with blankets or shirts, but these items also served other purposes. He used blankets to build nests, and shirts kept him warm outdoors. However, the idea of a "hat" as something to wear on one's head made no sense to Kanzi. He viewed it only as an extension of the hide-chase game and consequently did not learn the lexigram, though he seemed to understand the spoken word well.

Other lexigrams Kanzi did not know reflected a real confusion among similar items, such as "spoon." If Kanzi was asked to get a spoon out of the drawer, he always retrieved a utensil, but it could be any utensil. He did not seem to differentiate the function of spoons, knives, and forks. He preferred not to use a spoon himself and did so only when asked.

TEST 2

Kanzi's facility with English words raised the obvious question of exactly what sort of speech signals he was attending to. It seemed unlikely, given the wide variety of words Kanzi comprehended, that he was responding to intonation, stress, or other nonphonemic cues. Nonetheless, since pygmy chimpanzees do not speak English, it has been widely assumed that they lack the necessary neuronal structures to process speech at a phonemic level. The extra cues of stress and intonation, always present in normal speech, can be removed by using synthesized speech. The Votrax speech synthesizer used in the present study assigns a sound to each letter of the English alphabet. Words are formed simply by combining letters, as one does when a word is spelled. Certain parameters within the Votrax program alter the way a consonant is pronounced depending upon the adjacent vowels. The result is tolerably interpretable speech that sounds monotone, mechanical, and clipped. It is devoid of syllabic stress and intonation. In some cases, if one does not know the word being produced by the synthesizer, one cannot interpret it. Approximately 35% of the words produced by the Votrax synthesizer are not recognized by normal adults (Punzi and Kraat, 1986). According to Rentschler (1986), the types of sounds most difficult to identify when produced by a speech synthesizer are (1) nasals (such as the m and n sounds in man); (2) voiced continuants (such as the v in van and the z in zoo); and (3) voiced plosives (b, d, g).

The words Kanzi successfully recognized in the preceding test were now represented using the speech synthesizer. Kanzi successfully identified 104 of these words (see Table 3). Like human subjects, he appeared to have greater difficulty with voiced syllables than with unvoiced ones, particularly if the voiced syllable was a plosive. He was significantly more likely to miss the word if the initial syllable was voiced than if it was unvoiced. He was even more likely to be incorrect if the initial syllable was a voiced plosive (see Table 4). However, he was capable of identifying a large number of voiced plosives, as Table 3 illustrates. Kanzi was not more likely to misidentify words with nasals, and his vocabulary contained no voiced continuants.

There appears to be only one initial consonant that Kanzi could not identify when it was produced by the speech synthesizer; this was the glide in wash and water. Since there were only two words beginning with this sound in Kanzi's vocabulary, it is not possible to determine conclusively that he could not identify the synthesized version of these words. Kanzi's performance on the remaining items leaves little doubt that he is responding to the phonemic speech cues and not to stress or intonation. In fact, his ability to identify the synthesized speech is extraordinary. When the same words were presented to a normal 4-year-old hu-

Table 3

Comprehension of Synthesized Speech

100%		75%	Chance	
A-frame	Orange	Balloon	Away	Scrubby pine nook
Apple	Out	Bark	Bill	Sherman
Austin	Outdoors	Bread	Bowl	Shoe
Ball	Peaches	Bunny	Burrito	Soap
Banana	Peanut	Car	Can opener	Sour cream
Bean (green)	Pine needle	Cherry	Chicken	Towel
Bite	Play yard	Coffee	Clay	Wash
Blackberry	Potato	Coke	Coconut	Water
Blanket	Rain	Crisscross	Dessert	
Blueberry	Raisin	Egg	Dog	
Bug	Refrigerator	Groom	Gibbon	
Camper cabin	Rock	Gully gushers	Give	
Carrot	Salt	Hide	Go	
Cereal	Sandpile	Hot dog	Group room	
Chase	Shot	Jello	Head	
Cheese	Slap	Keepaway	Hilltop	
Childside	Snake	Linda	Hug	
Chow	Sparkler	Magnet	Jeannine	
Clover	Staff office	Matata	Kiwi	
Collar	Stick	Mop	Leaf	
Colony room	Straw	Mushroom trail	Lettuce	
Fire	Strawberry	Orange juice	Light	
Food	Sue's gate	Paint	Liz	
Funny face	Surprise	Shirt	Mary Ann	
Grab	Tickle	Sue	Mouth	
Hamburger	Toolroom	Sweet potato	Mulika	
Hammer	Toothpaste	Taco	Nail	
Hot	TV	Tomato	Observation	
Ice	Velvet plant	Toothbrush	room	
Juice		Trailer	Onion	
Key		Turtle	Open	
Kool-Aid		Umbrella	Orange drink	
Lemonade		Vacuum	Paper	
Lever		Yogurt	Peas	
M&Ms			Perrier	
Melon			Phil	
Milk			Pillow	
Money			Pinecone	
Mushroom			Pomegranate	
Oil			Rubber band	
Totals:	69	34		47

man subject, only 33 words were correctly identified on the first
encounter. Of course, Kanzi has heard these words more often; nonetheless, his accurate comprehension of them indicates that a species not
preadapted for speech can master a high degree of speech comprehension without specific training. Kanzi's comprehension apparently relies
on phonemic processing mechanisms similar to those used by human
beings.

Table 4
Types of Synthesized Speech Errors Made by Kanzi

	Correct	Incorrect
Initial syllable voiced	50	32
Initial syllable unvoiced	50	18
Initial syllable voiced plosive	16	16
Initial syllable unvoiced plosive	27	6

TEST 3

In both of the tests reported above, the experimenter knew the alternative Kanzi was asked to select on any given trial; however, she did not know where that alternative was in the test booklet, and she could not see Kanzi as he made his response. The purpose of the third battery of tests was to eliminate any possibility that the tester's knowledge of the correct item to be selected on a given trial could, in some unexplained manner, be cuing Kanzi to the correct response.

The cuing explanation is highly unlikely, given that Kanzi did make many errors on many words, as Tables 1, 2, and 3 indicate. Words that he knew were identified consistently across presentations and with different experimenters who were not familiar with his performance on given words on earlier trials. The consistency of errors on unknown words and lack of errors on known words is a strong indication that cuing was not occurring.

Nonetheless, because of the explicit criticism ape-language studies have received in the past (Sebeok & Umiker-Sebeok, 1980) and the lingering suspicion that Clever Hans has placed over the field of animal communication, we designed a test to eliminate all knowledge on the part of the experimenter by asking Kanzi to wear headphones. The target items were recorded in advance, and the experimenter did not know which was the target item Kanzi heard on any given trial; she simply noted his choice. On the 109 trials of this test, Kanzi made only three errors. Clearly, he had not been dependent upon cues from an experimenter who knew the target item.

TEST 4

In all the tests above, alternatives were randomly selected. This meant words that sounded like the target item were paired with it only by chance. Consequently, when given a choice between three words, which may or may not have sounded alike, Kanzi was able to select the correct word, even when the signal source was considerably degraded by synthesized speech. But what about words that sound very similar? Could Kanzi still select the target item correctly, or would his speech discrimination skills begin to break down? To answer this question 24 pairs of similar words were drawn from items in Kanzi's vocabulary (determined by his performance on tests with normal speech input samples). These 20 matched phonemic pairs were then presented to Kanzi, interspersed among 157 trials of nonmatched items. Each pair was presented four times, twice for each target word.

The results of this test (shown in Table 5) revealed that Kanzi could make accurate phonemic distinctions among pairs of words that shared initial syllables, such as ball-balloon, as well as among words that shared terminating syllables, such as head-bread. Kanzi correctly identified both target items in 21 of these 24 pairs. In some cases this meant he was able to differentiate pairs of words that shared both initial and final phonemes, such as clover-collar. These test results provide further support for the view that Kanzi is processing information phonetically and that he is processing the whole word as a unit, not just a portion of it.

The pairs that were the most difficult for Kanzi were also those that had double phonemic overlap—shot-shirt and lighter-light. The string-straw pair also proved difficult, but these items share a physical similarity as well as a phonemic similarity (both are long, pliable, and thin, and Kanzi plays with them in an identical manner).

SENTENCE COMPREHENSION

Kanzi's receptive ability in natural settings is considerably greater than has been demonstrated in controlled tests to date. He readily responds to complex sentences that require him to comprehend not just individual words but relationships between words. At present it is difficult, with blind experimenters, to test this capacity in ways that are comparable to the single-word data. As Kanzi carries out requests with real objects, it

Table 5

Phonetically Similar Pairs

A-frame	Apple
Ball	Bark
Ball	Balloon
Bread	Head
Carrot	Car
Cherry	Cheese
Clay	Clover
Clover	Collar
Give	Grab
Grab	Groom
Head	Bread
Hug	Hide
Leaf	Light
Lighter —————————	Light
Melon	Onion
Orange	Onion
Paper	Peaches
Peaches	Peas
Peanut	Peaches
Salt	Shot
Shot —————————	Shirt
String —————————	Straw
Toothpaste	Toothbrush
Turtle	Tickle

Note: Connected pairs are those Kanzi could not discriminate.

is possible to see his responses; hence cuing cannot be ruled out. He has not advanced to the point where he can listen to a complex request and then carry it out in the next room. Typically, after carrying out one of two requests such as, "Put the sour cream in the bowl," he begins to play with the available objects and ignores requests that he do specific things with them. He rebels just as young children rebel when given commands to do things they see no reason for and do not want to do. His vocabulary also does not lend itself to this type of testing, since most of the verbs reflect social games.

It would, of course, be possible to get Kanzi to carry out repeated commands if he received food rewards for doing so (and if he were deprived of enough food the rest of the day to motivate him sufficiently). However, this would be tantamount to teaching Kanzi specific responses to specific commands rather than probing the competency that has developed naturally. Consequently, we have avoided this situation.

In nontest contexts, however, it is possible to ask Kanzi to do only one or two things on any given occasion. By carefully avoiding situations in which the context might guide the behavior (for example, asking Kanzi to put the soap in the washer while pointing to the washer and handing him the soap), it was possible to determine Kanzi's approximate level of receptive comprehension.

Using this method, we obtained 310 instances of receptive comprehension across a three-month period in the fall of 1986, when Kanzi was 6 years of age. In each instance, we directed a vocal request composed of two or more words toward Kanzi when he appeared to be happy and in a cooperative mood. The request was made in English, and when they were available on Kanzi's keyboard, the speaker also touched lexigrams while voicing the utterance. The request was designed to be appropriate to the context but not determined by it. For example, Kanzi was asked to play a game of "grab lever" when other games (tickle, chase, etc.) were being played and when a number of objects were lying about in addition to the lever. He would not be asked to put the sour cream in the cooler in such a context; that request would be made as an area was being cleaned up and things were being placed in the trash, in the backpack, and in the cooler before departing. In both instances we took care not to use glances and gestures, and in many cases Kanzi had his back to the speaker and carried out the instruction without looking to the speaker for elaboration. Experimenters were asked to select utterances they thought Kanzi could understand based on their daily interaction with him. In some cases Kanzi showed comprehension of a sentence that was not planned as a test item but that met the other criteria. This is illustrated in the following example:

> Kanzi is playing with a ball near the riverbank, hitting it, tossing it around, slapping it, and so on. The experimenter asks (not intending to test Kanzi), "Are you going to throw your ball in the river?" and Kanzi answers by picking up the ball and throwing it into the river.

In this example there were a number of possible actions and a number of directions in which Kanzi could have thrown the ball. There were other objects that could be thrown; however, since Kanzi was playing with the ball at the time the utterance was produced, it is possible that he did not comprehend "ball" (although the single-word test data clear-

Table 6
Frequency of Different Sentence Types Directed Toward Kanzi

Action-object	107
Object-action	13
Object-location	8
Action-location	23
Total	151
Action-object-location	36
Object-action-location	9
Action-location-object	3
Agent-action-object	8
Total	56
Action-recipient	13
Action-object-recipient	19
Action-recipient-object	2
Object-action-recipient	2
Other	67
Total	103

ly show that he can). However, he must have comprehended "throw" and "river" to act as he did. Kanzi had never previously thrown his ball into the river, nor was it something he had watched others do. The action seemed to be initiated in response to the verbal suggestion, since Kanzi was not specifically directing the ball toward the river before this question.

In testing these utterances experimenters are also asked not to test Kanzi on any utterances used so frequently in a given context that he would perhaps have carried out these actions regardless of what was said to him. For example, if Kanzi was playing a game of hide and seek with a blanket, he would not be asked, "Can you cover your head with the blanket?" because this would be a probable event regardless of what was said to him.

Nearly all of the 310 utterances were unique, but on a few occasions two experimenters independently selected identical utterances. The types of utterances, and their frequency, that were directed to Kanzi are listed in Table 6. Forty of the utterances were classified by a second party, and reliability of classification across coders was 91%. Across all utterance types Kanzi responded appropriately to 298 utterances. An ex-

Table 7

Examples of Different Sentence Types Addressed to Kanzi

Action-object
"Would you please carry the straw?"

Kanzi looks over a number of objects that are on the table and selects the straw. He carries it as he goes to the next room with the caretaker.

Object-action
"Would you like to ball chase?"

Kanzi looks around for a ball, finds one in his swimming pool, takes it out, comes over to the keyboard with it, and comments "chase."

Object-location
"Would you put some grapes in the swimming pool?"

Kanzi selects grapes from among several foods and tosses them in the swimming pool.

Action-location
"Let's chase to the A-frame."

Kanzi is climbing trees and has been ignoring things that are said to him. When he hears this, he comes down rapidly and runs to the A-frame.

Action-object-location
"I hid the surprise by my foot."

Kanzi has been told that a surprise is around somewhere, and he is looking for it. When he is given this clue, he immediately approaches the speaker and lifts up her foot.

Object-action-location
"Kanzi, the pinecone goes in your shirt."

Kanzi looks around till he finds a pinecone and puts it in his shirt.

ample of each type of utterance and Kanzi's behavior that indicated he comprehended the utterance are given in Table 7. Although Kanzi heard some of these utterances, such as "Give me your bowl" or "Put this in the trash," at least once almost every day, many others were novel and had rarely, if ever, been uttered to him before this occasion. The specific utterances Kanzi heard often are so noted in the appropriate tables.

The most frequent type of utterance directed toward Kanzi was an action-object utterance. Typically, action-object sequences were present in full sentences, such as "Could you get the bread out?" but only the action-object part was judged as being critical to the test of comprehension, since other parts of the sentence were not subject to verifica-

Table 7 *(continued)*

Action-location-object
"Go to the refrigerator and get a tomato."

Kanzi is playing in the water at the sink. When he hears this, he stops what he is doing, goes to the refrigerator, and gets out a tomato.

Agent-action-object
"Jeannine hid the pine needles in her shirt."

Kanzi is busy making a nest of blankets, branches, and pine needles. When he hears this he immediately walks over to Jeannine, lifts up her shirt, takes out the pine needles, and puts them in his nest.

Action-recipient
"Kanzi, chase Kelly."

Kanzi was chasing Liz when he heard this. He immediately stopped, ran over to Kelly, and signed chase.

Action-object-recipient
"Kanzi, please carry the cooler to Penny."

Kanzi was playing. He stopped, looked around till he found the cooler, then carried it to Penny.

Action-recipient-location
"Kanzi, would you give Panbanisha an onion?"

Kanzi looked around till he found a wild onion, pulled it out of the ground, and gave it to Panbanisha.

Action-recipient-object
"Go play with the dogs on the childside."

Kanzi ran around to the childside part of the laboratory and began to play with the dogs.

---

tion. For example, in this sentence "could" could not be contrasted with another modal word; Kanzi was almost always the addressee, and the experimenter looked in his direction when speaking to him; and "out" was the only place that the bread could have gone if Kanzi picked it up. However, there were other actions he could perform on the bread, and there were other objects in the cooler.

Kanzi responded appropriately to all but 2 of the 107 action-object utterances directed to him, 99 of which were unique. The action-object components of the various utterances are listed in Table 8. There were 25 different action words and 65 different object words used in these combinations. As Table 8 illustrates, many of the action-object combi-

Table 8

Action-Object Utterances Directed to Kanzi

Action Word	Object Word	Action Word	Object Word
Bring	straw	Get	Ziploc bag
Carry	(orang's) blanket	Give	blackberries
Carry	cooler	Give	blanket
Carry	straw	Give	bowl**
Chase	bug	Give	hat
Chase	light	Give	umbrella
Chase	umbrella**	Grab	ball
Check	velvet plant**	Grab	head
Do	another one**	Grab	lever
Eat	hot dogs	Grab	mouth
Find	blueberries	Grab	potato
Find	can opener**	Grab	shoe
Find	glass	Hand	water toy
Find	hot dog	(What) happened	(to) ball
Find	lever**	(What) happened*	(to) paper
Find	nut	Hide	toy
Find	orange	Keepaway	hat
Find	stick	Like	potato
Get	apple	Like	rubber band
Get	ball**	Like	water
Get	blanket**	Look	(for ball)
Get	blueberry	Look	(at) funny face
Get	bowl**	Look	(for) grapes
Get	bread	Look*	(for) mushrooms
Get	can opener**	Oil	tootsies
Get	cheese	Open	backpack**
Get	clipboard	Open	banana
Get	Coke	Open	door
Get	cold water	Open	hot dog
Get	collar**	Open	orange
Get	dessert	Open	sour cream
Get	hamburger	Pick up	keyboard
Get	it	Pick up	pine needle
Get	keys	Show	hand
Get	knife	Slap	bug
Get	M&Ms	Slap	butt**
Get	mushroom	Take	blanket**
Get	paper	Take (carry)	hot food
Get	pot of food	Throw	ball
Get	shirt**	Tickle	keys
Get	sour cream	Use	rock
Get	spoon	Want	balloon
Get	stick	Want	food (while you wait)
Get	straw	Want	orange
Get	tape	Want	orange juice
Get	toothpaste	Wash	it
Get	trash**	Wash	tomato
Get	umbrella	Where is	can opener**
Get	watch	Where is	glass
Get	(more) water		

*Kanzi responded inappropriately to these requests.
**These requests were directed to Kanzi very often.

nations were composed of words that were not a part of Kanzi's productive vocabulary and were not on his keyboard (get clipboard, pick up keyboard). Also, a wide variety of sentence frames were employed in posing these different combinations. For example:

1. Will you carry the orangutan's blanket?
2. Maybe you can bring the straw?
3. Do you want an orange?
4. Kanzi, can you get the clipboard?
7. We might check the velvet plants.
8. Why don't you get a bowl?
9. Can you find the hot dog?

Action-object frames were sometimes posed in the inverse order, as in the following examples:

1. I want to ball chase with you.
2. Let's pinecone chase.
3. Why don't you guys hat chase?

Most object-action inversions were used because the symbol "with" was not on Kanzi's keyboard. He especially likes to engage others in action-oriented games with an object. In such games the goal was to either touch or tickle the other party with the object and was glossed as "ball chase," "umbrella tickle," since it was not possible to ask, "Can you tickle me with the umbrella?" if one was using the keyboard. Constructions using "with" were produced when only the spoken word was used, but at times the object-action order was also used in English. The object-action constructions are listed in Table 9.

Although it is not clear that Kanzi can understand all parts of sentences like those above, it is clear that he can select the critical words from a wide variety of sentence types and respond appropriately. It is also obvious that he is not responding to the action and the object as though they were independent entities. Thus, when he hears a sentence like, "Can you carry the orang's blanket?" he does not start carrying the first object he sees and then go touch the blanket. Instead, he looks around for a blanket and executes the carrying action upon the blanket.

Twenty-three of the utterances directed to Kanzi were of the action-location type. Again, the sentences posed were more complex than the action-location comprehension attributed to him. Most of the action-location combinations utilized fixed locations in Kanzi's environment that

Table 9

Object-Action Utterances directed to Kanzi

Object Word	Action Word
Ball	chase**
Hat	do chasing**
Hat	slapping
Lever	tickle
Pinecone	chase**
Shoe	grab
Shoe	tickle
Stick	chase**
Stick	break
Towel	keepaway
Turtle	find
Umbrella	chase
Umbrella	tickle

Note: Kanzi responded appropriately to all requests.
**These requests were directed to Kanzi very frequently.

Table 10

Action-Location Utterances Directed to Kanzi

Action Word	Location Word	Action Word	Location Word
Chase	(to) A-frame**	Go	(to) fourtrax
Chase	(to) childside**	Go	(to) gully gushers**
Chase	(to) crisscross corners**	Go	(to) hot food**
Chase	(to) M&Ms**	Go	(to) lookout point**
Chase	(to) raisins**	Go	outdoors**
Chase	(to) Rose**	Go	(to) T-room**
Chase	(to) tree house**	Go	(to) toolroom**
Drive	(to) river**	Go look	(in) toolsite
Go	(to) A-frame**	Look	(in) backpack**
Go	(to) car**	Look	(in) mouth
Go	(to) childside**	Push	away
Go	(to) crisscross**		

Note: Kanzi responded correctly to all of these utterances.
**These sentences were frequently addressed to Kanzi.

were on his keyboard and were traveled to frequently (such as A-frame, tree house, childside). We utilized 4 different actions and 20 different locations, and all combinations in this category were unique (see Table 10).

Of the 23 combinations, 20 involved travel (either chasing or going) to a location. Thus the combinations of this group are, for the most part, a single type moving through space (rapidly or slowly) to a named por-

Table 11

Object-Location Utterances Directed to Kanzi

Object Word	Location Word
Bottom	where (is)
Can opener	(in) backpack
Grapes	(in) pool
Lettuce	(in) food bin
Shirt	group room
Strawberry	(in) backpack
Tummy	where (is)
Water	(in) mouth

Note: Kanzi responded correctly to all of these utterances.

tion of that space. However, when we consider the object-location utterances, we find that location terms are not limited in these constructions to stationary entities in space (see Table 11).

The same is true when we look at the three-term relations action-object-location, action-location-object, and object-action-location. Here we find a much wider variety of terms being used as locations. Apparently the fact that Kanzi was always the presumed actor in action-location combinations limited the types of actions and locations that could occur.

In the most common three-term relation (action-object-location) listed in Table 12, there are 25 locations, and all but one of them (river) are temporary locations; that is, they are classified as locations only because of the way they are used in these utterances. Thus "trash" is used here to refer to the trash can in which an object (this) is placed, whereas in the action-object combinations it was used as an object to be obtained (as in get "trash" that was on the ground). As utterances moved to the three-term level, errors began to appear. In this case, three of the four errors involved the action word "put." In every instance the correct object was selected but not placed in the correct location.

Two other orders of these same three components also occurred (see Tables 13 and 14). The action-location-object term was typically used when the location referred to a fixed point in space and the reason for traveling to that point was to find some object, as in the sentence: "Let's go to gully gushers and look for turtles" (to which Kanzi responded by traveling to gully gushers and looking in places where turtles had been seen in the past). The object-action-location order is used when Kanzi is being told the location of an object, and in all cases that object is not a fixed location in space.

Table 12

Action-Object-Location Utterances Directed to Kanzi

Action Word	Object Word	Location Word
Bring	cooler	(to) me
Bring	friend	here
Dropped	grape	(by) foot
Hide	surprise	(in) shoe
Put	hot water	(in) hot dogs
Put	it	(in) backpack
Put	it	(in) bowl
Put	it	(by) group room door
Put	it	(with) juice
Put	it (juice)	(in) cooler
Put	it (water)	(in) mouth
Put	light	(in) backpack
Put*	melon	(in) backpack
Put	oil	(on) hands**
Put	orange drink	(in) backpack
Put	rubber band	(on) head
Put*	soap	(in) washer
Put	something	back
Put	sour cream	(in) cooler
Put	straw	(in) bin
Put	this	back
Put	this	(in) potty
Put	this	(in) trash**
Put	tomato	(in) refrigerator
Put*	toothpaste	(in) paper
Put	water	(on) it
Put	water	(in) lemonade
Put	water	(in) mouth
Remember	ball	(in) backpack
Remember	surprise	(in) can
Take	grape	(to) refrigerator
Take	shirt	off**
Take	sour cream	(to) refrigerator
Take	this	(to) potty
Take	water	(to) pool
Throw	ball	(in) river

* Kanzi responded incorrectly to these utterances.
**These sentences were directed to Kanzi frequently.

In nine of the action-object-location combinations the object was specified only by a general term such as "it" or "this." In most of these instances the item was probably somewhat salient given the context, and thus comprehension of "this" or "it" was aided to some degree. For example, the utterance, "Can you put it in the backpack?" was produced

Table 13

Action-Location-Object Utterances Directed to Kanzi

Action Word	Location Word	Object Word
Go	crisscross	(get) grapes*
Go	gully gushers	(look for) turtles
Go	mushroom trail	(get) grapes*
Go	play yard	(get) water*
Go	refrigerator	(get) food**
Go	refrigerator	(get) tomato
Go	Sue's gate	(get) surprise**
Go	trailer	(get) water and balloon*

Note: Kanzi responded correctly to all of these utterances.
*These items were not normally found at these locations.
**These sentences were directed to Kanzi frequently.

Table 14

Object-Action-Location Utterances Directed to Kanzi

Object Word	Action Word	Location Word
Ball	stays	here
Grape	hide	(in) shirt
Grape	hide	(under) stick
Grape	hide	(under) TV
Pinecone	go	(in) shirt
Rocks	will fall	out
Surprise	hide	(under) leaf
Surprise	hide	(under) rock
Surprise	hide	(in) shoe

Note: Kanzi responded correctly to all of these utterances.
**These sentences were directed to Kanzi frequently.

after Kanzi had just handed the experimenter a ball. Thus the object had already been singled out as one being acted upon. Nonetheless, it seems clear that Kanzi knows "it" must refer to a significant aspect of the situation, since there were other items available that he could have placed in the backpack.

In some cases, the referent of "it" could not be deduced from the context but had to come from the preceding clause or sentence, as in the examples, "If you don't want the juice, put it back in" or "Get some water. Put it in your mouth." Utterances with general terms were not tested intentionally. Instead, Kanzi responded to these remarks when they were uttered as part of the natural conversation directed to him daily. Kanzi's ability to comprehend all these utterances suggests at least some preliminary concept of words that refer in a general rather than a specific sense.

244

Table 15

Action-Recipient Utterances Directed to Kanzi

Action Word	Recipient Word
Chase	Kelly**
Chase	Orangutan
Go	Austin**
Grab	Jeannine**
Grab	Phil**
Hug	Jeannine
Hug	Kelly
Hug	Penny
Hug	Rose
Hug	Sue
Tickle	Phil
Wash	Madu

Note: Kanzi responded correctly to all of these utterances.
**These sentences were frequently directed to Kanzi.

Moreover, his ability to respond to a three-term relationship validates his response in the two-term action-object and action-location sequences and indicates that the correct response in those cases was not based on general semantic knowledge (such as when the name of an absent location is mentioned and the logical action is to travel to that location, or when someone mentions the name of an object that is not in her possession but is nearby and the logical action is to give her that object). If Kanzi's ability to respond to two-term relationships had been based solely upon his knowledge of single words, he would not have responded correctly to the three-term relationships.

This also applies to the two-term relationship action-recipient shown in Table 15 and the three-term relationship action-object-recipient (and action-recipient-object) shown in Table 16. Here we can see that Jeannine, Rose, Penny, and Sue are not just individuals associated with hugging, as the two-term relationships might suggest. In the three-term relationships Jeannine is the recipient of trash and a surprise, Penny is the recipient of a cooler, and Sue (or me) is the recipient of cherries.

In these combinations we see that, unlike the action-object combinations, the number of words in the action class is approximately the same as in the object and recipient classes. There are 16 actions, 19 objects, and 16 recipients, and every utterance is unique. These combinations, like the action-object-location combinations, provide evidence that Kanzi is responding to the relationships between words and that he

Table 16

Action-Object-Recipient Utterances Directed to Kanzi

Action word	Object word	Recipient word
Carry	cooler	(to) Penny
Get	cherry	(for) me
Get*	water	(for) me
Get	water	(for) plant
Give	ball	(to) Jeannine
Give	bowl	(to) Kelly
Give	chicken	(to) Sherman and Austin
Give	cooler	(to) Phil
Give	this	(to) Jeannine
Give	trash	(to) Jeannine
Give	water	(to) Mari
Hand	spoon	(to) me
Put*	food	(in) straw
Show	peanut butter	(to) me
Spit	water	(on) Mari
Take	pineapple	(to) Sherman and Austin
Take	straw	(to) orangutans
Throw	potato	(to) turtle
Use	lever	(on) bug

Action Word	Recipient Word	Object Word
Get	orangutans	out
Give	Panbanisha	onion
Go play*	(with) dogs	childside
Show	Jeannine	surprise

*Kanzi responded incorrectly to these utterances.

can respond to individual words in different ways depending upon their functional relation in the sentences directed to him. He can, for example, "Grab Jeannine" or "Give the trash to Jeannine," depending upon what is said to him. He also shows the ability to understand constructions in which Jeannine is the agent and the utterance is about something she has done, as in the utterance, "Jeannine hid the pine needles in her shirt." This utterance and others in which the agent is someone other than Kanzi are listed in Table 17. In this particular case, Kanzi's back was to Jeannine when he heard this utterance. He immediately turned around and approached Jeannine (although there were other individuals present) and put his hand down her shirt. He had not seen Jeannine hide the pine needles.

Table 17

Agent-Action-Object Utterances Directed to Kanzi

Agent Word	Action Word	Object Word
I	am going to throw	this
I	pick up	cube
Jeannine	hide	pine needles
Lever	open	coconut
Me	bite	tummy
Me	light	sparkler
Me	see	mouth

Note: Kanzi responded correctly to all of these utterances.

SELECTING PHOTOGRAPHS

The wide variety of utterances Kanzi has responded to in context suggests that his comprehension of speech goes beyond the single utterances measured in formal tests. However, it would be desirable to demonstrate syntactic competency in tests that are as tightly controlled as those used with single utterances. This is not easy to do, but a first step has been taken by asking Kanzi to look at complex photographs and select the one that matches the sentence he has just heard. For example, Kanzi might see photographs of Bill slapping a ball, Karen slapping a ball, and Bill putting pine needles on the fire. He would then be asked to select the photograph of Bill putting pine needles on the fire.

This approach has the advantage of being very similar to the single-item presentation format Kanzi is accustomed to. Since he is not confronted with a variety of real agents, objects, and locations, he is not so likely to become more interested in what he wants to do with the items than in what the experimenter would like to have done. The approach has some disadvantages also, the most significant being that it is often difficult to depict actions adequately in still photographs. Another disadvantage is that Kanzi is often so interested in new photographs of complex events that instead of pointing to one, he picks up all of them and looks at each one, often pointing to various things in the picture while vocalizing. Occasionally he takes all the pictures off in a corner and looks at them for several minutes before he can be persuaded to indicate which photograph corresponds to the sentence he has just heard.

Initial results using this method are shown in Table 18. Kanzi was presented with 34 sets of photographs of complex events. To keep this initial task as simple as possible, trials in which the photographs had overlapping alternatives were interspersed with trials in which there were no overlapping alternatives. If there were no overlaps, as was the case in Trial 1, Kanzi was still presented with a complex sentence. However, if he was able to match any item in the sentence with the same item in the photograph, he could be correct without comprehending the relationship between the sentence elements.

Nonetheless, even at the level of individual items most of these photographs were quite different from any used in previous tests with Kanzi. Normally each picture would contain only one salient item, such as a ball. The target picture for Trial 1 included a ball, a hammock, trees in the background, and Linda, who had a particular facial expression and was engaging in an action with the ball. On the first trial Kanzi seemed particularly excited about the photographs and looked at each of them for 30 sec or longer. He was especially interested in the picture of Bill biting Linda, in which Linda had a worried expression. He selected this photograph and took it with him to his nest, where he studied it for about 5 min before finally discarding it.

As Table 18 shows, Kanzi was able to choose the correct photograph on 76% of the trials. These data provide preliminary confirmation of his ability to respond to utterances in less structured settings. More testing of Kanzi's ability to understand novel utterances, out of context, is at present under way.

Conclusion

Although we certainly have not probed the limits of Kanzi's receptive competency in the tests described above, nonetheless there is evidence that Kanzi comprehends both individual words and simple sentences. His comprehension of individual words appears to be based upon their phonemic characteristics and not upon intonation, because removing these cues through the use of synthesized speech disrupts performance only slightly.

Kanzi's comprehension of sentences appears to be syntactically based in that he responds differently to the same word depending upon its function in the sentence. Moreover, he responds to all sentences as though a relationship among words is being communicated. In no instance does he react as though he has simply heard a number of single words. He responds reliably to both two-term and three-term relation-

Table 18

Identification of Complex Pictures

Linda holding ball*	Mary with ball in hammock
Rose biting tomato	Linda grabbing ball from Bill
Bill biting Linda	*Bill biting ball**
Bill grabbing Karen	Rose biting tomato
Mary pulling Karen	Jeannine patting Bill's ball*
Bill pulling Karen	*Jeannine biting Bill*
Bill putting pinecones on fire	Jeannine putting juice in backpack
Karen climbing tree*	*Jeannine biting juice**
*Jeannine hitting Bill**	Karen biting leaves
Bill biting leaves	Karen putting water on fire
Jeannine opening cooler	*Jeannine hitting Karen with stick**
Karen opening cooler	Jeannine pointing to A-frame
Bill standing on his head on cooler	Bill climbing up tree house
*Karen slapping Bill**	Karen going to A-frame*
*Jeannine opening cooler**	*Karen climbing tree*
Jeannine hugging Kanzi	Linda ball patting Mary's ball
Mary opening cooler	Bill drinking Coke
Karen tickling Mary	Linda drinking Coke
Rose tickling Kelly*	*Bill ball patting Linda's ball**
Jeannine tickling Mary	Jeannine hugging Mary
*Bill tickling Linda**	*Jeannine playing ball keepaway with*
Rose biting Karen	*Mary**
Karen climbing tree	Bill putting ball in backpack
Bill opening cooler	
Mary pulling Linda	
*Mary hitting Jeannine with stick**	

ships. The number of tokens within each class of terms is large, ranging from 20 to over 100. However, he has not yet shown a clear sensitivity to inversion of word order.

It is important to emphasize that Kanzi has acquired this capacity in an altogether natural manner. Since the age of 6 months he has been spoken to throughout the day in a normal fashion. People have commented on what he was doing, what they were doing, what was going to happen, what had happened, what they thought and felt. Kanzi, like a child, has listened to this frequent verbal input and has begun to comprehend.

Initially his comprehension was sporadic and faltering. By 3 years of age Kanzi was comprehending a large number of individual words but

Table 18 *(continued)*

Mary patting ball	*Mary biting Bill**
*Mary lighting fire**	Bill climbing in tree house
Linda putting sticks on fire	Rose biting Kelly
Bill grabbing Karen	Jeannine hugging Mary
Jeannine hitting pinecone with rock	Jeannine hitting Karen with stick*
*Bill hitting Karen with rock**	*Jeannine biting stick*
*Jeannine tickling Kanzi**	Bill biting leaves
Jeannine and Kanzi opening lock	Bill hitting table with rock
Mary tickling Jeannine	*Bill drinking Coke**
Linda putting sticks on fire	Mary drinking Coke
*Linda patting Mary's ball**	Karen biting leaves
Jeannine playing ball keepaway with Mary	*Bill biting leaves**
	Bill opening backpack
*Jeannine making fire with pine needles**	Jeannine biting Bill
Jeannine biting juice	Jeannine playing ball keepaway with Mary
Bill making fire with pine needles	*Jeannine patting Bill's ball**
Jeannine tickling Mary	*Jeannine hitting Karen with rock**
*Jeannine hitting Karen with rock**	Jeannine playing ball keepaway with Karen
Karen opening cooler	Jeannine hitting pinecone with rock
Karen hiding in tree	Bill hiding in trees
Bill opening backpack*	Karen putting water on fire
Bill hiding in tree	*Karen hiding in trees**

Note: The sentence Kanzi heard is in italic; the picture Kanzi selected is marked by an asterisk.

no two-term or three-term relations. Comprehension of complex relationships has progressed rather steadily across the past three years, culminating in the data presented here. However, at no time was Kanzi drilled on any specific command to facilitate comprehension or compliance, nor was he ever rewarded for complying with certain commands. Rather, his comprehension of things that are said to him has steadily increased across time so that he is able to comply with requests without the gestural assistance he required when he was younger. Many of the utterances directed to him that are reported here were completely novel in that none of the experimenters recalled asking Kanzi to do that particular thing in the past.

Kanzi's ability first to acquire language as a receptive skill and then to translate this understanding into productive competency sets him apart from other apes who have learned to use symbols. All previous studies have concentrated upon production as the primary skill. Production without comprehension fosters nonrepresentational symbol usage that is limited to requests and demands. Because Kanzi comprehended speech when he was not rewarded for doing so, and because he learned to associate the lexigram and the spoken word, again without being rewarded for doing so, he did not need the piecemeal approach that common chimpanzees and other apes have required to develop an understanding of reference.

Lack of syntactical structure has repeatedly been used as a means of seperating the utterances of apes from those of men. Apes' utterances have lacked syntactical stucture not because this is an innately human skill but because they have not been able to understand or respond to the structure others are using in communications directed to them. Use of syntactical structure is a natural outgrowth of understanding and responding to structured utterances. Kanzi is beginning to evidence structure in his combinations. For example, in two-element action-object constructions, Kanzi nearly always uses the action-object order (Savage-Rumbaugh, 1987a). As his utterances increase in complexity, it seems probable that he will continue to use the orders that he hears around him and that he understands.

Kanzi's ability to understand both words and sentences challenges the widely held assumption that speech processing is unique to humans. It suggests that the capacity to comprehend speech antedates the ability to produce it. The brain must have been ready to process language (both conceptually and phonemically) long before the vocal tract was ready to produce it. Indeed, it may be that pygmy chimpanzees in the field are producing a language of sorts but that we have not been able to decode it. Certainly the techniques of associating a specific sound pattern with a specific set of social circumstances (which are typically used to study primate call systems) are inadequate to the task of decoding a language-based system. Linguistic symbols tend to refer to absent referents and are not likely to bc decoded from an analysis of the ongoing social context, which emphasizes who vocalized to whom and when. Moreover, in a language system, sounds which are physically quite distinct, as revealed by spectrographic analysis, will be heard as the same word.

Kanzi appears to be the first ape who is truly acquiring language in the sense that he is learning to associate spoken words and symbols with events in his world simply by being enmeshed in a language environment. He is the first ape who has demonstrated comprehension of synthesized speech and complex sentences. His comprehension of speech seems to foster his acquisition of graphic symbols, since they are his only means of expression. Why have other apes not demonstrated similar skills? Why did Sherman and Austin's comprehension of speech remain limited to a few highly practiced phrases? The answers to these questions are not yet fully in hand. Speech was used around Sherman and Austin as frequently as it has been with Kanzi, but they were not exposed to the language environment until they were 2 years old. Perhaps early exposure to speech is critical to the development of this skill in apes. We are now rearing one infant of each species together, as we reared Kanzi, to attempt to determine to what extent Kanzi's unique capacities are the result of species variables and to what extent they can be attributed to environmental variables.

The research described in this paper and its preparation were supported by National Institutes of Health grant NICHD-06016, which supports the Language Research Center, cooperatively operated by Georgia State University and the Yerkes Regional Primate Research Center of Emory University. In addition, the research is supported in part by RR-00165 to the Yerkes Regional Primate Research Center of Emory University.

REFERENCES

Bates, E. (1979). *The emergence of symbols, cognition and communication in infancy.* New York: Academic Press.
Benedict, H. (1979). Early lexical development: Comprehension and production. *Journal of Child Language, 6,* 183–200.
Bloom, L. M. (1973). *One word at a time: The use of single word utterances before syntax.* The Hague: Mouton.
Brown, R. (1973). *A first language: The early stages.* Cambridge: Harvard University Press.
Chomsky, N. (1980a). Initial states and steady states. In M. Piatelli-Palmarini (Ed.), *Language and learning: The debate between Jean Piaget and Noam Chomsky* (pp. 107–130). Cambridge: Harvard University Press.
Chomsky, N. (1980b). Rules and representations. *Behavioral and Brain Sciences, 3,* 1–61.
Cleveland, J., & Snowdon, C. T. (1982). The complex vocal repertoire of the adult cotton-top tamarin (*Saguinus oedipus oedipus*). *Zeitschrift für Tierpsychologie, 58,* 231–270.

252

Fouts, R. S. (1972). *Ethology: The biology of behavior.* New York: Holt, Rhinehart and Winston.

Fouts, R. S. (1973). Acquisition and testing of gestural signs in four young chimpanzees. *Science, 180,* 973–980.

Gardner, B. T., & Gardner, R. A. (1971). Two-way communication with an infant chimpanzee. In A. M. Schrier & F. Stollnitz (Eds.), *Behavior of nonhuman primates* (Vol. 4, pp. 117–183). New York: Academic Press.

Gibson, D., & Ingram, D. (1983). The onset of comprehension and production in a language delayed child. *Applied Psycholinguistics, 4,* 359–375.

Goldin-Meadow, S., Seligman, M. E. P., & Gelman, R. (1976). Language in the two year old. *Cognition, 4,* 189–202.

Goodall, J. (1986). *The chimpanzees of Gombe: Patterns of behavior.* Cambridge: Belknap Press of Harvard University Press.

Greenfield, P. M., & Savage-Rumbaugh, E. S. (1984). Perceived variability and symbol use: A common language-cognition interface in children and chimpanzees (*Pan troglodytes*). *Journal of Comparative Psychology, 98,* 201–218.

Greenfield, P. M., & Savage-Rumbaugh, E. S. (1986). The rule-based use of combination of a pygmy chimpanzee. In S. Taylor-Parker and K. Gibson (co-chair), *Evolutionary perspectives on comparative ontogeny.* Symposium conducted as a presession of the International Primatological Society Congress, Gottingen.

Greenfield, P. M., & Smith, J. H. (1976). *The structure of communication in early language development.* New York: Academic Press.

Hediger, H. K. P. (1981). The Clever Hans phenomenon from an animal psychologist's point of view. In T. A. Sebeok & R. Rosenthal (Eds.), *The Clever Hans phenomenon: Communication with horses, whales, apes, and people. Annals of the New York Academy of Sciences, 364,* 1–17.

Huttenlocker, J. (1974). The origins of language comprehension. In R. L. Solso (Ed.), *Theories of cognitive Psychology.* Hillsdale, NJ: Erlbaum.

Jolly, A. (1985). *The evolution of primate behavior.* New York: Macmillan.

Kimura, D. (1961). Cerebral dominance and the perception of verbal stimuli. *Canadian Journal of Psychology, 15,* 166–171.

Kuhl, P. K., & Padden, D. M. (1983). Enhanced discriminality at the phonetic boundaries for the place feature in macaques. *Journal of the Acoustic Society of America, 73,* 1003–1010.

Kuroda, S. (1984). Interaction over food among pygmy chimpanzees. In R. L. Susman (Ed.), *The Pygmy chimpanzee: Evolutionary biology and behavior* (pp. 301–324). New York: Plenum.

Liberman, A. M. (1970). Some characteristics of perception in the speech mode. *Perception and Its Disorders, 48,* 238–254.

Liberman, A. M., Cooper, F. S., Shankweiler, D. P., & Studdert-Kennedy, M. (1967). Perception of the speech code. *Psychological Review, 74,* 431–461.

Lieberman, P. (1984). *The biology and evolution of language.* Cambridge: Harvard University Press.

Lock, A. (1980). *The guided reinvention of language.* London: Academic Press.

Lorber, J. (1980). Is your brain really necessary? Research news. *Science, 210,* 1232–1234.

McNeil, D. (1970). *The acquisition of language: The study of developmental psycholinguistics.* New York: Harper.

McShane, J. (1980). *Learning how to talk.* Cambridge: Cambridge University Press.

Miles, H. L. (1983). Apes and language: The search for communicative competence. In J. de Luce & H. T. Wilder (Eds.), *Language in Primates* (pp. 43–61). New York: Springer-Verlag.

Molfese, D. (1978). Left and right hemisphere involvement in speech perception: Electrophysiological correlates. *Perception and Psychophysics, 23,* 237–243.

Morse, P. A., & Snowdon, C. T. (1975). An investigation of categorical speech discrimination by rhesus monkeys. *Perception and Psychophysics, 17,* 9–16.

Nelson, K. (1973). Structure and strategy in learning to talk. *Monographs of the Society for Research and Development, 38,* no. 149.

Nelson, K. (1977). First steps in language acquisition. *Journal of the American Academy of Child Psychiatry, 16,* 563–583.

Nelson, K. (1978). How children represent knowledge of their world in and out of language: A preliminary report. In R. S. Siegler (Ed.), *Children's thinking: What develops?* (pp. 255–273). Hilsdale, NJ: Lawrence Erlbaum.

Oviatt, S. L. (1980). The emerging ability to comprehend language: An experimental approach. *Child Development, 51,* 97–106.

Pate, J. L., & Rumbaugh, D. M. (1983). The language-like behavior of Lana Chimpanzee: Is it merely discrimination and paired-associate learning? *Animal Learning and Behavior, 11,* 134–138.

Patterson, F. (1978). The gestures of a gorilla: Language acquisition in another pongid. *Brain and Language, 5,* 72–97.

Patterson, T. (1979). The behavior of a group of captive pygmy chimpanzees (*Pan paniscus*). *Primates, 20,* 341–354.

Premack, D. (1971). On the assessment of language competence in the chimpanzee. In A. M. Schrier & F. Stollnitz (Eds.), *Behavior of nonhuman primates* (Vol. 4, pp. 185–228). New York: Academic Press.

Punzi, L., & Kraat, A. (1986). *The effect of context on preschool children's understanding of synthetic speech—a pilot study.* Unpublished manuscript.

Rentschler, G. J. (1986). *The intelligibility of computer synthesized speech for language impaired children.* Unpublished manuscript.

Rescorla, L. (1976). *Overextension in early language development.* New York: Norton.

Rumbaugh, D. M. (Ed.). (1977). *Language learning by a chimpanzee: The LANA Project.* New York: Academic Press.

Sanders, R. J. (1985). Teaching apes to ape language: Explaining the imitative and nonimitative signing of a chimpanzee (*Pan troglodytes*). *Journal of Comparative Psychology, 99,* 197–210.

Savage-Rumbaugh, E. S. (1979). Symbolic communication—its origins and early development in the chimpanzee. *New Directions in Child Development, 3,* 1–15.

Savage-Rumbaugh, E. S. (1981). Can apes use symbols to represent their world? In T. A. Seabok & R. Rosenthal (Eds.), *The Clever Hans phenomenon: Communication with horses, whales, apes, and people. Annals of the New York Academy of Sciences, 364,* 35–59.

Savage-Rumbaugh, E. S. (1984a). Acquisition of functional symbol usage in apes and children. In H. L. Roitblat, T. G. Bever, & H. S. Terrace (Eds.), *Animal cognition* (pp. 291–310). Hillsdale, NJ: Erlbaum.

Savage-Rumbaugh, E. S. (1984b). Verbal behavior at a procedural level. *Journal of Experimental Analvsis of Behavior, 41,* 223–250.

Savage-Rumbaugh, E. S. (1984c). *Pan paniscus* and *Pan troglodytes:* Contrasts in preverbal communicative competence. In R. L. Susman (Ed.), *The pygmy chimpanzee: Evolutionary biology and behavior* (pp. 395–413). New York: Plenum.

Savage-Rumbaugh, E. S. (1986). *Ape language: From conditioned response to symbol.* New York: Columbia University Press.

Savage-Rumbaugh, E. S. (1987a). Contrasts in symbol acquisition between pygmy chimpanzees. Paper presented to the Society for Research in Child Development, Baltimore, April.

Savage-Rumbaugh, E. S. (1987b). Communication, symbolic communication, and language: A reply to Seidenberg and Pettito. *Journal of Experimental Psychology: General.*

Savage-Rumbaugh, E. S., McDonald, K., Sevcik, R. A., Hopkins, W. D., & Rubert, E. (1986). Spontaneous symbol acquisition and communicative use by a pygmy chimpanzee *(Pan paniscus). Journal of Experimental Psychology: General, 115,* 211–235.

Savage-Rumbaugh, E. S., Pate, J. L., Lawson, J., Smith, S. T., & Rosenbaum, S. (1983). Can a chimpanzee make a statement? *Journal of Experimental Psychology: General, 112,* 457–492.

Savage-Rumbaugh, E. S., Romski, M. A., Hopkins, W. D., & Sevcik, R. A. (in press). Symbol acquisition and use in three species, *Pan troglodytes, Pan Paniscus,* and *Homo sapiens:* Environmental and species variables. *Proceedings of the Chicago Academy of Sciences.*

Savage-Rumbaugh, E. S., Rumbaugh, D. M., & Boysen, S. (1978). Linguistically mediated tool use and exchange by chimpanzees *(Pan troglodytes). Behavioral and Brain Sciences,* 539–554.

Savage-Rumbaugh, E. S., Rumbaugh, D. M., & Boysen, S. (1980). Do apes use language? *American Scientist, 68,* 49–61.

Savage-Rumbaugh, E. S., Rumbaugh, D. M., & McDonald, K. (1985). Language learning in two species of apes. *Neuroscience and Biobehavioral Reviews, 9,* 653–665.

Savage-Rumbaugh, E. S., Sevcik, R. A., Rumbaugh, D. M., & Rubert, E. (1985). The capacity of animals to acquire language: Do species differences have anything to say to us? *Philosophical Transactions of the Royal Society of London, B308,* 177–185.

Savage-Rumbaugh, E. S., & Wilkerson, B. J. (1978). Sociosexual behavior in *Pan Paniscus* and *Pan troglodytes:* A comparative study. *Journal of Human Evolution, 1,* 327–344.

Savage-Rumbaugh, E. S., Wilkerson, B. J., & Bakeman, R. (1977). Spontaneous gestural communication among conspecifics in the pygmy chimpanzee *(Pan paniscus*). In G. H. Bourne (Ed.), *Progress in ape research* (pp. 97–116). New York: Academic Press.

Sebeok, T. A., & Umiker-Sebeok, J. (1980). *Speaking of apes: A critical two-way communication with man*. New York: Plenum.

Seidenberg, M. S., & Pettito, L. A. (1979). Signing behavior in apes: A critical review. *Cognition, 2,* 177–215.

Seidenberg, M. S., & Pettito, L. A. (1981). Ape signing: Problems of method and interpretation. In T. A. Sebeok & R. Rosenthal (Eds.), *The Clever Hans phenomenon: Communication with horses, whales, apes, and people. Annals of the New York Academy of Science, 364,* 115–129.

Seidenberg, M. S., & Petitto, L. A. (1987). Communication, symbolic communication, and language: Comment on Savage-Rumbaugh et al. *Journal of Experimental Psychology: General.*

Seyfarth, R. M., Cheney, D. L., & Marler, P. (1980). Vervet monkey alarm calls: Semantic communication in a free-ranging primate. *Animal Behavior, 28,* 1070–1094.

Snyder, L. S., Bates, E., & Bretherton, I. (1981). Content and context in early lexical development. *Journal of Child Language, 8,* 565–682.

Terrace, H. S. (1979). *Nim.* New York: Knopf.

Terrace, H. S. (1985). In the beginning was the "name." *American Psychologist, 40,* 1011–1028.

Terrace, H. S., Petitto, L. A., Sanders, R. J., & Bever, T. G. (1979). Can an ape create a sentence? *Science, 206,* 891–900.

Thompson, C. R., & Church, R. M. (1980). An explanation of the language of a chimpanzee. *Science, 208,* 313–314.

Thompson-Handler. N., Malenky, R. K., & Badrian, N. (1984). Sexual behavior of *Pan Paniscus* under natural conditions in the Lomako Forest, Equateur, Zaire. In R. L. Susman (Ed.), *The pygmy chimpanzee: Evolutionary biology and behavior* (pp. 347–368). New York: Plenum.

Wada, J., Clarke, R. I., & Hamm, A. (1975). Cerebral hemispheric asymmetry in humans. *Archives of Neurology, 32,* 239–246.

Waters, R. S., & Wilson, W. A., Jr. (1976). Speech perception by rhesus monkeys: The voicing distinction in synthesized labial and velar stop consonants. *Perception and Psychophysics, 19,* 285–289.

Wilson, E. O. (1975). *Sociobiology: A new synthesis.* Cambridge: Harvard University Press.

A Synthetic Approach to the Study of Animal Intelligence[1]

Alan C. Kamil

University of Massachusetts

Two Anecdotes

*I*t is 7:00 A.M. The sun has just risen over the botanical gardens, and my research team and I are about to give up our attempt to catch a male Anna's hummingbird with a discrete white spot behind his left eye. "Spot" has been defending a small, flower-rich territory, and we want to put a colored plastic band on his leg as part of our study of nectar-foraging patterns. To catch Spot we had arrived before sunrise and strung a mist net, 5 feet high and 18 feet long, across the middle of his territory. Mist nets, made of very thin black nylon thread, are designed to entangle any bird that flies into them. Unfortunately, a heavy dew at sunrise had collected on the strands of the net, and Spot saw it immediately. He had flown along it and even perched on it. Experience has taught us that once a hummingbird has done this, it will never fly into the net. So we were about to take down the net, but first we were having a cup of coffee. Spot was sitting on his

1. The ideas presented in this chapter have undergone a long, and still incomplete, development. During this time support has been received from the National Science Foundation (BNS 84–18721 and BNS 85–19010 currently), the National Institute of Mental Health, and the University of Massachusetts. I have also been stimulated by discussions, conversations, and arguments with many individuals. I would particularly like to thank Robert L. Gossette for first igniting my interest in the comparative

favorite perch, overlooking the territory from its southwest edge. Suddenly an intruding hummingbird flew into the territory from the northeast and began to feed.

Male Anna's hummingbirds are extraordinarily aggressive animals. Usually they will utter their squeaky territorial song and fly directly at an intruder, chasing it out of the territory. But that is not what Spot does. He silently drops from his perch and flies around the perimeter of the territory, staying close to the ground, until he is behind the other bird. Then he gives his song and chases the intruder—directly into the mist net. Spot pulls up short, hovers over the bird, utters another burst of song, and returns to his perch.

This anecdote raises many questions with interesting implications. For example, did Spot have a "cognitive map" of his territory that allowed him to understand that if he moved to a point behind the other bird he could force the intruder into the net? Since this is only an anecdote, it provides no definitive answer. But many more mundane empirical studies of nectar-feeding birds offer systematic data showing that they do possess considerable knowledge about spatial and temporal patterns of food production on their territories (Gass & Montgomerie, 1981; Gill & Wolf, 1977; Gill, in press; Kamil, 1978).

Consider this observation of chimpanzees reported by Goodall:

The juvenile female Pooch approaches high-ranking Circe and reaches for one of her bananas. Circe at once hits out at the youngster, whereupon Pooch, screaming very loudly indeed, runs from camp in an easterly direction. Her response to the rather mild threat seems unnecessarily violent. After two minutes, the screams give way to waa-barks, which get progressively louder as Pooch retraces her steps. After a few moments she reappears; stopping about 5 meters from Circe, she gives an arm-raise threat along with another waa-bark. Following behind Pooch, his hair slightly bristling, is the old male Huxley (who had left camp shortly before in an easterly direction). Circe, with a mild threat gesture towards Pooch and a glance at Huxley, gets up and moves away. Pooch has

study of learning, Daniel S. Lehrman and Robert Lockard for first directing my attention toward biology and ecology, and Charles Van Riper III for his guidance during my first research experience outside the cloisters of the laboratory. I would also like to thank Sonja I. Yoerg, Kevin Clements, and Deborah Olson for their comments and suggestions on a previous version of this chapter.

used Huxley as a "social tool." This little sequence can be understood only because we know of the odd relationship between the juvenile and the old male who served on many occasions as her protector and was seldom far away. (Goodall, 1986, p. 567)

There are many objections to the use of anecdotes such as these. As Thorndike (1898) pointed out, hundreds of dogs get lost every day and nobody pays much attention except the unfortunate dogs' owners. But let one dog find its way from Cambridge to London, or Boston to New Haven, and it becomes a famous anecdote. Anecdotes cannot provide definitive evidence about animal intelligence (or anything else). But it may be a serious mistake to completely ignore their implications, which can provide interesting hypotheses for rigorous test.

Furthermore, the two anecdotes related above are not isolated examples. Most fieldworkers have similar stories from their own experience. Books such as Goodall (1986) and Smuts (1985) are replete with them (see also Kummer, 1982; Kummer & Goodall, 1985). Much more important than the number of these anecdotes, however, is the fact that empirical data are being amassed to support their specific implications. The main point is that these anecdotes and supporting data suggest that the traditional psychological approach to the study of animal learning is too limited.

Psychologists have been studying animal learning for about a century. This century of experimental and theoretical work has produced some remarkable successes, particularly in understanding basic conditioning processes. However, these successes are limited in two major ways. First, they have been confined to a narrow domain. Recent research from a variety of settings has demonstrated that animals have mental abilities far beyond what they were given credit for just a few years ago. We must dramatically expand the range of phenomena addressed by the study of animal learning. Second, there has been an almost complete failure to place animal learning in any kind of comparative, evolutionary framework, primarily because of a failure to develop any detailed understanding of how animals use their ability to learn outside the laboratory. Recent developments in psychology and biology are beginning to suggest how this gap may be filled.

The expansion of the range of phenomena under study is already well under way, with the emergence of the cognitive approach to animal learning (Hulse, Fowler, & Honig, 1978; Roitblat, Bever, & Terrace, 1984) and diverse new techniques for exploring the capacities of animals

(Griffin, 1976, 1978). The development of a meaningful comparative approach is also beginning to emerge, thanks to developments in both psychology and biology.

My purpose in this chapter is to outline the beginnings of a new way to study animal intelligence. I have labeled this the synthetic approach because it represents an attempt to synthesize the approaches of psychology, ethology, and behavioral ecology. I have used the term intelligence, rather than more specific terms such as learning or cognition, to emphasize the breadth of the phenomena to be included. The synthetic approach builds upon previous successes but is much broader and more biological than the predominantly psychological approaches of the past. Its goal is to develop a full understanding of the intellectual abilities of animals, with particular emphasis on psychological mechanisms and functional significance.

What I am proposing is not a new theory. Rather, it is an attempt to outline a new scientific research program (Lakatos, 1974). According to Lakatos, research programs consist of two parts: a central core of laws, principles, and assumptions that are not subject to direct empirical test, and a protective belt of "auxiliary hypotheses" that relate the central core to observations and can be tested and perhaps rejected. The central core and its auxiliary hypotheses function to direct research toward certain problems and away from others. In these terms, I am urging two changes in the central core of the psychological approach to animal learning: a broadening of the discipline's domain and the adaptation of a biological and ecological approach to the study of learning. These changes could redirect attention to important and interesting facets of animal learning that have been ignored by the traditional psychological approach.

The Traditional Approach

The purpose of this section is to identify the central core of the psychological study of animal learning. There are two difficulties. First, the programs Lakatos discusses are from the history of physics, with explicit, usually mathematical, specifications of their central core. In the case of animal learning, the central core is less formalized and more difficult to specify. Another difficulty is that although it is easy to talk and write about "the traditional approach" to animal learning in psychology, in fact there have been a number of different approaches. Nonetheless, a few assumptions have been widespread, if not universal. Some of these assumptions formed the central core of the scientific reseach programs that have dominated animal-learning psychology and have directed attention away from important phenomena and issues.

GENERAL PROCESSES

One basic assumption has been that one or a very few general principles can account for all of animal learning. A variety of principles have been proposed, but the two dominant ones have been associationism and reinforcement theory.

Rescorla (1985) provides an extremely coherent overview of the associationist approach that is remarkable in the extent to which it agrees, in form, with Lakatos's description of a research program. The central core is the assumption that virtually all learning can be understood as the formation of an association between two events. The associationist approach then attempts to explain the diversity and richness of an animal's knowledge of its world not by hypothesizing a richness and diversity of learning mechanisms, but by weaving a web of auxiliary hypotheses around the central learning mechanism. Rescorla (1985) identifies three types of auxiliary hypotheses that serve this function: the complexity of the conditions that govern the formation of associations, a wide range of elements that can be associated, and multiple mechanisms by which associations can affect behavior. These auxiliary hypotheses have made associationism a powerful force for understanding some aspects of learning in animals, a force that is often underappreciated by those working in other areas.

The central core of reinforcement theory is that behavior can best be understood in terms of the strengthening or weakening effects of reinforcers and punishers on the responses that have preceded them. This was first clearly formulated by Thorndike (1911) and has been elaborated in many ways by others (Herrnstein, 1970; Skinner, 1938). Like associationism, reinforcement theory attempts to account for the richness and diversity of behavior by using a single principle with a web of auxiliary hypotheses. Among these hypotheses are the complexity of the effects of schedules of reinforcement and alterations in the definition of what constitutes a reinforcer. The study of reinforcement has made many important contributions to our understanding of learning.

Although associationism and reinforcement theory have proved to be powerful concepts, they have often been overemphasized. There are too many phenomena they cannot easily account for, including those studied by many cognitive animal psychologists and those beginning to be revealed by naturalistic studies of intelligence. The learning of associations between events and the effects of reinforcement must be investigated as part of any study of animal learning and intelligence. But these two principles in themselves cannot completely account for how animals adapt their behavior on the basis of experience.

RADICAL BEHAVIORISM

Two kinds of behaviorism need to be distinguished. Methodological behaviorism simply recognizes that behavior is what we must measure in experiments. Its central tenet is that all the mechanisms we may theorize about are known to us only through behavior.

Radical behaviorism goes beyond stating that it is behavior we seek to understand. According to the radical behaviorist, any theoretical constructs, especially about cognitive structures animals may possess, are not just unnecessary, but dangerous (Skinner, 1977); behavior can best be understood in terms of the functions that relate stimulus events to responses.

Radical behaviorism has been unremitting in its concentration on the similarities between species. For example, an often-quoted comment of Skinner's (1959) accompanies the cumulative records from several species: "Pigeon, rat, monkey, which is which? It doesn't matter . . . once you have allowed for differences in the ways in which they make contact with the environment, and in the ways in which they act upon the environment, what remains of their behavior shows astonishingly similar properties" (pp. 374–375).

The interesting aspect of this quotation is that it acknowledges the existence of differences between species but relegates them to the realm of the uninteresting. It provides a clear case of Lakatos's (1974) concept of a negative heuristic, directing research away from certain topics. For the synthetic approach, these differences are of interest. If they had been of more interest to the radical behaviorist, phenomena such as autoshaping and instinctive drift (see below) would have come as less of a surprise.

Another problem with the radical behaviorist position has been that it tends to be radically environmentalistic, regarding the organism as a tabula rasa upon which experience writes. This emphasis ignores the potential importance of the effects of genetics and evolutionary history. The emerging current view, particularly apparent in the cognitive approach to animal learning, is that organisms bring certain processes, such as attention and memory, to bear on problems. This in turn has serious implications for evolutionary analyses of animal intelligence.

COMPARATIVE GENERALITY

Another traditional assumption has been that the basic properties of animal learning are the same in a wide variety of organisms, which has justified the use of relatively few species in animal learning research. The logic underlying this assumption may have been that many of the psychologists studying animal learning were not primarily interested in the species they studied, but were using these species as convenient substitutes for humans. Therefore the only learning processes of real interest were those that could be generalized to our own species. This is a coherent, sensible approach, but it suffers from a basic flaw. The animals under investigation are biological entities, with their own evolutionary history. The way that evolutionary history might influence the outcome of learning experiments was not considered by most psychologists.

As reviewed below, there are special and substantial logical and methodological problems confronting the comparative analysis of learning and intelligence in animals. But to assume the absence of such differences, or at least their relative unimportance, has some major drawbacks because it places the study of learning outside the realm of modern evolutionary theory. Suppose there are, in fact, no important differences in the processes of learning among a wide variety of species—say, all vertebrates. This would imply that learning plays no adaptive role at all for vertebrates. Indeed, a number of ethologists (e.g., Lorenz, 1965) and psychologists (Boice, 1977; Lockard, 1971) have suggested that learning is relatively unimportant to animals in their natural environments. But more recent data have clearly demonstrated that learning and memory do function in crucial ways for foraging animals (Kamil, Krebs, & Pulliam, 1987; Kamil & Sargent, 1981; Shettleworth,

1984) and animals in social situations (Cheney, Seyfarth, & Smuts, 1986; Kummer, 1982). As is explained in more detail below, evidence for the functional significance of learning is evidence that there must be significant variation in intelligence between species.

EMPTY METHODOLOGICAL SOPHISTICATION

Bolles (1985a) suggested that an angry god put a terrible curse on psychology: "You will never discover anything about underlying causal processes, and you will never ever understand the overlying functional significance of anything. You will be forever doomed to be methodologists. You will content yourselves with teaching each other how to do experiments, and you will never know what they mean" (p. 137). According to Bolles, because of this curse psychologists have become more caught up with their procedures than with the animals they study.

Another way to express this problem is to say that psychologists have concentrated disproportionately on internal validity and ignored the issue of external validity. Internal validity refers to the internal logic of the experiment, including factors such as the absence of confounding conditions and the adequacy of controls. External validity refers to the extent to which the results of laboratory studies can be generalized beyond the laboratory situation. When one designs a single experiment, there tends to be a trade-off between internal and external validity. Well-designed and well-controlled experiments are generally carried out under highly artificial or constrained conditions, which limits external validity. But at some point, any area of scientific endeavor must be concerned with the issue of external validity.

For example, consider the study of language acquisition by children. At one time this field was dominated by laboratory research in highly constrained situations and theoretical work on transformational grammars. But at some point researchers began to ask whether the ideas developing from this laboratory work could deal accurately with the actual process of language acquisition as it occurs in normal circumstances. This in turn led to many naturalistic studies of language acquisition, whose results have had a large impact on theoretical ideas and laboratory research (Gardner, 1978).

The only external referent for animal learning research has been applied research with humans and animals. The applied work with animals immediately suggested problems (Breland & Breland, 1961), but they were largely ignored. The applied work with humans has had some success, but this too has been limited (Schwartz, 1984). What we need are additional external referents against which to judge the generality and importance of the information we have gained about animal learning and intelligence. As we shall see below, the absence of external criteria has caused particularly serious problems for comparative analyses of animal learning.

In summary, then, there are several problems with the traditional approach: a concentration on just a few general processes, with the possible elimination from consideration of many others; a concentration on behavior, ignoring the processes with which animals are endowed; the lack of an evolutionary, comparative framework; and the lack of substantial measures of external validity. These problems with the traditional approach have had particularly serious implications for the comparative analysis of learning and intelligence.

The Comparative Analysis of Intelligence

The traditional psychological approach to animal learning has largely ignored comparative questions, concentrating research on just a few species. This tendency has been documented and criticized many times over the past 35 to 40 years (Beach, 1950; Bitterman, 1960). Despite this, most learning research in psychology is still conducted with just a few species. Why has this criticism had so little effect?

One reason is the commitment to general processes. The assumption has been that just a few general processes can explain most learning in many species. If that were true, there would be no reason not to concentrate on a few available species. And of course the general principles of association and reinforcement have been demonstrated (but not studied in depth) in a wide range of species. One must wonder, however, to what extent the emphasis on general process has restricted the view of the animal learning psychologist.

Another important reason for the lack of comparative work among traditional animal learning psychologists is the substantial methodological and theoretical problems presented by any comparative analysis of learning. The major methodological problem involves the difficulty of measuring species differences in learning because of the learning/performance distinction. The major theoretical problem is due to the logical status of the so-called mechanisms of learning.

THE LEARNING-PERFORMANCE DISTINCTION

As Bitterman (1960, 1965) has so clearly articulated, the performance of a species in a particular situation is a joint function of its abilities and the particulars of the task presented. Thus the failure of a species (or an individual) to perform well on a particular test does not necessarily mean the species lacks the ability for which it is supposedly being tested. Rather, it may be that the situation is in some way inappropriate. A species may fail to solve a problem, for example, not because it is incapable of solution in a general way, but because the experiment was improperly conducted. In Bitterman's terms, some contextual variable, such as motivational level or response requirement, may have been inappropriate.

Bitterman's (1965) solution to this problem is "control by systematic variation," in which one systematically varies the contextual variables in an attempt to find a situation in which the species will perform well on the task. So, for example, one might vary motivational level, the intensity and nature of the stimuli, the response required, and so on. The problem, of course, is that control by systematic variation can never prove that a species difference exists. It is impossible to prove that there are no circumstances in which a species will learn a particular type of problem. Some untested combination of variables may produce positive results in the future.

This leaves a curious asymmetry in the interpretation of comparative-learning research. The meaning of similar results with different species is supposedly clear: the species do not differ in the learning ability being tested. The meaning of different results with different species is never clear. No matter how many failed attempts there have been, the skeptic can always claim, with impeccable logic, that the apparent difference may be due to something other than a species difference in learning abilities.

"MECHANISMS" OF LEARNING

The second problem that presents substantial challenges to the comparative analysis of intelligence is the logical status of what are commonly called the "mechanisms" of learning. In normal language a mechanism is machinery, like gears in a clock. The machinery is physical and can be observed directly. In comparative anatomy and physiology the mechanisms are also physical; respiration has a physically observable and measurable basis in trachea, lungs, and hemoglobin. In principle, learning mechanisms also have a physical basis in the brain. But that physical basis is as yet unknown in any detail, especially for more complex forms of learning. In any case, the way psychologists define learning (or cognitive) mechanisms is independent of the physical basis of these mechanisms.

The "mechanisms" of learning are known in terms of input-output relationships. That is, models are constructed that accurately predict output, behavior, from the input, previous experience. A successful model is then called a learning mechanism. The things we call learning mechanisms are not really mechanisms at all but hypothetical constructs, models that accurately predict behavior. What does it mean to say that the same hypothetical construct correctly predicts learning in two different species?

It certainly does not mean that the mechanisms of learning, in the physical sense, are identical in the two species. It is instructive, in this context, to look at an example from comparative physiology. There is considerable variety in the physical mechanisms of respiration, even among air-breathing vertebrates. The mechanisms (e.g., the lungs) are not inferred, they are directly observable. It is hard to imagine comparative physiologists arguing much about whether the differences between bird and mammal lungs are quantitative or qualitative, or whether we should use one mathematical model with changeable parameters or two different mathematical models. The differences are there to be directly observed and measured. In other words, some of the arguments about comparative interpretation of possible species differences in learning have their origin in the hypothetical nature of learning "mechanisms," not in the logic of comparative analysis per se.

Given the hypothetical nature of mechanisms of animal learning or intelligence, one of the central arguments of the traditional approach, that of qualitative versus quantitative differences, will often be impossible to resolve, and it misses the point in any case. For example, consider the argument over long-delay taste-aversion learning. Baron, Kaufman, and Fazzini (1969) have shown that as the delay between a bar press and a shock increases from 0 to 60 sec, the extent of suppression of bar pressing decreases. Andrews and Braveman (1975) have shown that as the delay between saccharin consumption and poisoning increases from a few minutes to 25 hours, the suppression of saccharin intake decreases. In describing these results, Mazur (1986) concludes that they "do not require the postulation of a different law to replace the principle of contiguity; they merely require the use of different numbers in describing the relationship between contiguity and learning" (p. 228). Although this statement is literally true—a single model can describe both sets of results with a change in parameter value—what does the word "merely" imply?

Clearly, it implies that the difference is "only" quantitative and therefore not of much interest (to Mazur). But how large does a quantitative difference have to be before it can escape the description "merely"? A difference between seconds and hours is a difference of more than a thousandfold. As Bolles (1985a) points out, a thousandfold difference in a biological system is never just quantitative. One can find

> on the skeletons of some snakes little bumps on certain vertebrae where the legs might be if the snake had legs. They are pelvic bumps, and it is my understanding that these bumps may be 1 or 2 mm in size . . . although a 1- or 2-mm leg is not much of a leg, it is actually about 1/1000th of the length of the legs of a race horse. So the difference in legs between a snake and a race horse is really only a matter of degree. (p. 393)

From a biological point of view, it does not matter whether one chooses to call the differences between taste-aversion learning and bar-press suppression qualitative or quantitative. The difference can be accounted for by postulating a single "mechanism" with a parameter or two whose values can be changed to accommodate the temporal differences. It can also be accounted for by postulating two "mechanisms." What matters is that there are differences, and these raise a large number of issues that need empirical attention. Since these issues are primarily evolutionary and functional in nature, the traditional approach is not likely to pursue them.

An analogy that may be useful in thinking about this problem is to compare learning mechanisms to computer programs. Suppose one were given two programs that solved arithmetic problems in compiled form, so that the programs could not be listed. How would one go about determining whether these programs were based on the same underlying algorithms? One would have to study the input-output relationships—give each program a set of standard problems and compare the speed and accuracy with which they solved the different problems. If the results for both programs were identical, it would seem highly likely that the programs were the same, although one could not be positive. Perhaps some other arithmetic test would produce results that were different for the two programs.

What would happen if the programs differed in some systematic way? For example, suppose that one program always took longer than the other, but only when division was involved. One would naturally be led to conclude that the programs used different algorithms for division. But wait! A theorist could claim that the difference was only quantitative— perhaps the slower program used the same algorithm but had a pause statement added to its division subroutine.

No analogy should be pushed too far. But my general point is that it would be very hard to know with certainty whether the two programs used the same algorithm. Furthermore, it would probably be impossible to tell the "evolutionary" relationship between the programs—whether they had been independently written or one had led to the other. This, of course, is the problem of homology versus analogy in the evolutionary study of traits.

There is one final point to milk from this analogy. One approach to the problem of comparing the two programs would be to attempt measurement at the molecular level and measure the activities of the microprocessor itself. Thinking about this brings out some interesting implications for the relationship between behavioral mechanisms and the physical processes instantiating them. At one level the mechanism for the two programs would be identical—the same processor, and so on, would be involved, even if the programs were written in different languages. But I am sure suitable measurements could be made that would reveal any difference. This suggests that knowledge of the events in the central nervous system that underlie the intellectual capacities of animals will be useful in understanding these processes. But it will have to be information of a certain type. I suspect it will be a long time before the neuroanatomy and neurophysiology underlying the complex processes involved in animal intelligence are understood at all. Behavioral work needs to proceed. The issues are too important to wait on the assumption that the physiological level of analysis will eventually solve these problems. In addition, without good understanding of the way mental processes function at the behavioral level, it is unlikely that physiological work can succeed (Kamil, 1987).

The Null Hypothesis

Many of the problems that the traditional approach encounters in the comparative realm can be seen quite clearly by examining the methods and conclusions of Macphail (1982, 1985), who conducted an extensive critical survey of the literature on the comparative study of learning in vertebrates. His conclusion was that there was no compelling reason to reject the null hypothesis "that there are no differences, either quantitative or qualitative, among the mechanisms of intelligence of non-human vertebrates" (Macphail, 1982, p. 330), and he has reaffirmed this more recently (1985). How does Macphail reach this conclusion?

One approach to this question would be to take each of the phenomena Macphail examined and decide how plausible his conclusions are. However, that would probably take a book as long as his. In any event, I want to raise a more crucial point. Does Macphail's basic approach to the comparative study of vertebrate intelligence have some basic flaw (or flaws) that calls his conclusion into question? One can argue that his logic forced the final conclusion.

The first problem with Macphail's analysis is his definition of intelligence. In his opening chapter, he avoids any explicit definition. In particular, he states that it would be best to leave open the question "whether intelligence is some unitary capacity, or better seen as a complex of capacities, each of which might be independent of the others" (1982, p. 4). Macphail says that a decision about this issue might bias his review. However, his review is in fact biased toward the unitary view. For example, in discussing the results of a comparative research program on reversal learning in birds conducted by Gossette and his associates (Gossette, 1967; Gossette, Gossette, & Inman, 1966), Macphail dismisses their findings. The reason for the dismissal is that different patterns of reversal learning between species were found with spatial and nonspatial cues. Macphail states, "If the ordering of species in serial reversal performance can be changed by altering the relevant dimension, it seems clear that serial reversal in itself cannot give a reliable measure of general intelligence" (Macphail, 1982, p. 223) In the concluding discussion of his last chapter, Macphail talks extensively in terms of general intelligence.

A second contributor to Macphail's conclusion is an extreme willingness to believe in the untested intellectual capacities of animals. If some apparently complex learning ability has been demonstrated in two distantly related species, Macphail is willing to assume it can be found in all species. For example, win-stay, lose-shift learning in object-discrimination learning set is best tested by looking for transfer from object-reversal learning to learning set. This phenomenon has been demonstrated in relatively few species (blue jays—Kamil, Jones, Pietrewicz, & Mauldin, 1977; rhesus monkeys—Warren, 1966; chimpanzees—Schusterman, 1962), and tests for such transfer have failed in at least two cases (cats—Warren, 1966; squirrel monkeys—Ricciardi & Treichler, 1970). The failure with cats is dismissed as apparently due to contextual variables, the failure with squirrel monkeys is not cited. The major implication of the discussion is that though most species have not been tested, they would show the phenomenon.

Another, perhaps more egregious example, is drawn from Macphail's (1985) discussion of languagelike behavior. Such behavior has been demonstrated in some primates using sign language or artificial language (e.g., Gardner & Gardner, 1969; Rumbaugh, 1977). Pepperberg (1981, 1983) has recently demonstrated similar behavior in an African gray parrot using "speech." Although the parrot has not achieved the level of performance shown by the primates (at least not yet), he has demonstrated capacities beyond what anyone (except Pepperberg) might have expected. Macphail (1985) concludes by saying, "As the single avian subject yet exposed to an appropriate training schedule, he [the parrot] gives good support to the view that the parrot's talent for language acquisition may not be significantly different from the ape's" (Macphail, 1985, p. 48). Macphail seems to be implying that the same would be true of every vertebrate species if only suitable testing procedures could be devised. This exceptional willingness to assume that species possess abilities for which they have not even been tested stands in marked contrast to Macphail's extreme unwillingness to accept apparent species differences that have been revealed.

The most important reason for Macphail's conclusion of no species differences among vertebrates in learning or intelligence is his extensive use of the contextual stimulus argument (Bitterman, 1960, 1965). As discussed above, whenever an explicit comparison of two species in the same learning task turns up differences, one can always argue that they reflect some performance factor (the effects of a contextual variable) rather than a difference in intelligence. Proving that there is no set of circumstances in which an animal can learn a particular task (e.g., that frogs cannot acquire language-like behavior) is impossible.

Thus Macphail's argument leaves us with two competing null hypotheses. One is the null hypothesis of no differences in intelligence among vertebrates. Macphail holds that this null hypothesis should be maintained unless clear, convincing evidence against it is obtained. But clear convincing evidence must prove the second null hypothesis that no contextual variable is responsible for the proposed species differences. This logic essentially makes it impossible ever to demonstrate that there are species differences in intelligence.

Macphail would probably say I have overstated his argument. He does not require absolute proof of the second null hypothesis through systematic variation, only some reasonable attempt at evaluating contextual variables. But who is to determine what constitutes reasonable? In fact, the problem of contextual variables can never be completely dealt with through control by systematic variation.

Macphail has performed a valuable service. His arguments have clearly demonstrated that the traditional approach to the comparative study of learning can never succeed. One can never be certain that a species lacks a particular learning ability. This lesson applies not just to the study of learning, narrowly defined, but to the study of animal intelligence in general. An alternative approach that avoids the problem of contextual variables must be found. As described later in this chapter, there are compelling biological reasons to believe that species differences in intelligence do exist. Given that Macphail's approach can never successfully demonstrate such differences, it is crucial to find an alternative approach that avoids the problem of contextual variables.

The Synthetic Approach to Animal Intelligence

In this section I will outline an alternative approach to the study of the mental capacities of animals. I have labeled this the synthetic approach because it represents an attempt to synthesize the approaches of psychologists and organismic biologists. The synthetic approach has three major aspects: (1) a broad definition of the phenomena of interest; (2) a comparative, evolutionary orientation; which leads to (3) an emphasis upon the importance of studying learning and its effects both in the laboratory and in the natural environment of the species being studied.

BROAD DEFINITION OF THE PHENOMENA OF INTEREST

Using the term animal intelligence is a calculated gamble. It has the substantial advantages of communicating the general topic of interest to a wide audience in many different fields and of emphasizing the broad range of phenomena to be included. But it also carries a substantial disadvantage. It is a term that has been used and abused in many ways in the past. When technical discussion begins, then, there is a risk of misunderstanding based on people's assuming different definitions of animal intelligence.

I want to be explicit about the definition of animal intelligence I am using. The synthetic approach defines animal intelligence as those processes by which animals obtain and retain information about their environments and use that information to make behavioral decisions. Several characteristics of this definition need to be emphasized.

First of all, this is a broad definition. It includes all processes that are involved in any situation where animals change their behavior on the basis of experience. It encompasses the processes studied with traditional methods such as operant and classical conditioning. It also includes processes such as memory and selective attention, which animal cognitive psychologists study (Roitblat, 1986). It includes processes involved in complex learning of all sorts, including that demonstrated in social situations. It also includes the study of more "specialized" learning, such as song learning and imprinting.

Second, the definition emphasizes the information-processing and decision-making view of animals. This makes it very consistent with the approach of animal cognitive psychologists. It also makes the synthetic approach consistent with behavioral ecology (Krebs & Davies, 1978, 1984), which emphasizes the adaptive significance of the behavioral decisions of animals.

Third, this definition assumes that animal intelligence is multidimensional, not unidimensional, in accordance with recent thinking about human intelligence (Gardner, 1982). It also prohibits any simple ordering of species in terms of general intelligence. Species that are very good at some problems may be bad at others.

Fourth, this definition offers the possibility of conceptually integrating environmental and genetic influences on behavior, thus avoiding the nature/nurture controversy. It is generally recognized that no behavior is determined completely by either genetic or environmental variables alone. However, this realization does not seem to have had much effect on animal learning research in psychology, which still tends to ignore the idea that the learning abilities of animals are part of their biological heritage. The synthetic approach regards learned behavior as the result of experience. But these effects of experience are determined by the intellectual capacities of the organism, which in turn depend upon the expression of genetically and ontogenetically determined abilities.

This focus on processes instantiating behavior obviously entails rejecting most types of behaviorism, but not methodological behaviorism. The primary way to learn about these processes is by studying behavior. There is no desire to throw away the considerable methodological sophistication that has been developed over the past century, only to redirect that sophistication.

COMPARATIVE, EVOLUTIONARY ORIENTATION

There has been considerable disagreement and confusion about the importance, role, and purpose of comparative research on animal learning. Some have viewed animal learning research as primarily a way of understanding basic mechanisms that would, at least in the long run, lead to fuller (or even complete) understanding of our own species. For these scientists, comparative research has been relatively unimportant. Others have viewed comparative research as important but have adopted approaches in conflict with evolutionary theory (Hodos & Campbell, 1969). For example, Yarczower and Hazlett (1977) have argued in favor of anagenesis, the linear ranking of species on a trait. But given the complexity of relationships among existing species, it is hard to see how such linear ranking would be useful, though it is possible.

The synthetic approach adopts a view of comparative research on animal intelligence that is based upon modern evolutionary theory. The essence of the approach is to assume that the various processes composing animal intelligence have adaptive effects and to use this assumption as a starting point for research, particularly comparative work. In this framework the goal of research is to develop a full understanding of animal intelligence at all relevant levels of explanation, including developmental, mechanistic, physiological, phylogenetic, and ecological levels. For comparative work, this sets the goal of understanding patterns of similarities and differences among species. The evolutionary framework offers several new research strategies for the study of animal intelligence, discussed in the last section of this chapter.

One important implication of the synthetic approach is that both qualitative and quantitative differences between species are of interest. This is important for two reasons. First, the distinction between qualitative and quantitative differences is often a matter of individual judgment. Second, examining the comparative study of morphological traits clearly shows that the distinction between qualitative and quantitative differences is blurred. Understanding qualitative differences, particularly the relationship between qualitative differences and the ecology of the species in question, is a crucial part of developing a full understanding of the phenomena of interest.

For example, consider once more the comparative physiology of respiration. Those writing about the comparative study of learning often use respiration, or some other physiological system, as an analogy that may offer some guidance (e.g., Bolles, 1985a; Revusky, 1985). At some levels the respiratory system is the same in a wide variety of animals. For example, fish, amphibians, reptiles, birds, and mammals all use various hemoglobins to bind oxygen and transport it through the circulatory system. But at other levels respiratory systems differ dramatically. Many amphibians utilize a positive-pressure ventilation system to move air through the lungs. Mammals utilize negative-pressure ventilation in which pressure in the thoracic cavity is slightly lower than atmospheric pressure. Birds, in contrast, have a flow-through lung ventilation system that requires two respiratory cycles for the complete passage of a breath of air. These differences are related to various ecological correlates of the different niches of these organisms (Hainsworth, 1981). Revusky (1985) uses the analogy between learning and respiration to argue for the existence of a general learning process. But the substantial variation in the respiratory systems of different animals can be used to reach another conclusion: that full understanding requires the analysis of differences among species as well as similarities.

THE EMPHASIS ON BOTH LABORATORY AND FIELD

Because the synthetic approach is evolutionary in orientation, it necessarily views events in the field, under natural conditions, as crucial. That is, it is assumed that the intellectual capacities of animals serve important biological, adaptive functions. Therefore studies of learning, memory, and so on, under natural conditions can throw considerable light upon animal intelligence. In most cases coordinated laboratory and naturalistic research will be the most informative.

This coordinated approach to laboratory and field research on animal intelligence is important for two reasons. First, it addresses the problem of external validity raised earlier. If the principles of animal intelligence derived from laboratory research prove useful in the field, this will increase our confidence that important mechanisms of animal behavior have been successfully identified. Second, it is important for theoretical reasons. Since the synthetic approach depends heavily on identifying the specific ways animal intelligence affects biological success, field research will be necessary. These issues will permeate the rest of this chapter.

THE PLACE OF GENERAL PROCESSES IN THE SYNTHETIC APPROACH

The emphasis on general learning processes has been so pervasive that explicit discussion of their place in the synthetic approach could be valuable. Two extreme views about general processes can be identified (Bitterman, 1975). The extreme general process view is that a single general process is responsible for all learning. The extreme antigeneral process view, perhaps best exemplified by Lockard (1971), holds that there is no generality, that learning in each species is unique.

The synthetic approach views both these positions as too extreme. On the one hand the available evidence, especially the research of Bitterman and his colleagues with honeybees (e.g., Abramson & Bitterman, 1986; Bitterman, Menzel, Fietz, & Schafer, 1983; Couvillon & Bitterman, 1984) clearly demonstrates impressive similarity in basic associative learning among diverse species. On the other hand, the demonstration of a general learning process present in many species does not rule out the possibility of important, significant species differences, both qualitative and quantitative.

Assume that animals use a host of processes to obtain environmental information and that some of these are quite general across species, others widespread but less general, and others very limited in distribution. A research program based upon the assumption of general processes would appear successful—general processes would be found. However, the less general processes would remain undiscovered. Furthermore, and more important for any comparative, evolutionary study of animal intelligence, differences among species and the adaptive role of cognitive processes outside the laboratory would remain unknown.

Arguments for Increased Breadth

The synthetic approach calls for two broad changes in the traditional psychological approach to animal learning: increasing the breadth of phenomena being studied, and placing these phenomena in an evolutionary, ecological framework. In this section I will present the arguments for increased breadth.

COGNITIVE PROCESSES IN ANIMALS

Perhaps the greatest challenge to the traditional approach from within psychology has been the emergence of the cognitive approach to animal learning. This development has been thoroughly documented in a number of publications (Hulse et al., 1978; Riley, Brown, & Yoerg, 1986; Roitblat, 1986; Roitblat et al., 1984). The cognitive approach emphasizes the internal states and processes of animals.

Organisms are assumed to have internal cognitive structures that depend on their individual development as well as their evolution. External objects cannot enter directly into an organism's cognitive system, and so they must be internally encoded—that is, "represented." Accordingly, much cognitive research involves techniques for studying the representations used by an organism, the processes that produce, maintain, and operate on them, and the environmental and situational factors that affect them (Roitblat et al., 1984, p. 2).

One important area of cognitive research focuses upon the "memory codes" animals use. For example, in a symbolic matching-to-sample task, the animal is first presented briefly with a single stimulus, the sample. Then it is presented with an array of test stimuli. Choice of one of the test stimuli will be reinforced. Which stimulus is correct depends upon which sample stimulus was previously presented. There are at least two ways the animal could code the sample information: retrospectively, by remembering the sample itself, or prospectively, by remembering which test stimulus would be correct. Roitblat (1980) found that errors tended to be directed toward test stimuli resembling the to-be-correct test stimulus, implying a prospective code. Cook, Brown, and Riley (1985) have obtained data in the radial maze implying that rats use both retrospective and prospective memory in this spatial task.

Another cognitive issue that has received a great deal of attention is animals' ability to time the duration of events. One procedure that has been used to study timing is the "peak procedure" of Roberts (1981). On most trials, rats receive food for bar pressing after a signal has been present for a fixed duration. On occasional probe trials, the signal remains on for a much longer period. When the rate of bar pressing on these probe trials is analyzed as a function of time into the trial, the response rate is highest at that point in time when food is usually presented on nonprobe trials. The process underlying this ability to gauge time appears to have many of the properties of a stopwatch. For example, the clock can be stopped or reset (Roberts, 1983).

Another cognitive ability that has been extensively studied is counting. The major methodological problem facing research on counting, or sensitivity to numerosity, is how to demonstrate that behavior can be brought under the discriminative control of number and not any of the many other attributes that may correlate with number. Although not every study has addressed this problem, it has long been recognized (Koehler, 1950; Thorpe, 1956). Fernandes and Church (1982) presented rats with sequences of either two or four short sounds. If there were two sounds, the rat was reinforced for pressing a lever on the right. If there were four sounds, the rat was reinforced for pressing the lever on the left. Not only did the rats perform accurately, but they maintained this accuracy when nonnumerical aspects of the sequences, such as stimulus duration and interstimulus intervals, were varied.

Davis and Memmott (1983) demonstrated sensitivity to sequentially presented stimuli with a much different procedure. Rats were trained to respond on a variable-interval food reinforcement schedule until they were responding steadily. They were then exposed to three unsignaled shocks during each session. Responding was initially suppressed, but after some time responding accelerated after the third shock, even though there was considerable variation in when during the session the shocks could occur. For example, in control sessions in which there were only two shocks, one early and one late, there was no acceleration of responding after the second shock, which came near the end of the session.

The existence of cognitive abilities such as counting, timing, and memory coding clearly challenge the traditional approach, especially radical behaviorism. The nature and implications of this challenge have been discussed in many places in the literature (e.g., Roitblat, 1982, and replies; Riley et al., 1986). The cognitive approach is an alternative research program to radical behaviorism and also can be claimed to include associationism, since modern theories of association are very cognitive in nature. Furthermore, as I will discuss below, the various aspects of the cognitive approach fit very well with the synthetic approach, particularly when it comes to comparative, evolutionary issues.

COMPLEX LEARNING IN ANIMALS

The cognitive approach has begun to emphasize more complex forms of animal learning, but many examples of research on complex learning remain to be integrated within the cognitive approach. In some cases these areas of research predate the emergence of the cognitive approach by many years.

One clear example of this is provided by the literature on object-discrimination learning set (Bessemer & Stollnitz, 1971). In an object-discrimination learning set (ODLS) experiment, animals are given a series of discrimination problems to solve. Each problem is defined by the introduction of a new pair of stimuli, one arbitrarily designated as correct. Of main interest is an improvement in the speed of learning new problems, especially above chance choice on the second trial of new problems. Many primate species (Bessemer & Stollnitz, 1971), as well as several avian species (Hunter & Kamil, 1971; Kamil & Hunter, 1969), have been shown to reach high levels of performance on the second trial of new problems.

The model that best accounts for ODLS performance in primates is a cognitive model. The basic idea is that the animals learn a pattern of choices descriptively labeled "win-stay, lose-shift." That is, on Trial 2 of a new problem, they remember two aspects of what happened on Trial 1: which stimulus was chosen and whether they received reinforcement. Then if they remember reinforcement (win) on Trial 1, they choose the same stimulus on Trial 2. If they remember nonreinforcement (lose) on Trial 1, they shift their choice on Trial 2. The results of many experiments on long-term and short-term memory, on the effects of switching stimuli between Trials 1 and 2, of positive transfer from reversal learning to ODLS, and of stimulus preferences on Trial 1 are all consistent with this model.

Despite this impressive literature, the ODLS phenomenon has been largely ignored by those working on animal learning. It apparently lies outside the realm of phenomena traditional workers are willing to consider. Given the apparent involvement of long- and short-term memory, and strategy learning, it is particularly surprising that animal cognitive psychologists have ignored ODLS.

There are many other examples of complex learning in animals that are generally ignored, in the sense that no consistent attempt has been made to integrate these phenomena into a systematic cognitive-based scheme. These include evidence for categorical learning by pigeons (Herrnstein, 1985), detailed spatial representational systems in a variety of organisms (bees—Gould, 1987; primates—Menzel & Juno, 1982, 1985), and various forms of reasoning in chimpanzees (Gillan, Premack, & Woodruff, 1981).

These phenomena suggest that the cognitive approach needs to be expanded. At least to an outsider like me, it appears that many of the issues of central concern for animal cognitive psychologists originate in procedures used in the past. A good example of this point is provided by research on selective attention in animals. Some psychological work on selective attention has attempted to determine whether attention could account for certain phenomena such as reversal learning (Bitterman, 1969; Mackintosh, 1969). Other research has attempted to demonstrate attention to abstract dimensions, such as color or line orientation in matching to sample tasks (e.g., Zentall, Hogan, & Edwards, 1984). These types of research are very different and perhaps in the long run less informative than direct attempts to study selective attention and its characteristics. One area in which selective attention and its effects have been examined is research focused upon the detection of cryptic, hard-to-see prey. Selective attention appears to play a substantial role in prey detection (Bond, 1983; Dawkins, 1971a, 1971b; Pietrewicz & Kamil, 1981). Animal cognitive psychology needs to broaden its scope and focus more directly on the information-handling processes of animals, with less focus on the particular issues generated by methodological developments of the past. The broad definition of intelligence offered by the synthetic approach would hasten this process.

EVIDENCE FROM THE FIELD: SOCIAL KNOWLEDGE

The emergence of behavioral ecology in the past 20 years has led to a dramatic increase in our knowledge of the behavior of individual animals in the field (see Krebs & Davies, 1978, 1984). This literature contains many examples of data demonstrating that animals know a great deal about their environments, especially in two contexts—foraging and social behavior. In this section I discuss some of the data on social relationships. Data on foraging behavior will be reviewed later.

As I indicated at the very beginning of this chapter, many anecdotes based on observations in the field suggest that animals possess considerable knowledge about their world, particularly social interactions. Because anecdotes have generally been regarded as scientifically unacceptable, they are most often unreported. As Kummer (1982) has observed, this is unfortunate. It has left each fieldworker aware only of his or her own observations.

My own experience confirms this. After observing the behavior of "Spot" described at the beginning of this chapter, I filed the incident away and for a long time never discussed it with anyone. One night, with some hesitation, I told the story to a group of fieldworkers. It turned out that another hummingbird researcher had seen a similar incident in another territorial species. Every fieldworker present that evening had stories that suggested animals possess more knowledge of their environment than typically considered by the laboratory researcher.

Although these are only anecdotes and their scientific validity is limited, it is time to take their implications seriously and begin to design experiments to test the implications. For example, Goodall (1986) reports many observations of the chimpanzees at Gombe that indicate these animals are acutely aware of the social relationships of their group. In Goodall's terminology, animals manipulate others and assess others' interactions. Are there any more systematic data to support these implications?

Kummer and his associates have tested some of these ideas in their research program with hamadryas baboons. Hamadryas baboons have a single-male, multiple-female social system in which males "appropriate" females. Kummer, Gotz, and Angst (1974) found that if a male was allowed to watch another male with a female, this inhibited the tendency of the observing male to attempt to take over the female, even if the observing male was dominant to the other male. Something analogous to a concept of "ownership" appears to be present.

Even more intriguing, Bachmann and Kummer (1980) found that male hamadryas baboons assess the relation between another male and a female. They tested twelve baboons, six of each sex. In the first stage they tested all possible different-sex pairs for grooming preference. This allowed the experimenters to construct a hierarchy of preference of each animal for each of the opposite-sexed animals. They then allowed males to watch another pair for 15 minutes. At the end of the 15 minute observation period, they gave the observer a graded set of opportunities to attempt to appropriate the female. They found that the observer assessed the relationship between the male and female he had been observing. The probability of the observer's attempting to appropriate the female depended on the female's preference for the original male. If that preference was weak, appropriation was more likely.

The research program of Cheney and Seyfarth is generating similar kinds of data for vervet monkeys. Cheney and Seyfarth (1980) conducted playback experiments in the field during which the scream of a juvenile was played through a hidden loudspeaker to groups of females that included the juvenile's mother. Mothers responded more strongly to these calls than the other females did. More surprisingly, the other females often responded by looking at the mother before the mother herself had reacted. This indicates that the females recognized the relationships of other females and young.

More recent data indicate that vervets have knowledge about other social relationships. Cheney and Seyfarth (1986) recorded the probability of agonistic encounters between members of a vervet group as a function of recent social interactions. There were two main findings. First, they found that individuals were more likely to behave aggressively toward other group members who had recently fought with their own kin, indicating that they know their own kin. Kin recognition is well known in many species. Second, Cheney and Seyfarth found that individuals were more likely to interact aggressively with others whose close kin had recently fought with their own kin. This indicates that vervet monkeys know about the relationships of other monkeys in their group. This appears to be learned, since monkeys under three years of age did not show the effect. How the relationships are learned is unknown.

Cheney and Seyfarth (1985) have argued that primate intelligence may have evolved primarily to deal with social relationships. Monkeys and apes clearly recognize social relationships and remember recent affiliative and aggressive interactions. But when tested for similar nonsocial knowledge, the monkeys appear surprisingly unresponsive. In various field experiments, vervets failed to respond to signs of predators. Cheney and Seyfarth's (1985) argument seems premature because these experiments on nonsocial knowledge may have failed to produce positive results for many reasons other than the monkeys' lack of knowledge. Nonetheless, their more general point about the importance of cognition in social settings deserves careful attention, not only in primates but in many group-living animals.

CONCLUSIONS

It is clear that a trend toward studying more complex forms of animal learning is well under way. It is important that this trend continue. Many unanticipated intellectual abilities have been revealed, and this implies that there are more waiting to be discovered.

Griffin (1976, 1978) has argued that interspecies communication offers an important tool for investigating the knowledge animals possess about their world. This is certainly true, and it is encouraging to see the technique being used with more species, including not only apes (Savage-Rumbaugh, this volume) but birds (Pepperberg, 1981, 1983), dolphins (Herman, Wolz, & Richards, 1984), and sea lions (Schusterman & Krieger, 1986).

There are two general suggestions about how this search for complex processes in animals should proceed that I would like to make at this point. First, some research should concentrate primarily on what animals know, without worrying too much, for the time being, about how they acquire the knowledge. For example, the research of Premack and his associates with Sarah, a chimpanzee trained to use plastic symbols as a medium for communication, indicates that Sarah understands many relationships among stimuli. Although this research tells us little about how Sarah acquired this knowledge, it begins to tell us some of the things any complete theory of animal intelligence will have to be able to explain.

Second, it is important to continue to test animals in relatively unconstrained situations. It is quite possible that by restricting attention to experimental situations in which animals had few response alternatives and had to deal only with a few simple stimuli, psychologists have underestimated the abilities of their subjects. For example, the research of Menzel and Juno (1982, 1985) has demonstrated one-trial discrimination learning and extensive long-term memory for the spatial location of many objects in group-living marmosets, in marked contrast to the relatively poor performance of marmosets in more traditional experimental settings (e.g., Miles & Meyer, 1956). The distinguishing features of the procedures of Menzel and Juno (1982, 1985) were probably the lack of constraints on the behavior of the marmosets and the use of knowledge about the natural foraging environment of these marmosets in designing the problems. These two characteristics were probably crucial to making it possible for the animals to demonstrate what they knew about their environment.

Arguments for a More Biological Approach

In this section I will review three areas of research—biological constraints on learning, "specialized" learning, and learning under natural conditions. The results of research in these three areas, considered together, provide convincing evidence that learning must be considered in a biological, evolutionary framework.

BIOLOGICAL CONSTRAINTS ON LEARNING

The phenomena that are usually called biological constraints on learning indicate the intrusion of biological factors into standard, traditional conditioning situations. Breland and Breland (1961) were the first to recognize the importance of constraints in operant-conditioning situations. They observed what they called instinctive drift, a tendency for "natural behaviors" of animals undergoing operant conditioning to intrude upon and interfere with the emission of the response being reinforced. The Brelands clearly recognized the fundamental importance of their observations, which they viewed as a "demonstration that there are definite weaknesses in the philosophy underlying these [conditioning] techniques" (Breland & Breland, 1961, p. 684). However, their findings had little effect at the time. The later discoveries of taste-aversion learning, autoshaping, and species-specific defense reactions had more impact.

Taste-aversion learning was first reported by Garcia and Koelling (1966). In essence, taste-aversion learning suggests that some stimuli are more associable than others, challenging the often implicit assumption of associationists that stimuli are generally equipotential (Seligman, 1970). These studies show that many animals are more likely to associate intestinal illness with gustatory (or olfactory) stimuli than with external stimuli. Garcia and Koelling (1966) proposed that these results demonstrate that rats may have a genetically coded hypothesis: "The hypothesis of the sick rat, as for many of us under similar circumstances, would be, 'it must have been something I ate.'" (Garcia & Koelling, 1966, p. 124).

The phenomenon of autoshaping was first reported by Brown and Jenkins (1968). Brown and Jenkins found that if they simply illuminated a light behind a pecking key for a few seconds, then presented food, the pigeons began to peck the key even though these pecks had no effect on the presentation of the reinforcer. Although they felt that an appeal to some species-specific disposition was necessary, and though Breland and Breland reported many similar findings in less constrained situations, Brown and Jenkins do not cite the Brelands. The implication that species-specific predispositions affect the key peck has been confirmed. Jenkins and Moore (1973) showed that the topography of the pigeon's key peck depends on the reinforcer used. Mauldin (1981; Kamil & Mauldin, 1987) found that three different passerine species each used species-specific response topologies in an autoshaping situation.

The concept of species-specific defense reactions originated in a seminal paper by Bolles (1970). Bolles argued that many of the results of avoidance-conditioning experiments could best be understood in terms of the innate species-specific responses of the species being tested, such as fighting and fleeing. The opening sentence of his abstract was, "The prevailing theories of avoidance learning and the procedures that are usually used to study it seem to be totally out of touch with what is known about how animals defend themselves in nature" (Bolles, 1970, p. 32).

I have been brief in describing these developments because there are already so many extensive reviews of biological constraints available in the literature (e.g., Seligman & Hager, 1972; Hinde & Stevenson-Hinde, 1973). And there is still considerable controversy about the extent to which these phenomena require abandoning any of the central assumptions of the traditional approach. For example, Revusky (1985) argues against radical behaviorism but also contends that taste-aversion learning can be encompassed in a general associationist approach (see below).

There can be no doubt that these "biological constraints" on learning demonstrate that the evolutionary history of the species being studied can affect the outcome of a conditioning experiment. Whether the differences between taste-aversion learning and other aversive conditioning are considered qualitative or quantitative, differences that seem most explicable on functional grounds do exist. The form of the response in a Skinner box depends on the natural repertoire of the animal, as do the results of avoidance-learning experiments. However, the impact of these findings on the psychological study of animal learning has been limited.

The very label given to these phenomena, biological constraints on learning, reveals this limited impact. The label implies that there is some general process, learning, that is occasionally constrained by the biology of the organism (Kamil & Yoerg, 1982). Surely a broader view is justified. The animal comes to the learning situation with a set of abilities that determine what behavioral changes will occur. These abilities are part of the animal's biological endowment. (I do not imply that they are completely genetically determined—clearly ontogenetic factors play an important role.) In that case a functional, evolutionary approach is necessary.

"SPECIALIZED" LEARNING

The value of a functional approach to the study of learning can be seen clearly in the literature on specialized learning. Specialized learning appears in specific biological contexts and plays very specific roles. Examples include song learning, imprinting, and homing/migration. In each of these cases, available data demonstrate that the phenomena in question meet any reasonable definition of learning—changes in behavior based on experience. The data also show important species differences in learning, which can often be related to differences in the natural history of species.

Naturalistic studies of nest and egg recognition by gulls and terns suggest the existence of important differences in learning among closely related species that correlate meaningfully with natural history (Shettleworth, 1984). Royal terns nest in dense colonies where it is difficult to discriminate among nest sites. Their eggs are highly variable in appearance, and they learn to recognize their own eggs. Herring gulls build elaborate nests that are spaced farther apart, and they learn to recognize their nests but not their eggs. By the time the chicks are old enough to wander from the nest, the parents have learned to recognize them (Tinbergen, 1953). Yet another pattern is shown by kittiwakes. These birds nest on cliff ledges, and their chicks do not (cannot) wander from the nest site. Parent kittiwakes recognize only their nest sites and do not discriminate their own eggs or young from those of others (Cullen, 1957).

As Shettleworth (1984) has pointed out, these kinds of differences do not necessarily result from differences in learning *ability*. It may be that all the species have the same ability to learn to recognize their eggs, young, and nest sites, but natural circumstances of the species vary so as to favor one type of learning. For example, kittiwakes might learn to recognize their eggs if their eggs varied as much in appearance as do those of royal terns. The necessary experiments, such as placing eggs that vary in appearance in kittiwake nests, have not been carried out. However, this consideration does not apply to all examples of specialized learning.

In the case of song learning, at least some of the necessary experiments exploring differences in learning abilities have been done. Many male passerine birds sing songs that function both to attract a mate and to defend a territory against other males (Kroodsma, 1982). In many species these songs are acquired through experience. Chaffinches, marsh wrens, white-crowned sparrows, and many other species must hear adult song when young to sing appropriately when mature. In many cases there are "dialects" of birdsong—different versions are observed in the same species in different geographical areas. The dialect an adult male sings often depends upon which dialect he heard during development.

The findings of Kroodsma and his associates on differences in song learning between eastern and western marsh wrens (currently classified as two subspecies) provide particularly clear evidence on differences in song learning between these two populations of marsh wrens. Kroodsma and Verner (1987) found that the normal repertoire size—the number of different songs sung by a single individual—varied considerably between the two populations. Eastern birds had repertoire sizes of about 30–60 songs while western birds had repertoire sizes of 120–220. While this could represent a difference in learning ability, it could also be the result of differences in early experience. It seems likely that the eastern wrens hear fewer songs when young than do western birds.

Kroodsma and Canady (1985) have performed the experiment necessary to distinguish between these possibilities. They raised eastern and western marsh wrens in identical laboratory environments. All subjects heard 200 tutor songs during development. Eastern birds learned 34–64 different songs, while the western wrens learned 90–113 songs under identical conditions. Furthermore, Kroodsma and Canady (1985) found significant differences in the size of the song-control nuclei in the brains of the two groups. Eastern birds had smaller song-control areas. The differences in song learning ability and neuroanatomy appear to be associated with several ecological differences between the populations, including year-round residency and high population densities in the western population.

Thus the evidence on song learning among passerine birds clearly demonstrates that species differences in ability exist. Many such differences are known, and they appear to correlate with natural history and ecology (Kroodsma, 1983; West & King, 1985). The finding that two subspecies of wrens learn different things from the same experience is particularly noteworthy. There can be important differences in specialized learning among extremely closely related animals. The question is whether such differences can be expected in more general types of learning.

The discussion of general and specific adaptations by Bolles (1985a) provides a good framework for this discussion. He points out that some adaptations are common, but unrelated, evolutionary adjustments to common circumstances. The phenomenon is called convergence, and color vision is an illustration of it. Full spectrum color vision pops up here and there in the evolutionary tree . . . it appears in some mammals, in most birds, in some fish, and in some of the arthropods. Animals in between are more or less color-blind . . . One way to think of color vision is that it has been discovered or invented several times independently. (p. 394)

Bolles (1985a) contrasts these reversible adaptations with others that apparently are not reversible, such as feathers:

Only birds have feathers. But the feather idea was apparently stupendously successful, because there are no birds without feathers. Once feathers came upon the scene, that was it, all descendants were stuck with feathers. Some birds (e.g., penguins) have funny feathers. . . . [Feathers] may change shape and size and color and waxiness and so on, but evidently if you have feathers you can depend upon all your descendants having feathers. . . . Is associative learning like feathers? Is the ability to learn such a stupendous advantage that once in possession of it, there is no way back? (pp. 394–395)

There can be little doubt that some specialized forms of learning are like color vision. Song learning appears scattered, albeit fairly widely, among passerines, varying significantly in its characteristics. The same may be said of imprinting. But are there forms of learning that are like feathers?

Bolles suggests that associative learning may be like feathers. The similarity in basic conditioning processes among widely different species suggests that this is so. The same argument can be made about the law of effect. The effects of reinforcement have also been demonstrated in many species. However, several points must be made about the analogy between feathers and learning.

First of all, even if some kinds of learning are like feathers, this does not mean there are not important differences between species in the learning. Although all feathers have certain features in common, they also vary. They are different at different stages of a bird's life and on different parts of a bird's body. And there are substantial variations be-

tween avian species. A large part of understanding feathers is understanding this variation. We need to examine even the most general kinds
of learning for significant variation. To do so will require knowledge of
the function of learning. I will return to this point later.

Second, even if there are general kinds of learning, this does not necessarily settle the question of homology and analogy. These concepts are
labels for two very different possible evolutionary reasons for similarity
between species. Homology is similarity through common evolutionary
origin or descent. Its counterpart is analogy—similarity despite separate evolutionary origin because of similar adaptive pressure (see Atz,
1970, for a discussion of the difficulties of applying these concepts to behavior). General forms of learning, unlike feathers, may have arisen two
or more times during evolutionary history. For example, the similarities
Bitterman and his co-workers have found between associative learning
in honeybees and mammals may be the result of analogy, or convergence (Abramson & Bitterman, 1986). It can be argued that the world is
structured in such a way that any learning mechanism that accurately
and efficiently predicted events would have to have certain characteristics, namely those that associative learning shows. (Dennett, 1975, has
argued that the law of effect must be part of any adequate and complete
psychological theory. This philosophical argument implies that evolution may have invented the law of effect any number of times.)

Third, it would be premature at this time to attempt to decide whether any particular kind of learning is general. Biological variation, whether in general adaptations like feathers or in more specialized adaptations like color vision, requires some understanding of the function of
the trait in question. Variation in feathers and in color vision relates to
adaptive functioning. For example, in the case of color vision one can
hypothesize that honeybees have color vision because they feed from
colorful flowers (and this is exactly what made von Frisch, 1954, so sure
that honeybees did have color vision).

The problem is that in the case of possibly general processes of learning, we have little idea of their specific functions. One can reasonably
speculate that association learning is useful for an animal because it allows accurate prediction of future events. One can reasonably argue that
the law of effect is useful because it allows the animal to obtain resources
like food or water. But these are very general arguments and do not easily lead to the selection of particular species for study on ecological
grounds. What is needed is some more definitive and specific idea of

how learning and cognitive processes actually function under natural conditions. Fortunately, for the first time recent developments in behavioral ecology are making data relevant to this problem available in a substantial way.

LEARNING IN THE FIELD

Certain kinds of learning have long been known to occur in the natural world of animals: song learning and imprinting are the outstanding examples. But these are specialized forms of learning. Is there any evidence that the types of learning psychologists have typically been interested in occur outside the laboratory?

Many have maintained that learning in a more general sense is not important to animals under natural conditions (Boice, 1977; Lockard, 1971). This presented a problem to anyone attempting an evolutionary, adaptive approach to learning. If learning is unimportant in the field, why is it so evident in the laboratory? Do animals carry around what Boice called surplusage—unneeded and unnecessary abilities?

The problem appears to have been methodological, at least in part. Learning is much more difficult to observe than is learned behavior. Imagine a bird eating a monarch butterfly and subsequently throwing up. After that experience, it will simply avoid eating monarchs (Brower, 1969). The scientist watching birds would have to see the brief first encounter to understand that later avoidance of monarchs was learned. This raises the second problem. The identification of learning requires documenting changes in the behavior of individuals over time. Until relatively recently, there were very few extended field studies of known or marked individuals. In the past 20 to 30 years such studies have become much more common, thanks in part to the emergence of behavioral ecology. These studies have revealed that animals in their natural environments face many problems that they appear to solve through learning and cognition (see Krebs & Davies, 1978, 1984, for reviews of behavioral ecology; Shettleworth, 1984, for an explicit discussion of the behavioral ecology of learning). For example, bumblebees learn how to handle different flower species and which flowers are most profitable (Heinrich, 1979); nectar-feeding birds remember which flowers they have emptied (Gass & Montgomerie, 1981; Kamil, 1978); food-caching birds remember the locations of their stored food (Kamil & Balda, 1985; Shettleworth & Krebs, 1982) as well as the contents of the caches (Sherry, 1984); and young vervet monkeys learn the social relationships among members of their groups (Cheney & Seyfarth, 1986). In light of the accumulating evidence, it is difficult to conceive of anyone's believing that learning is not important in the natural world of animals outside the laboratory.

In addition to these empirical developments, important theoretical developments in behavioral ecology have emphasized the potential biological importance of learning. A variety of models have shown that if animals are sensitive to many of the features of their environment, they can increase the efficiency of their behavior. For example, the original "diet" selection model of MacArthur and Pianka (1966) assumes that predators know the nutritional value and density of their prey and the time required to handle it. Given that they possess this information and that they can rank prey types in terms of the ratio of nutritional value to handling time, a relatively simple rule can determine which prey types should be eaten whenever encountered and which ones should never be eaten in any given set of circumstances. Although this model has not been completely successful in predicting selection among prey types, it has had considerable success (for recent reviews see Krebs, Stephens, & Sutherland, 1983; Schoener, 1987). Studies stimulated by this model have shown that animals respond adaptively to changes in the density of their prey (e.g., Goss-Custard, 1981; Krebs, Erichsen, Webber, & Charnov, 1977) and learn to rank different prey types as the model predicts (Pulliam, 1980). Other models have similarly predicted learning effects that have been confirmed by subsequent experiments (see Kamil & Roitblat, 1985, for review; see Stephens & Krebs, 1986, for detailed presentation of foraging theory, especially chap. 4).

There can be no doubt that animals use learning to modify their behavior under natural conditions and that such learning can have very important adaptive implications. This is good news for the student of animal learning: the phenomena we have been interested in are biologically significant. However, we must also recognize the implications of this conclusion, the most central being that the study of learning must be placed in a biological context, and we must deal with the thorny problems this outlook raises.

In summary, then, three types of research indicate the need for a biological approach to learning: (1) biological constraints, which clearly show that the evolutionary history of the species can affect the outcome of conditioning experiments in a variety of ways; (2) studies of specialized learning, which indicate that there can be significant variation in learning mechanisms that correlate with the ecologies of the species being studied; and (3) evidence from behavioral ecology, which shows that general forms of learning are of adaptive significance and may also, therefore, vary in ways that correlate with ecology.

The Implications of an Adaptive Approach to Intelligence

In earlier sections of this chapter, I argued that learning is adaptive and proposed that the synthetic approach should operate under that assumption. This assumption has important comparative implications, primarily that there *must be* significant variation in intelligence among species. Why is this a necessary implication?

Let us return to the feather analogy used by Bolles (1985a). He pointed out that learning might be like feathers—such a stupendously successful adaptation that, once developed, it could not be lost. Some might be tempted to use this analogy to argue that some adaptations are so successful that they simply do not vary significantly among species that possess them. This conclusion is not supported by available evidence on successful adaptations.

Feathers represent an extremely successful adaptation. But not all feathers are the same. Different types of feathers serve different functions and have different structures. Some feathers, such as down, serve as insulation. Other feathers function primarily in flight. Still others, the filoplumes, apparently serve as sensory organs, sensitive to the position of other feathers. Furthermore, within a feather type there can be considerable between species variation in structure between species that is related to special adaptations. For example, the underside of an owl's wings has a velvety pile produced by special processes of the barbules, which reduces the sound of the wings when the owl swoops down on prey. Birds of the open sky have long primary flight feathers best suited to fast, straight flight, whereas woodland birds have shorter primaries that increase maneuverability. Diving birds have overlapping feathers that reduce drag (Lucas & Stettenheim, 1972; Spearman & Hardy, 1985).

The list of functional variations of feathers is extremely long, even without mentioning perhaps the biggest source of variation, the evolution of brightly colored feathers for interspecific display.

The point of this discussion of more than you (or I) ever wanted to know about feathers is that traits with adaptive functions vary between species, in ways that make sense in terms of the ecology and adaptations of the organisms they serve. If animal intelligence is adaptive—and as I have already stated, ample evidence of this is emerging—then intelligence must vary between species. The variation may be qualitative or quantitative; intelligence may consist of a complex of processes. But differences there must be. I cannot think of a single adaptive trait that does not vary in some way between species, often closely related species—the structure of the eye, the forelimb or hind limb, the stomach, the lungs. Why should animal intelligence be any different?

One reason animal intelligence could be different has been proposed by Shettleworth (1982, 1984)—the distinction between function and mechanism. Shettleworth argues that because natural selection selects only among outcomes, not among the processes that produce them, any of a number of different mechanisms may be selected in any given situation. While this is true in global terms, it may well be false when examined in detail. Different mechanisms are unlikely to produce exactly the same outputs. In fact, as long as we are limited to input-output studies of the mechanisms of intelligence, we will classify two mechanisms producing the same results as the same mechanism (as would evolution).

However, as in the computer program example explored earlier, different mechanisms are likely to have different input-output relationships. If the input-output relationships differ, detailed analysis may prove that one mechanism is more functional than the other for problems the species faces. In that case natural selection will favor the more functional mechanism.

Returning to the main argument, my analysis of Macphail's approach to the evolution of intelligence among vertebrates suggests that his analysis is based upon prevailing but unproductive assumptions and definitions. Macphail recognized this possibility when he pointed out that "even the tentative advocacy of [the null] hypothesis is in effect a *reductio ad absurdum* which merely indicates that comparative psychology has followed a systematically incorrect route" (Macphail, 1982, p. 334). That is exactly my contention. The challenge is to devise an alternative approach that can be used to investigate the evolution of animal intelligence while avoiding the snares that entangled Macphail and others.

Another potential problem with the literature upon which Macphail's analysis is based must also be noted. It is quite conceivable, perhaps even likely, that some mechanisms of intelligence are widespread throughout broad segments of the animal kingdom while others are not. Indeed, one could argue that the literature on classical conditioning demonstrates that the associationistic mechanisms involved are widespread whereas the literature on song learning, for example, demonstrates narrow distribution of song-learning mechanisms. It may be that the psychological study of animal learning has concentrated upon general mechanisms, ignoring those with more limited distribution. But some of these mechanisms of limited distribution may be more general, across tasks, than very specific forms of learning like song learning. In particular, some more complex forms of learning—so far little studied outside a few primate or avian species—deserve comparative attention (Humphrey, 1976).

Research Strategies

The purpose of this section is to propose a set of research strategies to further our knowledge of animal intelligence. In outlining these strategies I have been guided by the two criticisms of the traditional approach developed earlier: that we know relatively little about the intellectual capacities of animals and that we understand very little about how these capacities function or evolved. I have also sought to develop a set of strategies that will avoid the problems revealed by analysis of Macphail's review of the comparative literature on animal learning.

There are two components to any strategy for studying animal intelligence: selecting the procedures to be used and selecting the species to be studied. These are not unrelated problems. Research will proceed most readily if there is a good match between the task employed and the species under study.

These suggested research strategies originate from several considerations: (1) the characteristics of research that has produced good evidence for complex intelligent processes in animals; (2) the decision-making processes that are being revealed by laboratory and field research in behavioral ecology; and (3) an examination of the biological approach to comparative research.

DEVELOPING A NATURAL HISTORY
OF ANIMAL INTELLIGENCE

One important step to developing a new approach to the comparative study of animal intelligence will be to develop a natural history of animal intelligence. This would consist of a detailed study of intelligence under natural conditions. The focus would be upon the problems animals are faced with in the field and how they use their mental capacities to solve them. In many cases field experiments or laboratory work closely coupled to natural history would be necessary.

I have already referred to many examples of field data that demonstrate or suggest how intelligence is used to solve the problems nature presents to animals. These include timing in hummingbirds, spatial memory in food-storing animals, and knowledge of social relationships in primates. The two major arenas for the operation of animal intelligence are foraging and social behavior. These areas need to be examined much more closely, and in a wider variety of species, from the point of view of the functional significance of animal intelligence.

USING NATURAL HISTORY TO CHOOSE
SPECIES AND DESIGN PROCEDURES

Once the study of natural history has revealed a particular problem that is (or might be) solved by learning in the field, this knowledge can be used to select species for study and to design experimental procedures for testing. This is a strategy ethologists have used with considerable success in studying "specialized" learning such as song learning, imprinting, and migration. There are also a number of examples of this approach dealing with processes that may be more general. These include the detection of cryptic prey (Bond, 1983; Pietrewicz & Kamil, 1981); spatial memory in food-caching parids (Sherry, 1984; Sherry, Krebs, & Cowie, 1981; Shettleworth & Krebs, 1982) and nutcrackers (Balda, 1980; Kamil & Balda, 1985); and pitch perception in starlings (Hulse, Cynx, & Humpal, 1984).

Another approach has been to design experimental situations to test models of natural behavior, particularly optimal foraging models. For example, there have been tests of patch selection (Smith & Sweatman, 1974), within-patch persistence (Cowie, 1977; Kamil & Yoerg, 1985; Kamil, Yoerg & Clements, in press), and collecting food to be brought to a central place (Kacelnik, 1984; Kacelnik & Cuthill, 1987). One problem with some of these studies is that researchers sometimes fail to consider whether the species they choose to study are appropriate for the model they wish to test.

This raises the general point of evaluating ecological validity. It is relatively easy to argue that laboratory tasks should reflect the problems animals normally face in nature. But it is not so easy to judge how well any particular task meets that requirement. The best way to address this issue is to collect laboratory data that can be compared with effects known to occur in the field. For example, when Pietrewicz and I were first developing our procedure for studying cryptic prey detection by training jays to detect cryptic moths in slides, we collected data that could be checked against phenomena known to occur in the field. We found that the moths in the slides were least detectable by the jays when shown in their species-typical body orientation (Pietrewicz & Kamil, 1977). The jays slow their search immediately after finding a moth (unpublished data), a result identical to the "area-restricted search" often observed in the field (Croze, 1970). They also search more slowly when the prey are more cryptic (Getty, Kamil, & Real, 1987; Kamil & Olson, in preparation), an effect also analogous to data collected in the field (Fitzpatrick, 1981). These isomorphisms between laboratory and field mean that when we investigate parameters that cannot be studied under natural conditions, there is some reason to believe the results are applicable to the field.

We hope that adopting this research strategy based upon natural history will have two effects: first, that it will lead to a clearer and fuller understanding of animal intelligence; second, that it will change the focus of research on animal learning and cognition, making it more animal oriented and less process oriented. This will allow greater integration with organismic biology. It will also focus more attention on a crucial evolutionary issue, the adaptive significance of animal intelligence. But it will not solve the problem of contextual stimuli and the difficulty of establishing that species differences in learning or cognition even exist. However, the synthetic approach does suggest some ways around this problem.

USING EXTERNAL CRITERIA TO MAKE
COMPARATIVE PREDICTIONS

One way to minimize the problem of using contextual stimuli as an alternative explanation for species differences is to have some external criterion that predicts differences among a number of species. For example, Rumbaugh and Pate (1984) have used an index of encephalization to predict species differences among seven nonhuman primate species on a complex learning task. The encephalization index accurately predicts the performance of the species. Since there are many predictions, supported in detail by the comparative data, contextual stimuli do not provide a likely alternative explanation. The probability that contextual stimuli will produce a ranking of nine species by chance is exceedingly small. Thus the use of an external criterion to make a priori specific predictions provides an explicit alternative to the null hypothesis of no species differences. If this alternative makes many predictions and these are supported, then contextual stimuli cannot be taken seriously as an explanation.

Indexes of brain size or encephalization provide one source of external predictions. These indexes may be particularly useful for comparing closely related species, as in Rumbaugh's research program. Natural history and ecological considerations can provide another source of a priori predictions of species differences in animal intelligence. If some animals face specific foraging or social problems that others do not face, and if learning is used to solve these problems, then a comparative prediction is at least implicit. For example, do food-storing birds have a greater ability to remember spatial locations than other birds? Are animals that utilize food resources that are renewed on a strong temporal schedule, like trap-lining hummingbirds, better at timing? Are animals that live in stable, long-lasting social groups better able to learn about social relationships either between themselves and others or among others?

The key to overcoming the problem posed by contextual variables is generating multiple predictions about species differences. The ecological approach leads to such multiple predictions because of the processes of convergence and divergence. Divergence refers to differences between closely related species owing to differences in their ecologies. The differences in the beaks of the Galápagos finches are the classic case.

Convergence refers to similarities between distantly related species because of similar ecological pressures and adaptations. For example, nectar feeding has evolved independently among many groups of birds, including the hummingbirds of North and South America, the honey creepers of Hawaii, and the sunbirds of Africa and Asia. Many of these birds have decurved beaks that are well suited to extracting nectar from flowers.

The ways convergence and divergence can be used to generate multiple predictions can be seen by considering a specific example. Suppose one hypothesized that nectar feeders should have particularly good spatial memory (Kamil, 1978) or timing ability (Gill, in press). This hypothesis could be tested by comparing closely related animals, only some of which feed on nectar, such as the Hawaiian honey creepers, which vary enormously in foraging specializations. Any supporting evidence could then be tested with other groups of nectar-feeding birds. It could also be tested by doing comparative research with other groups that include nectar feeders, such as bats.

The strategy of selecting species for study based upon convergence and divergence can be applied to many aspects of animal intelligence. For example, if the social context has been crucial for the evolution of learning, as Cheney and Seyfarth (1985) suggest, then at least some of the phenomena observed in group-living primates should be found in some avian species. Many birds have long life spans spent in stable groups with established genealogies (e.g., Florida scrub jays—Woolfenden & Fitzpatrick, 1984; bee eaters—Emlen, 1981). Some of these groups have been studied for as long as 20 years. The findings reported suggest that these birds may be making judgments of the sort described for primates, but the appropriate data have not been collected. It would be important to collect them.

USING SPECIFIC PROCESSES TO GENERATE MULTIPLE PREDICTIONS

Another way to minimize the interpretive problems posed by contextual variables is to design several experimental procedures, each measuring the same intellectual ability, and test two or more species with all the procedures. The species tested should be chosen with some external criterion so that specific predictions are made in advance. Then if the results of each of the procedures indicate the same ordering of the species, contextual variables are unlikely to be responsible.

One example of this strategy can be found in ongoing research on spatial memory in Clark's nutcrackers. These birds are known to use spatial memory in recovering their caches (Balda, 1980; Balda, Kamil, & Grim, 1986; Kamil & Balda, 1985). This memory is remarkable in at least two ways: it is long lasting and of large capacity. We have found that nutcrackers perform better than pigeons in an open field analogue of the radial maze (Balda & Kamil, in press). Data collected by Olson (in preparation) indicate that the nutcrackers also perform better than pigeons in a spatial operant task. As data from different settings accumulate and are consistent in showing that nutcrackers remember spatial locations better than pigeons, our confidence that there is a species difference in cognitive ability increases.

Conclusions

In this chapter I have argued for a new, broader approach to studying the evolution of the cognitive capacities of animals. This synthetic approach is based upon several arguments. (1) Data from the natural world of animals as well as from the laboratory clearly show that the intellectual capacities of animals are greater than previously thought. This means that we need to use a broad definition of animal intelligence. (2) The traditional psychological approach to the study of animal learning has been defined too narrowly, and its logic has prevented meaningful comparative, evolutionary analysis. (3) The literature on several phenomena, including constraints on learning and "specialized" learning, indicates that an approach based on research strategies drawn from biology and behavioral ecology can be useful in analyzing the evolution of animal intelligence. (4) As a prerequisite to engaging in a meaning comparative analysis of animal cognition, we must develop hypotheses that make multiple and detailed predictions about species differences in intelligence. Natural history and behavioral ecology are important sources of such hypotheses.

We have a great deal yet to learn about the cognitive abilities of animals. If we adopt a broad approach, using the best of what psychology and biology have to offer, we are most likely to succeed in our efforts to understand these abilities and their evolution. The next twenty years of research on these problems should be very exciting.

REFERENCES

Abramson, C. I., & Bitterman, M. E. (1986). Latent inhibition in honey bees. *Animal Learning and Behavior, 14*, 184–189.

Andrews, E. A., & Braveman, N. S. (1975). The combined effects of dosage level and interstimulus interval on the formation of one-trial poison-based aversions in rats. *Animal Learning and Behavior, 3*, 287–289.

Atz, J. W. (1970). The application of the idea of homology to behavior. In L. R. Aronson, E. Tobach, D. S. Lehrman, & J. S. Rosenblatt (Eds.), *Development and evolution of behavior*. San Francisco: W. H. Freeman.

Bachmann, C., & Kummer, H. (1980). Male assessment of female choice in hamadryas baboons. *Behavioral Ecology and Sociobiology, 6*, 315–321.

Balda, R. P. (1980). Recovery of cached seeds by a captive *Nucifraga caryotactes*. *Zeitschrift für Tierpsychologie, 52*, 331–346.

Balda, R. P., & Kamil, A. C. (in press). The spatial memory of Clark's nutcrackers (*Nucifraga columbiana*) in an analog of the radial-arm maze. *Animal Learning and Behavior*.

Balda, R. P., Kamil, A. C., & Grim, K. (1986). Revisits to emptied cache sites by nutcrackers. *Animal Behaviour, 34*, 1289–1298.

Baron, M., Kaufman, A., & Fazzini, D. (1969). Density and delay of punishment of free-operant avoidance. *Journal of the Experimental Analysis of Behavior, 12*, 1029–1037.

Beach, F. A. (1950). The snark was a boojum. *American Psychologist, 5*, 115–124.

Bessemer, D. W., & Stollnitz, F. (1971). Retention of discriminations and an analysis of learning set. In A. M. Schrier & F. Stollnitz (Eds.), *Behavior of nonhuman primates* (Vol. 4.) New York: Academic Press.

Bitterman, M. E. (1960). Toward a comparative psychology of learning. *American Psychologist, 15*, 704–712.

Bitterman, M. E. (1965). Phyletic differences in learning. *American Psychologist, 20*, 396–410.

Bitterman, M. E. (1969). Habit reversal and probability learning: Rats, birds and fish. In R. Gilbert and N. S. Sutherland (Eds.), *Animal discrimination learning*. New York: Academic Press.

Bitterman, M. E. (1975). The comparative analysis of learning. *Science, 188*, 699–709.

Bitterman, M. E., Menzel, R., Fietz, A., & Schafer, S. (1983). Classical conditioning of proboscis extension in honeybees (*Apis mellifera*). *Journal of Comparative Psychology, 97*, 107–119.

Boice, R. (1977). Surplusage. *Bulletin of the Psychonomic Society, 9*, 452–454.

Bolles, R. C. (1970). Species-specific defense reactions and avoidance learning. *Psychological Review, 77*, 32–48.

Bolles, R. C. (1985a). The slaying of Goliath: What happened to reinforcement theory. In T. D. Johnston & A. T. Pietrewicz (Eds.), *Issues in the ecological study of learning*. Hillsdale, NJ: Erlbaum.

Bolles, R. C. (1985b). Short term memory and attention. In L. Nilsson & T. Archer (Eds.), *Perspectives on learning and memory*. Hillsdale, NJ, Erlbaum.

Bond, A. B. (1983). Visual search and selection of natural stimuli in the pigeon. *Journal of Experimental Psychology: Animal Behavior Processes, 9*, 292–306.

Breland, K., & Breland, M. (1961). The misbehavior of organisms. *American Psychologist, 16*, 681–684.

Brower, L. P. (1969). Ecological chemistry. *Scientific American, 220* (2), 22–29.

Brown, P. L., & Jenkins, H. M. (1968). Auto-shaping of the pigeon's key peck. *Journal of Experimental Analysis of Behavior, 11*, 1–8.

Cheney, D. L., & Seyfarth, R. M. (1980). Vocal recognition in free-ranging vervet monkeys. *Animal Behaviour, 28*, 362–367.

Cheney, D. L., & Seyfarth, R. M. (1985). Social and non-social knowledge in vervet monkeys. In L. Weiskrantz (Ed.), *Animal intelligence*. Oxford: Clarendon Press.

Cheney, D. L., & Seyfarth, R. M. (1986). The recognition of social alliances by vervet monkeys. *Animal Behaviour, 34*, 1722–1731.

Cheney, D. L., Seyfarth, R., & Smuts, B. (1986). Social relationships and social cognition in nonhuman primates. *Science, 234*, 1361–1366.

Cook, R. G., Brown, M. F., & Riley, D. A. (1985). Flexible memory processing by rats: Use of prospective and retrospective information in the radial maze. *Journal of Experimental Psychology: Animal Behavior Processes, 11*, 453–469.

Couvillon, P. A., & Bitterman, M. E. (1984). The over-learning extinction effect and successive negative contrast in honeybees (*Apis mellifera*). *Journal of Comparative Psychology, 98*, 100–109.

Cowie, R. J. (1977). Optimal foraging in great tits (*Parus major*). *Nature, 268*, 137–139.

Croze, H. J. (1970). Searching image in carrion crows. *Zeitschrift für Tierpsychologie*, Suppl. 5, 1–85.

Cullen, E. (1957). Adaptations in the kittiwake to cliff-nesting. *Ibis, 99*, 275–302.

Davis, H., & Memmott, J. (1983). Autocontingencies: Rats count to three to predict safety from shock. *Animal Learning and Behavior, 11*, 95–100.

Dawkins, M. (1971a). Perceptual changes in chicks: Another look at the "search image" concept. *Animal Behaviour, 19*, 566–574.

Dawkins, M. (1971b). Shifts in "attention" in chicks during feeding. *Animal Behaviour, 19*, 575–582.

Dennett, D. C. (1975). Why the law of effect will not go away. *Journal of the Theory of Social Behaviour, 5*, 169–187.

Emlen, S. T. (1981). Altruism, kinship and reciprocity in the white-fronted bee-eater. In R. D. Alexander & D. W. Tinkle (Eds.), *Natural selection and social behavior: Recent research and new theory*. New York: Chiron Press.

Fernandes, D. M., & Church, R. M. (1982). Discrimination of the number of sequential events by rats. *Animal Learning and Behavior, 10*, 171–176.

Fitzpatrick, J. W. (1981). Search strategies of tyrant flycatchers. *Animal Behaviour, 29*, 810–821.

Frisch, K. von (1954). *Dancing bees: An account of the life and senses of the honey bee* (trans. Dora Ilse). London: Methuen.

Garcia, J., & Koelling, R. A. (1966). Relation of cue to consequence in avoidance learning. *Psychonomic Science, 4,* 123–124.

Gardner, H. (1978). *Developmental psychology.* Boston: Little, Brown.

Gardner, H. (1982). *Frames of mind: The theory of multiple intelligences.* New York: Basic Books.

Gardner, R. A., & Gardner, B. T. (1969). Teaching sign language to a chimpanzee. *Science, 165,* 664–672.

Gass, C. L., & Montgomerie, R. D. (1981). Hummingbird foraging behavior: Decision-making and energy regulation. In A. C. Kamil & T. D. Sargent (Eds.), *Foraging behavior: Ecological, ethological, and psychological approaches.* New York: Garland Press.

Getty, T., Kamil, A. C., & Real P. G. (1987). Signal detection theory and foraging for cryptic or mimetic prey. In A. C. Kamil, J. R. Krebs, & H. R. Pulliam (Eds.), *Foraging behavior.* New York: Plenum.

Gill, F. B. (in press). Temporal sensitivity in trap-lining hermit hummingbirds. *Animal Behaviour.*

Gill, F. B., & Wolf, L. L. (1977). Nonrandom foraging by sunbirds in a patchy environment. *Ecology, 58,* 1284–1296.

Gillan, D. J., Premack, D., & Woodruff, G. (1981). Reasoning in the chimpanzee. 1. Analogical reasoning. *Journal of Experimental Psychology: Animal Behavior Processes, 7,* 1–17.

Goodall, J. (1986). *The chimpanzees of Gombe: Patterns of behavior.* Cambridge: Harvard University Press.

Goss-Custard, J. D. (1981). Feeding behavior of red-shank, *Tringa totanus,* and optimal foraging theory. In A. C. Kamil & T. D. Sargent (Eds.), *Foraging behavior: Ecological, ethological, and psychological approaches.* New York: Garland Press.

Gossette, R. L. (1967). Successive discrimination reversal (SDR) performance of four avian species on a brightness discrimination task. *Psychonomic Science, 8,* 17–18.

Gossette, R. L., Gossette, M. F., & Inman, N. (1966). Successive discrimination reversal performance by the greater hill myna. *Animal Behaviour, 14,* 50–53.

Gould, J. L. (1987). Landmark learning by honey bees. *Animal Behaviour, 35,* 26–34.

Griffin, D. R. (1976). *The question of animal awareness: Evolutionary continuity of mental experience.* New York: Rockefeller University Press.

Griffin, D. R. (1978). Prospects for a cognitive ethology. *Behavioral and Brain Sciences, 1,* 527–538.

Hainsworth, F. R. (1981). *Animal physiology.* Reading, MA: Addison-Wesley.

Heinrich, B. (1979). *Bumblebee economics.* Cambridge: Harvard University Press.

Herman, L. M., Wolz, J. P., & Richards, D. G. (1984). Comprehension of sentences by bottlenosed dolphins. *Cognition, 16,* 1–90.

Herrnstein, R. J. (1970). On the law of effect. *Journal of the Experimental Analysis of Behavior, 13,* 243–266.

Herrnstein, R. J. (1985). Riddles of natural categorization. In L. Weiskrantz (Ed.) *Animal intelligence*, Oxford: Clarendon Press.

Hinde, R. A., & Stevenson-Hinde, J. (1973). *Constraints on learning*. New York: Academic Press.

Hodos, W., & Campbell, C. B. G. (1969). *Scala naturae*: Why there is no theory in comparative psychology. *Psychological Review, 76*, 337–350.

Hulse, S. H., Cynx, J., & Humpal, J. (1984). Cognitive processing of pitch and rhythm structures by birds. In H. L. Roitblat, T. G. Bever, & H. S. Terrace (Eds.), *Animal cognition*. Hillsdale, NJ: Erlbaum.

Hulse, S. H., Fowler, H., & Honig, W. K. (1978). *Cognitive processes in animal behavior*. Hillsdale, NJ: Erlbaum.

Humphrey, N. K. (1976). The social function of intellect. In P. P. G. Bateson & R. A. Hinde (Eds.), *Growing points in ethology*. Cambridge: Cambridge University Press.

Hunter, M. W., & Kamil, A. C. (1971). Object-discrimination learning set and hypothesis behavior in the northern bluejay. *Psychonomic Science, 22*, 271–273.

Jenkins, H. M., & Moore, B. R. (1973). The form of the autoshaped response with food and water reinforcers. *Journal of the Experimental Analysis of Behavior, 20*, 163–181.

Kacelnik, A. (1984). Central place foraging in starlings (*Sturnur vulgaris*). 1. Patch residence time. *Journal of Animal Ecology, 53*, 283–300.

Kacelnik, A., & Cuthill, I. C. (1987). Starlings and optimal foraging theory: Modelling in a fractal world. In A. C. Kamil, J. R. Krebs, & H. R. Pulliam (Eds.), *Foraging behavior*, New York: Plenum.

Kamil, A. C. (1978). Systematic foraging by a nectar-feeding bird, the amakihi (*Loxops virens*). *Journal of Comparative and Physiological Psychology, 92*, 388–396.

Kamil, A. C. (1987). Sensory biology and behavioral ecology. In A. M. Popper & J. Atema (Eds.), *Sensory biology of aquatic animals*, New York: Springer-Verlag.

Kamil, A. C., & Balda, R. (1985). Cache recovery and spatial memory in Clark's nutcrackers (*Nucifraga columbiana*). *Journal of Experimental Psychology: Animal Behavior Processes, 11*, 95–111.

Kamil, A. C., & Hunter, M. (1969). Performance on object-discrimination learning-set by the greater hill myna (*Gracula religiosa*). *Journal of Comparative and Physiological Psychology, 73*, 68–73.

Kamil, A. C., Jones, T. B., Pietrewicz, A. T., & Mauldin, J. (1977). Positive transfer from successive reversal training to learning set in blue jays. *Journal of Comparative and Physiological Psychology, 91*, 79–86.

Kamil, A. C., Krebs, J. R., & Pulliam, H. R. (1987). *Foraging behavior*. New York: Plenum.

Kamil, A. C., & Mauldin, J. E. (1987). A comparative-ecological approach to the study of learning. In R. C. Bolles & M. D. Beecher (Eds.), *Evolution and learning*. Hillsdale, NJ: Erlbaum.

Kamil, A. C., & Olson, (in preparation). The effects of crypticity upon the speed and accuracy of prey detection.

Kamil, A. C., & Roitblat, H. L. (1985). The ecology of foraging behavior: Implications for animal learning and memory. *Annual Review of Psychology, 36*, 141–169.

Kamil, A. C., & Sargent, T. (1981). *Foraging behavior: Ecological, ethological and psychological approaches.* New York: Garland Press.

Kamil, A. C., & Yoerg, S. I. (1982). Learning and foraging behavior. In P. P. G. Bateson & P. H. Klopfer (Eds.), *Perspectives in ethology* (Vol. 5). New York: Plenum.

Kamil, A. C., & Yoerg, S. I. (1985). Effects of prey depletion on patch choice by foraging blue jays (*Cyanocitta cristata*). *Animal Behaviour, 33,* 1089–1095.

Kamil, A. C., Yoerg, S. I., & Clements, K. C. (in press). Rules to leave by: Patch departure in foraging blue jays. *Animal Behaviour.*

Koehler, O. (1950). The ability of birds to "count." *Bulletin of Animal Behaviour, 9,* 41–45.

Krebs, J. R., & Davies, N. B. (1978). *Behavioural ecology: An evolutionary approach.* Sunderland, MA: Sinauer.

Krebs, J. R., & Davies, N. B. (1984). *Behavioural ecology: An evolutionary approach,* 2nd ed. Sunderland, MA: Sinauer.

Krebs, J. R., Erichsen, T. J., Webber, M. I., & Charnov, E. L. (1977). Optimal prey selection in the great tit (*Parus major*). *Animal Behaviour, 25,* 30–38.

Krebs, J. R., Stephens, D., & Sutherland, W. (1983). Perspectives in optimal foraging. In A.H. Brush & G. A. Clark, Jr. (Eds.), *Perspectives in ornithology.* Cambridge: Cambridge University Press.

Kroodsma, D. E. (1982). Song repertoires: Problems in their definition and use. In D. E. Kroodsma & E. H. Miller (Eds.), *Acoustic communication in birds* (Vol. 2). New York: Academic Press.

Kroodsma, D. E. (1983). The ecology of avian vocal learning. *BioScience, 33,* 165–171.

Kroodsma, D. E., & Canady, R. A. (1985). Differences in repertoire size, singing behavior, and associated neuroanatomy among marsh wren populations have a genetic basis. *Auk, 102,* 439–446.

Kroodsma, D. E., & Verner, J. (1987). Use of song repertoires among marsh wren populations. *Auk, 104,* 63–72.

Kummer, H. (1982). Social knowledge in free-ranging primates. In D. R. Griffin (Ed.), *Animal mind–Human mind.* Berlin: Springer-Verlag.

Kummer, H., & Goodall, J. (1985). Conditions of innovative behaviour in primates. In L. Weiskrantz (Ed.) *Animal intelligence.* Oxford: Clarendon Press.

Kummer, H., Gotz, W., & Angst, W. (1974). Triadic differentiation: An inhibitory process protecting pair bonds in baboons. *Behaviour, 49,* 62–87.

Lakatos, I. (1974). *The methodology of scientific research programs.* Cambridge: Cambridge University Press.

Lockard, R. B. (1971). Reflections on the fall of comparative psychology: Is there a message for us all? *American Psychologist, 26,* 168–179.

Lorenz, K. (1965). *The evolution and modification of behavior.* Chicago: University of Chicago Press.

Lucas, A. M., & Stettenheim, P. R. (1972). *Avian anatomy: Integument.* Agricultural Handbook 362, Washington, DC: United States Department of Agriculture.

MacArthur, R. H., & Pianka, E. R. (1966). On optimal use of a patchy environment. *American Naturalist, 100,* 603–609.

Mackintosh, N. J. (1969). Habit-reversal and probability learning: Rats, birds and fish. In R. Gilbert and N. S. Sutherland (Eds.), *Animal discrimination learning*. New York: Academic Press.

Macphail, E. M. (1982). *Brain and intelligence in vertebrates*. Oxford: Clarendon Press.

Macphail, E. M. (1985). Vertebrate intelligence: The null hypothesis. In L. Weiskrantz (Ed.), *Animal Intelligence*. Oxford: Clarendon Press.

Mauldin, J. E. (1981). *Autoshaping and negative automaintenance in the blue jay (Cyanocitta cristata)*, robin (*Turdus migratorius*) and starling (*Sturnus vulgarius*). Ph.D. diss., University of Massachusetts, Amherst.

Mazur, J. E. (1986). *Learning and behavior*. Englewood Cliffs, NJ: Prentice-Hall.

Menzel, E. W., Jr., & Juno, C. (1982). Marmosets (*Saguinus fuscicollis*): Are learning sets learned? *Science, 217*, 750–752.

Menzel, E. W., Jr., & Juno, C. (1985). Social foraging in marmoset monkeys and the question of intelligence. In L. Weiskrantz (Ed.), *Animal intelligence*. Oxford: Clarendon Press.

Miles, R. C., & Meyer, D. R. (1956). Learning sets in marmosets. *Journal of Comparative and Physiological Psychology, 49*, 219–222.

Olson, D. (in preparation). Spatial memory during nonmatching to sample in nutcrackers and pigeons.

Pepperberg, I. M. (1981). Functional vocalizations of an African gray parrot (*Psittacus erithacus*). *Zeitschrift für Tierpsychologie, 55*, 139–151.

Pepperberg, I. M. (1983). Cognition in the African gray parrot: Preliminary evidence for auditory/vocal comprehension of the class concept. *Animal Learning and Behavior, 11*, 179–185.

Pietrewicz, A. T., & Kamil, A. C. (1977). Visual detection of cryptic prey by blue jays (*Cyanocitta cristata*). *Science, 195*, 580–582.

Pietrewicz, A. T., & Kamil, A. C. (1981). Search images and the detection of crypic prey: An operant approach. In A. C. Kamil & T. D. Sargent (Eds.), *Foraging behavior: Ecological, ethological, and psychological approaches*. New York: Garland Press.

Pulliam, H. (1980). Do chipping sparrows forage optimally? *Ardea, 68*, 75–82.

Rescorla, R. A. (1985). Associationism in animal learning. In L. Nilsson & T. Archer (Eds.), *Perspectives on learning and memory*. Hillsdale, NJ: Erlbaum.

Revusky, S. (1985). The general process approach to animal learning. In T. D. Johnston & A. T. Pietrewicz (Eds.), *Issues in the ecological study of learning*. Hillsdale, NJ: Erlbaum.

Ricciardi, A. M., & Treichler, F. R. (1970). Prior training influences on transfer to learning set by squirrel monkeys. *Journal of Comparative and Physiological Psychology, 73*, 314–319.

Riley, D. A., Brown, M. F., & Yoerg, S. I. (1986). Understanding animal cognition. In T. J. Knapp & L. C. Robertson (Eds.), *Approaches to cognition: Contrasts and controversies*. Hillsdale, NJ: Erlbaum.

Roberts, S. (1981). Isolation of an internal clock. *Journal of Experimental Psychology: Animal Behavior Processes, 7*, 242–268.

Roberts, S. (1983). Properties and function of an internal clock. In R. L. Mellgren (Ed.), *Animal cognition and behavior*. New York: North-Holland.

Roitblat, H. L. (1980). Codes and coding processes in pigeon short-term memory. *Animal Learning and Behavior, 8,* 341–351.

Roitblat, H. L. (1982). The meaning or representation in animal memory. *Behavioral and Brain Sciences, 5,* 353–372.

Roitblat, H. L. (1986). *Introduction to comparative cognition.* San Francisco: W. H. Freeman.

Roitblat, H. L., Bever, T., & Terrace, H. (1984). *Animal cognition.* Hillsdale, NJ: Erlbaum.

Rumbaugh, D. M. (1977). *Language learning by a chimpanzee: The LANA project.* New York: Academic Press.

Rumbaugh, D. M., & Pate, J. L. (1984). The evolution of cognition in primates: A comparative perspective. In H. L. Roitblat, T. G. Bever, & H. S. Terrace (Eds.), *Animal cognition.* Hillsdale, NJ: Erlbaum.

Schoener, T. W. (1987). A brief history of optimal foraging ecology. In A. C. Kamil, J. R. Krebs, & H. R. Pulliam (Eds.), *Foraging behavior.* New York: Plenum.

Schusterman, R. J. (1962). Transfer effects of successive discrimination-reversal training in chimpanzees. *Science, 137,* 422–423.

Schusterman, R. J., & Krieger, K. (1986). Artificial language comprehension and size transposition by a California sea lion (*Zalophus californianus*). *Journal of Comparative Psychology, 100,* 348–355.

Schwartz, B. (1984). *Psychology of learning and behavior,* 2nd ed. New York: Norton.

Seligman, M. E. P. (1970). On the generality of the laws of learning. *Psychological Review, 77,* 406–418.

Seligman, M. E. P., & Hager, J. L. (1972). *Biological boundaries of learning.* New York: Appleton-Century-Crofts.

Sherry, D. F. (1984). Food storage by black-capped chickadees: Memory for the location and contents of caches. *Animal Behaviour, 32,* 451–464.

Sherry, D. F. , Krebs, J., & Cowie, R. (1981). Memory for the location of stored food in marsh tits. *Animal Behaviour, 29,* 1260–1266.

Shettleworth, S. J. (1982). Function and mechanism in learning. In M. Zeiler & P. Harzen (Eds.), *Advances in analysis of behavior,* Vol. 3, *Biological factors in learning.* New York: Wiley.

Shettleworth, S. J. (1984). Learning and behavioral ecology. In J.R. Krebs & N.B. Davies (Eds.), *Behavioral ecology,* 2nd ed. Sunderland, MA: Sinauer.

Shettleworth, S. J., & Krebs, J. (1982). How marsh tits find their hoards: The roles of site preference and spatial memory. *Journal of Experimental Psychology: Animal Behavior Processes, 8,* 354–375.

Skinner, B. F. (1938). *The behavior of organisms.* New York: Appleton-Century-Crofts.

Skinner, B. F. (1959). A case history in scientific method. In S. Koch (Ed.), *Psychology: The study of a science.* New York: McGraw-Hill.

Skinner, B. F. (1977). Why I am not a cognitive psychologist. *Behaviorism, 5,* 1–10.

Smith, J. N. M., & Sweatman, H. P. A. (1974). Food searching behavior of tit mice in patchy environments. *Ecology, 55,* 1216–1232.

Smuts, B. B. (1985). *Sex and friendship in baboons.* Hawthorne, N.Y.: Aldine.

Spearman, R. I. C., & Hardy, J. A. (1985). Integument. In A. S. King & J. Mc-Lelland (Eds.), *Form and function in birds,* Vol. 3. New York: Academic Press.

Stephens, D. W., & Krebs, J. R. (1986). *Foraging theory.* Princeton: Princeton University Press.

Thorndike, E. L. (1898). Animal intelligence: An experimental study of the associative processes in animals. *Psychological Monographs, 2* (whole No. 8).

Thorndike, E. L. (1911). *Animal intelligence: Experimental studies.* New York: Macmillan.

Thorpe, W. H. (1956). *Learning and instinct in animals.* Cambridge: Harvard University Press.

Tinbergen, N. (1953). *The herring gull's world.* London: Collins.

Warren, J. M. (1966). Reversal learning and the formation of learning sets by cats and rhesus monkeys. *Journal of Comparative and Physiological Psychology, 61,* 421–428.

West, M. J., & King, A. P. (1985). Learning by performing: An ecological theme for the study of vocal learning. In T. D. Johnston & A. T. Pietrewicz (Eds.), *Issues in the ecological study of learning.* Hillsdale, NJ: Erlbaum.

Woolfenden, G. E., & Fitzpatrick, J. W. (1984). *The Florida scrub jay: demography of a cooperative-breeding bird.* Princeton: Princeton University Press.

Yarczower, M., & Hazlett, L. (1977). Evolutionary scales and anagenesis. *Psychological Bulletin, 84,* 1088–1097.

Zentall, T. R., Hogan, D. E., & Edwards, C. A. (1984). Cognitive factors in conditional learning by pigeons. In H. L. Roitblat, T. G. Bever, & H. S. Terrace (Eds.), *Animal cognition.* Hillsdale, NJ: Erlbaum.

Subject Index

Author Index

322